Italian and Italian American Studies

Stanislao G. Pugliese
Hofstra University
Series Editor

This publishing initiative seeks to bring the latest scholarship in Italian and Italian American history, literature, cinema, and cultural studies to a large audience of specialists, general readers, and students. I&IAS will feature works on modern Italy (Renaissance to the present) and Italian American culture and society by established scholars as well as new voices in the academy. This endeavor will help to shape the evolving fields of Italian and Italian American Studies by re-emphasizing the connection between the two. The following editorial board consists of esteemed senior scholars who act as advisors to the series editor.

REBECCA WEST
University of Chicago

JOSEPHINE GATTUSO HENDIN
New York University

FRED GARDAPHÉ
Queens College, CUNY

PHILIP V. CANNISTRARO[†]
Queens College and the Graduate School, CUNY

ALESSANDRO PORTELLI
Università di Roma "La Sapienza"

Queer Italia: Same-Sex Desire in Italian Literature and Film
 edited by Gary P. Cestaro
 July 2004
Frank Sinatra: History, Identity, and Italian American Culture
 edited by Stanislao G. Pugliese
 October 2004
The Legacy of Primo Levi
 edited by Stanislao G. Pugliese
 December 2004
Italian Colonialism
 edited by Ruth Ben-Ghiat and Mia Fuller
 July 2005
Mussolini's Rome: Rebuilding the Eternal City
 Borden W. Painter Jr.
 July 2005
Representing Sacco and Vanzetti
 edited by Jerome H. Delamater and Mary Anne Trasciatti
 September 2005
Carlo Tresca: Portrait of a Rebel
 Nunzio Pernicone
 October 2005
Italy in the Age of Pinocchio: Children and Danger in the Liberal Era
 Carl Ipsen
 April 2006
The Empire of Stereotypes: Germaine de Staël and the Idea of Italy
 Robert Casillo
 May 2006
Race and the Nation in Liberal Italy, 1861–1911: Meridionalism, Empire, and Diaspora
 Aliza S. Wong
 October 2006

Women in Italy, 1945–1960: An Interdisciplinary Study
  edited by Penelope Morris
  October 2006
Debating Divorce in Italy: Marriage and the Making of Modern Italians, 1860–1974
  Mark Seymour
  December 2006
A New Guide to Italian Cinema
  Carlo Celli and Marga Cottino-Jones
  January 2007
Human Nature in Rural Tuscany: An Early Modern History
  Gregory Hanlon
  March 2007
The Missing Italian Nuremberg: Cultural Amnesia and Postwar Politics
  Michele Battini
  September 2007
Assassinations and Murder in Modern Italy: Transformations in Society and Culture
  edited by Stephen Gundle and Lucia Rinaldi
  October 2007
Piero Gobetti and the Politics of Liberal Revolution
  James Martin
  December 2008
Primo Levi and Humanism after Auschwitz: Posthumanist Reflections
  Jonathan Druker
  June 2009
Oral History, Oral Culture, and Italian Americans
  edited by Luisa Del Giudice
  November 2009
Italy's Divided Memory
  John Foot
  January 2010
Women, Desire, and Power in Italian Cinema
  Marga Cottino-Jones
  March 2010
The Failure of Italian Nationhood: The Geopolitics of a Troubled Identity
  Manlio Graziano
  September 2010
Women and the Great War: Femininity under Fire in Italy
  Allison Scardino Belzer
  October 2010
Italian Jews from Emancipation to the Racial Laws
  Cristina M. Bettin
  November 2010
Anti-Italianism: Essays on a Prejudice
  edited by William J. Connell and Fred Gardaphé
  January 2011
Murder and Media in the New Rome: The Fadda Affair
  Thomas Simpson
  January 2011
Mohamed Fekini and the Fight to Free Libya
  Angelo Del Boca; translated by Antony Shugaar
  January 2011
City and Nation in the Italian Unification: The National Festivals of Dante Alighieri
  Mahnaz Yousefzadeh
  April 2011
The Legacy of the Italian Resistance
  Philip Cooke
  May 2011

New Reflections on Primo Levi: Before and After Auschwitz
    edited by Risa Sodi and Millicent Marcus
    July 2011
Italy on the Pacific: San Francisco's Italian Americans
    Sebastian Fichera
    December 2011
Memory and Massacre: Revisiting Sant'Anna di Stazzema
    Paolo Pezzino, translated by Noor Giovanni Mazhar
    February 2012
In the Society of Fascists: Acclamation, Acquiescence, and Agency in Mussolini's Italy
    edited by Giulia Albanese and Roberta Pergher
    September 2012
Carlo Levi's Visual Poetics: The Painter as Writer
    Giovanna Faleschini Lerner
    October 2012
Postcolonial Italy: The Colonial Past in Contemporary Culture
    Edited by Cristina Lombardi-Diop and Caterina Romeo
    January 2012
Women, Terrorism and Trauma in Italian Culture: The Double Wound
    Ruth Glynn
    February 2013
The Italian Army in Slovenia: Strategies of Antipartisan Repression, 1941–1943
    Amedeo Osti Guerrazzi, translated by Elizabeth Burke and Anthony Majanlahti
Italy and the Mediterranean: Words, Sounds, and Images of the Post-Cold War Era
    Norma Bouchard and Valerio Ferme
    September 2013

The Failure of Italian Nationhood

The Geopolitics of a Troubled Identity

Manlio Graziano

THE FAILURE OF ITALIAN NATIONHOOD
Copyright © Manlio Graziano, 2010.
All rights reserved.

First published in hardcover in 2010 by PALGRAVE MACMILLAN® in the United States—a division of St. Martin's Press LLC, 175 Fifth Avenue, New York, NY 10010.

Where this book is distributed in the UK, Europe and the rest of the world, this is by Palgrave Macmillan, a division of Macmillan Publishers Limited, registered in England, company number 785998, of Houndmills, Basingstoke, Hampshire RG21 6XS.

Palgrave Macmillan is the global academic imprint of the above companies and has companies and representatives throughout the world.

Palgrave® and Macmillan® are registered trademarks in the United States, the United Kingdom, Europe and other countries.

ISBN: 978-1-137-34722-0

The Library of Congress has cataloged the hardcover edition as follows:

Graziano, Manlio, 1958–
 [Italie, un état sans nation? English]
 The failure of Italian nationhood : the geopolitics of a troubled identity / Manlio Graziano ; [translated to English by Brian Knowlton].
  p. cm.—(Italian & Italian American Studies Series)
 Includes bibliographical references and index.
 ISBN 978-0-230-10413-6 (alk. paper)
  1. National characteristics, Italian. 2. Nationalism—Italy—History. 3. Regional disparities—Italy—History. 4. Group identity—Italy—History. 5. Italy—Politics and government. 6. Italy—Politics and government—1994– 7. Italy—Social conditions. 8. Italy—Ethnic relations. I. Title.

DG442.G7513 2010
945.092—dc22   2010007421

A catalogue record of the book is available from the British Library.

Design by Scribe Inc.

First PALGRAVE MACMILLAN paperback edition: August 2013

10 9 8 7 6 5 4 3 2 1

Contents

Preface to the English Edition   ix

Introduction to the English Edition   xi

Introduction   1

Foreword: The "Original Sin"   13

Part I: The Original Characteristics

1. How Premature Development Became a Factor of Backwardness   27
2. The Phantom Nation   35
3. The Northern Question   43
4. Inventing Ancestors   49
5. The Unhappy Consciousness of Italian Development   55
6. A Culture without a Nation   61
7. The Difficult Italianization of the Piedmont   69
8. The Difficult Piedmontization of Italy   75
9. The Moderate Social Bloc   81

Part II: The Permanencies

10. Transformism   91
11. Internationalization Crises and Transformism   99
12. Emerging Sectors and Transformism   105
13. The Southern Question   111

Part III: Identity and Sovereignty

14. A Counter-Reformist Identity   121
15. A Civil "Guelph" Religion   129
16. The Quest for a Civil Italian Religion   137
17. A Petit-Bourgeois Fatherland   145

18	A Country of Limited Sovereignty	153
19	Identity and Development	161
20	The Failure of "Democratic Nationalization"	167
21	Italian Metamorphoses	177
22	Between Europe and the Mediterranean	183
23	The Internationalization Crisis of the 1990s	191
Conclusion		199
Biographies		203
Notes		217
References		249
Index		259

Preface to the English Edition

This book, written by an Italian purposely for a foreign public, was first published in France, where I live and work, in 2007. It attempts to explain the profound changes that are under way in Italian politics and, more generally, in Italian society. This book comes out in the United States just a few months before the 150th anniversary of the unification of Italy, and, with unpremeditated irony, illustrates why Italy was never really unified. People who, for different reasons, are interested in current Italian affairs are usually eager to understand the nature of "Berlusconi-ism," a cultural, political, and social phenomenon that has lasted, by now, for longer than 10 percent of the entire time that the Italian state has existed. The brilliant thinker and politician Piero Gobetti, killed by fascists in 1926 at the age of twenty-five, described fascism once as the "autobiography" of the Italian nation. Today, it is possible to describe "Berlusconi-ism" as the most recent version of this country's autobiography.

This is the reason why almost no changes have been made to the original version of the book, published when Italy was ephemerally led by a center-left government. That short period was exceptional; since then, Italy has recovered its "normality," which is the actual subject of this book.

This book, therefore, lacks any reference to the 2008 global economic crisis, which substantially modified the character of international relations, upon which Italy is, as I have tried to demonstrate, particularly dependent. But since this is a study of historical and structural trends and not an "instant book," the 2008 crisis did not compromise any analysis done before this date.

I want to take advantage of this short introduction to the American edition to thank all the people who made this publication possible: Professors Stanislao Pugliese, of Hofstra University, and Osvaldo Croci, of Memorial University of Newfoundland, who submitted the text to Palgrave; Chris Chappell and Samantha Hasey, from Palgrave; Brian Knowlton, my very patient translator; Professor Vera Negri Zamagni, whose expertness is exceeded only by her kindness; and my friends Constance Cooper and Paolo Rampini, who encouraged—and helped—me unfailingly.

Manlio Graziano
Paris, February 1, 2010

Introduction to the English Edition

This book by Manlio Graziano proposes a historical interpretation of the present difficulties and strengths of Italy, making use of an original approach. The author covers the last two centuries of Italian history, mixing chronology with themes, without sticking to the mere succession of events, and referring often to the present. He adopts an interdisciplinary viewpoint, putting together culture, politics, and economics, with the aim of giving a comprehensive view of Italian society. Graziano has not cultivated a single historical discipline at the expense of others because he believes that a more global assessment of the issues at stake is necessary to the understanding of a country like Italy; he can do this because he possesses an extensive and rare capability of reading and processing different types of literature. The result is a book that touches upon many of the most important passages of the history of unified Italy in a highly readable form, which I consider particularly suitable to a foreign audience not interested in too many details if unnecessary to illustrate the arguments discussed. Also, the long-run view offered by the author is particularly adequate to represent the "path dependence" that underlies his basic argument.

The thrust of Graziano's thesis is summarized in the book title: Italy, a territory of strong municipal traditions, has unified and modernized without ever becoming a "nation." The author starts by pointing out that the unification of the country in 1861 was a surprising process covering areas that were not at all prepared for this event, much less capable of becoming active partners in it, as a result of the cultural and economic backwardness produced by the decline of the once flourishing Italian city-states. Indeed, there was such a widespread awareness of this at the time that the Risorgimento writer and politician Massimo D'Azeglio proclaimed "after having built Italy, we have to build the Italians." Unfortunately, the bourgeois class, which in central and northern Europe led the national modernization of their countries, was, in Italy, insufficient to the task, and even the decision to adopt a centralized model of government, à la France, served only to mask the many shortcomings of local territories, without paving the way to the effective building of a nation.

Having clearly analyzed these initial conditions, Graziano tries to answer the following question: Was the Italian state able to overcome its unfavorable beginnings at some point in time? His negative answer is built up through a discussion of the efforts put in place to this end in the various periods of Italian history. During the liberal years of the second half of the nineteenth century, the much criticized "trasformismo" of Italian politics (the less than neat political coalitions that were formed in Parliament) is seen as the only way to govern a country with such diverse cultural and economic conditions. The fascist dictatorship is judged as an effort to produce a coherent government for a country that was no longer amenable to a peaceful democratic coexistence, while the never-ending north-south dualism is seen as a failure to build a common set of rules of behavior, in spite of the unified legislation in existence. The long discussion that Graziano offers of the ambiguous role of Catholicism is of great interest in this context: on the one side he recognizes that the Catholic identity could be a deeply unifying element of the Italian nation, though hardly a really distinctive element because of the well-known supranationality of Catholicism; on the other side he points out that the many efforts to contrast Catholicism by building alternative secular identities were unsuccessful, but served to increase divisions.

On the whole, we can say that the picture Graziano offers of successive Italian governments shows how they tried to bypass the problem rather than facing it, putting in place strategies to keep the country together without lessening the differences. In this context the present political move toward "federalization" is explained as an acknowledgment by the Italian elites of the failure to make Italy a nation, but it also offers the chance to raise some extremely interesting final thoughts.

Indeed, if the lack of an effective national identity could have been a handicap for Italy in the past, in the present transition of the European nation-states toward entrusting increasing shares of sovereignty to the European Union, Italy might suffer less and be better equipped to live under a "glocal" regime: global institutions on the one side and local governments on the other side. The author speaks in this connection of an "advantage of backwardness." It should never be forgotten that in Italy practically nothing is brand new because nearly everything has been experimented with in some other form in the past. So the present "local" dimension has in Italy antecedents in the premodern times that were quite advanced and flourishing and could easily be revived within an entirely new framework.

As every good book does, this one too opens up a number of questions previously not raised. The book's thesis implies a counterfactual, namely, that a country in modern times can produce better political and economic results if it enjoys a stronger national identity. Indeed, a cohesive nation can express a more coherent and sustained set of policies, both domestically and in the international arena, but it can also breed a tendency toward warfare and economic protectionism. The lack of a strong national identity did not spare Italy the horrors of two world wars. This book raises questions that are relevant today not only for Italy.

Vera Zamagni
University of Bologna, 2010

Introduction

In 1987, Prime Minister Bettino Craxi announced that Italy, having surpassed the gross domestic product (GDP) of Great Britain, had become the fifth world power. This declaration was followed by a storm of polemic, in particular from the British, who accused ISTAT (the Italian Office of National Statistics) of having modified its method of calculating the GDP to their advantage. This was, to some extent, true. But it was also true that the Italian economy was proving, at that point, to possess a dynamism superior to not only that of Thatcher's Britain, weakened by a strong dose of liberal medicine, but also that of France, where the Italian "*nouveaux condottieri*," as *L'Express* had labeled them two years previously, were seizing hold of the media, the banks, the insurance sector, and even one of the symbols of French national pride, the famous sugar company Béghin-Say.

In reality, the ruse was not so much falsification of the figures as the fact that, while the other countries were restructuring their economies and their public administration, Italy was managing to sidestep the obstacles by playing the cards of low wages, devaluation of the lira, and public debt.

Twenty years later, Italy had fallen to seventh place among the major powers; in 2006, its GDP was not more than 78 percent of Great Britain's, and in 2004 it was overtaken by China.[1] From 2001 to 2005, Italy was recorded as having the weakest rate of growth in Europe, and its share of global trade fell from 5 percent in 1987 to 3.6 percent in 2005, which was the level at the beginning of the 1960s.[2]

The main political and economic players tried to place the blame for this downturn on each other: in the second half of the 1990s, when the ruse of artificial growth had ceased to work, it was the so-called "First Republic" and its figurehead, Bettino Craxi, that found themselves on trial. Then, the two opposing coalitions, born out of the crisis, held each other accountable for the feeble economic performance of the country, without the slightest allusion to their own responsibility, nor a nod toward the influence of the global economy, unless in order to absolve themselves.

And yet, ten years after Craxi's triumphant statement, Sergio Romano suggested that the problem was structural; at the end of the period of the "economic miracle," Italy, to his mind, had strong chemical, iron and steel, and information technology industries, and had the potential to be a civil nuclear power. "All of these assets have disappeared over the years," he concluded.[3]

* * *

In this book we will be studying Italy with reference to structural elements that are verifiable and quantifiable.

In 1859 through 1861, Italy came together out of an unusual combination of factors, predominantly international ones, with the major powers realizing the benefits of adding a new pawn to their geopolitical chessboard. It was not born, like many other nation-states, from the bourgeois struggle against the limitations that hampered its own development. This singular trajectory—at least among the great and middle powers—has meant that in Italy the prevailing cultural and political inclination is more oriented toward official and, even more often, unofficial diplomatic maneuvering than toward the necessities of the economy.

Among the ruling classes of the country, concern for immediate particular interests has nearly always predominated over the necessity of defining the *general interest*. Consistently with this habit, politicians have managed public resources for the sake of privileging first and foremost their electoral "clients," even if this means contradicting the rules of development. Thus from the end of World War II to the end of the 1980s, the small peasantry, artisans, shopkeepers, transporters, and small-scale bankers (all in sectors of low productivity) were sheltered from specific legislation. When this policy of protectionism was revealed to be unworkable, the tendency was to absorb the excess workforce into public administration.

All of these factors have flowed into the persistent low productivity of the country: the industrial horizon has always been dominated by small businesses; transport and distribution networks are among the most fragmented in Europe; the organization of the education system and of research remains among the most inefficient;[4] and, finally, the number of public-sector employees—at 3.36 million in 2006—is less than that of France, but more than that of Germany in relation to the population, and much greater than that of countries whose economic results have been among the best in the whole of the European Union (EU) in recent years, such as Spain and Ireland. Together, these conditions have contributed to the progressive decline of Italian industry, so much so that we may speak of the "eclipse" or even, to quote Luciano Gallino in 2003, the "vanishing" of Italian industry.

Gallino underlined the fact that the weakness of industrial production was not without geopolitical consequences. In the twenty-first century, he wrote, as in previous centuries, and perhaps even more so, a country that lacks a large manufacturing industry "risks becoming a sort of colony, subordinated to the economic, social and political needs of other countries possessing such an industry."[5] Italian passivity in international relations can also be explained by this fundamental structural characteristic.

In a text from 1993 entitled *Stato senza nazione*, Zeffiro Ciuffoletti, referring to the period after the unification, suggested a link between the lack of "nationalization of the masses" and the lack of industrial development in the country.[6] Furthermore, in their text about the history of Italian foreign policy, Giuseppe Mammarella and Paolo Cacace returned insistently to the connection between the "lack of clear vision of national interests" and "the interrelation between foreign and domestic politics."[7]

* * *

Examining the structural characteristics of the country will help us to avoid the risk of getting lost in what Bollati has defined as "the ethnic ether."[8] It equally means we can avoid the tendency to moralize, which never actually changes the facts of reality.

In this book we will be principally concerned with what is "constant" in the physiognomy of the country, knowing full well that "constant" does not mean "immutable." On the contrary, we are forced to put the most emphasis on the idea of *process*, on the transformation of different phenomena. For example, "crises of internationalization" are present throughout the whole history of unified Italy, defined by its traumatic collisions with major upheavals in the global economy and international politics; nevertheless, it is obvious that, with each collision, as much its subject as its object changed—both in form and dimensions. The crisis of 1866 was, like that of 1992, a "crisis of internationalization" that had a significant impact upon the political and economic face of the country; but the national and international contexts, the personalities and the factors involved can in no way be compared.

* * *

One section of this book will be devoted to the "crossing of the desert" from 1494 to 1861. Our aim will be to understand in what way the country's "original characteristics," its fundamental elements, have determined how contemporary Italy came together and took shape. Our aim will be to understand why, on the eve of 1861, very few leaders of the ruling classes of the different Italian states were contemplating the possibility of the unification of the peninsula, indeed, why most of them actually opposed any impetus that led in this direction.

Educated by the lessons of 1848 through 1849, the Lombards feared that a union with the Piedmontese would remove them from the geopolitical orbit of central Europe without actually freeing them from their status as a political minority, which they suffered as part of the Austrian Empire. The Piedmontese, who had not participated in any essential moment in the life of Italy up until that point, were thinking only of a dynastic extension of their territory, which would bring to the house of Savoy the rich regions of northern Italy, as well as a loose confederate link with the other parts of the peninsula. The Sicilians were struggling for their own independence. The Neapolitans were determined to protect the integrity of their kingdom, which was threatened by separatism and the local potentates. The Pope, quite simply, identified unification with the loss of his temporal power, and when his fears were realized, he excommunicated the whole of the political community, withdrew inside the walls of the Vatican, and ostracized the nascent state. Last but not least, regarding the unitary patriots, since the failed revolutions of 1848 and 1849, either they had signed on to Cavour's "diplomatic revolution" or they had squandered their energy and credibility in the fabrication of implausible insurrections.

* * *

The exceptional circumstances leading to the unification of Italy will be the subject of a special analysis at the beginning of this book, because they help us to understand one of the main characteristics of the country: its constant subordination to the interests of other great powers. When the military alliance between France and the Kingdom of Sardinia against Austria in 1859 provoked the unintended result of insurrections in central Italy and Sicily, Great Britain swapped its initial caution for unreserved support for unification. Therefore, from its very birth, Italy was often to be an instrument used by the major powers. Trying to find a place in the shadow of whichever power enjoyed the most prosperity at any given moment, Italy has been pitched from one alliance to another according to the dynamics of interests that were hardly ever its own.

At the beginning of the twentieth century, the German chancellor Bernhard von Bülow expressed his annoyance at Italy's habit of "waltzing" with Germany's enemies. From that day on, the vagaries of Italy's foreign policy were regularly denounced. What have been rarer, however, are attempts to explain why it vacillated so.

The outstanding performance of the Italian officers who, in the centuries before unification, were in the service of France and Austria; the undeniable brilliance of Garibaldi's armies; the demonstrable heroism of soldiers abandoned by the state after September 8, 1943; and even the political and diplomatic qualities of two "Italians" who led other countries, Napoleon Bonaparte and Sonia Maino Gandhi, spare us the temptation of creating an "ethnic" link between the foreign policy of the country and its population. If the problem does not reside in the Italian "character," then it resides in other factors of a historical nature, be they economic, social, cultural, or institutional, or as is most likely, all of these put together.

* * *

In this book we will try to clarify systematically the link between a weak national identity and an uncertain presence on the international stage.

While other countries pursue power politics in order to serve national interests, in Italy there has been, since the unification, a trend to support the need for the country to pursue power politics in order to discover what its interests actually are. Each time this trend announces itself, it reveals the lack of a guiding principle in foreign policy—that is, the lack of a sense of aim and initiative when attempting to act on the international stage. Each time this trend resurges, Italy heads straight toward risking new humiliation.

We may note quite rightly that the phrase "lack of national interests" encourages a degree of confusion, in the sense that it could lead one to think that Italy does not have its own interests. In reality, the problem is the exact opposite; across the Italian peninsula there exist a great number of disparate interests that, incapable of identifying themselves in collective will, create a host of divergent foreign policies, potential or actual. The major cities, the regions, the different productive sectors, the economic groups more open toward international markets, those who are oriented more toward the domestic market, the Catholic movements (often laying claim to differing positions, even while serving ultimately the same cause): all these particular interests rarely manage to synthesize their will with the general interest.

The form of political action that is designed to cater to multiple interests and that, instead of achieving a general synthesis, seeks out short-term provisional and partial synthesis is referred to as "transformism."

* * *

This book will give ample space to the question of transformism. We could even say that it is a book about transformism, if this did not suggest that it is, by the same token, a book on the weak identity of Italians and on the wavering trajectory of the foreign policy of their country.

This is not another history of Italy. In fact, it is rather an attempt to sketch out a history and an analysis of the social and political mechanisms that govern Italy as a unitary state and their correlation with the social psychology of Italians. A history, because we are retracing the abiding nature of these mechanisms throughout the whole existence of the country; an analysis, because we are trying to understand the reasons for their existence.

It is necessary to try to establish a reason why a country born without an identity, without a well-defined international role, established upon political structures that were transformist in essence, found itself, almost 150 years later, still suffering from a weak identity, an unstable international position, and a transformist employment of political power. We locate this reason in the *country's endemic low productivity*.

A country like the Italy of 1861, with an essentially rural economy and very little industry, all of which was of small or very small proportions, could only ever be a country of low productivity. The fragmentation and the isolation of the bourgeoisie as well as its fundamentally agricultural identity as a result made it difficult for different interest groups to align themselves in powerful coalitions capable of acting as figureheads for the general interest. In addition to this, the international patronage of the country had, to some extent, absolved the ruling classes of the necessity of strategically evaluating their own development. As they were not being solicited by active coalitions of interests, the political community operated through a process of carefully co-opting the productive sectors of society, and welcoming them with transformist initiatives, with the ultimate aim of preserving the stability of social relations and avoiding all potential social dislocation.

One of the first consequences of transformism was that general productivity remained low. The second consequence, strongly linked to the first, was that the social dislocations were almost always imposed from abroad.

* * *

The history of Italy is also the story of a long succession of "crises of internationalization." These crises were brought about by changes in international economic and political relations, which in turn had brutal repercussions for the internal stability of Italy. Another constant is that the greater the attempts to keep the influence of foreign upheaval from Italy, the worse the problem became.

The chapter devoted to the internationalization crisis of 1866, which marked the end of the internal balance of powers upon which Italy had been founded, examines what was, to some extent, the prototype of a long series of transformations generated, or at least stimulated, by international events. The end of the free-trade cycle in the 1880s, the French conquest of Tunis in 1881, the expansive Belle Époque period, the Eastern Crisis, World War I, German rearmament in 1935, the Keynesian cycle resulting from the Great Depression, and the beginning of the new free-trade cycle from the second half of the 1970s: there we have a brief list of some of the major international upheavals that had violent repercussions for the Italian nation.

Only once did the breach of stability come from within; at the end of the 1960s, when major strikes meant the end of the social compromise of low salaries, one of the keys—indeed, for many, the only key—to the "economic miracle" of the 1950s and the 1960s. But on this occasion, the opposite happened: in the absence of major international upheaval, the temporary crisis was overcome by the transformist co-optation of the Italian Communist Party (PCI) in the governmental majority, which put a halt to salary growth, and by a phase of economic expansion contrived by the "competitive devaluation" of the lira.

The lowering of salaries and the depreciation of the currency were the two shortcuts that allowed Italy to harbor, for another ten years, the illusion that it could exist without a radical overhaul of its structures in order to ensure a systematic increase in productivity.

* * *

Encountering the "European constraint"—to employ a phrase happily coined by Guido Carli—was the most recent crisis of internationalization faced by Italy, and ultimately triggered the cataclysm of the 1990s.

The members of the European fellowship—who were, we should note, also direct competitors—agreed upon the objective of preventing Italy from enjoying the sort of "unfair" competition it had endured so often before through the devaluation of the lira. At the end of the 1970s, the members of the European Economic Community employed a relatively "soft" method, by obligating the Italian currency to adhere to the European Monetary System, all the while giving it some special dispensation. Despite this favorable treatment, the impact of this ruling was brutal, and one of its many consequences was the exit of the PCI from the governmental majority.

During the 1980s, the public debt took on unheard of proportions, which allowed families to multiply their revenue and business concerns to conquer foreign markets, which were, at the same time, in the process of restructuring. Nevertheless, the 1980s was also the period when Germany ceased to be a "political dwarf" and provoked a sudden acceleration of the European process. Franco-German cooperation, signified by the Maastricht Treaty and the single currency, was also the sign that, for Italy, the period of special treatment was definitively over.

Very few observers have suggested that the coincidence of timing between the Italian crisis, the signing of the Maastricht Treaty, the collapse of the Soviet Union, the breakdown of Yugoslavia, and also the beginning of the Japanese "squandered decade" was not down to chance. If we consider, as Sergio Romano did, that the

Italian state was "the greatest entrepreneur to the west of Dnepr,"⁹ the coincidence becomes understandable. The combined pressure of German strength and international free trade had shaken the structures of all countries with a mainly state-governed economy, which had stood firm up until that point thanks to the geopolitical safety net assured by Yalta.

Italy welcomed the "European constraint" wholeheartedly. Any other option meant the risk of isolation from the motor of development moving through the rest of Europe. The regionalist factions that had developed in the 1980s expressed, whether consciously or not, a determination to maintain their link with the rest of Europe, with Italy or without her. Although everyone was aware of the risks, and although everyone was aware that liberalization was the only possible solution, people were equally convinced of the fact that it was up to "others" to suffer the burden of this decision and sacrifice themselves for the good of the country.

To put an end to the deadlock, it was necessary, as Federico Rampini said in 1996, to summon the European "bogeyman,"[10] who alone was capable of conquering all opposition. Among the most vociferous resistors were the major Italian political parties, born in the state-capitalism era and incapable of playing the liberal role put upon them by the new free-trade era. The "Clean Hands" judges were, to a certain extent, the "secular arm" charged with administering the European verdict that condemned this torpid political system.

* * *

In his book on Italy in Europe, Mario Monti remembers having said one day to Margaret Thatcher that Italians needed Maastricht because they had "never had a Margaret Thatcher."[11]

In France, some commentators think that Mitterrand's liberal awakening in 1983 left behind few concrete measures and a considerable amount of antiliberal doctrine. In Italy, not only was there no Thatcher, but there was not even a Mitterrand. We could even go so far as to say that in Italy the situation was exactly the inverse: Mitterrand became liberal while maintaining a language that was "Socialist;" in Italy, the country continued to be "Socialist" while using a liberal vocabulary. The reason lies in the fact that the political and economic players were inexorably linked to the state; even the largest private industries received loans and orders from the state, profited from the mass acquisition of public shares at an attractive price, exported successfully due to the favorable value of the lira, and ultimately got their credit from state-owned banks.

Silvio Berlusconi presented himself as a free-marketer. In reality, he is no such thing, neither by his origins—the Socialist Party led by Bettino Craxi having assisted considerably in the domestic expansion of his business—nor through his political actions. Under his second government, tax came to represent, in 2005, 45.4 percent of the wage in comparison to an average of 37.3 percent in the Organization for Economic Cooperation and Development (OECD) countries; in the same year the level of debt as a percentage of GDP had increased by 2.5 points compared to the year before, reaching a total of 106.4 percent. The current account surplus went from 6.6 percent of GDP in 1997 to 0.4 percent in 2005. In addition, between 2001 and 2004 productivity decreased by 0.1 percent, whereas in Germany it increased by 11.8 percent and in France it increased by 8.9 percent: according to the Global Economic Forum, in 2005 Italy was forty-seventh in the global rankings of productivity. Growth, having remained fixed below 1 percent from 2002, reached a level of stagnation at 0 percent in 2005. As a result, Italy's part of the global market fell from 4 percent to 3 percent between 2001 and 2005.[12]

* * *

One cannot help but stand up and take notice when a new paradox emerges in which the right wing acts as the party of laxity and the left wing presents itself as the party of discipline. This new paradox was accompanied by another that saw the left wing and the pacifists greet the Italian military mission to Lebanon with enthusiasm, while the right wing and the nationalists expressed trepidation. An Italian in hibernation since the 1960s, reawakening in 2007, would surely feel disoriented.

The problems encountered by the second government of Romano Prodi (2006–2008) must not be attributed exclusively to the strength of the far left in the coalition, as suggested by the Anglo-Saxon press and the employer's federation, but rather they should be attributed to the risk of alienating the electorate by attacking its social status. It is a difficulty encountered by the left and the right, by every government; indeed, it is the challenge of all politicians subject to the judgment of the voters. The Italian particularity, when it comes to this issue, is that the left wing as well as the right wing are culturally strangers to the free-market mentality and any profound change is only possible if it is imposed by a foreign "bogeyman" at the gates.

The first and certainly the most important step in the Italian turnaround was the weakening of protectionism under the first government led by Giuliano Amato, in 1992. Many public assets were privatized and public expenditure was subject to the biggest reduction in the entire history of the Italian Republic. Some of the "historic" institutions—for example, the famous "Cassa per il Mezzogiorno"[13]— were dismantled, as well as one of the biggest state conglomerates in the Western world, the Institute for Industrial Reconstruction (IRI).[14] The Italian market was fully opened to external competitors, many diverse sectors were deregulated, and vast reform of the public administration as well as an initial reorganization of the banking system began.

We must remember that Amato had had the good fortune to be prime minister when the parliamentary right to veto was almost nonexistent: 205 out of 630 deputies were in fact prosecuted on May 18, 1993,[15] and consequently they were ready to vote for any government rather than risk the dissolution of the parliament, and probably time in prison. This "extraparliamentary" character of the government broke down the traditional transformist mechanism, and Amato was able to submit the country to European guidelines. This submission brought about more structural changes than forty years of democratic elections.

Some other transformations induced by the European process concerned the political field more directly. From the unification until 1994, the Italian political system always centered around a single party; with the exception of a short period in the mid-1870s, two opposing coalitions never presented themselves before the electorate with the same chances of success. After its victory in 1876, Agostino Depretis' *Sinistra* became the "single party of the bourgeoisie,"[16] and the *Destra* progressively ceased to be a real party of opposition and eventually disappeared. In the decades that followed, debate about the possibility of having several parties was even the subject of theoretical discourse. Benedetto Croce, to name but one example, suggested in two essays from 1912 and 1928 that such a thing was artificial. Between the publication of Croce's first and second text, fascism had imposed *de jure* the single-party system. In the postwar period, the Communist Party never represented a real danger to the monopoly of the Christian Democrats (DC), as the international stage did not allow it any access to power.

The changes on the international stage in the 1980s and 1990s altered the situation. Thanks to her relationship with Europe, Italy not only avoided a fate like that of Yugoslavia or the USSR, or even that of Argentina in 2001, but also became a "normal country,"[17] at least in the sense that two coalitions could now compete for power.

Governmental stability was the other important modification to take place in Italy over the last decade, at least with the Silvio Berlusconi governments. After Alcide De Gasperi in the period between 1948 and 1953, Berlusconi was the second president of the Italian Counsel to be in office for an entire term; the government he led from June 2001 to April 2005 was the longest lasting in the entire history of the republic: 1,414 days, which is more than a third longer than the former record, held by Bettino Craxi, for some 1,083 days between 1983 and 1987. Very few commentators have noticed that this shift occurred in all the major European countries, in which the process of Europeanization had imposed greater stability. Italy became a "normal country" in the sense that it became less Italian and more European.

* * *

Among the permutations of recent years, one of the most striking is the emergence of a "personalization" of politics. This phenomenon does not simply stem from the European process, but is also part of the "natural" evolutionary trend of parliamentary politics, discernible in many different countries with diverse customs and institutions. In Italy this trend was worsened by the frenetic search for a "substitute" for traditional politics, at least from the 1970s onward. Used for the first time by Craxi, provoking both skepticism and sarcasm, the "personalization" card was abundantly played during the years of the great crisis, especially by Silvio Berlusconi. The latter certainly took it up a notch, and his adversaries have been equally vocal in contributing to his iconization, even if contemptuously. For this reason we have too often seen Berlusconi as the man being talked of, without interrogating Berlusconi-ism—a social and psychological phenomenon whose roots lie, we might say, in the whole history of Italy.

Since the birth of this country, numerous political leaders and intellectuals—not to mention the Catholic Church—have praised frugality, and considered it as a sort of Italian fatality: the nationalists and the Fascists went so far as to transform it into virtue, as a moral crutch to be used in the fight against the "five meals a day" nations, as Mussolini used to refer to the "rich countries." In the postwar period, the DC and the PCI competed fiercely for the virtue of temperance, right up until the second half of the 1970s, when these two parties began their governmental collaboration under the twin mottos of "austerity" and "sacrifice."

But meanwhile—since the time when it was said that the sun was the only industry that suited Italy, the time of "proletarian Italy," the time when the frugality of the rural family was held up as an example to the whole of the nation—an essential change had occurred in the lives of Italians: they had ceased to be the beggars of neorealist movies—they had gotten rich. The immigrants, the *sciuscià*, and the bicycle thieves[18] were now coming from the Balkans, from North Africa, and from the Far East, and all trying to land on the Italian coast.

Many within the political and intellectual communities failed to recognize these changes and, more to the point, failed to understand them. This created a division between the Italians who wanted to benefit from their new conditions without feeling guilty and their political and intellectual leaders. Some years before Berlusconi gave his name to this phenomenon, the president of Fiat, Gianni Agnelli, visited a secondary school where he was greeted with enthusiasm by the students, who excitedly suggested that he grab the reins of the country himself and kick out the "petty politicians." This welcome left the political community flabbergasted, in particular the left wing, for whom Agnelli still personified the "enemy of the people".

The shades of this new climate were recognized by Bettino Craxi. In abolishing one part of the mechanism of index-linking salaries, Craxi launched a challenge to the trade union power that was tightly linked to the PCI. In the referendum on this issue, 54.3 percent of the electorate voted with the Socialist prime minister and against the unions and the PCI. We could say that Berlusconi-ism was born on that day.

* * *

Fifteen years after the beginning of the lengthy Italian crisis, the polemic about the political "caste"—that is, despite the Indian metaphor, the "untouchables" who are ready to defend their privileges at any cost—is resurfacing, along with the threat of another great political turmoil.

There exists a long tradition of the myth of the "antipolitical" that took root in the whole history of postunification Italy. A minister of the last Prodi government, Tommaso Padoa Schioppa, noted that "artists, administrators, lawyers, advertising executives, trade unions, and entrepreneurs are as much a ruling class as the government." We return once more therefore to the problem of the ruling classes and, as Padoa Schioppa would suggest, to the issue of bad habits, and the worst habit of all, that of trying to solve the mystery of their own historical weakness through finding a scapegoat.

In recent years, studies on the absence of an Italian sense of civicness have become more common. Some have attributed this to "amoral familism,"[19] others to the Counter-Reformation, some to the rampant cult of individualism sanctioned by the "Berlusconian way of life," and others to the political parties and the so-called cost of politics. Some have spoken of the limited resources of "social capital," meaning, in sociological terms, "a sense of the responsibility towards others and institutions—solidarity and participation."[20] In sum, a general observation is that there is great reluctance from individuals to sacrifice even a small part of their own particular interests in the name of the general good.

The Italy of today is still characterized by marked "political fragmentation"— the absence of a "center" already observed by Giacomo Leopardi in 1824. In addition to having introduced certain corrections and, in certain cases, certain solutions to some of the structural problems of the country, the European process has offered a place in which this fragmentation—inherited from its history and its geography—has been acknowledged and, little by little, has begun to disappear. Italy became, for a while, a sort of model of supranational integration, of polycentrism, of voluntary (and sometimes even eager) cession of sovereignty in the framework of a new plurality of institutions that leaves behind the traditional concept of a "Europe of regions."

From the phase of stop and go experienced in Europe between 2005's referenda in France and the Netherlands (but probably from the "Letter of the Eight" in 2003) and the election of Nicolas Sarkozy in 2007, media campaigns used fear of a possible return to 1992 as a warning to the political community. When the European process slows down, Italy risks falling back into bad habits, which are now less likely to succeed, given that the ministers and central bankers can no longer use the ruse of competitive devaluation. On the other hand, when the European process speeds up again, the squabbles of Italy's political leaders, the backwardness of the country's infrastructure, the low wages, and the burden of public debt and increasing taxation are all factors capable of preventing the country from following the continental pace.

The problematic national identity of Italy, from whichever angle it is examined, has been and is of geopolitical significance.

Foreword

The "Original Sin"

All'Italia indifferente fu imposta la rivoluzione da motivi esterni e da contingenze di politica europea
[External causes and European political situation imposed the revolution to an indifferent Italy.]

—*Piero Gobetti (1923)*[1]

Italy's External Origins

At the moment of its unification, Italy was one of Europe's most backward countries, in both economic and financial terms. Agriculture, which accounted for 56.7 percent of gross domestic product (GDP), employed 70 percent of active workers, while industry, which contributed 20.3 percent to GDP, employed only 18 percent, with most of those working at home and in sectors using low-level technologies (notably textiles). The state, indebted to the tune of 500 million lira (about 2 billion euros at the 2002 equivalent), had neither the capital nor, as we will see, the political will to foster a shift from a largely traditional phase, involving modest forms of manufacturing, to an industrial phase.

Modern industrial establishments were exceedingly rare (there were only ten blast furnaces on the peninsula), and even if they were nearly all linked to railway construction, the rail network itself remained very limited (1,829 kilometers), relying heavily on imported equipment. The banking system, without the stimulation of the industrial demand, managed to attract only 1.4 percent of national revenue and included almost none of the medium-term credit establishments that are indispensable to industrial financing. The backwardness of industry was also linked to low primary-sector productivity: by some estimates, revenue per hectare amounted to barely 80 lira, compared to the equivalent of 170 lira in France and 213 lira in England, while wheat production was a mere nine hectoliters, compared to fifteen in France and thirty-two in England.[2]

Given a demographic growth rate weaker than the continental average, and modest industrial development, the process of urbanization was extremely slow, despite an urban tradition far more ancient than in most other European countries. Thus Naples was the country's most populous city, with 447,000 inhabitants, followed by Turin (250,000), and Rome and Milan (each with 185,000). The lack of a well-qualified labor force weighed further on development, more than other factors, as both an effect and a cause of the country's backwardness. While 54 percent of the working population was illiterate, only a mere 12 percent could truly read and write. Of the 15 million people age eighteen or older, only 120,000, or 8 percent, had completed any secondary education. Finally, per capita revenue was only one-third that of France, and one-fourth that of Great Britain.

Italy was not the only European country with economic and social indicators that trailed countries like France and Great Britain. Backwardness is a relative concept and cannot be measured purely by statistical data. But Italy's backwardness became a first-order geopolitical handicap at the very moment when the new state pretended to rank among the great powers, regardless of its grave structural deficits. This made the country appear, as Bismarck sarcastically proclaimed, "like a creature of great appetite but weak teeth."

The Italy of the second half of the nineteenth century displayed none of the characteristics that typically give rise to an "autonomous" or "national" unification movement. The historic rupture that led to the integration of the different parts of the peninsula was provoked by an extraordinary set of circumstances far beyond anyone's expectations. In his reflections on the *Risorgimento*—Italy's "rebirth"— Antonio Gramsci ascribes this unexpected development to a "determined historic European connection:" the reciprocal weakening of the two great continental powers—France and Austria—and the emergence of a third great power, Prussia.[3] In other words, the formation of the Italian state resulted in large part from the spreading seismic waves that were shaking Europe's geopolitical balance of power.

Count Cavour and Napoleon III, with the hypotheses they concocted in 1858, hardly foresaw the unification of the country; moreover, the Piedmontese ruling class was far from possessing the force required to imagine such a solution. That is why it had to hastily "invent" a political product lacking cultural or popular bases in hopes of achieving within mere decades what neighboring countries had spent centuries constructing.

The Piedmont's domination of the other regions—heavy-handed for the Mezzogiorno, but humiliating as well for Lombardy, one of Europe's most evolved regions—and its subsequent co-option by the great-power concert, imposed the need on this new Italy to have a direction even before it had an identity. Having lacked a direction *a priori*, the fruit of a rational political plan—which existed only in the minds of the *patrioti*, who had played a negligible role in the country's birth—it was necessary to look for a direction *a posteriori*. Thus was invented the legend of an Italy that *"si è fatta da sé"*—had made itself—and thus too was forged the religion of the *Risorgimento*, a mythical epic in which a few powerful actors had managed to bend reality to their will.

"Artichoke" Politics

A number of historians have recently established a relationship between the absence of the masses in the national movement, the "heterogenesis" (external origins) of the Italian state, and the persistence, in a unified Italy, of some distinctive traits of the Savoyard political tradition.

From the thirteenth to the sixteenth century, the House of Savoy had enlarged its borders in the direction of Italy, not by dint of its material or spiritual wealth, but by a form of diplomacy practiced without hesitation, always able to draw advantage from rivalries among its neighbors—the Guelphs and Ghibellines, the Italian republics and the empire, France and Austria. The foreign policy of the Savoy constantly evolved through ambiguity and by playing one side against another.

One of the rare countries where the post-Napoleonic Restoration truly deserved its name was the Piedmont, where the civil code and the gains that it brought were abolished. It is highly likely that the Savoy's rigid adherence to the principles of the Restoration and its hostility to any unitary notion were two reasons why, at the Congress of Vienna, their kingdom became seen as a balancing factor against a total Austrian domination of the peninsula. Two other reasons were its geographic situation as a buffer state between France and Austria, and the fact that since it was largely French in language and culture, it was supposed to be exempt, by its very nature, from any temptation toward Italian "nationalism."

The reattachment of Genoa and of all of Liguria was indisputably the essential factor in strengthening the Kingdom of Sardinia, making it a symbolic counterweight to Hapsburg hegemony on the peninsula. For all that, Turinese diplomacy played no role in the annexation, which was decided in the first treaty, even before the Piedmont delegation arrived in the Austrian capital.

Despite that, the Piedmontese rulers attributed the "conquests" achieved in Vienna to politics based on the old scheme of dynastic expansion characteristic of Savoyard politics: that of the "artichoke," whose leaves are eaten one after the other.[4] They considered it perfectly normal, in the literal sense of the word, that their state should be able to grow by profiting openly from the quarrels between the great powers. For the same reason, they did not consider themselves the slightest bit indebted to the country—France—that had supported the enlargement of the Sardinian kingdom and that directly guaranteed its independence vis-à-vis Austria. To the contrary, since France was in a position of weakness and Austria in a position of strength, the best tradition suggested that Turin should profit, purely and simply, by turning toward the latter in order to gain advantage at the expense of the former. Thus, until the 1830s, Charles Albert continued to claim French territories beyond the Alps, even while confiding in Metternich that he would enjoy "his most beautiful day when he could march alongside Austrian soldiers against France and Louis-Philippe."[5]

In reality, Austrian soldiers had no intention of marching against France. This demonstrates how misapprehended international affairs remained in the eyes of the Piedmontese ruling class: for its members, the "balancing of power" consisted simply of the atavistic habit of jumping from one side of the balance to the other. The new European situation had definitively deprived the Italians of any option of turning the neighboring powers against each other. Therefore Piedmont was no longer able to apply its traditional politics and found itself at the rearguard of the national movement.

Between Myth and Reality

The historian Francesco de Sanctis was the first to sense, from the early years of the new kingdom, the need to use history as a political weapon by celebrating an imaginary compromise between the moderates and the democrats as a sort of founding act of the unified kingdom. His objective was to give ideological legitimacy to the new state against those who would deligitimize it (above all, the Catholic Church) by giving it a certain consistency in the eyes of the masses, who were indifferent or even open to the clerics' arguments. With de Sanctis, the syncretic vision of the *Risorgimento* arose and placed in the same Olympus such diverse and irreconcilable figures as Victor Emmanuel, Mazzini, Garibaldi, and Cavour. Little by little this political weapon became a sort of collective and retrospective myth: the king, the liberals, and the ordinary people marching together, arm in arm, toward the common objective of "making Italy."

In fact, the kings had been fiercely hostile to anything remotely suggestive of unification, to the point that the Piedmontese censor had banned, as late as the 1840s, the very use of the words "Italy" and "nation", always replaced by a more anodyne "country." The liberals and the masses, for their part, felt little common bond. The former saw no way that their elevated ideals could possibly have anything to do with the mundane needs of the latter, while the latter were left baffled by the obscure formulas employed by the former.

If this triad—the king, the liberals, and the people—was but a chimera, invented *a posteriori* (the way the Galls were for the French or the Goths for the Germans), then just who were Italy's true "founders"? Put another way: Did any force exist in Italy capable of leading a national movement?

Theoretically, yes. For example, the thousands who, under Napoleon, had held civil or military posts—young, ambitious, talented people, sensitive to the political and cultural problems of their era, regretful that this was not an epoch in which a career was offered to people of talent. The latter could only reject the "intellectual hell" that dominated in Turin (the phrase comes from Camillo Benso, the Count of Cavour, who was peremptorily asked to leave the kingdom after having published in Paris in 1846 an essay on the railway system in Italy and its unifying role in the peninsular market). Indeed, their influence within the army played a determining role during the insurrections of Naples in 1820 and Piedmont in 1821. But the resounding failure of both the revolts sufficed to exclude them from among those who might have been able to take leadership of an eventual Italian national unification process.

For a while the hope of a "patriotic" Pope was the hypothesis most discussed in Italian intellectual circles. The *neo-guelfi* (neo-Guelphs) argued that the Pope could use his moral authority to bring together the "Italian race," which was politically divided, but united by ties of blood, religion, and language. But when several armies from different states of the "Italian race" began pursuing the routed Austrians in April 1848, Pope Pius IX declared that he "rejected the disconcerting suggestions contained in newspapers and other writings by those who would make the Roman Pontiff the president of a certain new republic to be constituted with the support of all the peoples of Italy."[6] This about-face by a Pontiff who had seemed at first to support the liberals' aspirations was not, however, the only reason for the failure of the neo-Guelph plan. In fact, as Gramsci observed, the great powers probably would not have accepted that "the cultural function of the Church and its diplomacy, already sufficiently encumbering ... gain further strength by basing itself on a large territorial state and a proportionally important army."[7]

The bourgeoisie was actually the only class with any direct and immediate interest in achieving a unified national market. But with isolated exceptions, this class produced few theories and even less action toward this end.

A Weak and Fragmented Bourgeoisie

The modern idea of nation arrived in Italy on the tips of the bayonets of the revolutionary French bourgeoisie: the standardization of institutions and of legal codes, the adoption of the decimal metric system, and the improvement of communications that, after the Napoleonic conquest, was applied to the entire peninsula left a concrete taste for the benefits to be gained from national unification.

In March 1816, Marshal Heinrich Joseph de Bellegarde, governor of Lombardy, wrote in a dispatch to Vienna that after Napoleon, the Italians would never again accept a simple reconstitution of the small states of yesteryear. In particular, Bellegarde added, Milan, as the capital of the former Italian kingdom, had acquired considerable political importance.[8]

Notwithstanding his confusion between "the" Italians and a small minority of them, Count Bellegarde had seized on a key point: the political importance of Milan. But he had attributed to it a certain scent of Italianness that was not actually so clearly discernible. It is true that while the first revolts against the Viennese-imposed order had broken out in Naples and in Turin, the true capital of the liberal political movements was Milan.

Il Conciliatore, a journal founded in September 1818 by Count Federico Confalonieri, comprised a group of young people with liberal political aspirations and a shared interest in economic and educational reform. In ensuing years this tendency produced numerous offshoots. Among them, the group gathered around the *Politecnico*, another journal created in Milan in 1839 by Carlo Cattaneo, was doubtless the one that placed greatest emphasis on the link between industrial progress and the expansion of constitutional liberties. Moreover, the agrarian transformation had favored the development in Lombardy of a conspicuously larger bourgeoisie than in other regions of Italy, beginning in the mid-eighteenth century.

The Austrian Empire, which after 1815 included also Lombardy and Veneto was not about to impede the development of the Lombardian bourgeoisie, if only because of the wealth it could amass through taxation. Indeed, the budget of the

"Lombard-Venetian Kingdom" was always positive, whereas that of the Austrian Empire, as a whole, was in deficit at least until 1860. Among the advantages benefiting the Lombardian bourgeoisie at the end of the Napoleonic wars were the resumption of exports to Great Britain, the respect of property that originated under the Italian kingdom, an administrative system far more modern than those of the other Italian states, and a road network that was considerably improved, especially in the direction of the Alps—not to mention the thirty-four years of uninterrupted peace from 1814 to 1848.

While the sociological connotations of what one calls the "bourgeoisie" are often eclectic and problematical, one can accept, at least with circumspection, the assertion that the incidence of bourgeoisie over the entire population of the Kingdom of Italy in Napoleonic times was 2.5 to 3.5 times greater than the rate calculated for the entirety of the peninsula eighty years later.[9] That being said, although the Lombard bourgeoisie was among the most numerous, wealthiest, and most industrialized in Italy and in Europe, it did not take the lead in the process of national unification. Despite its admiration for the French example, it was undermined by its fragmentation and by the absence of real links to any political power that might have directly represented its interests.

Since the end of the independence of the Duchy of Milan (1494), Lombardy had been subjected in turn to domination by the French, the Swiss, the Imperial power, the Spanish, the Austrians, the French, and once again by the Austrians, before finally being conquered by the French in 1859 and ceded to the Piedmontese. Its "unpolitical" characteristic is perhaps one of the reasons for Milanese superiority vis-à-vis Rome, Florence, Turin, and Naples; but it may also constitute one of the reasons for the hesitation and political division of the Milanese bourgeoisie at the time of the *Risorgimento*. None of the democrats and only a few liberals were interested in allying themselves with the backward and reactionary Piedmont, to which they preferred the Austrian Empire and its opening to more promising markets Even Carlo Cattaneo, who was later to lead the anti-Austrian insurrection of 1848, had not hesitated earlier to support Metternich's plan for a closer economic union between Austria and northern Italy. The Milanese revolt of 1848 was, in its origins, a simple manifestation of the fact that people were fed up with the "annual pillage," denounced by Cattaneo, which had filled the Austrian tax collectors' coffers with "two thousand of our millions."[10]

The impossibility of providing a unitary administrative, fiscal, and military framework for the common interest left private interests free to play any angle in pursuit of immediate benefit. Thus municipal jealousies—like the rivalries between Bergamo and Treviglio that ultimately blocked for many years the completion of the rail line between Milan and Venice—combined with sporadic capitalist initiatives and limited use of scientific and technical advances. Even when the result was to express a semblance of a common interest, it did not necessarily amount to a national Italian character. When the need was seen to open to new markets from the base of a large unitary grouping, the inclination was to turn where satisfaction seemed most rapidly attainable. Thus, in the 1830s, the Milan Chamber of Commerce manifested its need for opening to new markets through a desire to adhere to the German *Zollverein* (Customs Union). If these were the realities of the Lombard bourgeoisie—the most developed, the most entrepreneurial, and the most numerous in Italy—one can imagine what the situation was in the rest of the country.

The absence of the masses in the national process must be linked to this fundamental circumstance. In fact, the bourgeoisie of the peninsula felt a more acute fear of "the people" than of "the tyrants." There were three essential reasons for this: the bourgeois were few in number; they had very strong social kinships with large property owners; and they had begun to become conscious of their own existence as a class only after the French Revolution. Nevertheless, the principal causes of their weakness were their fragmentation and their small numbers. Because of these factors, during the *Risorgimento* process and even afterward, private interests and regional divisions outweighed any national feelings.

It thus becomes difficult to pose the problem of an Italian "passive revolution" in terms of a lack of political will, as has often been done. The only class objectively interested in a unification of markets was lacking in economic power, political energy, and historic tradition. Under these conditions, the Italians might never have achieved national unity if an external event had not unsettled the country's situation, and that of Europe. The "heterodirection" (external direction) thus becomes key to reading contemporary Italian history.

"Diplomatizing the Revolution"

In 1821 the traditional duplicity of the House of Savoy manifested itself, with two different kings applying two different policies. Victor Emmanuel abdicated because of the insurrection, and Charles Albert—the self-proclaimed regent—accepted the constitution and named as minister of war the head of the conspiracy, Santorre di Santarosa, in order to prepare for the inevitable conflict with Austria. Charles Felix, the legitimate heir, dismissed Charles Albert and Santarosa and called on the Austrians to come to his aid. Charles Albert, fearful of losing his right to the succession, renounced the conspirators and, when he became king in 1832, went so far as to exclude them from the traditional amnesty.

When the insurrection of 1820 erupted in Naples, the equilibrium established in Vienna in 1815 was still too recent for the English to respond to the insurgents' calls for help. Unable to profit from dissensions among the great powers, the Italian insurrection of 1820 through 1821 foundered.

International influence in the affairs of the peninsula was clear during the two revolutionary crises that shook Europe shortly afterward. The French revolution of 1830 gave rise, in 1831, to a series of small uprisings, which were almost immediately put down. And in 1848, after the insurrections of Paris, Vienna, Budapest, and Prague, the antifiscal furies that, from the beginning of the year, had the Milanese boycotting tobacco and lottery games—following the model of the Boston Tea Party—turned into armed revolt.

For some years Charles Albert, having lost all hope of annexing a part of Switzerland, and having realized that the Austrians were not disposed to back his expansionist aims in the direction of France, had turned toward Lombardy, long coveted by the House of Savoy. This is the reason why, fearful of the risk of a republican contagion in Turin, he decided to march on the Lombard capital on March 24, 1848, to seize the initiative from the liberals. Thus, divisions among anti-Austrian parties, Piedmontese indecisiveness and military insufficiencies made Milan the first insurgent capital of the Empire to be brought back, on August 6, under the authority of Vienna.

Nonetheless, Austrian revanchism and the proclamation of the Tuscan and Roman republics—the latter under highly popular leaders like Mazzini and Garibaldi—forced the Piedmontese to resume the war with the goal of reestablishing order in the interior under the cover of "national" action. This decision was surely made less painful by the certainty that England and France, as Denis Mack Smith reminds us, guaranteed that the Piedmontese kingdom would suffer no territorial loss, even if it should be defeated yet again.[11] "We cannot win," Massimo d'Azeglio frankly acknowledged to Silvio Spaventa a few days before hostilities resumed, "but we will fight anew: our defeat will be the defeat of this party that pushes us today to resume the war, and between a defeat and a civil war we choose the former."[12]

If defeat was the goal, it was achieved barely three days later, ingloriously, at Novara: the king abdicated, but the dynasty was safe. As Mack Smith notes, the hypothesis that Italy was created "by itself" was revealed as manifestly absurd. As the Tuscan liberal Bettino Ricasoli bitterly remarked: "Italy no longer does anything by itself."

The *sine qua non* of Italian unification was thus the modification of the geopolitical framework that emerged from the Congress of Vienna. This order suffered in the second half of the century: industrialization, having spread to other regions, began to transform the relationships between the powers. This new phase was marked by three major conflicts: the Crimean War, the American Civil War, and the war between Prussia and France. The conflict on the shores of the Black Sea, according to Paul Kennedy, put an end to the diplomacy of the European concert and caused each of the "flank" powers—that is, Russia and England—"to feel less committed to intervention in the center."[13] Prussia, not yet the hegemonic power of the German world, and Austria, still wrestling with numerous problems engendered by its years of decadence, left France to emerge as the dominant power in continental Europe, even if this was a domination by default.

It was as this new international context was coming to a head that Count Camillo Benso di Cavour, now prime minister in Turin, launched his strategy of trying to "diplomatize the revolution."[14] The English and the French, aiming to placate Austria, did everything in their power to engage Piedmont in the Crimean War, thereby lessening any temptation it might have to take advantage of the situation to attack Lombardy. Cavour was thus invited to the Congress of Paris of 1856, during which the "Italian question" was dealt with rather summarily. The brief references to it had no practical consequences; nevertheless, Cavour obtained two relatively significant results: the increase of Turin's prestige in Italy, as the Piedmontese kingdom was the only and the first state on the peninsula to be represented in an international assembly, and, above all, the possibility of testing its allies' intentions and availability regarding a possible campaign against Austria. The "diplomatization" of the Italian question was thus, from that point on, in motion.

Gramsci observes that Cavour was not only a diplomat but, above all, a political creator.[15] The origins of his creation, a unitary Italy, were thus diplomatic and international—not national. As Sergio Romano points out, this "original sin" was to mark its history.[16]

An Italian "Miracle"

In the mid-1850s, Napoleon III concluded that conditions were in place for the "Vienna order" finally to be modified. The major obstacle was, obviously, Austria. Therefore the "Italian question" served primarily as a pretext to weaken Vienna. As to Cavour, who was perfectly aware of the geopolitical constraints facing the kingdom and the Savoy family's traditional politics, he explicitly offered the French the geostrategic advantage of controlling the Po Valley.

The relationship—equivocal, to say the least—between the head of the Turin government and democratic terrorism circles led some historians to suspect him of inspiring, directly or indirectly, the attack on Napoleon III perpetrated by Felice Orsini on January 14, 1858. While this was never proved, the attack clearly could not have come at a better moment for those on either side of the Alps. Amplifying the revolutionary threat through his resort to spectacular police measures, Cavour sought to demonstrate that, absent a diplomatic solution to the "Italian question," it was going to be difficult to contain all the bombers roaming around Europe and taking the French emperor as their favored target. In France, Orsini's act helped put in motion the process of unraveling the treaties of 1858, supplying Bonaparte with an occasion to prepare public opinion for a decision bound to be far from popular.

Between July 1858 and January 1859, the pacts between France and Piedmont were sealed. The map of a new Italy was drawn up, providing for the birth of three states: the north plus Emilia was attributed to Piedmont, which would cede Savoy and Nice to France, the center to Napoleon III, and the south to Lucien Murat, the son of the last king of the Napoleonic Kingdom of Naples and Sicily, Joachim Murat. These three states were then to be confederated under the presidency of the Pope. Each protagonist had grounds for satisfaction: Bonaparte because he felt he had "reconquered" the peninsula, and Cavour, who, considering the thought of unification as so much nonsense ("*corbellerie*"),[17] hoped for the birth of a homogeneous state, limited to the rich northern regions and led by Turin.

The war and its consequences confirm the validity of the thesis that society's history is the terrain on which countless wills and forces confront and collide, with a result rarely corresponding to the protagonists' initial plans. In fact, the war provoked not only the expected intervention of France, but also insurrection in Emilia and Tuscany, which proclaimed their allegiance to Piedmont; the deep anxiety of the Pope, of whom Napoleon III was the international protector; the threats of Berlin in Paris and, last but not least, a completely new English perspective on the Italian question. All these factors, even if separately predictable, completely transformed the landscape when they arose all at once. The emperor, just as the revolutionaries had foreseen,[18] decided not to pursue the routed Austrians, instead signing an armistice with them in Villafranca, near Verona, on July 8, 1859.

The events of 1859 through 1860 were a sort of archetype of the Italian attitude on the international stage—imposed by objective circumstances, but nearly always presented as the result of an autonomous and subjective choice—consisting of relying on its own weaknesses as if they were elements of strength. Having furnished Napoleon III with a troop contingent significantly smaller than promised, and after having been accused by Victor Emmanuel of "playing at making revolution in central Italy," Cavour resigned after the French-Austrian armistice, slamming the door and denouncing the king as a "traitor" for having signed it.

Yet, these mutual recriminations between the two heads of the Piedmontese executive did not prevent them from reversing roles later. Victor Emmanuel, who had signed a treaty guaranteeing the return of the "legitimate sovereigns" to Florence and Modena, took his own turn at "playing at making revolution" with Garibaldi, even as he assured Pope Pius IX and the king of the Two Sicilies of his respect for the integrity of their states—and this just twenty days before the departure of the Garibaldinian "Red Shirts" for Sicily. Cavour, who had returned to power under the insistent pressure of the English ambassador in Turin, reached agreement with Napoleon III to exchange central Italy for the Savoy (fatherland of the king) and Nice (fatherland of Garibaldi). Later, using as a pretext the risks inherent in a breakthrough by the Garibaldinian "bands"—which he had done nothing to stop—he finally obtained from the French emperor the authorization to traverse—and to annex on his way through—Romagna, Marche, and Umbria, which belonged to the states of the Church, thus achieving the unification of the peninsula.

Several "historical determined connections" thus contributed to the success of this "Italian miracle": an official alliance with France, which was trying to resolve its historic rivalry with the Germanic world; a permanent sort of blackmail exercised against France itself, based on its weaknesses and fears; an unscrupulous game between the varied revolutionary movements; and finally, the room for maneuver that the Mediterranean policy of the British Empire allowed (and sometimes encouraged). Among all these factors, the latter was doubtless the most important.

An English Creation

Having crossed the Mediterranean for Algeria in 1830, colonial France pursued its expansion under the Second Empire in the direction of Africa and the Far East. In 1854 Ferdinand de Lesseps obtained from the viceroy of Egypt, Mohammed Said Pasha, a concession to begin excavation for the Suez Canal. Work began in 1859. To satisfy the demands of an expansionist and Mediterranean politics, the French fleet was reinforced, to the point that in 1859 it raised apprehensions in London.

From 1859 to 1860, Great Britain's attitude regarding the "Italian question" passed through three distinct and apparently contradictory phases that might appear contradictory but which make sense given traditional Anglo-Saxon pragmatism: a first phase, during which London wanted to prevent any modification of the *status quo* that had served well enough for nearly five decades; a second, following the armistice of Villafranca, during which English diplomats grew concerned at the possible expansion of French hegemony on the peninsula; and finally a third, marked by the insurrections of central Italy and Garibaldi's expedition to Sicily, which was seen as the definitive collapse of French ambitions, and in particular as the occasion to integrate the peninsula in a stable manner into a new balance of power more favorable to the ambitions and interests of the British crown.

It was for that reason that the British ambassador in Turin "imposed" Cavour's return; he was the only man positioned to successfully lead the annexation of the former states of central Italy. It was also for that reason that the warships of the Mediterranean fleet "protected" the vessels of the Garibaldinian fleet from any threat by the Neapolitan navy. And when the Pope and the former king of Naples, exiled to Rome, threatened to add an international political-military alliance to the pontifical anathema against the new state, the British made public a fiery declaration justifying Italian unification in the name of the principle of nationality. This declaration, along with the immediate recognition of the new state, signified that Italy was henceforth placed under the protection of the Empire of Her Gracious Majesty. Compared to the subalpine kingdom that had served since 1815 as a buffer state between France and Austria, unified Italy offered added value in its fortunate geopolitical position.

Having long made the government of the Two Sicilies a pillar of their regional hegemony, the English now gladly abandoned a contested and vacillating king of Naples for a young and dynamic Kingdom of Italy whose future Mediterranean ambitions, at times openly encouraged by other powers, were likely to conflict with French designs without constituting the slightest threat to English supremacy.

Thus opened what Sergio Romano calls Italy's "historic cycle of Mediterranean policy"[19] under the shadow of Great Britain. It would continue, almost without interruption—if not without numerous infidelities—until 1935.

"Determined Historical Connections"

Among the varied protagonists of the *Risorgimento*, those who, like Cavour, played an active role managed to do so by rapidly adapting their actions to the actual movements of the international balance of power. Others, like Garibaldi, played a role that was, in truth, passive.

Nonetheless, it is the character of Garibaldi who most fascinates those who have written the history of the *Risorgimento*. In 1854, even before the actions that would reinforce his aura—the Expedition of the Thousand, the Aspromonte and Mentana battles—he received a particularly warm welcome from workers groups during a visit to London. After 1860 the figure of Garibaldi became the prisoner of a hagiography in which appreciation for his undeniable military qualities became jumbled with sentimental considerations.

But some aspects of the "Red Shirts" expedition of the Thousand to Sicily seem to justify the fear, expressed decades later by Prime Minister Giolitti, that "such beautiful legends"[20] might be spoiled if they were better known: for example, the Mafia's decisive support in the conquest of Palermo, or the Camorra's support before the triumphal entry into Naples.

It was a series of exceptionally favorable circumstances that, along with Garibaldi's military genius and undeniable charisma, made it possible—for the first and last time—for an Italian military expedition to produce a lasting political result. We can briefly list some of these: the Palermo insurrection of April 4, 1860; the king's unofficial support for an expedition to Sicily; the exclusively verbal opposition of Cavour who, far from stopping Garibaldi, secretly forwarded arms to him and arranged for him to be protected by Admiral Persano's fleet; the interests of the Genoese naval company Rubattino, which placed its ships at the disposal of the expedition; the benevolent neutrality of two English warships anchored just off Marsala; the dispatch, following the conquest of Palermo, of four thousand new "volunteers" under the command of military officers close to Turin; the English government's clearly negative response to the French request to organize a joint maritime blockade in order to discourage any landing by the Red Shirts in Calabria; the decision by most Neapolitan naval officers not to block the general's march toward the capital of the kingdom; and the allegiance to Garibaldi of the southern property owners, convinced of the necessity of "changing everything so that everything will remain unchanged."[21]

It thus required the support of the king, the distraction of the government, England's benign neglect, the weariness of the enemy, and the favorable reception of the ruling classes and of local mafias for the Sicily expedition to achieve a different outcome from defeats such as Gianicolo, Aspromonte, Bezzecca, and Mentana.[22] Despite everything, the new kingdom adopted the adventure of the Expedition of the Thousand as the foundation of its national legitimacy. Thus the myth of "the sacred rabble of Garibaldi" having awakened "Italian civilization" from its "secular lethargy"[23] began to spread. In the end, this legend served as the foundation of a conviction that Italy's creation was marked, as Sergio Romano writes, not by a plan but by an act, not by an idea but by an intuition. The country, as Romano says, thus remains subject, in its most difficult moments, to a fascination with the decisive gesture, the thundering oration, the Providential man.[24]

From Garibaldi to Berlusconi, by way of Mussolini and De Gasperi—all actors in "the most difficult moments" of the country's history—the passivity of the masses has focused attention on a few individuals and on the happy few who bask in their aura. Political psychology, anthropology, and even hagiography have thus ended up pushing aside the study of "determined historic connections."

Part I

The Original Characteristics

Chapter 1

How Premature Development Became a Factor of Backwardness

"One, None, and a Hundred Thousand"

Postunitary Italy, far from presenting a well-defined face, is the unstable combination of some particular characteristics. The first of these is the fragile dialectic between the various geographical pieces that make it up: the "thousand bell towers," the regional particularities, the use of dialect as a badge of local identity, the relations between the center and the periphery—most particularly, between the north and the south, ever a source of jealousies, haggling, and friction.

When, beginning in the 1880s, the governments of the *Sinistra* attempted to bind up certain of these divisions, they began by co-opting emerging interest groups, or those previously excluded from power (the southern elites, above all), and did so simply by juxtaposing them to the already dominant interest groups. Political institutions thus became the venues of incessant bargaining. The formation of these fragile and temporary alliances between particular and sectoral interests was referred to as "transformism," a process that has accompanied the entire history of united Italy. This fragmentation hampered the search for a national "common interest" and consequently prevented the development of any long-term national strategy.

The impossibility of defining objectives not at the mercy of such transactions hindered the formation of national political parties able to represent alternative interests in any enduring way. The problem, which Francesco de Sanctis described as early as 1877—"We are now at the point where there are no solidly constituted parties, except perhaps for those based on regions and on clientele, Italy's two scourges," he said[1]—was a constant of Italian history up to the 1990s. Until that time, the peninsular political system, lacking viable alternatives, always pivoted around a sort of "single party"—at times surreptitious, at times official. The liberal monarchy, fascism, and the Christian Democratic republic all experienced, under different forms, governmental mechanisms incapable of any change except by traumatic rupture. Opposition parties were thus always forced to choose between "subversivism" (different from subversion, which they never practiced) and more or less open collaboration with power; they sometimes managed simultaneously to be both subversive and governmental.

In the early years of the country's existence, these opposition groups, though kept at a distance from official political life, possessed a capital that the forces of the government and the administration lacked: identity. The democrats, the Catholics, and the Socialists benefited from having strong and clear identities, which were even more salient in contrast to the governing powers, which lacked any clearly defined personality.

The fragmentation of the ruling class, the fortuitous character of unification, the mistrust of politics, and the "pragmatism" of the transformist governments thus deprived this new creature of a clearly defined national character. At the beginning of the Italian adventure, the country's new leaders—the *Destra*—were preoccupied with building from nothing the structures of a new state with suddenly enlarged borders, and they had little time to abhor any ideological vacuum. But this changed once Italy found itself projected into the center of a system of international relations in which it supposedly had a role to play; the difficulty of defining a plausible national identity began to pose a major problem when compared to other countries that had constructed their own over centuries. From that point forward, any shift in the international order had repercussions for Italy, provoking a more or less serious internal crisis that aroused new doubts about its identity.

Dynamic Constants

The constants of postunitary Italian history reflect realities rooted deeply in the social life of the country. Yet, unless one analyzes their interconnections, there is a risk of magnifying them as pure manifestations of political folklore, or of using them as ideological cover for otherwise unmentionable struggles between conflicting interests. Through most of the history of unitary Italy, that has been true of the north-south "dualism": detached arbitrarily from other factors, the "southern question" has given rise to partial interpretations, used by some in the ruling southern classes as an ideological alibi to solicit every sort of public assistance.

These unilateral visions produced other risks. To continue with the example of the north–south "dualism," other inequalities in the country's interior have often been neglected, such as the existence of a center and a northeast, with their own distinct characteristics. The social and economic phenomenon referred to, appropriately, as the "Terza Italia," ("Third Italy")—an industrial area that notably includes Veneto, Emilia, and Tuscany, as well as the Adriatic regions—has arisen and asserted itself, despite the ruling class's near-sightedness.

A too-hasty analysis of these factors leads to a further misunderstanding: their unchanging aspect ends up completely overshadowing their dynamic aspect. In other words, the fragility of national identity, transformism, state control, clientelism, regional divisions, de facto "single-partyism" and interference by the Church crop up so regularly that they can leave the impression that Italian society of the past century and a half has scarcely evolved at all.

In reality, it is clear that these factors, appearances notwithstanding, never remain static. Even those that lend themselves most readily to folkloric representations of the supposedly eternal "Italian genius"—the Mafia, for example—have undergone radical transformations through their history, always linked to the radical transformations of the conditions with which they have interacted. The Mafia arose, according to certain interpretations, as a sort of feudal agent defending the "oppressed," but it was "baptized" only after Italian unification, and today represents a veritable multinational entity with both licit and illicit interests.[2]

The same can be said of other strictly political factors. As one historian has noted, the "law" of transformism appears only when one assesses the history of Italy on the basis of an external model, namely, on the basis of a level of institutional functioning that one supposes the country could have attained and that it has failed to reach because of its defects.[3]

Nearly all recent studies on the relationship between north and south in Italy find that the gap between the two regions can be viewed as a consequence of unification, to the extent that unification—by bringing the regions under the same, uniform institutional framework—tended to institutionalize the gap. At the same time, if one considers the dynamic aspect, it becomes clear that over the past fifty years the difference between the two has remained essentially constant, which means that in relative terms the south has developed at rates comparable to the north.[4] This reading of "dualism" undercuts the conventional wisdom on the situation of the Mezzogiorno.

A Heavy Heritage

Generally those who have sought to explain the traditional weaknesses of the Italian ruling class without resorting to shortcuts like fatalism, moralism, or even racism, have insisted on the backwardness—or backwardnesses—of the country. We should keep in mind that the notion of backwardness is relative and based on multiple factors. It necessarily implies a comparison with other entities presumed to be more advanced, or examined under different points of view. It also supposes, naturally, the existence of a competition, of whatever nature.

Italy, even while expressing fairly early on a subjective will to compete with the other powers of the "European Concert," found itself from its very birth in objective competition with those powers, by reason of its history, its "geopolitical capital," and the uses the other powers sought to make of it. In the Middle Ages, Italy was the leading capitalist country in the world, both chronologically and in terms of its importance. That conferred certain responsibilities: the commercial expansion led by the Venetians and the Genoese, the financial importance of the Lombard and Florentine bankers, the prodigious cultural splendor dispensed by the universities, the literary schools, the centers of pictorial and musical arts, all left a concrete heritage, of which the use of Tuscan as the lingua franca of many intellectual and commercial circles was long the most salient sign. If we add to that the role of universal spiritual power played by one of the peninsular states and, no less important, the aura of ancient Rome, we can see that the *Risorgimento* myth of a "Third Rome" was far weightier than anything the bards of Italy's "manifest destiny" could support.

The Italian colonies present on the Adriatic, in Malta, in Tunis, in Alexandria, in Istanbul, in the Aegean, and even on the shores of the Black Sea endowed unified Italy, virtually, with a far from negligible political capital that it could have used, at least proportionately, the way de Gaulle used the Francophone community. Although there were no substantial initiatives to this end, the inheritance of the past nonetheless helped the new country occupy a space—and not just geopolitically or geoeconomically—with which others, and Italy itself, would henceforth have to deal.

The ruling class in Piedmont that now found itself in command, preoccupied with internal concerns and accustomed to dealing with other powers from a subordinate position, reacted slowly to the new international reality. Relations with the outside world were perceived without the problem of the *saltus* really being raised—and consequently, without necessary connections to internal problems being made. The theoretical awareness of the gap between ambitions and the means to achieve them emerged slowly among most of the ruling class: yet, it was precisely this gap that was to mark the subsequent history of the country and make its backwardness a problem without a solution.

The *Destra*, despite a rich theoretical tradition far superior to the disordered eclecticism of the *Sinistra*, lost its bearings once unification was achieved. Not only had the imperatives of centralization drained it of its decentralizing liberalism, but also the *Destra* incorporated the interests of a dispersed class of property owners who were weak, few in number, and, with rare exception, insensitive to the requirements of industrial development. Its conservatism was dictated not only by its will, however understandable, to preserve the social relationships from which it drew its wealth, but also by the quite natural sociopsychological reflex through which all human groupings tend to persevere with the mechanisms that made their success possible.

One idea originating in England, and to which the property owners were evidently sensitive, was that "the Italians' steam is their sun,"[5] as the industrialist Richard Cobden told Massimo d'Azeglio in 1847. During the debate on the commercial treaty with France of 1863, the deputy Carlo de Cesare explained to the chamber his free-trade choice by noting that "the climate, the air, the sun, the countryside of Italy will never permit us to become eminently industrial like the English and the French. One struggles in vain against the laws of nature."[6] The preeminence of "natural" social relationships, deemed so because of their bond to the earth, led several representatives of the *Destra* to posit a sort of "agrarian fatalism" as one of the "laws of nature."

When the first serious difficulties appeared, coming on top of the crisis of the southern *brigantaggio*, the need for a more profound consideration became clear. Thus one observer went so far as to describe unification as a distortion of the laws of history and geography and to observe, as did the southern liberal Giustino Fortunato, that the new country had a cumulative "lag of several centuries vis-à-vis other civilized nations."[7] Once the problem of Italy's "lag" or backwardness was posed in these terms, a small minority began the search for its causes, and the means to attack it.

A "Too-Early" Comer

Among the paradoxes of Italian history, one of the most singular is that the country, generally considered as a "late comer," is in truth a "too-early comer," if one can put it that way. The decline and then the decadence of the peninsula after the Renaissance are in direct relationship to the precocity of its development: too much commerce, too much production, too much wealth, and cities that were too large for the economic, political, or military conditions of the era.[8]

Without wading into the debate on the causes of Italian decadence, let us briefly consider a few points that may illuminate the political factors in contemporary Italy and of the social psychologies behind them.

It is necessary first to set aside a few simplifications. While the conditions for the decadence of the richest Italian cities were present by the end of the fourteenth century, it would be inexact to suggest that the Italian economy of the Renaissance was decadent. At the end of the fifteenth century, for example, Florentine banks kept capital reserves two to three times what the bankers Peruzzi and Bardi used in the thirteenth and fourteenth centuries. More significantly, as the economics historian Vera Zamagni states, at the end of the seventeenth century, Bologna was the most highly industrialized city in Europe.[9] The decline thus stretched out over a very long period, and it was not until the seventeenth and eighteenth centuries that we can really speak of decadence.

Thus the prevailing notion that the great geographical discoveries of the late fifteenth century constituted the direct and immediate cause of Italian decline must be considered with caution. They doubtless catalyzed—but did not provoke—a process rooted in developments at least a century earlier. When one considers the reasons for decline in their entirety, both economic and political, it becomes clear that many of them are linked to "excess" growth, that is, a physiological defect of capitalism that Italian development highlighted for the first time in history: overproduction.

Among the causes of Italian weakening, Vera Zamagni cites above all the accumulation in a few hands of the wealth engendered by prosperity.[10] This accumulation was due to several causes, starting with the substantial stability of an internal market that, as the misery of the masses persisted, offered few prospects for enlargement outside those guaranteed by the rich merchants, bankers, aristocrats, and princes of the Church, ever more refined and demanding. Then, the increasingly limited dimensions of the world market on the one hand and of technological capacities on the other probably made it difficult to contemplate major investments that would render productivity more extensive or intensive, and this further encouraged the tendency toward what we now would call nonessential consumption.

According to Maurice Aymard, the technological deficit also contributed to inflexibility in different sectors of production. This was true notably in the countryside, in the face of increased demand provoked, again, by growth. Supply shortages pushed up wheat prices, in turn leading to increased salaries for manufacturing jobs, and consequently, a transfer of capital into agriculture, where development potential could be realized only slowly.[11]

Finally, we must not forget the rigidity of corporations, which tend to perpetuate means of production and levels of remuneration even when they are no longer appropriate.

The "corporations of artisans and tradesmen" began appearing in the second half of the twelfth century, at first simply as associations for defense and mutual assistance; but later, they rapidly became a necessity of economic life in towns and cities, the inevitable consequence of the closed nature of communal markets. The proliferation of autonomous communes—born in just a few decades on the bases of the old Roman cities—had the corollary effect of producing a complete division of work between country and city. Thus each commune, needing to establish a vital relationship with the surrounding countryside, found itself in a state of near-constant hostility, open or latent, with the neighboring commune, typically thirty to forty kilometers distant. In these conditions, the city and the countryside had no choice but to preserve at all costs their mutually indispensable economies. Toward that end, they created mechanisms to regulate, limit, or prevent free competition within the commune. Clearly this artificial equilibrium—which allowed the artisan or small merchant to forecast the precise quantity of merchandise that he would be certain to sell to his restricted and guaranteed clientele—could not be maintained in an era when certain cities had reached far higher levels of development. It was at that moment, in the second phase of the communal age, particularly between the second half of the thirteenth century and the first half of the fourteenth, that corporations became major impediments to growth, a key cause of the decline of certain regions to the profit of others with more flexible and lower-cost labor forces.[12]

At this stage of economic and social evolution, the potential offered by the organization of the state began manifesting its clear superiority over the cities: the internal monopoly guaranteed by communal organization was overwhelmed by this newer form of organization that could regulate, protect, and encourage commerce both internally and externally. That gave rise, in effect, to converging movements of the commercial bourgeoisie toward the absolute state (helping it extend the means of communication and defend against the nobility and competitors), and of the absolute state toward the commercial bourgeoisie (furnishing it, through taxes and credit, with the means to finance its administration and its wars).

This tendency toward the formation of national states (as they would be called much later) took shape at a time when the decline of the Italian states had already reached a relatively advanced stage. But the new economic problems alone do not sufficiently explain this missed rendezvous that, in the final analysis, would prove fatal for Italian development.

When the Europe of the fifteenth century—this "hodge-podge of petty kingdoms and principalities, marcher lordships and city-states,"[13] as Paul Kennedy describes it—began witnessing the formation of the first states of a certain size, the Italian cities, which had developed far beyond the limits of the old, small communes, arose as a final insuperable obstacle preventing the constitution of an absolute Italian state. The great modern monarchies, on the other hand, had the good fortune not to encounter, on their paths toward unification, any serious urban obstacle.[14] It is not by chance that the south, where urban civilization was much less developed, had been the only region on the peninsula to unify, for better or for worse.

Of course, other factors contributed to this outcome: demographic movements, growth in external trade, the expansion of the monetary economy, the appearance of new competitors in central and southern Europe as well as in Mediterranean trade, the threat presented by Turkish advances, and finally, geographic discoveries, although their real effects would become clear only much later.

But if one wanted to synthesize this abortive process, one could say that each of the five city-regions that then dominated on the peninsula—Milan, Florence, Rome, Venice, and Naples—was too strong to allow one of its rivals to impose hegemony on it and too "weak" to succeed in imposing it. Thus began a period characterized by a long series of debilitating wars, with frequent appeals to foreign powers and the progressive deferment of any hope of being able to manage the creation of a central power or, at a minimum, to reform a fragmented market. These initial characteristics marked the history of the peninsula so profoundly that they would remain present even after unification.

Chapter 2

The Phantom Nation

The Origins of the Nation

Before proceeding further, a rapid digression is indispensable regarding the "national question" in general and the "crisis of the nation-state" in particular. The debate surrounding the "nation" gave rise to concepts as varied as the nations themselves. Even more so, for the concept of nation changes not only in space but also with time. The key is not to define the supposedly true nature of a "nation"— and of its political form, the nation-state, which does not exist—but rather to find a political and historical meaning that might help us pierce the mystery of the Italian nation.

To say that the great national states—France, England, Spain—were born in the fifteenth century is to employ a sort of diachronic contraction, but one unlikely to satisfy those who seek the "true nature" of the particular political entity that we call a "national state." In fact, these states were termed "national" only *a posteriori*, and for two good reasons: (1) the concepts of "nation" and of "nationality" appeared only much later, and (2) these states hardly possessed the attributes now considered characteristic of a "nation."

"The state," says the *Enciclopedia Einaudi*, "becomes a nation when the community that it organizes in the interior of a fixed territorial, economic and social space becomes conscious of its own historical, cultural and linguistic identity as a civilization with well-defined borders."[1] If we follow this definition, we must recognize that at the point when the borders of France, Great Britain, and Spain were becoming settled, the process of "nationalization," far from being consecrated by unification, was only beginning. National identity is acquired through the superposition of heteroclite elements (creating what later would be called "national specificities"), nearly always *imposed* by state power, with the principal aim of creating uniform conditions to allow a market with much larger borders to exist.

The "nation," as a political and juridical concept, began taking a defined form only at the end of the eighteenth century. With the French Revolution, it became the foundation of French political sovereignty, a role that had belonged, during the Ancien Régime, to the person of the king. This coincidence between the birth of the "nation" and the bourgeoisie's assumption of political power is hardly a matter of chance. Sieyès himself explained that the nation and the bourgeoisie are but one: "The Third (Estate) thus embraces everything that belongs to the nation; and everything that is not the Third cannot be viewed as being of the nation."[2] So it should not be surprising that the Napoleonic Wars, the first attempt at bourgeois unification in Europe, were fought under the banner of the nation. Nor should it be surprising that, having modified social relationships in the conquered countries, they would have awakened "national" sentiments there, at times taking the form of collaboration and at times opposition to the French armies.

The supposed contradiction between a sort of "civilizing mission" of nationalism and its "thirst for domination" is in fact an inevitable consequence of the contradictory nature of the bourgeoisie. This class has always combined its particular national interests with its universal interests, everywhere attempting to create favorable conditions for its businesses. The implementation of the "principle of nationality" at Versailles in 1919 confirms that pure national states have never existed, but that all states have adopted the "national" form as a political cover for their modernization and expansion.

Denationalization and Renationalization

Since evolutions in international relations have brought the hypothesis of European unification out of the realm of pie-in-the-sky theoretical speculation, the inadequacy of the national state has become a major political problem for the leaders of all affected countries.

Italy—where the political crisis of the 1990s combined with a weak national consciousness—brought this crisis of the nation-state into sharp focus, further fueling the misconception that it was purely an Italian problem. Perhaps this misconception slowed awareness of the problem in other European countries; in any case it sparked a particularly rich and in-depth debate on the causes of the national deficit in Italy and on the true Italian particularities behind it.

The Gulf War of 1991 sparked a debate by several newspapers and commentators on the lack of a foreign policy sufficient to the new international conditions. The country had been pulled into the conflict through no initiative of its own and without a clear vision of its implications. The term "renationalization"— which first appeared in the German debate on reunification, but with an opposite meaning—led in Italy to a demand that national interests be redefined to give the country greater autonomy in foreign policy choices. The point was to make Italian interests more visible, but to do so first by better defining their nature and by asserting, without nostalgia or inhibition, a sense of national pride.

As these themes were raised by men and political forces largely considered conservative, the debate risked succumbing to the very cleavages that it meant to overcome in the name of an overarching national interest. It was partly toward this end that, in 1993, the review *Limes* was created, with an editorial council that included figures of every political stripe.

From its very first issue, the review declared an ambition of "searching for the national interest" in a geopolitical debate.[3] In October 1994, an editorial in an issue devoted entirely to this debate[4] held that the end of the so-called "First Republic" and the difficulties in birthing a second could be attributed to "denationalization"—that is, the pretension, supposedly dating from the end of World War II, of building national institutions "on the denial of the nation." The fact that, for a half century, the national question has remained "buried away in a well-guarded warehouse of collective repression" had not produced entirely negative results, the editorial writer held: in truth, the political and military cover provided by the United States had allowed Italy to practice a "discreet and parasitic" geopolitics, cunningly managing its interests in the Mediterranean and in Eastern Europe. Thanks also to its low profile and its adaptability, the author concluded, Italy had become "one of the richest countries in the world."

If one accepts the argument of the *Limes* editorialist that one condition for Italy's enrichment was the capacity of its postwar governments to thrive parasitically in a particularly favorable geopolitical context, the logical conclusion is that the end of this balance could not help but affect the general situation in the country. From the moment the Berlin Wall fell, this "parasitic" foreign policy ceased to be profitable and an urgent need arose to redefine the nature and means of the "national interest." For it was then that the "geopolitical limits" of Italy's economic and commercial power—as the *Limes* editorialist put it—could be seen in the collapse of "the illusion that Italian industry can spread through the world merely by its intrinsic virtues, without a country-system to support its penetration into external markets."[5] It was only at this moment that the imbalance between a well-performing economy and a weak and vacillating "country-system" became the crucial problem at the center of the Italian political struggle, and the object of a veritable tidal wave of critical speculation.

National Europeanism

This gap between the dynamic economic power of Italy and political structures incapable of supporting its interests in the face of international competition is not, however, an exclusively Italian occurrence. Being composed of men, states, along with their bureaucracies, their institutions, their political parties, their trade unions, and their economic groups, are ever vigilant, as is any living organism, about their own preservation and reproduction. Toward that end, they sometimes tend to encroach on one another's areas of competence. One could almost say that a degree of confusion about roles and prerogatives constitutes a physiological "anomaly" common to every political system. In Italy, in any case, this "anomaly" has often produced a pathological degeneration: Fascism went so far as to codify this, by superimposing the roles of the party and the state, and by the latter's seizure of key economic sectors; the republic roughly maintained this confusion, despite a strictly liberal constitution, by perpetuating organic links between a Christian Democratic "party-state" and the key centers of economic control. It is thus not surprising that once this mechanism ceased functioning in one direction—from politics toward the economy—it began functioning in the opposite direction. The ascension to the highest offices in the state of Carlo Azeglio Ciampi (former governor of the Bank of Italy), of Romano Prodi (former chairman of IRI, Italy's biggest state holding company), and of Silvio Berlusconi (former chairman of Fininvest) are only the most conspicuous examples.

This blurring of genres has benefited Italian capitalism in moments of crisis and reconstruction. But it has nearly always led to a tangled system of intermixing and of mutual impediments. These are provoked by the asynchronous movements of the particular interests of the state, its bureaucracy, and its institutions, and of the parties, the trade unions, the economic groups, and so on. These "conflicts of interest," when not disturbing the mechanisms that allowed Italy to become "one of the richest countries in the world," have been condemned, at most, as strains on an ideal democratic model. At a certain stage of international competition, however, these distortions have been viewed not only as "immoral," but also as "antieconomic." Only when they reached the latter level had their "immorality" led them before the courts.

Consider the example of corruption in the assignment of public markets. So long as international competitors lacked the means to penetrate the Italian market, the misappropriation of public funds was considered merely a sort of supplementary "tax" aimed at regulating internal competition. But once foreign competitors gained the economic strength to begin knocking at the peninsula's doors, this "tax" ended up strangling productive activity. Since it was also an essentially protectionist mechanism, it ultimately had the effect—taken with other protectionist practices, such as the systematic devaluation of the lira—of provoking countermeasures by the international economic and political community. Those in turn led to the progressive marginalization of Italian products. The situation became intolerable when the international balances that had guaranteed Italy's "impunity" disappeared, and Rome found itself standing alone before a European Union that demanded the end to illicit practices and the opening of markets. It was then that the "geopolitical limits" of Italian economic and commercial power created an urgent need for a rapid and radical solution.

To simplify, there were effectively two currents of thought confronting each other. A large part of the productive bourgeoisie—in particular, the small and medium bourgeoisie of Lombardy and the northeast—lined up with the "pessimists of reason": since the state had proven itself unable to defend their interests, they would have to find their political representation beyond the state, in Europe or in local realities, or in a privileged linkage between local realities and European institutions, bypassing state mediation. In Brussels, important industrial and commercial sectors began engaging in ever more intense dialogues with foreign diplomats, completely eliminating the institutional filter, or else substituting for it.[6]

The hypothesis of the "optimists of will"—that is, of those who subscribed to the need to bet on the state's redemptive capacities and thus of rediscovering the geopolitical frontiers of the Italian *nation*—based this on another bit of evidence, no less troublesome for the peninsula's various interest groups: if Italy undeniably needed Europe, what concrete reasons could support the hope that Europe still needed Italy? The response, from those holding this view, lay in the reestablishment of a state sufficiently strong and credible to become an indispensable partner in the great political negotiation under way on the European construction site. If this approach was to stand any chance of success, however, it was necessary above all for Italy to avoid giving the impression that it was a country whose various parts were available to the highest bidder.

These two theses, considered in their pure theoretical formulations, appear radically opposed, and incompatible. That did not prevent the two political formations which represented the most extreme versions—the Northern League and the former Fascist National Alliance—from reaching governmental and electoral agreements, almost without interruption, within the center-right coalitions.

The accession to the European Monetary System (1978) and the subsequent signing of the Treaty of Maastricht (1991) drastically reduced the number of "heterodox" options available, notably the possibility of a competitive devaluation of the lira. From that point on, despite some bitter disagreements and oratorical jousting, at times bordering on the grotesque, all the Italian political groupings have been, to varying degrees and at varying times, Europeanist, federalist, and national, with the partial exception of the Northern League, which sometimes added—for purely extortionate purposes—a secessionist nuance. The neo-Fascist party headed by Gianfranco Fini was, for its part, anti-European, so long as it continued to see itself as being excluded *a priori* from any possibility of directly controlling power. Once this possibility became reality for the first time with the electoral coalition of 1994, not only did it throw overboard all its Mussolinian-derived ideological bric-a-brac but also it converted to Europeanism—moderate and nationalist, to be sure, but still in phase with the imperatives of Italian economic power. This proves that, polemical excesses aside, there simply was no other path possible but the one indicated by Brussels.

The editorial board of *Limes* was quite aware of this. In the issue mentioned, General Carlo Jean gave concrete dimension to the geopolitical quest for a national identity: "Interests cannot be mapped in concentric circles of decreasing intensity," he wrote. "The only objective parameters allowing us to identify them are the size of economic exchange and the number of Italian citizens in the various zones."[7] Based on the first of these two parameters, most observers agreed that Italy's interests lay, above all, in Europe.

According to data furnished by Patrizio Bianchi,[8] in 1992 to 1993, 41.7 percent of direct foreign investment by Italian industry went to Western Europe, 27.1 percent went to Eastern and central Europe and the former USSR, for a total of 68.8 percent of all investment abroad. Investments for corporate control amounted to 74.3 percent of all investments for the whole of Europe. The objective for the "optimists of will" was therefore not to disengage from the European process, but rather to try to more effectively advance Italian interests within Europe, or as Jean put it in a frank and direct manner: "We cannot permit Italy to be useful to Europe unless Europe is useful to Italy."

Unfortunately for the "optimists of will," in 1994 the season of national Europeanism had not yet arrived. If it were to have any hope of following the rhythms and meeting the deadlines of the European process, Italy still had many exams to pass, many companies to privatize, much debt to reduce, many tangles to unravel. It was in no position to insist that Europe demonstrate, any more than Bianchi's data had already done, how it could "serve Italy." The immaturity of this line of reluctant Europeanism was one of the principal reasons—perhaps *the* principal one—for the very early end of Silvio Berlusconi's first attempt to rule the country. Thus "passive Europeanism" became, paradoxically, the only way for Italy to overcome its backwardness and lessen the fluctuations due to the gap between its economy and its politics.

Northern Europeanism

In an essay published in the August 1996 issue of *Limes*, Jacopo Turri analyzed four ways that the risks posed by the Northern League might evolve: a "Belgian" model, involving increasing autonomy for the regions, which, however, would not dare go to the point of a rupture; a "Czechoslovak" model, characterized by a peaceful and consensual separation; a "Soviet" model, born from the implosion of the state "envelope"; and a "Yugoslav" model, where separation would carry "worrying and bloody" implications.[9]

None of these four models applied to the Italian case. In fact, the author himself imagined a fifth hypothesis—even though he termed it extremely unlikely—of a "neutralization of the League" through its co-option within the system and its transformation into one of the elements of a new political balance built on bipolarity. Ultimately this "co-option" took place: it was one of Silvio Berlusconi's fundamental achievements, and it helped propel him to victory in the elections of May 2001.

The long and durable governmental collaboration between the Northern League and the center-right beginning in 2001 should not make us forget that the party of Umberto Bossi had been, in December 1994, the parliamentary faction responsible for the fall of the first Berlusconi government, nor that it later assured, along with the parties of the center-left, the survival of the government of Lamberto Dini until the elections of 1996. Thus when, in June 1995, the League created a "Parliament of the North," with the objective of writing the constitution of the "Italian federal republic," the head of the opposition at that time, Silvio Berlusconi, termed the initiative a "grotesque bit of buffoonery," while the head of the Democratic Party of the Left (PDS; the former Italian Communist Party) and future prime minister, Massimo D'Alema, termed it a "normal political initiative, lacking any subversive character."[10] A few months later the same D'Alema explained that the League had much in common with the left, above all a "strong social contiguity," as Bossi's grouping was in the majority among the workers of the North.[11] Even after the electoral victory of the center-left in 1996, the new prime minister, Romano Prodi, offered the League the chairmanship of two parliamentary committees, including the one in charge of regional affairs.[12]

The apprehensions regarding the "secessionist" threats of the League redoubled in intensity when the grouping, electorally weakened, flatly renounced any possibility of an alliance with the left and again became the object of Silvio Berlusconi's earnest attentions. Virulent campaigns ensued, and they were all the more virulent because everyone knew that the elections of 1996—when the center-right forces victorious in 1994 had increased their electoral pull—had been carried by a center-left coalition only because of the electoral division between Berlusconi's

"House of Liberty" coalition and the Northern League. It was at that moment that a certain number of leftist intellectuals discovered the virtues of "republican patriotism," in order to oppose the "risks of the disintegration of the nation."

In fact, the exaggeration of the risks represented by the League was often the form taken in the political battle over assuring its support—or demonizing it when it was moving toward the opposite pole. Rare were those who grasped the real motivations; among them was Sergio Romano, who said: "If Italy does not enter into Europe on the first of January 1999, the unity of the nation is in danger. He who truly believes that the country's northern regions would accept, tomorrow, being left in the bosom of Piraeus, Andalusia and Estremadura, while seeing themselves separated, perhaps irremediably, from the Tyrol, the Carinthians, Bavaria and the Alpine departments of France, well, this man would be committing a serious political error."[13]

In this utterly explicit "egoism," one finds the reasons for the strength of the League starting in the late 1980s, but one also finds their antithesis, which is to say, the reasons that led to its electoral weakening, starting precisely in January 1999. To simplify, the regionalist movements reflected the fierce determination of a few of the most dynamic economic groups to remain bound to Europe (if only to be rid of the parasitic burden). A sort of direct relationship was thus established between the strength of the League and the delay in the movement toward European integration. And vice versa, for, even as the various steps in the rapprochement to the European process were taken by the "country-system" as a whole, the determination of one part of these groups changed direction toward the "passive Europeanism", their principal aim still being not to lose contact with the Tyrol, the Carinthians, Bavaria, and the Alpine departments of France.

"Passive Europeanism" thus seemed to satisfy this demand. In the wake of his victory in 1996, Romano Prodi confirmed his government's intention to adapt his country as quickly as possible to the criteria of the Maastricht Treaty.[14] This decision was supported not only by the will of the head of government but also by the opening of credit from Europe, and from Germany in particular, which culminated on November 24, 1996, with the readmission of the lira into the European Monetary System, a sort of holding room on the path to the common currency.

That is why, little by little, the League lost part of its electoral influence, to the benefit of the parties of "national Europeanism," which had been hunting on more or less the same ground, geographically and socially. In the elections of 1996, this open competition resulted in what was called a "vendetta of the North" between the League and Forza Italia, with the result not only of allowing the center-left to win the elections but also of excluding from the first Prodi government any representation of Milan (outside the existing links between Minister Antonio Maccanico and Mediobanca[15]), or of Lombardy and the northeast. The political convulsions that flowed from the crisis of the 1990s thus raised anew the existence of an unresolved "southern question."

Chapter 3

The Northern Question

"The Particular Interest"

In his "Prison Notebooks," Antonio Gramsci contends that all Italian intellectual life up to the twentieth century was no more than a "phenomenon of French provincialism":[1] it pretended to have its foundations in historic antecedents in Italy, but in fact these antecedents were well rooted in the culture and traditions of France.

When national identities are invented, reciprocal borrowing is the rule. But for the Italian ruling classes and intellectuals, France was long the almost exclusive reservoir of ideas, taste, institutions, and symbols. The centralism, the system of prefects and of education, the literary, philosophical, and scientific trends, even the flag of the Cispadane Republic—everything was based on the French model. Remarking on this "intellectual and moral hegemony of foreign intellectuals," Gramsci concludes that in Italy there is no "national intellectual and moral bloc."[2]

His undeniably perceptive observations notwithstanding, Gramsci sometimes overestimates the capacity of intellectuals to influence historic events, either positively or negatively. In observing the process of *Risorgimento*, one might better explain the cultural hegemony of the "moderates" by the very nature of a national "revolution"—which was meant to take place without provoking ruptures or, above all, involving the masses. In short, by hoping to have a revolution without a revolution, the Italian bourgeoisie condemned itself to seeking awkward compromises with the old dominant groups, thus perpetuating its own divisions and all the constraints caused, among other factors, by structurally unequal regional realities.

The intellectuals who committed themselves to the *Risorgimento* were not in a position to forge a national identity; at times, they even explicitly refused to do so, as was the case with Vincenzo Gioberti. But it is not enough to merely say this; one must also seek to identify the "objective responsibilities" that help determine the subjective responsibilities evoked by Gramsci. It is in seeking these that one finds the elemental basis of a connection between an Italian "national question" and the "northern question": indeed, the only bourgeoisie within the geographic confines of the peninsula that was truly in a position to support the cause of national identity was the Lombard bourgeoisie. And yet, it did not do so.

As the historian Giorgio Rumi noted,[3] when one deals with the question of Italian decadence, one often returns to Milan and its incapacity to become the "European bridgehead of the country," its incapacity to play a significant role in the political life of the country. And this incapacity is a constant of Italian history, at least up to its most recent Berlusconian variation.

Civil Magnificence and Political Impotence

The social psychology of the northern Italian elites—who placed the jealous defense of their territory's dynamism above all nonepisodic involvement in any other activity[4]—has been solidifying for centuries. In a text presented at the Sixth Italian Scientific Congress of 1844, Carlo Cattaneo dates from the time when the ancient Roman municipalities reappeared—between the late first millennium and early second—the first wave of transformation of the serfs into the free peasants, transformation that, in subsequent centuries, spread through all of Europe.[5] This emancipation of feudal law, achieved in the name of old Roman right, allowed numerous Lombard cities to give birth to a civilization founded on what Cattaneo calls the "occupations of peace": commerce, trade, and industry. Even in modern times, Cattaneo proudly points out in another text,[6] "the streets of Paris and of London carry the names of Lombard bankers; and 'Lombard,' in France, meant banker."

This historic phase culminated with the Duchy of Milan, whose state power and territorial expansion were proportional to the prosperity of its economic activities. Still, we must again point out that the appetites born from this exuberance were behind the decadence that was to follow. Like all Italian states—too weak to absorb others, too strong to let themselves be absorbed—Milan relied on foreign assistance and entrusted its political ambitions to the army of the king of France Charles VIII. Despite the multiple and successive twists and turns of Ludovic Sforza himself, the Lombard capital lost forever its political independence and, at the same time, lost some of its importance relative to other great cities of the north—Venice, Genoa, Turin—which, themselves, maintained their role as political capitals.

Thus opened a new phase in Milan's historic existence, characterized by the divorce between its economic strength and its political power. As Rumi put it, then began "a destiny of civil magnificence and political impotence."[7] The seeds of the Lombard social psychology that have been transmitted down through the centuries were sown.

Control of the ancient duchy of the Sforzas passed into Spanish hands in 1535. The decadence that followed brought economic decline and a shrinking of borders. According to Cattaneo, it was a certain "contempt for the trades and for business"—which the Spaniards considered "work suitable for infidels and the impure castes"[8]—that led to this decadence. The Austrian conquest, two centuries later, did not restore the city's political prerogatives, but favored a rebirth of the hardworking traditions of the local populace, returning a certain degree of administrative autonomy to the municipalities while simultaneously abolishing feudal rights, which were replaced by a modern cadastral system within a substantially unified commercial space. Vienna's solicitude allowed the Lombards to return to their old traditions of productive intensity.

According to Cattaneo's calculations, the Lombard peasants enjoyed productivity rates twice those of their French counterparts. Besides, the city of Milan alone employed some 450 engineers, while the French Department of Bridges and Highways (Ponts et Chaussées) employed only 568 for the entire country.[9] This pride in producers who were "more brave than lucky"[10] strengthened the conviction that Lombardy was summoned by a singular destiny to give birth to not just any sort of civilization, but precisely to an "economic civilization" that could compensate for the loss of political supremacy.

In fact, this conviction reflected reality: Lombardy was not only the most prosperous region south of the Alps; it was the richest in all the Austrian Empire. But this conviction also reflected the real state of things, in that "political impotence"—along with "civil magnificence," to be sure—left the dominant Lombard classes without a state of their own to count on. This obliged them to engage with the central authorities in a sort of permanent negotiation. This situation gave rise to a series of reciprocal dependences which—when examined in all their complex and often conflicting intertwinings, marked by suspicion, subtle calculations, ruses, and collusion—might help us unravel the tangle of the Italian nation.

The Social Psychology of Lombardy

For a long time the "northern question" was merely the rhetorical, polemical counterpart to the more famous "southern question." It became a real political problem only when Milan found itself no longer satisfied to play its traditional role as "moral capital" and began demanding greater involvement in the management of political power.

The early beginnings of this came in the late 1970s and the early 1980s, and its causes were the same as those that later were to provoke the upheaval of the Italian political panorama. At that time, the "northern question" manifested itself in two apparently distinct forms: the stormier of the two, and thus the one bound to arouse the curiosity of the media, had to do with the local electoral lists referred to as "civic" lists (i.e., not linked to existing political parties), which, while existing more or less throughout Italy, in the north ultimately federated themselves into several leagues, and finally into the Northern League; the other form, reminiscent of the course of an underground river, led in 1983 to the nomination of Bettino Craxi as head of the government, the first Milanese president of the council in all the history of unitary Italy.

The League's "folkloric" forms of public activity masked the distant roots of the "northern" factor. For the historian Marco Meriggi, the League's anticentralism and antifiscal polemic can be seen as a resurgence of a trait that has recurred through the history of these regions, where development and wealth are concentrated to the highest degree.[11]

For these reasons, it can be difficult to understand Italian political events of the latter part of the twentieth century if one ignores certain constants in the social psychology of the north, and particularly of Milan. They can be classified as a sort of regional version of a quite Italian virtue, almost a sort of survival instinct, which consists in attempting to transform a weakness into a source of strength. The absence of local institutions of state and the subordination of the Milanese elites to the great political and cultural realities of Vienna, Paris, and Madrid was transformed into a prideful demand for material and civic wealth; this legitimized the resentment against the political center and its fiscal pressures.

To this attitude we must add the mix of fear and defiance in the face of a national revolutionary movement, capable of encouraging popular demands that, as French experience shows, can sometimes hardly be contained. The resultant mixture describes a dominant Lombard class firmly astride its prerogatives, certain of being able to use its money to constrain Vienna, threatening if need be to join the Italian national cause, so long as the latter does not produce consequences inimical to commerce.

Lombardy, like every other region, saw the birth of numerous political currents, representing even more numerous and disparate economic and social interests. But most of these currents were infused, one way or another, with the same social psychology that we have just described. In a study devoted to the "State of Milan,"[12] Fausto Fonzi describes some of the characteristics of the Lombard radical movement (the far left wing of the time) in a way that would not seem entirely out of place in describing the uninhibited syncretism of certain recurrent themes of the "Lombardism" of the 1990s. This movement, he writes, was able to reconcile "the interests of the rural and shop-owning bourgeoisie to the poetry of Cavallotti" and to unite socially heterogeneous forces thanks to a rather fluid demagogy, nourished by a form of municipalism with antisouthern and moralistic accents, and confronting fiscal and centralizing pressures.

In 1899 the Lombard radicals used their talent for rallying disparate interests under their banner to promote a municipalist alliance based on themes that had been used against Vienna during the time of the Lombardo-Venetian Kingdom, namely, the demand for autonomy and the denunciation of the waste by central state institutions of resources extorted from the hard-working north. This alliance—opposed by the most-protected sectors of the economy, notably the cotton industry and electricity producers—included not just radicals, but free-trade industrialists, Socialists, and a part of the Catholic world. These groups, as one can see, were of a heterogeneous and even conflictual nature, but all were close to an autonomist tradition with strong local roots.

With the rhetoric that surrounded them, the elections of 1899 ended a period of five years of troubles and contradictions, during which Milan had been the theater of a dialectic of conflicts and agreements characteristic of advanced countries. First the bourgeoisie sought, and gained, the support of the proletariat against Crispi and his Abyssinian War of 1896; then it begged the support of the armed state against the riotous proletariat in 1898; finally, an important part of the free-trade bourgeoisie again gained the support of the proletariat by seducing its political leaders with the myth of "municipal socialism," this supposed "prelude of the socialist society to come," preached by Filippo Turati.[13]

In short, at the end of the nineteenth century, some of the constants of the social psychology of the dominant Lombard classes—the defense of the particular prerogatives of different municipalities; the feeling of being subjected to a sort of systematic pillage of wealth produced; the polemic against the "foreign" capital of the pillagers—had ample political echoes. The ideologies that resulted, however, were merely the forms in which this social psychology was historically incarnated.

Chapter 4

Inventing Ancestors

Plebeian Jacqueries

The idea that production and good administration are more important than the management of public affairs is a legacy from the Lombard bourgeoisie to the rest of the country.[1] In the early decades of unified Italy, the productive bourgeoisie remained largely at a distance from political power and made no attempt to define a vision of the whole, a general "national" perspective. It thus remained prisoner to its own regional and cultural divisions, the two often going hand in hand. The absence of a coherent ideological horizon left room for a sort of ersatz conscience that Giulio Bollati has identified in history and in the invention of the "national character."[2]

Bollati wanted to avoid the traps of the "pure idea or ethnic ether,"[3] and proposed measuring and verifying the concrete manifestations of Italian social psychology. His first step was to define the historic circumstances and the temporal space in which the *Italian* made his first appearance as a social species unto its own, between the late eighteenth and early nineteenth century. Previously, the author suggests, Italians were nothing more than a highly confined group of speakers of a capricious and often arbitrary language that had outlived its past glory. The inhabitants of the peninsula had almost nothing in common on a cultural level and, in their near totality, were ignorant of even the most elementary rudiments of the spoken language—or, as we shall see, the written—used by the confined group mentioned above.

The principal characteristic of the history of this mass of uncultivated natives was precisely its lack of history: they had scarcely played any role in the diverse historic processes that had unfolded on the peninsula. Or more precisely, they had participated the way slaves participated in the construction of the great classic civilizations.

This phenomenon has been explained in various ways. According to Galli della Loggia, for example, the resigned and passive submission of the Italian peasant masses stemmed from the fact that they were politically controlled not by a feudal-type aristocracy, as in the classic European model, but by cities and by the Church.

As everywhere else, this control was based on a relationship of forces; but it also depended on the prestige enjoyed by the communes and on the Church's ability to remain close to rural communities and thereby neutralize any temptation they had to revolt.[4] Thus, in the absence of serious peasant movements in medieval and early modern Italy, it was the urban plebes—from the Vespers of Palermo to the Revolt of the Ciompi, from Cola di Rienzo to Masaniello—who were the protagonists of sporadic episodes of rebellion.[5]

In the cases mentioned, conflicts were more often provoked by profound political crises than by social crises, as with the German peasant revolt of 1525 or the French peasant reaction during the "*grande peur*." The explosions of Italian anger mentioned above were brief, indecisive, and quickly subdued. They were not the action of a class or of a coalition of classes, but rather of an ambiguous mass of the lower classes, of "plebes" without history, roots, defined interests, or premeditated designs.

It is notable that such keen observers of Italian reality as Giuseppe Prezzolini, Luigi Barzini, and Indro Montanelli employed nearly identical images to draw a sort of "analogical portrait" of Cola di Rienzo as a paradigm of one form of the Italian political struggle, comparing him to Benito Mussolini. "He embodied the inflamed and angry temperament of the ignorant and frustrated commoners," wrote Montanelli. Di Rienzo, he added, was "a typical Italian troublemaker who, when he speaks, gets drunk on his own words and ends up believing them, thus losing all sense of reality and proportion."[6]

Naturally, analogies between Cola di Rienzo and Mussolini must be viewed with caution, given the differences between the two periods. Nonetheless, once one starts in this direction one must not stop with external coincidences, one must consider the symptomatic conditions that surrounded the birth, six hundred years apart, of these two very similar political phenomena: first is the existence of a sort of social and political sediment that filters into any space vacated by state authority and generates the sort of banditism that, Prezzolini says, Italians idealized as a revolt against the established order; next comes the composite pragmatism of the political "programs" built on this slippery, viscous mire; and finally, the readiness of Italians to succumb in times of crisis to a fascination with the "providential man"—these three factors are often found in Italian history.

Fabricating Ancestors

Each country, at the moment when it creates its national identity, discovers a certain number of more or less legendary figures in its past who are then raised to the rank of ancestors. But the question arises: How are these figures chosen?

The shadow of Rome, of course, extends over much of Italian history. But, as Theodor Mommsen pointed out, the Italians, divided, undisciplined, and defeated in almost all their wars, can be considered heirs of the Romans—who for their part unified the civilized world by force of arms and law—only in the way that maggots can be considered heirs of the carrion of a once proud and noble horse.[7]

Classical writers—Virgil, above all, but also Cicero and Titus Livius—"explained" Rome's greatness as flowing from the particular favor that the *Urbs* enjoyed among the gods. Augustine and other fathers of the Church "explained" it as providential design. To Dante, the divine seal on the "Eternal City" made collaboration between the Church and the empire indispensable. This insistence on the providential character of Rome contributed to the creation of a myth, more political than religious, that others through the ages have drawn upon, from Petrarch to Machiavelli, from Alfieri to Mazzini, from Carducci to Mussolini. Still, there is no Roman who, in Italian mythology, fills the role occupied by, for example, Vercingetorix in French mythology.

One explanation could stem from the fact that national ideologies began forming during the eighteenth century, at a time when they had, first, to distinguish themselves from the French model. Thus, instead of Greco-Roman mythology, or the mythology of the Mediterranean world, upon which France had a corner, it was the rustic thatched cottages of northern Europe that were celebrated. The new national cultures were forged by opposing "their bodies to the threat of the universal monarchy imposed by Rome," in the words of Fichte,[8] where, behind Rome, one must read Paris.

Divided between their admiration for philosophical and revolutionary France and their desire to free themselves from its domination, Italian intellectuals thus hesitated between several myths. Those drawn to the "thatched villages" of northern Europe summoned up a mythical peasant who, however, had one major drawback—he could easily be compared to other, actually existing, peasants. The actually existing peasants could not boast of the imaginary characteristics that their mythical "colleagues" own and, moreover, had to be kept at a distance from the creation of unitary Italy. The result was a sort of latent schizophrenia that would do nothing to strengthen the "feeble popular legitimation of the Italian state."[9]

Mythical Peasant and Empirical Peasant

There was no shortage of rebellions against such-and-such a baron or this-or-that feudal lord during the history of modern Italy: The revolt of the Calabrian peasants of 1459 through 1464 comes to mind, as do at least seven other major rebellions, between 1512 and 1584 in Calabria, Abruzzi, and Basilicata. These, however, were isolated and generally ephemeral episodes that did not evolve into "national" uprisings of the sort seen in Germany or France.

A particular and unique cultural overlap between the ruling classes of the countryside and of the communes made the Italian peasantry a doubly submissive class, almost incapable of an autonomous social presence. For a very long time, property owners in other countries generally shared with their serfs a state that one might call cultural nonexistence. They exercised absolute control over their subjects in matters economic, juridical, and military, but barely differed from them in terms of knowledge or, in some cases, the way they lived. In Italy, to the contrary, the progressive integration of property owners into urban economic life led to their cultural integration as well, thus adding this particular form of superiority to the other types of domination. In this double oppression was the sort of total cultural submission of the peasants that Galli della Loggia describes; they were reduced to a state of political insignificance and "covered, anthropologically, with discredit."[10]

We mentioned the "overlapping" between the ruling classes of the city and those of the country: the former "offered" the latter the cultural instruments of their domination, the latter brought to the city the "minor tradition" of a popular culture of which they, too, were the guardians. That explains the persistence of the "agrarian cultural paradigm" that feeds some in the intelligentsia aiming to prepare the terrain for a national Italian ideology.

This "peasant ideology," nonetheless, is neither exclusively nor specifically Italian. Almost everywhere, the second phase of identity construction is that in which the *real peasant* continues to be treated as a negligible quantity, but the *literary peasant* begins assuming the "coelacanth function"[11]—a living fossil, guarantor of the reconstitution of the ancestors—embodied until then by a "people" lacking concrete reference. In the eyes of the urban intellectual sitting at his desk by the fireplace, the peasant becomes the most authentic expression of the relationship between a nation and its land, and his mores become ethical references.

At this stage of the construction of identity, Italian intellectuals were far from being an exception. The real Italian specificity is manifested by the discovery of the deep roots of "ancient peasant civilization" decades before other European cultures—late in the eighteenth century—when the process of forming national unity was still in gestation. Unequal economic development was reflected—in the medium or, more often, the long term—by an unequal ideological development whose effects were sometimes surprising. Thus, in Italy, the particular mixture of capitalism's precocious rise (and precocious fall), and the way it then increasingly trailed behind other potential competitors, led to a singular phenomenon of anticipation, which one might define as a sort of "Italian path to Catonism."[12]

The Italian Path to Catonism

For centuries, as we have seen, peasants had been condemned by their subordinate cultural state not only to political insignificance but to "anthropological discredit." Testifying to this discredit is the lexicon in which nouns relating to the peasant condition have often become adjectives used to describe someone crude or grubby: *villano, rustico, cafone, zotico*. From Tommaso Garzoni (1585) to Giuseppe Baretti (1769), literature, too, offers evidence of the disdain with which real peasants are viewed.[13]

It may be of interest to note that in apparent opposition to this "anthropological discredit," only a few years after Garzoni's work was published, the Bolognese writer Giulio Cesare Croce published *Le sottilissime astuzie di Bertoldo* (1606) and *Le piacevoli e ridicolose semplicità di Bertoldino* (1608), two books that, according to Prezzolini, defend "the countryman against the city, the wisdom of tradition against academic culture" and even "poor nations against rich nations."[14] While G. C. Croce himself affirmed in his autobiography that "sod and soil are [his] Latin,"[15] his work does not seem to step beyond the confines of the republic of letters. Besides their evident references to situations typical of the Commedia dell'Arte, certain of the adventures experienced by the peasant hero Bertoldo reproduce those of *fabliaux* peasant heroes like *Brunain, la vache au prêtre* or, especially, *Le Vilain mire*, in which the protagonist is supposed to illustrate more a character than a social condition, and whose place, clearly allegorical, might even be occupied by an animal. Croce does not want to depict a social situation, but simply to comment, in burlesque fashion, on the most obvious faults of men and women.

It would not be until the end of the eighteenth century that a small number of Italian intellectuals would suddenly discover that the soul of the fatherland is embodied in country people. Bollati even gave us the precise dates of this phenomenon: from 1796 to 1800, between Bonaparte's two Italian campaigns. At that moment, certain property owners tried to turn a revolutionary dynamic into an antirevolutionary defense, by adopting "the French model, but reversed in such a way that it functioned against the social consequences of the French model."[16]

Previously partisans and detractors of the French Revolution had fought in the name of ideas and had totally ignored the real forces behind those ideas. This attitude persisted so long as the real Italian forces were not pounded, directly or indirectly, by the waves unleashed by the French storm; that is to say, until, in Bergamo and in Friuli, for example, sentiments of revolt began to spread among peasants who had been struck by the winter famine of 1793 to 1794; during these riots, the French example was openly evoked.

Bollati tells us that it was at that moment that, for the first time, the shrewdest aristocrats—Paolo Greppi, Federico Manfredini, and, above all, Francesco Melzi d'Eril, who were far from being anti-French, since they saw Napoleon's France as the best guarantee against the revolutionary tide—began asking themselves how best to use "the incalculable resource of all these men on whom, unfortunately, we will have to rely to save Italy," in Greppi's own words.[17]

We can rather approximately situate the birth of an Italian "rural ethic" in Naples, sometime around the Parthenopean Republic of 1799. Its authors were two of the protagonists of this experiment, Vincenzio Russo and Vincenzo Cuoco. The former was the voice of abstract rhetoric of the republican government, of antimodernism so radical that it was almost an apology for pauperism, and at the same time, a partisan of extremely moderate social reforms. The latter, a survivor of the bloody repression that had followed the reconquest of Naples, arrived at the conclusion that rhetorical abuses detached from the people's real interests had, in the end, helped Cardinal Ruffo build his counterrevolutionary army on an ample mass base, principally of peasants.[18]

The connection between the problem of popular participation in the "common cause" raised by Greppi and the failure of this first "passive revolution" in Italian history provides us some insight, beyond the ideological representations, into the complex network of relationships between the objective situation, the wishes of the ruling classes, and the role of intellectuals, who have often become the unhappy conscience of a poorly understood process.

Chapter 5

The Unhappy Consciousness of Italian Development

The Discovery of the Real People

According to Paolo Greppi, at the end of the eighteenth century Italian landowners found themselves caught between the Napoleonic armies and the peasant masses who, he said, seemed ready at any moment to "cry, 'To the winner go the spoils' and to help the French pillage the rich"[1]; so it was urgent, he continued, for these same landowners to persuade the ministers of the various peninsular states to deploy "two armies in the field, each of one hundred thousand men."[2] In the notes of this gentleman of Lombardy, Bollati sees evidence of three capital discoveries: first, the existence of a country of seventeen million inhabitants; next, the possibility, even the obligation, for landowners to federate out of common interest; and finally, the necessity, if this federation is to survive, to transform the peasants into consenting citizen-soldiers and turn them away from any temptation to rebel.[3]

None of Greppi's wishes came to pass, for reasons worth further analysis, but of these the most important surely is the polyphony (indeed, the cacophony) of reactions to the suggestions coming from revolutionary France. Even if one considers only those who did not militate against the Napoleonic armies, at least two dissonant refrains emerge: first, the pragmatic realism of the Greppi's, the Melzi d'Eril's, and other Lombard landowners; and, second, the idealism—ranging from sentimental purism to dogmatic rigorism—of the leaders of the Parthenopean Republic of 1799.

The lawyer Vincenzio Russo can be considered an archetype of metaphysical revolutionary idealism. After having been arrested and banished from the Kingdom of Naples, he wrote from Rome, where he had taken refuge during the ephemeral republic of 1798 to 1799, a sort of radically antimodern manifesto. The theoretical postulate of his platform was that "he who extends commerce beyond simple barter has forged the first links in the chain of slavery." Russo went on to preach the destruction of Italy's leading ports, "a source of corruption," and the disappearance of the great cities, "favorable to despotism."[4] While the real people of Rome revolted against the French troops barely two weeks after their arrival,

Russo's notion of ideal humanity was rooted in the "sterile regions": he cited the mountain folk of Switzerland and the Apennines as models to follow.

One of his political adversaries was his friend Vincenzo Cuoco, a fellow leader of the Neapolitan revolution of 1799. With Cuoco, the speculative bent of the southern intellectuals, which in Milan had come into contact with the hard core of social and political conflicts, transformed itself, to a degree, into the "consciousness from without" introduced to a ruling northern class whose empiricism often prevailed over coherent theoretical thought. It was not the first time, nor would it be the last, that the "philosophy" of the south would come to the rescue of a northern "pragmatism" lacking in great concepts.

Although he was critical of the dogmatic fervor of Vincenzio Russo, it was from him that Cuoco borrowed the notion of a "peasant philosopher," in order to forge a "prototype of an Italian" whose health and vigor emanated precisely from his rural origins. This ideological reversal of the relationship between city and countryside could be explained by the possibility—rendered concrete by the conscription of the masses—of resolving the problem of a national army, a problem that had haunted partisans of Italian unity since Machiavelli. It was no longer a question, as had been the case for Greppi, of improvising a military mobilization to face the French, but rather of laying the bases of an institution on which the legitimacy of a state would reside. Vincenzo Cuoco thus threw himself into the pedagogical task of explaining to the landowners that the time for disdain of the people was past, for it would henceforth be their responsibility to ensure the continuity and the defense of property. Instead of disdain, it was now time to seek consensus: It was necessary for the "predominant class" to share with "the servant class" all "the benefits of civil life."[5]

Other intellectuals, such as Berchet, Borsieri, Gioberti, and, especially, Manzoni, undertook the task of accompanying this peasant in his encounters with industrial civilization.

Philanthropic Paternalism

Invisible to eighteenth-century observers, the peasant masses haunted the nightmares of landowners late in that century and early in the next before transforming themselves, during the Napoleonic domination, into "wild beasts to be tamed." Once the Austrian occupiers had again interposed their military and police shield between the landowners and the masses, "it was no longer necessary (it was *not yet* necessary) to manage their warlike energies."[6] The intellectual avant-garde could deny historical evolution, but it could not go so far as to force the subordinate classes back into the void from which the French Revolution had pulled them. Instead, it adopted an air of philanthropic paternalism in their regard.

According to Gramsci, the intellectuals' attitude of "paternal and 'god-like' protection" comes across as a sort of "relationship between two races," a rapport established on the model of the "Animal Protective League or the Anglo-Saxons' Salvation Army vis-à-vis the cannibals of Papua New Guinea."[7] The so-called "literature of humbles" that resulted—Manzoni is its most illustrious representative—reflects the intellectuals' self-satisfaction, their sense of superiority.

Bollati notes that Manzoni represents, better than most, the fundamental puzzle of the *Risorgimento*, namely, the "crossing of two vectors running in two opposite directions": on the one side, the objective necessity of channeling a country's every energy toward the goal of constructing an independent state, and on the other, the tendency of the ruling classes to "constrict, control, conserve" these same energies, if only to stay on top of economic development so rapid that it risks becoming subversive.[8]

The Augustinian concept of peace as "*tranquillitas ordinis*"[9] was the most suitable representation of the thread from which the "revolutionary" weaves of the Lombard bourgeoisie were made; thus the Catholic intellectuals became almost naturally their avant-garde. Manzoni and other writers shared the privilege of rinsing the liberal laundry in the papal Tiber,[10] notably with Niccolò Tommaseo and, especially, with Vincenzo Gioberti, to whom one owes the "neo-Guelph" hypothesis of Italian unification. Manzoni meantime played an absolutely exceptional role in the attempts to build a national ideology—indeed, a unique role—serving as a sort of bridge between the often fanciful romantic national archeology and the more concrete needs of a nation that was starting to construct itself, beginning with its language.

Although considered the most eminent Italian representative of this movement, Manzoni was in reality a "critical" romantic. If he fully embodied the spirit of the new literary movement, he was far more reticent about embracing all its ideologies and symbols. For him, real humanity of the sort that must be offered as both example and model—especially for future Italians—was to be found not among history's active figures, but among their victims. "Guilt" resides not only among "the emperors, the kings, the conquerors, the factious and the ambitious"[11]; it is also found among those who cling to the fatal pretension that man can find within himself the source of morality, can be the artisan of his own destiny. Manzoni contends that this sin of pride inevitably produces a quest for possessions that can never be fully sated and that can lead to certain evils, given the nature of human instability. In the end, man must submit to the only certain and immutable law—that which is revealed by God.

The Manzonian man, who draws his moral qualities from the unhappiness of experience, is torn by a struggle between pride and punishment that is part of his condition. It goes beyond history and, a fortiori, beyond social classes. Nonetheless, tossed out the door of philanthropic solidarity, social realities find their way back in through the window of this imaginary construct: the man frozen in a historical immobility is none other than the peasant; centuries have passed, leaving him still in place, tirelessly carrying out the tasks that have befallen him.

"The Curse of the Proletariat"

The political immobility of the countryside, Galli della Loggia asserts, was a "constant" of Italian life at least until the second half of the nineteenth century, mainly due to an extremely prolonged "stagnation" in social relationships, which would prove to be a fundamental element of Italian backwardness.[12] The linkage between rural immobilism and the incapacity to solve the problems that left Italy lagging behind other European powers is particularly interesting; it allows us to verify the conservative—rather, "antimodern"—character of Manzoni's ideology.

As we have seen, a reactionary current always spreads within parts of the intellectual elite as capitalist development advances. In Italy, beyond the doctrinaire fanatics of antimodernity, à la Vincenzio Russo, who had only the most glancing understanding of capitalism, there existed a grouping sufficiently familiar with this new social organization to want to save the country from it. The Italian example is not isolated: The "populist" movement of late-nineteenth century Russia took up the same concept, evoking the existence of a "Russian exceptionalism" that would allow it to move directly from a primitive community to a collective economy without passing through capitalism. But while this movement "toward the people" in Russia led numerous intellectuals to join directly in action and propaganda, in Italy such practical gestures were rare and isolated; the dominant intellectual attitude was essentially, as we have seen, one of condescending paternalism.

The two most important episodes of the Italian version of the movement "toward the people"—those of 1844 under the brothers Bandiera and that of Pisacane in 1857, all of them linked more or less to Mazzini—ultimately led to a mobilization of the rural plebes, but a mobilization whose target was the very people who had come to "liberate" them. For Gramsci, the structural reason for the Pisacane failure was the absence of a platform, of a party, of a cadre trained to lead a new state.[13] And that brings us back to the heart of the problem: the separation between the supposed "national revolution" and the real "nation."

To the empirical observation on the masses' absence from the national unification movement, Denis Mack Smith adds an important thought: The masses were absent so long as the "civil war" between the old and new ruling classes did not affect the conditions of their social existence, but when it did, he adds, the peasants nearly regularly constituted a counterrevolutionary force.[14] Thus the national Italian movement could no longer afford simply to ignore, to channel, or to mythicize the peasant masses; it had to prevent them from being in a position to do harm.

The more developed countries had already recognized the impossibility of proscribing class struggles, so the ruling Italian classes and their ideologues simply proscribed the classes—or at least the system, which seemed, in its development, to have provoked class struggles. In 1819, the Milanese landowner Giuseppe Pecchio, writing in the *Conciliatore*, described the misdeeds effected by large landholdings, as well as the excessive use of machines in manufacturing. This observation resulted from a study of industrialization in England where, Pecchio wrote, "two years ago, the numerous population of factory workers rose up against the tyranny of the bosses."[15] In 1829 another former contributor to the *Conciliatore*, Gian Domenico Romagnosi, in an article on "British pauperism,"[16] denounced "the veritable slavery of the factory, absolutely analogous to the serfdom." In 1841 the Piedmontese count Carlo Ilarione Petitti di Roreto questioned whether industrial innovations were really always useful, particularly for an agricultural country like Italy.[17] Behind his philanthropic preoccupations, Petitti did not hide another concern, raised by the ever-growing masses of "proletarians: a term selected to designate the little people living day-to-day" who "are in a state of latent war against their employers."[18] Even for Cesare Correnti of Milan, an organizer of the 1848 uprising, "the curse of the English proletariat"[19] had to be exorcised.

Most prominent in this chorus of anticapitalist doubt—with the remarkable absence of Cavour and Cattaneo—were thinkers, like Gioberti, who framed their concepts in a broader philosophical context. For the latter, "an insufficient consideration of the moral ingredients of wealth is the cause of numerous economic errors and makes a great number of questions almost insoluble."[20] Like some of the other authors mentioned above, Gioberti displayed his admiration for English power and wealth, but he turned the problem upside down: it was not a question of avoiding the British model, but rather of proposing the Italian model to the British. The "turbulent democracy" into which the "Chartists' abject faction" risked plunging England could be averted by embracing the "propensities of Oxford,"[21] that is, by reintegrating the Roman Catholic family. The reference to Chartist movement is symptomatic: the return to Rome of the British prodigal son not only would help replace "the moral ingredients" of capitalist wealth but also would spare it the agonies of class struggle. This, then, was the model proposed for Italian development.

An Imaginary Crucible

Paul Kennedy, in describing the situation of the different powers on the eve of World War II, wrote that Mussolini's Italy was one of the rare cases in all the history of human conflict when a country's entry into war did more damage to its allies than to its adversaries.[22] What might at first seem like a "bon mot" or a paradox is in fact a thesis amply illustrated by a minutely detailed summary of the structural fragility of Italy in the 1930s: a fragility due, according to Kennedy, to the persistent dependence on small farming.[23]

Under Mussolini, the peasantry's "Catonist" function—as a rampart of social stability—reached its apogee. It was no accident that the "virtues of rural life" and of corporatist ideology were being glorified at the same time. But the resurrection of corporatist theory from the fogs of medieval history was an ideological operation, one that cannot be attributed to fascism. It dated back another fifty years, when Catholic social circles, pointing to the experience of the Catholic Friendship Society of Joseph de Maistre, gave birth in June 1874 to the movement of *l'Opera dei Congressi*, the Work of the Congress. Opposed to capitalism, bearers of an individualistic and conflictual conception of social relationships, they exalted the virtues of rural society, while viewing the cities as hotbeds of corruption and impiety. *Rerum Novarum*, the encyclical promulgated by Pope Leo XIII in 1891, offered a systematic framework for this social doctrine, founded on an unyielding opposition to liberal economy, a reevaluation of the corporatist system, a condemnation of capitalism, and a demand for a "just salary." The first "modern" Catholic labor union, the Italian Confederation of Labor (CIL)—founded in 1919 to stem the rapid rise of the General Confederation of Labor (CGL), the trade-union organization linked to the Socialist Party—included in its platform "the abolition of salaried workers and the collaboration between the classes, organized at the trade-union level according to the corporatist and social-political model."[24]

Starting in the first half of the nineteenth century, even before the Church had expressed its position *ex cathedra*, these theses had been spread through Italy by some renowned Catholic intellectuals. Following the logic of "moderate hegemony," not only was there an a priori rejection of any identification between a nation and a single class—namely, the bourgeoisie—but also the very possibility of such an approach was ruled out. Therein resides one reason for Italy's uncertain national aspect: the clear and firm demand for such identification had, after all, constituted a prime force behind the French revolutionary bourgeoisie.

Rather than do everything in their power to regain lost terrain, the leading Italian classes satisfied themselves with contemplating the country's backwardness and, indeed, transforming it into a specific native virtue, into a distinctive characteristic of a supposed national identity. In doing so they went beyond even the traditional distinctions between Catholic and secular culture. Taking a stand against the "theory of rights," and in particular against the "right to well-being," Giuseppe Mazzini demanded an Italian specificity not too different from what the Catholics proposed: the Italian nation should be founded not on rights, but on duties, he said, and the first of these should be to renounce any private or personal demands in order to let them all meld jointly in the crucible of the Motherland.[25]

The final paradox largely explains the deficits that Italy had to overcome, painfully, throughout its contemporary history: at the very moment when the unitary state became a reality, the rural myth of the ancient agricultural civilization confronted the harsh reality of a war led by the Italian army against the peasants of the south and pursued by fiscal means against the peasants of the entire country. The new state thus came into being as an entity that was foreign, even hostile, to a large majority of the "real" Italian people. Even the official language of the new state was unknown to 97.5 percent of the population, according to the "rough" calculation of Tullio De Mauro. From that point forward, the ability to speak Italian was a "distinctive sign of one's class."[26] After fifty years spent trying to paper over the social differences in the *mare magnum* of the "people," nothing could more strikingly symbolize the gap between the planned Italian identity and its actual realization—leaving the real people, in every way, as foreigners in their own country.

Chapter 6

A Culture without a Nation

Linguistic Dirigisme

At the moment of Italian unification, the ruling Piedmontese class faced an unexpected reality: Rather than governing a small, semi-French, mostly homogeneous, subalpine region, it now had to govern an almost entirely Mediterranean entity, disparate both geographically and in human terms. Deeply pragmatic, these first rulers wasted no time contemplating their difficulties, but instead plunged straight into what they considered the most urgent tasks facing them. The thorniest of these, in their eyes, was the survival of the new state.

In the early years of unitary Italy, the fear that this barely constructed edifice might collapse under the concentric attacks of the Catholic powers (Austria and France) and of the Bourbons of Naples, exiled in the Pope's court, outweighed all other concerns. Thus, instead of any discussion of the formation of a "nation," the ruling classes gave immediate priority to the creation of the state, which is to say the establishment of an administration and of a coercive, unitary governing apparatus.

Paradoxically, it was precisely these coercive structures that proved to be the most rapid and effective, at least in the short term, in a first "nationalization" of the masses. Indeed, they succeeded, just years after the new state's birth, in giving rise to movements of rebellion that involved the real masses of the entire country. The extremely unpopular wheat tax provoked, in December 1868 and January 1869, a wave of revolts that spread from Lombardy through the entire peninsula, forcing the army to intervene.[1]

But the best-known case was the contribution that mandatory military service—especially during World War I—played in diffusing the "national" language. Beginning in 1915, peasants from every region of Italy found themselves at the fronts, communicating together for the first time, with army chaplains often serving as intermediaries and interpreters. The language that provided a common vehicle for communications was a new and original Italian, impregnated with dialects and military jargon, in which the Piedmontese dialect of the old hierarchies and the southern accents of the new ones predominated. It thus took nearly sixty years of unitary life and a world political catastrophe for a "national" language to begin to be understood (if almost never practiced) by a majority of the Italian people.

A particularity of the Italian dialects—certainly the most original one—is that their diffusion was, so to speak, "democratic." In the other national entities that sprung into being in the nineteenth century, a scholarly language, used by the political, economic, and cultural elites, existed in opposition to the popular forms of speech; in Italy, on the contrary, dialects were used by every social category not only in private life but often in official and public occasions as well. The first Italian king hated speaking Italian; his prime minister, Camillo Benso di Cavour, felt much more at ease with French or even English, and ministerial meetings were regularly conducted in Piedmontese, until *after* unification.

In 1868, Alessandro Manzoni was named to head the Commission of the Ministry of Public Instruction, in charge of linguistic questions. For decades Manzoni had dreamed of being able to contribute to the birth of the new unitary language, but his wish had collided with another of his dearest hopes—for the revolution to take place without a revolution. As the linguist Giacomo Devoto emphasizes, the demand that unitary political institutions be linked to a unitary language encountered a key obstacle in "the social immobility accompanying the national revolution."[2] The persistence of dialects, adds another linguist, Tullio De Mauro, was the consequence of "the plurisecular stagnation of the economic, social and intellectual life of the country."[3]

Manzoni favored a language imposed from top to bottom: Florence should thus have fulfilled the centripetal role played in France by Paris, in Spain by Madrid, and in England by London. This policy, later described as "*dirigiste*," proved illusory, and not just for the reasons mentioned by Devoto. Even the notion of sending Tuscan teachers across the national territory to serve as "missionaries of the language" failed in the end, principally because of the clear lack of structure in the Italian educational system in the early decades of the unitary experience. According to a ministerial inquiry of 1910—fifty years after unification—two-thirds of all classrooms were "inadequate" and half of the sixty thousand teachers were "insufficient"; in some cities, the law explicitly authorized placing illiterate teachers in charge of classes when necessary; and under the pretext that students did not understand Italian, their teachers generally spoke in a dialect.[4] Della Loggia quotes the Economic Archives of Italian Unification as saying that in Tuscany, the land of the "language missionaries," only 20 percent of those who had attended school could actually read.[5] According to De Mauro, Manzoni's "dirigiste" proposition ultimately engendered "a new purism and a new pedantry"[6] that had no practical effect on language training or on a national conscience.

A Dead Language

As we have seen, the linguistic tools used for centuries by the various populations that were now brought together under the virtual name of "Italians" created more division than cohesion. The persistence of dialects is like a dust cloud left by the peninsula's history of fragmentation; the Italian language, for its part, was just one more sign of not only regional and local divisions (sometimes even divisions between a city's neighborhoods)[7] but also of social divisions. As asserted by Carlo Gozzi, Manzoni himself, Luigi Settembrini, Antonio Gramsci, and others, Italian was for centuries a "dead language," resuscitated with the goal of becoming the *koinê*—a standard language—of populations of disparate origins and languages, a little like Hebrew for the state of Israel.

After the fall of the communes and the affirmation of the principalities, writes Gramsci, Italian became "yet again, a written and not a spoken language, of the learned and not of the nation,"[8] like Latin before it. The same intellectuals who, even in the nineteenth century, saw the resurrection of Italian as offering a heretofore absent "linguistic motherland," actually used it almost exclusively in their writing, and often as a second language, after French or a dialect.

Before unification, the "language question" had remained in the domain of artistic production; with unification, it was supposed to be rethought with a view to serving the communications needs of the new Italians. The failure of the Manzonian approach shows that it had become impossible to favor any other approach based on personal preferences. The theses of the "dirigistes" were opposed by the "liberal" theses of the man considered the most eminent linguist of his time, Graziadio Isaia Ascoli, who placed his hopes for the diffusion of the national language in the improvement of the cultural, economic, and social conditions in the country.[9]

In fact, it was not until certain major upheavals shook the bases of "social immobility" that the Italian language started, however slowly, to become the collective patrimony of the Italian people. As with other social phenomena, the moments when this historic movement sped up or slowed down (such as political unification, the world war, or the "economic boom" of the 1950s) were also the moments when the propagation of the Italian language sped up or slowed down.

Tullio De Mauro describes four social processes that were largely responsible for the progressive linguistic unification of the country: the actions of the organs of the unitary state, industrialization, urbanization, and interregional demographic exchanges. In fact, the rural flight, which underlay the migration toward cities and industrializing countries—is simply the flip side of industrialization. If industrialization was the most important social vector of linguistic unification, then clearly the "agriculturalist" policy adopted by the first unitary governments (despite Cavour's resistance) retarded any benefits that the "invisible hand" could have brought—in language, too—to the puny and vacillating "visible hand" of the state.

As for the latter, the institution on which Manzoni's hopes largely resided—schools—probably contributed the least to the diffusion of the Italian *koinê*. In contrast, the establishment of a unitary bureaucratic apparatus played a hardly negligible role. On the one hand, it favored the concentration in Rome of a ruling class, drawn from the regions, which was forced on a daily basis to use the common language; on the other hand, by conferring tasks on the peripheral organs of the new state, it established them as outposts of the Italian language.

Nonetheless, as we have seen, it was compulsory military service that played the central role in the diffusion of the language. If a schools inspector in Palermo province in 1864 could deem "satisfactory" an attendance rate of 30 percent for boys and 18 percent for girls[10]—this, though attendance supposedly was "obligatory"—the state was far less yielding in dealing with those who sought to avoid mandatory military service, going so far as to deport, or even summarily execute, draft dodgers.

During the first decade of the twentieth century, one could see empirical evidence that a direct and proportional relationship existed between the end of "social immobility" and the spread of instruction: During this period of the first "economic miracle" on the peninsula, the avoidance rate for mandatory schooling fell rapidly, to 25 percent. Moreover, the zones of "linguistic conservation," the countryside, began to depopulate, as people moved to the centers of "linguistic innovation,"[11] that is, the cities. "Thus," wrote the linguist Matteo Giulio Bartoli in 1930, "the cities, which yesterday were the cradles of dialectal variety, will become their tombs."[12]

The "Italian Genius" Abroad

As to the role played by eighteenth-century intellectuals in the global diffusion of Italian culture, Gramsci raises the question of whether "the cosmopolitanism of Italian intellectuals" is of the same nature as "the cosmopolitanism of other national intellectuals."[13] The response, as emerges throughout his writings, is negative: in the Italian case, he states, cosmopolitan character and national character are opposed and mutually exclusive.

Catholic universalism also weighed on this, with an absolutely singular character in comparison to the Church of Rome's other "national" experiences. The demand for a centralist approach to counter feudal division could certainly not be satisfied in Italy by a Church that was itself directly or indirectly feudal; nonetheless, writes Amadeo Bordiga, the Italian communes, managed by artisans, bankers, and merchants with relationships across Europe, viewed the Church's universal influence as a sort of subsidiary political network.[14] To this "passive" function—the Church used by the nascent Italian bourgeoisie as a sort of facsimile of the universal Roman Empire—one must add the "active" function, linked to the needs for defense, development, and independence in the face of the great European monarchies. These necessities, Gramsci writes, "led the Church to turn ever more to Italy to seek the bases for its supremacy and to the Italians for the personnel to man its organizational apparatus."[15]

This character of the Catholic Church, both Italian and universal, in Galli della Loggia's view, explained the intrinsically antinational role that it played from the Middle Ages to 1929, the year the Concordat was signed. Its independence vis-à-vis the state and society was facilitated by the lack of state unity in Italy, and so the Church militated actively against such unity.[16] Thus della Loggia continues, Italians were subjected to a double-negative consequence: the Church was an obstacle to their national plans, and they were unable, in contrast to other Europeans, to count on "the precious support of a national Church."[17]

Whatever the cause, the absence of a state, of a central political power capable of offering a national perspective to the wide sweep of the intellectual energies of the peninsula, lay behind the emigration of the most active and gifted of Italians. In order to be able to exercise their talents, the latter found themselves having to put themselves in the service of some foreign power, thus losing all specifically "Italian" character. The reason Christopher Columbus sailed in the service of Spain and not of an Italian republic, Gramsci observes, "must be sought in Italy and not among the Turks or in America," those generally blamed for the decadence of the peninsula.[18]

Leaving aside the emigration of laborers, which began on a massive scale only late in the nineteenth century, the Italians who gained fame and importance outside their native land in the most disparate areas were like the "adventurers" described by Giuseppe Prezzolini. This group, as Prezzolini wrote, would—had they grown up in a "civil and well-ordered society"—have become "ministers of state and the most distinguished of diplomats, eminent generals or admirals, professors capable of arousing their students' intellectual curiosity, excellent writers rich in ideas"; yet all of them, Prezzolini concluded, for want of a supportive state, elected to try their chances abroad.[19]

Among a great number of examples, Gramsci recalls that, in the war of Flanders in the late sixteenth century, a large number of military men, many of particular genius, were Italians.[20] One might also cite two other illustrious examples, both of them paradigmatic, yet verging on the paradoxical. The first is that of the fate of Prince Eugene, the only representative of the Savoy family who is still famous through much of the Christian world for his military virtues.[21] Another example is the battle of Lissa in 1866, where Italian admirals in the service of the Austrian Empire prevailed rather easily over the quite new military fleet of the Italian kingdom commanded by Admiral Persano.

This "cosmopolitan function of the cultivated Italian classes"[22] had a prejudicial effect on the birth of an Italian cultural identity, a prejudice that men of letters inherited and in turn passed on through the centuries.

The "Foreign Genius" in Italy

As to the defeat of 1866, Pasquale Villari observed that its reasons should not be sought so much in the "quadrilateral" of Mantua, Verona, Legnago, and Peschiera, as in the "quadrilateral of 17 million illiterates and of 5 million Arcadians."[23] As conservative as he was, Villari did not content himself, as did some of his contemporaries, with snide references to the cultural inadequacies of the lower classes; he was equally critical of the shortcomings of the ruling classes, imbued over the centuries with a cultural education that was dominated, as Gramsci put it, by "emphasis, the declamatory style, and stylistic hypocrisy."[24]

During the same period when, in France, a generation of men "of science, of arts and of crafts" began to rally together in the pursuit of "common ideas of common interests"—thus giving birth to a veritable "party of philosophers"[25]—in Italy, each intellectual was entrenched in his own garden, protecting it fiercely from any outside influences. In France, by bringing together their scattered energies, philosophers had applied themselves to studying their times, with the conviction that it was only by exploring the limits within which one operates that one learns to move beyond them. In Italy, all the cultivated classes remained prisoners of their situation, even when the French armies brought them the "liberty" that they had not managed to achieve on their own.

In the eighteenth century, Italian cultural circles remained essentially under French influence. After the "Great Century," France's political, economic, and cultural influence radiated across virtually all the so-called civilized world. But its effects were particularly important in Italy, because it did not enrich and complete a vibrant local culture, but, in a sense, replaced it, filling the voids left by an inadequate national tradition. Inasmuch as the Italian language was arbitrary and very rarely used even by representatives of the "cultivated classes," another linguistic *medium* was needed to foster the circulation of ideas and of men as well as of merchandise, which even then had long ago spilled beyond the narrow confines of the "shadow of the local bell tower" within which one spoke one's own dialect. This medium was, quite naturally, French.

The linguist Melchiorre Cesarotti observed, regarding the end of the century, that there "was no even slightly cultivated person for whom [the French language] was not familiar and almost natural: the library of worldly women and men is only French."[26] During Napoleon's domination of the peninsula, the historian Carlo Denina, analyzing the junction between the subjective demands of the nascent Italian bourgeoisie and the existing cultural and political conditions, went so far as to propose the outright adoption of French as Italy's national language.[27]

Most of the authors responsible for the literary glory of the eighteenth and nineteenth centuries had to struggle to achieve a mastery of Italian that equaled the ease with which they had mastered French and their own dialect. Vittorio Alfieri recounted in his autobiography how he had first written in French before "sinking into the grammarian's abyss" in order to put himself "in a condition to know [his] language, as a man of Italy."[28] Francesco de Sanctis writes that Alfieri had decided to go live in Florence to *"disfrancesizzarsi"* (de-Frenchify) and *"intoscanirsi"* (Tuscanize) himself; and once, after having worked and reworked some verses, he cried out: *"Gira, volta, ei son francesi"* (Turn them and turn them again, they are still French!).[29] Manzoni, in a personal letter, compared the "ease" with which he had written the *Lettre à M. Chauvet sur l'unité de temps et de lieu dans la littérature* (1820), in French, with the "suffering endured" during the rewriting of *Promessi Sposi*.[30] Before becoming a celebrated writer and the author of important dictionaries of the Italian language, Niccolò Tommaseo, born in Sibenik, on the Dalmatian coast, where Venetian dialects competed with Croatian, began his apprenticeship as a writer in dialect and in Latin, displaying "a skill that his first compositions in Italian did not manage to equal."[31] Having noticed, during a stroll in Rome, that Giovanni Verga expressed himself "with difficulty and with numerous imperfections" in Italian, whereas he spoke easily in Sicilian with some sailors he chanced to meet, the writer Edoardo Scarfoglio wondered "why Verga doesn't have the Sicilians he writes about speak in Sicilian."[32] Through the first half of the twentieth century, several of the most celebrated writers—Gabriele D'Annunzio, Filippo Tommaso Marinetti, Giuseppe Ungaretti, and Curzio Malaparte, for example—continued to write with equal ease in French or Italian.

One might say, as Sergio Romano did, that the entire history of Italian literature in the eighteenth and nineteenth centuries is marked by a certain linguistic precariousness, by a sense that the relationship between the artist and his principal tool was, in a real way, artificial.[33] But, as Gramsci reminds us, "Every time the question of language resurfaces one way or another, it is because a series of other problems are lining themselves up at the front of the stage." The most important of these was "the development and the enlargement of the ruling classes."[34]

Chapter 7

The Difficult Italianization of the Piedmont

A Rib of France

When he arrived in Turin in 1831, the Tuscan writer Cesare De Laugier noticed with some amazement a sign, in the direction from which he had just come, that read "Road to Italy." When he asked the significance of this, he was told in French: "Do you not realize you're in Piedmont, and not in Italy?" In an 1855 text, the historian Cesare Balbo recalled that the elder members of his family, when they left the Piedmont, would say that they were going to Italy.[1]

The Piedmont is hardly the only region with few ties with Italy. What is particular is that the country's unification began in this region, which, as the federalist Enrico Cenni put it in 1861, had "the palest color of Italianity."[2] According to Galli della Loggia, "from a geolithic point of view," this was a veritable case of outside "interference" in Italian affairs; it contributed to making the pursuit of a national identity problematic and laborious.[3]

The Piedmont administrative region as we know it today is a recent creation, born in 1912 by joining the "statistical provinces" created in 1864 into "statistical regions" of no administrative character whatsoever. The name "Piedmont," in the beginning, had a purely geographical meaning ("at the foot of the mountains"). In the twelfth century, when it first appeared, it still had its original connotation and referred only to the territory reaching from the Alps to the upper reaches of the Po. It later expanded to include the entire area at the foot of the Alps, from Aosta to Nice, and some territories that today are Piedmontese—the plains east of the Sesia, Asti, and the Montferrat—have not been part of it for long.

Simply put, the Savoy dynasty anchored its power to an ethnic and territorial continuity that has existed, one might say, forever. The Roman administrative division established under Augustus gave rise to the province of the Cottian Alps; its capitals were Susa (now in Italy), Briançon, and Saint-Jean-de-Maurienne (now in France). This unity was confirmed by the episcopal subdivision in the Middle Ages, which had supplanted the administrative organization of the Roman Empire. It was subjected to the vicissitudes of war between the Francs and the Lombards, yet, it never gave birth to any "natural" border along the crest of the Alps.[4]

The Savoy dynasty worked to reassemble the feudal mosaic. It used as its base communications routes that were often shared but that depended on control of the peaks through which trade transited between northern and southern Europe: Mont Cénis and the Saint Bernard passes. This family, with its ancient Burgundian roots, whose authority extended to the Rhone and the banks of Lake Geneva, considered itself a repository of the frontier culture that united the French, Italian, and Swiss worlds. When, in the wake of the peace of Cateau-Cambrésis in 1559, Emmanuel Philibert transferred the capital of the duchy from Chambéry to Turin, there was no particular sense that it had changed countries, all the more so since the new capital lived entirely under French influence.[5]

The decision to transfer the capital to Turin indicated a fundamental political reorientation. This was not, however, dictated by a supposed Italian national vocation, but rather it was due to the uncomfortable position of the duchy, which existed as a sort of earthenware pot lodged between the cast-iron vessels of France and the Empire. After the Hundred Years War, the political homogenization of the French kingdom and the wars of Italy, Savoy's western possessions found themselves under objective threat. Thus the choice of bilingualism, along with other measures geared toward a progressive "Italianization" of the duchy, had an eminently political significance. This held not only a defensive character vis-à-vis France but also a view toward later enlargements of the kingdom, which were certainly more likely in the direction of a weak and divided Italy—and, conceivably, of Switzerland—than of a strong and centralized France.

Finally, to the extent that one can speak of an "Italian choice," one cannot do so before the eighteenth century. It was then that Charles Emmanuel and his entourage broke the precarious bilingual equilibrium and encouraged the use of Italian. The attestation of Cesare de Laugier shows, nevertheless, the point to which Piedmontese life remained foreign to these measures, which went against the entire historic and cultural tradition of the region.

The National State of Savoy

In a famous passage of his *De vulgari eloquentia*, from 1303, Dante Alighieri definitively excludes (*"et si quis dubitat, illum nulla nostra solutione dignamur"* [if anyone doubts it, we would not consider this worthy of a response]) Piedmontese from the list of commonly spoken Italian tongues.[6] As we have seen, Montaigne largely confirmed this judgment 250 years later. For the former Florentine prior, as for the chairman of the Parliament of Bordeaux, this was an empirical observation; modern linguistic studies would later provide scientific confirmation. Linguists grant Piedmont the particular status of "border land," with all the ambiguity the term implies; the specific political calculation involved added to the ambiguity.

The choice of bilingualism for the duchy of Savoy carried with it (and, in a way, implied) a fundamental contradiction. On the French side, it merely institutionalized the use of a language already widely employed, even among the lower classes, in view of an effective political unification. But on the Italian side, it was a juridical fiction, to the extent that there was an attempt to impose by decree a language hardly known outside intellectual circles, and even intellectuals were highly divided as to its use.

Constanza Arconati noted that, three centuries after the arrival of the dukes in Turin, the "three national languages [of Piedmont] are French, Piedmontese and Genovese," even though, as she underlines, "only French was understood by everyone."[7] As we have seen, the princes of Savoy themselves used Piedmontese and French as "national languages": the use of dialect helped to create a sort of familiarity with their subjects, even the most humble of them, paradoxically facilitating their sociocultural integration in their chosen region.[8]

But it was not just Piedmont's linguistic specificity that marginalized the region in comparison to the rest of the peninsula. There was also the fact that Piedmont had not experienced the urban flowering that was such a salient characteristic of Italian history, and that while in the rest of communal Italy the first collective emancipations of serfs dated to the thirteenth century, Emmanuel Philibert's sixteenth-century attempts to abolish the significant remains of servitude in his state collided with a highly conservative social and historic framework.

According to Bollati, the effort at renewal, which stemmed from a desire to follow modern Europe's footsteps, led not to the birth of the early core of a future national state, but to "a veritable national state itself," on the model of the great monarchies.[9] State structures were transformed and consolidated; the goal was to reinforce the principle of subordinating private interests to a central power. Parliaments were the key instrument of this action, while the creation of provinces, prefectures, and a Council of State helped in forming a modern administrative structure. As we will see, this evolved form of state was to constitute Piedmont's specific contribution to the Italian cultural panorama of the eighteenth century, and would be a particularly important trump card for Turin during the nineteenth-century process of Italian unification. But it was in terms of military organization that the process of modernization begun by Emmanuel Philibert left the most enduring mark, from at least three viewpoints: of the independence of the state; of the subjection of feudal potentates; and in the birth of an alleged Piedmontese specific "nature"[10].

As for this last aspect, it was the military tradition that, according to Balbo, explained the "greater solidity and the lesser vivacity"[11] of the Piedmontese when compared to the Lombards. This "natural" quality intermingled with the nature and history of the dynasty: the habit of commanding and obeying the confidence "in the calming values of bureaucratic regularity"[12] were legacies that Piedmont transmitted to Italy. This heritage was to prove vitally important during Italy's critical moments, but would be a major handicap in times when Italy was at its most dynamic.

Piedmont's Lag

According to Piedmontese historians of the first half of the nineteenth century, the region's "natural" quality reflected a mixture of military tradition, administrative solidity, and social conservativism. If this correlation of factors indeed underlay

Piedmont's social order, it clearly was destined to morph from a stabilizing element into a multiplier of instability once any of the factors entered into crisis. That has been the case each time the jealously preserved principle of social homogeneity has collided with some new historic development. So it was in the eighteenth century, when certain eastern regions were incorporated into the Kingdom of Savoy whose social relationships dominating in the countryside differed significantly from those typifying rural Piedmont.[13] And so it was certainly when Piedmont felt the shocks of various international upheavals: whether political catastrophes like occupation under Napoleon; or new conditions emerging in world markets, as in the 1870s, when the end of the free-trade cycle gave a *coup de grace* to the "agriculturist path to economic development" that the Piedmontese had followed.

It is important to recall that Piedmont's lag behind the rest of Italy proved both a blight and a blessing for the House of Savoy. There is no doubt, for example, that the region's social conditions at the point when the capital was transferred to Turin were among the peninsula's worst. Yet this immaturity put the duchy in a potentially favorable situation compared to the other Italian states; while the others found themselves at the start of a phase of senescence, the duchy could be seen as having a certain youth, with prospects of considerable growth and development. Moreover, from the end of the sixteenth century, Piedmont-Savoy appeared (along with Venice, which was possibly even less Italian than Turin) to be the only Italian state that had maintained its independence in the face of the omnipresent Spanish guardianship ratified at Cateau-Cambrésis.

But the Savoys' objectives were not national, they were territorial and dynastic, and their policy of state reform must be placed in this strategic perspective. Even at this point, Piedmont's development lagged behind the rest of the peninsula. When Victor Amedeus II reformed the administration of his state, developed the University of Turin, and fought against abuses by the clergy and the nobility, notes Procacci, the Medici still reigned in Florence, Naples had yet to regain its independence, and Habsburg reformism had not yet reached Milan. But the advantage was only apparent, and it was transitory. Rather than anticipating the great reforms of the eighteenth century, the Kingdom of Piedmont attempted to create for itself structures worthy of a "great European monarchy," but based (though with a few decades' delay) on the classic scheme of absolutism. Thus, by opting for a protectionist mercantilism, the Savoy king completely ignored the liberalization of land and merchandise that was taking shape in Lombardy and Tuscany, and he encouraged the trends toward the integration of a nearly invisible bourgeoisie with the diffusion of the "bourgeois gentilhommes" who financed the public debt even as they shed their entrepreneurial vestments.

Moreover, the new "ruling class," created to manage the apparatus of absolutism, was composed of skillful, hardworking, and meticulous executors, but, as Quazza writes, men lacking "the general capacities of judgment that politics demands."[14] Finally, the reforms engendered a malaise among the traditional nobility by accelerating a process that marginalized them, to the benefit of a "service nobility." The result was that the old dominant classes felt threatened by change even though other social classes did not feel advantaged.

Thus some of the factors that had touched off the decline of France from the end of the seventeenth century to the beginning of the eighteenth century found their way to the Piedmont, aggravated by the latter's backwardness vis-à-vis the rest of Italy and of Europe. The signing of a concordat with the Church, the resumption of persecutions of the Jews and the Waldensians, the arrest of certain intellectuals like Alberto Radicati di Sostegno[15] and Pietro Giannone, and the dismissal from the university of these same professors who had supported the reform process were, from the first half of the century, among the telltale signs of a stunningly rapid regression: Turin, as Procacci writes, rapidly became the grayest of Italian capitals, the best protected against the spread of the Enlightenment, by imposing the barrier of censorship, "the barracks and the Boeotia of enlightened Italy,"[16] Piedmont's noninvolvement in the tumultuous and changing history of the rest of the peninsula made possible this original process, which helps understand the seeming mystery that allowed this region, "politically and intellectually underdeveloped"[17] in the eighteenth century, to take a role, a century later, leading the unification of Italy.

Chapter 8

The Difficult Piedmontization of Italy

Piedmont as a Political Party

In 1824 Giacomo Leopardi wrote that "as the nation has no center, there is not really an Italian public."[1] The situation had not greatly changed thirty-seven years later. When Italy unified, it suffered from two main defects, as Sabino Cassese put it: that of being "a state without a nation" and that of suffering from a "chronic weakness of its ruling class."[2] As we go forward, let us keep in mind this correlation between the absence of a "center," the weakness of a national "ruling class," and the absence of an "Italian public."

The notion of a "center" involves several characteristics, including the geographic, cultural, and economic senses; the Italy of 1861 lacked all three at once. The principal reason, as we have seen, lay in the very conditions of the process of unification, which resulted not so much from the work of politicians emerging from the struggles of the *Risorgimento* as from a fortuitous mixture of several exceptional circumstances. It was thus necessary to create from scratch a new ruling class, and to do so with men lacking both in experience and in national vocation.

It would not be accurate, however, to suggest that the Italy of the 1860s was completely lacking in political leaders with a sense of the "national interest," as we understand that term today. To the contrary, the problem was that there were too many of them. There was a Piedmontese "national" ruling class, a Lombard "national" ruling class, another from Emilia, and others from Tuscany, Rome, Naples, and Sicily, just to mention the most important of them. As the preunitary states were at such highly different stages of development, the organization of interest groups within the new Italian state entity occurred not "horizontally," which is to say through the representation of the interests of the various classes, but "vertically," that is, through the representation of the interests of the regions. This was evident even at the level of parliamentary groupings: within the *Destra*, there was notably a standing Piedmontese delegation, a Tuscan faction *(called Consorteria)*, a Lombard faction and an Emilian faction.

In this struggle between regional parties, it was Piedmont—the least Italian of all the regions—that assumed the leading role. Nonetheless, most historians agree that there was little alternative to Piedmontese leadership. They offer several explanations. First, it was the ruling class of Turin that managed to turn the international situation to advantage and pull off the process of unification. Second, as we have seen, only Piedmont had succeeded in its political independence. Third, independence had guaranteed a continuity of institutions and customs that, bolstered by the Albertine Statute of 1848, had helped insert Piedmont, and later Italy, into the current of European liberalism. Fourth, the tepid response, even the overt hostility, of other regions of the peninsula to the unitary concept meant that parts of their ruling classes were excluded from the subsequent Italian experience. Last but not least, Piedmont was sufficiently weak, sufficiently small, sufficiently peripheral, and sufficiently not very Italian that the local ruling classes of the other states of the peninsula could accept its hegemony as a lesser evil.

All the arguments for some other center for national political life faced corresponding major handicaps. Rome was a sort of natural center for obvious historic, cultural, and geographic reasons; Naples was the most populous city on the peninsula, and capital of the largest state; Milan's economic weight was too great; Florence, in addition to its tradition and its certified "Italianity," had long been the most liberal capital. The affirmation of one of them would have constituted, in the eyes of all the others, a much more cumbersome weight and a far harder obstacle to surmount than the choice of the subalpine capital. To all that one must add the desire to confront Europe with a fait accompli, in order to avoid what seemed the imminent risk of having the peninsula's barely achieved unity placed in question. All these factors made the new state more an enlargement of the old Piedmont than a new and original political organism.

Since political distinctions, at the dawn of unitary Italy, were based not on class, but on region, differences over the economic and social choices to be made seemed less urgent than those involving the relationship between the dominant region and the other centers of local power. In this regard, the debate in Turin revolved around two principal options and a secondary option. The first, advocated by Cavour, foresaw a rebalancing of the new political entity around Rome, and this in the medium term. For the second, the unitary process demanded the assimilation of the other states to the state of Piedmont, to its institutions and to its laws, with a view to creating a "certain identity of thought and of feelings around the fundamental problems of the state."[3] The third, minority view, was represented by those who were nostalgic for *"Piemons felix"*; for them, the supposedly harmonious development of the Kingdom of Savoy would be definitively disturbed by this union against nature with "unhappy populations lacking morals, lacking courage, lacking education."[4]

Cavour eventually prevailed, and in March 1861 the new Italian Parliament approved the principle of Rome as capital. But this did not mean that the opponents of Rome had forgotten their reluctance, nor that the functionaries and military men of Piedmont did not storm the rest of Italy as if it were a conquered land.

That is why the "Piedmontization" of Italy was seen as abusive by the other regions—even as "the last of the barbarian invasions"[5]—and behind it came the most serious and murderous of all the wars fought by the Italian armies in the nineteenth century: that against the *brigantaggio*.

Centralism and Decentralization

Proposals advanced by certain Piedmontese liberals even before 1848—calling for the establishment with other states of the peninsula of a customs union, the construction of a national rail network, the unification of currencies, and the standardization of measures—showed that at least some members of Turin's ruling class were aware that the only path to development had to involve the formation of a national market.

In the 1840s, the Piedmontese state promoted development with ever more evident determination. This acceleration is confirmed by a study of Turin's budget from the Restoration until 1850: between 1820 and 1830, public spending rose by 10.15 percent; from 1830 to 1840, by 11.3 percent; and then in the years from 1840 to 1850 it took a spectacular leap, 262.44 percent.[6] Beginning in the 1850s, this process continued under Cavour's direction, as new approaches were adopted on customs, fiscal, and administrative matters.

Cavour's superiority flowed from the realization that any political option is effective only to the extent that it takes account of the constraints imposed by "determined historic connections." His ability to adapt, rapidly and without particular scruple, to even the most unexpected of new circumstances allowed him to preserve a basic strategic perspective for the productive Italian classes.

His capacity for adaptation was suddenly tested by the unexpected unification; one could almost speak of a theoretical conversion. Though in his previous political programs he had always advocated the principle of self-government, Cavour did not hesitate to drop this and become the fiercest partisan of centralism the moment that regional autonomy seemed to lure those who might be tempted to challenge unification.

Nevertheless, Cavour exploited every facet of this ambiguous oscillation between self-government and centralization in order to accelerate the unification process once that had become a concrete possibility. When he returned to power in January 1860, after the Villafranca episode, he began by criticizing the "expeditive method" by which the annexation of Lombardy had been undertaken. In a speech to parliament on May 26, 1860—the day Garibaldi began the siege of Palermo—he promised to create a commission to ensure the specific needs of the regions that chose to unite with Piedmont.

Between his May 26 speech and his letter of December 18—with its centralist and resolutely unitary tone—the prime minister had availed himself of every nuance available on his political palette in order to construct a complex system of alliances between the different parts of the peninsula. He had first soothed the irritated and disappointed Lombards, even as he coaxed the Emilians and the Tuscans while winking in the direction of the Sicilians, who were rebelling over the disrespect shown by the regime in Naples to their historic identity. Later, when Piedmontese laws began to be applied in the annexed states, the commission that had been promised in May quickly drowned in a sea of vague and timid proposals, to the great relief of the many Piedmontese who had supported the *Risorgimento* on the condition that the supremacy of their laws and traditions be explicitly recognized. The progressive decline of the regionalist approach could only benefit the different municipalities, whose autonomy would most likely be greater in relation to a central government than in relation to regional capitals.

The axis around which this oscillating policy revolved was Cavour's perseverance in asserting the need to shift the capital of the new kingdom to Rome. In his conception of a balance of power à l'italienne, Rome perfectly fulfilled the requirement of a capital that was not too strong, not too peripheral, not identifiable with a specific dynasty, and having a nonnational governmental tradition. Rome was a "neutral" city, equidistant from "strong" cities—though strong for different reasons—like Milan and Naples, either of which would have upset the precarious unitary balances had it been given an excessively important role. But it was also distant from Turin, which, by virtue of the spread of its laws, its institutions and its personnel throughout the peninsula, was no longer the modest city—the "lesser evil"—of the preunification period.

It would take another forty years for a "Roman party" to begin to appear, with its policy of conquest and occupation of the state, and for its opposite, an anti-Roman polemic.[7] Those forty years were dominated by a slow transition from "Piedmontization" to the nationalization of the state administrative machine.

Italy Under Piedmontese Guardianship

The state of emergency in the early years of the new state's existence justified, even in the eyes of the Lombard Stefano Jacini, a "temporary dictatorship."[8] For the federalist and southerner Gaetano Salvemini, a centralized administration was an absolute necessity, considering the administrative anarchy of southern Italy.[9]

This centralized regime, however, proved to be far from "temporary." To the contrary, it became an almost distinctive mark of Italian political life. It survived the transformist earthquakes, was raised to the level of a state religion by fascism, and, finally, was surreptitiously preserved by the republican regime despite the great decentralizing principles set out in the Constitution of 1948. Even in June 2006, Italians rejected, in a referendum, a constitutional reform calling for the devolution of greater powers to the regions, a reform sought by the center-right coalition and fiercely resisted by the center-left coalition.

Thus unification took political responsibilities away from the regional capitals, without, however, managing to grant them to a strong central power. It is true that the essential policy lines undertaken by Cavour were, in a certain measure, determined by events themselves. Still, it is impossible to deny that their application gave rise to a sort of heterogenesis of ends. With the sacrifice of democrats as potential political personnel, the thus-impoverished ruling class had to deal, without the necessary practical experience, with problems far exceeding its capacities of adaptation and response. What is more, "Piedmontization" soon transformed into a force of conservation, indeed of self-conservation.

The determination of Cavour and of the moderates to free themselves from all democratic and Garibaldian interference was both an inspiration and a necessity of the strategy of unification. To be sure, the most determined elements of the Italian national avant-garde were found in the camps of the democrats and the republicans. But their actions had led to a litany of failures, whereas Cavour's strategy had been crowned with success. Not only were the democrats, with their subjectivism and unpredictability, incapable of developing a strategy based on the interests of a class aspiring to become a national ruling class, but they constantly risked undercutting that strategy. Gramsci emphasizes that the moderates represented a relatively homogeneous social group, which means that their politics saw relatively modest swings, whereas the democrats, as Gobetti put it, comprised "a people of originals, of unemployed and of civil servants,"[10] and thus had such large swings of position that the moderates could easily exploit them.[11]

The "Piedmontization" of public life extended into the administration of the state from its summit to its periphery, from the formalization of juridical continuity between the Piedmontese and Italian kingdoms to the holding of plebiscites, from the decision to maintain the dynastic continuity of Victor Emmanuel to the choice of prefects; it included the laws of 1859—extended to the entire peninsula in 1865—and the men given ministerial responsibilities in the different postunitary executives.

By Emilio Gianni's calculations, of the fifteen Italian governments in the period 1861 through 1876, the men of Piedmont occupied 28.8 percent of the posts, followed by Tuscany with 11.6 percent, Emilia with 10.3 percent, and finally the south with 11.6 percent. Of the eight presidents of the Council of Ministers, five were Piedmontese (Cavour, Rattazzi, La Marmora, Menabrea, and Lanza) and three were "Piedmontized" (Farini, Minghetti, and Ricasoli). The same trend can be seen in those who held the principal ministries: interior, foreign affairs, and justice.[12]

But if governments change, bureaucracy endures. It is thus extremely significant that the "central core" of the latter was based on the ancient Piedmontese bureaucracy, facilitated by a superior familiarity with legislation largely transferred from the Kingdom of Sardinia to Italy and by the political support it enjoyed.

Despite the supposed desire to keep it "temporary," Piedmont's predominance continued for several decades. Even at the end of the century, one-quarter of senior civil servants were Piedmontese, and among military officers, the figure was a still higher, 36 percent, even though the population of Piedmont was a mere one-tenth of the total Italian population.[13] As for the prefects, in 1861, 30.5 percent had come directly from the former Piedmontese bureaucracy, a percentage that rose to 45.8 percent in the years of administrative unification (1865–66), before sinking again to 27.5 percent in 1871.[14]

Given these conditions, it is not difficult to see why, in the early years of the kingdom, political struggle took on the color of a struggle between regions and, more specifically, of a struggle for or against Piedmontese occupation of the state. It was not until the end of the liberal regime and fascism that Piedmont finally lost its predominant role in Italian public life.[15]

Thus the most delicate period in the formation of the new state was based largely on a single regional experience. The process of integration that ensued was not seen by the affected populations as a process of adhesion to a common national state and common national values. The "Italianization" of the country continued, but very slowly, at a rate inversely proportional to the influence exercised by Piedmont and the Piedmontese.

Chapter 9

The Moderate Social Bloc

The "Brigantaggio"

As with the analogous movement in Germany, Italian unification took place by "iron and by blood," but unlike in Germany, it was mostly the iron and blood of others. The French war against Austria of 1859, the 1866 war between Prussia and Austria, and finally, the Franco-Prussian War of 1870 were truly the founding acts of unified Italy. But one must also mention another war, entirely Italian, which left a deep impact on the unitary experience: the war against the *brigantaggio*.

According to Prime Minister Bettino Ricasoli, this anti-Italian guerrilla movement consisted of "escapees from every prison" and of "soldiers and apostles of European reaction."[1] These two groups were, undeniably, a part of the *brigantaggio*, but in reality its nature was more complex and heterogeneous, which would lead later to highly disparate interpretations.

To begin with, it had a history. Brigandage, both solitary and gang banditry, had for centuries been the only form of peasant revolt. Giuseppe Prezzolini found references in the literature to outlaws who were beloved by the "poor and the deprived" because they had had the courage to break with the established order.[2] In studying the southern peasants of the second half of the nineteenth century, it is important to keep in mind their "two-headed" character: having played a decisive role in weakening the power of the king of the Two Sicilies, these peasants, almost without ceasing, continued their guerrilla war against the new Italian army of occupation.

To be sure, these peasants were transformed into "soldiers of European reaction." Their hatred for "progress" and the influence of the Church were two sides of the same coin. In fact, the juridical abolition of feudal life at the start of the nineteenth century had merely rendered their existence even more pitiable. Following the abolition of grazing rights on state-owned land and their usurpation by the nobles and the bourgeois, the peasants lost the last physical spaces they had been free to exploit. They then fell deep in debt and were left with no choice but to borrow at usurious rates. The members of the new bourgeoisie, for their part, having devoted their capital to the purchase of land and to more profitable investments, brought few technical improvements to agricultural production; they dealt with their competition, feeble as it was, merely by intensifying their exploitation of the peasants' manual labor.[3] All these factors strengthened the image of the

Church in the peasants' eyes, the Church that reminded them of the virtues of a time when feudal lords still had obligations and responsibilities to them.

The spread of capitalist social relationships was at the origin of the break between peasants, on the one side, and property owners on the other, with their retinue of lawyers, shopkeepers, employees, and minor intellectuals. The "alliance" of 1860 between the Jacquerie and the "democratic revolution" could have been merely tactic and temporary. When the police of the Kingdom of the Two Sicilies took flight, Jacquerie no longer knew any restraint and the "democratic revolution" quickly changed its priorities. Denis Mack Smith affirms that Garibaldi rapidly realized that "his only chance" of lasting success lay in the support of property holders, and he quickly launched a policy of widespread repression.[4]

The actions of the intellectuals and military men of Piedmont (as well as the "Piedmontized"[5]) sent to "pacify" the south were dictated, quite simply, by fear, by concern, and by misconceptions. The fear: all those who had put their eggs in the basket of unification were haunted by the specter of 1799—the counterrevolutionary Jacquerie organized at the highest level and with international support. The concern: the imponderable attitude of the democrats vis-à-vis the Jacquerie.[6] The misconceptions: a profound misunderstanding of the southern situation and a conviction that applying philosophical and economic principles that had seemed logical in the north would overcome all the problems. It is now clear that those misconceptions shaped the practical steps taken to confront the fears and the concerns that, in fact, had very real foundations.

Among these misconceptions was the notion that it was poor governance by the Bourbons that had kept the supposedly untapped richness in the south from being developed. This idea, according to Salvatore Lupo, was in turn supported by a typically positivist conviction that would leave a deep and lasting impression on the history of the country: the notion that economic development is "natural", and that imbalances therefore reflect "anomalies that imply inadequacies more than they demand remedies."[7]

But this conviction had a flip side, as Sergio Romano put it: "a sort of racism toward those who appear irremediably corrupt and allergic to liberal therapy."[8] The lieutenant of the King, Luigi Carlo Farini, contrasted the civic virtues of the Bedouins to the "barbarity" of the "*cafoni*," the southern peasants. Even the Garibaldians considered the southern peasants as "Bedouins," speaking an "African-like" language.[9]

The resignation of the very popular Liborio Romano (elected in eight districts) from the Council of Lieutenancy; the purging of the local bureaucracy, where the Garibaldian petit bourgeoisie had begun to install itself; the dissolution of the 100,000-strong Neapolitan army, suddenly reduced to joblessness; the liquidation without severance of the Red Shirt army; the law suppressing most religious orders (which destabilized the liberal clergy): one way or another, all these measures ultimately fed the growth of banditism. Thus, among the "scum" denounced abroad by Ricasoli, one found, along with the "apostles of reaction," the newly jobless created by the new regime, but also some of those who had cooperated in putting the new regime in place or who, at the very least, had been disposed to support it; and, above all, was the mass of angry and exasperated peasants.

Only when the war against the *brigantaggio* ended did the "southern question" officially arise, that is the ascertainment that if Italy was now undeniably a juridical entity, the Italian nation itself was still far from reality.

The "Great Fear" of 1860

The "southern question"—which was the point of contact between two very different stages of development—arose during the rigid administrative centralization of 1859 to 1865. According to one witness with a privileged perspective, Cavour's personal secretary Isacco Artom, the cause of regional autonomy ran aground precisely over "the question of Naples"[10]: the fear of peasant revolts in the south was the real reason for abandoning any plans for decentralization; all other causes were subordinate.

Undeniably, the largest part of the Italian bourgeoisie—of whatever regional origin, economic power, or political leaning—was shaken, and sometimes genuinely terrified, by the upheavals of 1859 to 1861. But what exactly was it that inspired such fear?

"Fear of revolution" was on everyone's mind, but it was a vague fear, not entirely justified by actual circumstances. To be sure, there were memories of 1848 to 1849 and the "specter of communism."[11] But again, these fears must be attributed more to French intellectual and moral influence than to the actual state of social life in Italy, where the industrial proletariat was practically nonexistent. In fact, the democratic revolutionary tempest of the midcentury had provoked two sorts of opposite reactions: while in the other Italian states repression had raged, to varying degrees of severity, in the Piedmontese kingdom the task of reestablishing calm and quieting the democrats' passions was left to the Statute, a sort of constitutional chart.

According to Charles Albert's juridical counselor, Federigo Paolo Sclopis, the charter could open the way to the integration of the "educated middle classes" in the management of public affairs.[12] At the same time, the liberal choice had allowed the Piedmontese kingdom to absorb a large part of the energetic elements—a sort of intellectual avant-garde of the bourgeoisie—whom the other governments of the peninsula had banned.[13] While only a small number of them had lastingly integrated the structures of the Piedmontese state,[14] these exiles exerted significant influence, directly or indirectly, on the Piedmontese culture of the 1850s, as seen in the moderates' developing hegemony and in the concomitant decline in the democrats' influence.

The democrats having been left on the margins of political life after 1848, the question on the origins of the "great fear" remains. It was certainly fanned by the threat of peasant revolts. But the real risk was not one of a "rural revolution"; the social conditions for this were missing, as was a serious political plan of action and leaders capable of imposing it. The real risk was represented by the "specter of 1799,"[15] which, as it developed, took on the contours of an organized and permanent Jacquerie.

The defense of property and of the barely achieved unification seemed worth the sacrifice of some vaguely decentralizing principles. "The aim is clear, and it is not open to discussion," wrote Cavour on December 14, 1860, at the moment of his "Jacobin adaptation": "to impose unity on the most corrupt, the weakest part of Italy. And as to the means, no doubt is permitted: moral force and, if it proves insufficient, physical force."[16]

Beginning in March 1861, an occupation army of 120,000 men proceeded to reconquer southern Italy, using summary methods and violence of every sort that left thousands of victims in its wake. This intervention had been demanded—and carried out, so long as they were still in positions of responsibility—by the democrats themselves.

Moderate Hegemony

By 1849 Cavour had become convinced that a "democratic revolution" in Italy had little chance of succeeding. He had reached this conviction through an analysis of the social bases of the democratic party: lacking support among the masses, he wrote, it could count on support only from the middle and, to an extent, the upper bourgeoisie, "and they have many interests to defend." Had the social order been truly threatened, he said, he was persuaded that even the most extreme republicans would have been in "the front ranks of the conservative party."[17]

Cavour saw rather lucidly what the real situation was regarding a question—that of the "democratic revolution"—that historians would later spend more than a century sorting through. He understood that the radical democrats' social base was still too young, too limited, and too timid to achieve a real unity of interests that could be translated into a substantial plan of action. Facing a murky outlook, these new societal groups increasingly found ways to accommodate themselves to a reality that allowed them to satisfy their immediate interests. This might have been less enticing in terms of grand ideals, but it was certainly more attractive in terms of the conditions of their material existence.

These new groups had begun taking on social weight under the absolute monarchies at the end of the eighteenth century, with the establishment of a professional bureaucracy in which recruitment was based on ability, not birth. The French contamination and the adoption of the civil code—with its repercussions on social relationships—meant that the influence and the role of these bourgeois sectors gradually grew. The Restoration seemed to frustrate their political ambitions, leading some of the most dynamic elements to embrace the cause of the democratic revolution, yet economic evolution continued to strengthen their influence. The subjectivist idealism of the doctrinaire democrats, who failed to understand the correlation between economic facts and political facts, was lost in their vague theoretical constructions. Their futile attempts to force reality to conform to their fantasies gave rise to senseless abortive uprisings that ended up decimating the revolutionary avant-garde.

The ever-starker contradiction between the economic emergence of these new bourgeois groups and the political failure of those who should have been in their front ranks was synthesized by Turin's liberal choices, with its policy of integrating the middle classes in public affairs, and by the strategy of Cavour's "diplomatic revolution." In political terms, this choice translated as the *"connubio"* (marriage) of 1852, the parliamentary alliance between the center under Cavour and the center-left under Rattazzi.

If, as Rosario Romeo attests, the evolution of primitive accumulation is behind the development of new layers of society, and if their development in turn explains the need to integrate them into the management of public affairs, it is indispensable for us to ponder, however briefly, the question of primitive accumulation in the Italy of the eighteenth and nineteenth centuries, while noting that findings on this subject are far from unanimous.

To Romeo, for example, it goes without saying that the sources of capitalist accumulation in Italy were less numerous than in other countries, since trade and colonial exploitation must be excluded. It was, rather, the revolutionary actions of the French occupiers, he continues, that allowed the bourgeoisie to appropriate a good part of the ecclesiastical property and that erased all juridical distinction between feudal property and bourgeois property.[18]

According to Vera Zamagni, the elements of capitalist transformation of the countryside gave the agricultural economy a much larger role than that of a simple producer of foods and raw materials: they encouraged the birth of rural industries, enlarged the markets for services (transport, credit and insurance), favored the rise of entrepreneurial aptitudes, and stimulated the importation of machines and of raw materials. Moreover, the increase in agricultural productivity made possible the forceful eviction of country labor, which could then be put to use in other activities.[19] This latter aspect corresponds, according to Marx, to a fundamental stage in the process of primitive accumulation.[20]

We must also underline the importance of what Franco Bonelli calls "externally induced agricultural accumulation". The increase of revenues in more industrially advanced European countries had provoked a demand for products—raw materials and semifinished products, food products, and to some extent even services—that the Italian economy was in a position to provide.[21]

This expansion of wealth and economic activities thus upset the existence of the traditional social classes—notably by making the nobility more bourgeois[22]—while giving rise to other, more numerous classes. Beyond the big property owners, who were traditional beneficiaries of this "agrarian surplus," there were a growing number of actors occupied in new industrial or semi-industrial activities linked somehow to agricultural accumulation. And there were others who profited indirectly from the new wealth, including those in commercial activities or financial and liberal professions (bookkeepers, notaries, lawyers) linked to the multiplication of properties. Here, in flesh and blood, were the "middle classes" that Sclopis envisaged integrating into the management of public affairs and who would constitute, under Cavour, the real actors of Piedmontese acceleration in the 1850s.

The Structural Bases of Moderate Hegemony

According to Indro Montanelli, another result of the terror of a popular revolt was the creation of a "closed oligarchy."[23] Piedmontese electoral law, extended little-changed to the rest of the country, reflected the criteria that had inspired the concession of the statute, that is, the desire to co-opt the "middle classes." The proof of this is that the democrats had accepted it since 1848 because, as one of their more radical members, Angelo Brofferio, put it, it opened the doors to "industry, to art and to intelligence of every sort."[24] Moreover, the Piedmontese electoral corps could brag of far broader bases than those that existed in France under the July Monarchy, which was considered a "bourgeois monarchy" *par excellence*. And while the electoral law of 1861 foresaw, in keeping with Cavour's desire, a reduction in the number of electoral districts in the turbulent south, these same democrats did not oppose this either. It was only much later that the latter, by then transformed into the *Sinistra*, would have become the almost exclusive representatives of the interests of the new bourgeois classes, particularly in the south. These groups would gradually but surely be involved in the management of "public affairs" from 1876, the date of the massive entry of the southern bourgeoisie into the executive, and 1882, the date of the new electoral law that tripled the number of voters.[25]

The cultural hegemony of the moderates had become firmly established in the 1850s, at the point when the promises implicit in the statute, in the electoral law, and in the "*connubio*" had seemed to translate into a sort of "Get rich!" invitation extended to all levels of the Piedmontese bourgeoisie.

With a population equivalent to only 11.2 percent of that of the peninsula,[26] in 1857 Piedmont and Liguria provided 18.1 percent of total agricultural production (while Lombardy furnished only 15.3 percent); in 1859, 46.4 percent of the entire Italian rail network was on the territory of the two regions of the Savoy kingdom (28.5 percent of it was in the Lombard-Venetian Kingdom). In 1858 they were also leaders in imports (36.9 percent of the total, compared to 21.5 percent for Lombardy-Venice) and exports (30.9 percent to 26.6 percent); also in 1858, 37.9 percent of all employees in the mechanical industry were concentrated in the Turin and Genoa regions, while only 15.1 percent were in the two Italian regions of the Austrian empire.[27]

Beyond the numerous polemics that have muddled this discussion, it seems rather clear that the question of Piedmontese hegemony can be explained by these three fundamental, and fundamentally linked, factors: (1) an exceptional concentration of intellectual energy in Turin and Genoa; (2) Cavour's political acuity, which provided a national strategy in the framework of international constraints; and (3) the capacity for these influences to spread socially as Piedmont rapidly gained tangible economic supremacy over the other Italian regions (which, let us not forget, were in a concomitant phase of economic slowdown).

Piedmontese hegemony, in any case, entered into crisis at the very moment of unification, because the material conditions that had determined it changed abruptly. As the newly unified country engaged increasingly with the world market, Piedmont's economic power, which had seemed so vigorous compared to the other Italian states, suddenly looked pallid in comparison to the other powers. In 1840 the Italian states accounted for 10.8 percent of the total economies of the six leading European powers; this rate declined inexorably for the rest of the century to 10.5 percent in 1850, 10.05 percent in 1860, 8.6 percent in 1870, and 8.3 percent in 1880.[28] And if one makes the comparison to the most dynamic economy of the era, that of the United States, the gap is even clearer and more dramatic. In 1830 the two countries' relative shares of world industrial production were approximately equivalent (2.3 percent for the Italian states and 2.4 percent for the United States), but by 1860 American industrial power was 2.9 times that of Italy, and in 1880, 5.9 times.

Thus the bases of the implicit pact proposed by Cavour to the Piedmontese (or Piedmontized) bourgeoisie had collapsed at the very moment when that pact had achieved its goal.

Part II

The Permanencies

Chapter 10

Transformism

The Co-opting of Emerging Social Strata

The question of transformism, long buried in history books, resurfaced suddenly in the 1990s as a result of the Italian political crisis.[1] Curiously, this reference to transformism occurred at the very moment when the Italian system was experiencing something unheard of: a democratic transition from one coalition to another. From 1861 to 1994, never had one majority been replaced by another following an electoral verdict. This *de facto* "monopartyism" had often been considered the most blatant proof of transformism—as a mechanism through which the party in office could keep power, and as a solution to the impasse created by lack of a dialectic.

Before examining whether the changes on the Italian political horizon in the 1990s affected the nature of transformism, we should first make some semantic clarifications. "Transformism" does not mean transformation; the term transformism does not represent simply a change in the head of state or the migration of politicians from one coalition to another. These are but symptoms of a far more complex phenomenon linked inextricably to the weakness and inadequacies of the Italian ruling class.

Aside from the small group of commentators who, like Benedetto Croce or Rosario Romeo, have relativized the importance of transformism, historians and specialists have generally considered transformism a physiological characteristic of Italian political life and have tried to define its contours.

The American historian Raymond Grew has pointed out that some traits typically considered as transformist are not exclusive to the Italian experience. Their quasi-institutional character, he suggests, is what distinguishes Italy and discourages the formation of national political parties. The absence of national parties in turn prevents specific local problems from being connected to national, more general problems.[2] Thus, according to Grew, the tradition of the *Risorgimento* would have created—in the "new" Italy where interests invariably had multiplied—a system physiologically incapable of representing the general interest.

For Antonio Gramsci, "the whole of political Italian life since 1848 is characterized by transformism." Having considered its temporal dimensions, Gramsci explained the phenomenon as the process of the "the elaboration of an ever-expanding ruling class . . . through gradual but continual absorption of active elements coming as much from opposing groups as from allied groups."[3] This analysis was confirmed in the 1990s by all those who had associated transformism with the weakness of the social base of power and with the problematical necessity of widening it: thus the co-opting of new elites and new interest groups was the only way the Italian ruling class could think of to regenerate itself.[4]

In light of this, many historians have wondered whether the so-called *connubio* (marriage) between Cavour and Rattazzi in 1852 should be thought of as the prototype of transformism. Clearly, if we consider the *connubio* as one stage in the process of the integration of the "middle classes" that began with the granting of the statute, we can only conclude that it was a form of transformist co-optation. This practice resurfaced in 1860, with the absorption of local notables, Neapolitan soldiers, and former Garibaldians into the ruling class. Obviously it would occur again in 1876, when the term "transformism" was coined by Agostino Depretis to justify his "transformation of the parties" into what Raffaele Romanelli would call the "single party of the bourgeoisie."[5]

Transformism, Grew concluded, is therefore a factor of stability and continuity, to the extent that it prevents one government class from being replaced by another "in the revolutionary sense,"[6] exactly as Gramsci had written some thirty years earlier.[7]

Thus, although the term "revolution" has been used too often—from the "parliamentary revolution" of Depretis in March 1876 to the "revolution of the *mani pulite*" in 1992, by way of the "Fascist revolution" of 1922—in no case did one class substitute for another in the "revolutionary sense"; rather, changes took place within the ruling class. The arduousness of these changes was proportional to the resistance of the old group in power, reluctant to accept the integration of new social strata. The contrary is also true, as the *connubio* and other examples demonstrate. Rosario Romeo reminds us that Cavour had taken to heart the words of Chateaubriand, who said that "in the major revolutions, the talent that collides head on with the revolution is crushed; only the talent that follows it can master it."[8] Transformism has been the only method used throughout Italian history to try to "master" the political, economic, and social contradictions of the country.

The Impossible Conservative Party

In March 1886 a representative of the liberal *Destra*, Silvio Spaventa, established a causal link between the "disorganization of the parties" and the "disorganization of the social classes" represented by those parties just before the rise to power of the *Sinistra*.[9] At that time—March 1876—Agostino Depretis had presented his new government to the Chamber of Deputies, with a speech rich in democratic sentiment: beyond the rhetorical demagoguery borrowed from Mazzini, this speech concealed, according to Sergio Romano, "the interests of the new social strata, eager to consolidate their wealth." According to Romano, who cites the memoirs of Fernando Martini, a close collaborator of Depretis, the latter was aware of the necessity of opening up to these social strata, but feared that this operation could endanger the structures of the young state. Thus, in its origins, the transformist process was not really an ambitious project for renewing the country, but an attempt to consolidate gains "through enlarging the social base of the nation and the legitimacy of power." Seen from this angle, transformism was responding, in Romano's eyes, to "a physiological necessity of the political country."[10]

Other historians have emphasized the purely defensive character of the operation: a convergence of the liberal right and left toward the center in order to isolate and reduce the intrinsically subversive extreme wings. The seditious elements that the transformist operation was designed to curb were on the one side the Catholic Church and on the other the far left—republican and socialist. The country having been unified without (and against) them, they were not only strangers to the system, naturally enough, but also its declared enemies.

In fact, the far left of the 1870s and the 1880s represented an even lesser threat than the democrats in the time of Cavour. It was the remnants of the preceding democratic tradition, stripped of their bourgeois social base, that had merged into the *Sinistra*. Now, wrote Gramsci, this left wing represented nothing more than the "miserable, impoverished, illiterate" part of the country and could express itself only through "sporadic, disjointed, hysterical forms, a series of anarchist, subversive gestures, with neither consistency nor a concrete political direction."[11] Moreover, Gramsci added in another note, even the most superficial of analyses showed that in the 1870s the economic and social conditions hardly existed to create a socialist party that could genuinely threaten the liberal state.[12]

Only the Catholic Church was a serious danger in the eyes of the liberal ruling class; subjectively, because of the personal convictions of the men of the *Sinistra* (a number of them having anticlerical political backgrounds), and objectively, because of the violently hostile attitude of Pius IX and part of the ecclesiastical hierarchy toward the new state.

Several elements suggest that this supposed danger was, in fact, less than had been claimed. First, after unification, and especially after 1870, the "Pius IX generation" had bet heavily on what could be called "a strategy of refusal," implying a nostalgic, if fading, hope for a reestablishment of the pope's temporal power.[13] In other words, Catholic energies were largely concentrated upon the goal of reconstituting the pontifical states, not conquering Italy. It was only after the defeat of Napoleon III's France that the idea of a role in Italian affairs began, timidly, to emerge. Nonetheless, this idea long remained embryonic, largely because of the opposition from those who complained of the plundering inflicted by the Italian state.

Another reason a Catholic uprising was unlikely: in Italy, the Church lacked a homogeneous social base. Without this, it could not create a synthesis of interests and establish an alternative strategy to the power in place. At the moment of unification, the Church represented—the landowning clergy aside—a part of the *Ancien Régime* nobility, the small and negligible mass of the Roman *Lumpenproletariat* whose revenue was assured by public charity, and above all, the great majority of the peasantry. The church's influence upon the latter merely kept them away from the parliamentary political system.

The only attempt to create an English-style two-party system came from a group of property owners—"the national conservatives," to use Stefano Jacini's definition[14]—who proposed to Catholics the idea of forming a large conservative party with an essentially peasant base. A more relevant example came from Spain, where the clergy, allied to the landed classes, helped mediate between the peasants and the ruling class, and did this so well that universal suffrage, introduced in 1899, could be used in a conservative direction. It was, however, from Italian particularity that the project failed: in fact, it occupied the same social ground as the "single party of the bourgeoisie," whose interests and objectives it shared. The only significant difference with the former—the idea of integrating the peasant masses into political life through universal suffrage—became meaningless the minute the Church withdrew all support, direct or indirect, for the conservative project.

The main reason the Church did not respond to the conservatives' solicitations was that it wanted to preserve its autonomy of judgment and action in order to assimilate its defeat—stinging, but temporary—and prepare its revenge. According to Edoardo Soderini, Leo XIII was less interested in a conservative party than in one like the German *Zentrum*, which was more unmistakably Catholic and capable of acting upon the political scene without necessarily linking itself to a right-wing, even an extreme right-wing, position.[15] The weakness of the conservative platform, moreover, led the Catholic hierarchy to fear a double reduction of its autonomy: first at the hands of the conservatives themselves, and then at the hands of the traditional liberal groups that seemed likely to absorb the conservative party. The Pope's consideration of possible parliamentary action by the Catholics[16] showed that he was guided not by a "fundamental opposition to a liberal state," as Croce[17] affirmed, but by the fear that a Catholic party, emerging prematurely, could be swallowed up in the political morass and lose its specific identity. The Pope thus preferred to play the card of temporal power, giving him much more leverage to negotiate with the Italian state, than to risk eventual dilution in the existing system.

The traditional strength of a bimillennial organization like the Catholic Church comes from its capacity to build very long-term strategies. Thus, to secure the resources indispensable to its survival, and indeed its revival, the Church ended up constructing its social base from the network of credit institutes created in Rome and in northern Italy beginning in the 1880s. Only after forming this base could the Church transform its traditional influence over the rural masses into a real plan of action and into direct competition with the socialists for the loyalty of the nascent working class. From that moment, the Church could count on its own forces, without outside help, and thus begin the slow march toward the Concordat and the Christian Democrat Party.

The Constant Characteristics of Transformism

In texts dealing with the Italian crisis of the 1990s, different definitions of transformism sometimes refer to the same object, and the same definition can suggest different objects. Nearly all specialists agree, however, on the description of the phenomenon, while disagreeing on names and dates.

According to Roberto Cartocci, for example, the transformist practice was dominant between 1945 and 1992, meaning until the moment when the first Giuliano

Amato government had partly interrupted the "perverse relationship" between the government, the parties, and the parliament. Amato himself, as Treasury minister in the Craxi government, referred to government activity thus: "Everyone bargains with everyone, all procedural activity is a bargain, and at each bargain either we come to a halt or something goes missing."[18] For Gianfranco Pasquino, equally, the "centrality of Parliament" signified only a central place for transactions between the government, the opposition, and "a good number of powerful interest groups."[19] Sergio Romano adopted the same timeframe as Gramsci: Italy, he wrote, was governed from 1848 by large transformist coalitions that preserved power by expanding as much to the right as to the left, through a constant traffic of favors that was as systematic as it was lacking in strategic vision.

Interestingly, the British historian Seton-Watson described the Depretis era in much the same way. The post-1876 parliament, he wrote, "became the marketplace for the distribution of functions; the government was considered a dairy cow, from which it was possible to milk a job, a title, a new railway line, or a new import tax, in exchange for votes to support the majority."[20]

Other similarities between the two periods are too numerous and striking to be simply the result of chance. Among them, the lack of a true opposition, and thus of any possibility of take over between opposing forces, is probably the most telling. But there are other "coincidences" worth underlining: for example, the frequency of governmental crises even amid an incontestable stability of power, only paradoxical in appearance.[21] One could also cite the constant growth of southern representation in governments, and a curious resemblance between the personal characteristics of some of the protagonists of the two eras: sometimes discreet, prudent, disinterested, yet at the same time clever mediators in the most complex, even shameless, bargaining; models, we could say, of private virtue and public vice.

Structurally the two periods are characterized foremost by a huge increase in public spending and by growing state intervention in the economy. Under the *Sinistra*, Vera Zamagni has calculated, the incidence of public spending on gross domestic product (GDP) had increased by up to 20 percent by the end of the 1880s.[22] Similarly, during the republican period, it did nothing but increase, reaching 57.8 percent of GDP in 1993 (with the public debt–GDP index reaching 119 percent that year). At the same time, the growing participation, direct or indirect, of the state in economic affairs had contributed to creating what Cassese called a "capitalism without capital that is not public, and with very few capitalists."[23]

Regarding Italy in the first few decades after unification, one must not overlook the thousands of jobs created in both central and local bureaucracies. These new recruits had a political interest in the survival of the apparatus that was providing them a living. Similar hypertrophic enlargement of the public administration was seen between 1970 and 1990, when the number of civil servants (all levels included) went from 1,779,004 in 1971 to 2,325,304 in 1992 (an increase of 23.5 percent), the year when a rapid decrease began to be seen.[24] In both cases, it was the sudden need to deal with the exigencies of the global market that provoked the transformist rupture.

The Transformist Rupture

We have spoken up to now of "physiological transformism," which takes place through that almost daily practice of parliamentary and governmental bargaining, and with the progressive enlargement of the bases of power. There is, however, another kind of transformism that is more traumatic, characterized by the collapse of political regimes, and that is regularly accompanied by a "transformism of the masses."

The structural fragmentation of the ruling class does not constitute a critical problem so long as the political parties and the governmental coalitions manage to represent most interest groups through transformist mechanisms. However, this same fragmentation can prove lethal once the implicit pact linking the ruling class to its clients dissolves. In fact, if the negotiation between disparate interests is the mechanism that resolves, technically and temporarily, the problem of forming a majority, this same mechanism feeds a permanent state of conflict, which explodes every time the negotiation grinds to a halt.

We return finally to the structural problems of the various economic sectors: the difficulty of finding a common interest and a corresponding political agenda. If this proves impossible, each sector is obliged to bypass the obstacles by trying to create a short-term synthesis, for example, through an exchange of favors.

The fact that each economic group tries to influence the successive political syntheses by promoting its own interests is part of the rulebook in all industrialized countries; it is not in itself a crisis factor. It becomes such, Arrigo Cervetto wrote in 1969, once a particular interest has sufficient strength to provoke a rupture in the balance, but not yet enough to create a new balance.[25] This was Italy's situation at the end of the expansion of the "economic miracle"; experiencing a crisis marked by the imbalance between those groups oriented toward the global market and those sectors assisted by internal protectionism. A similar crisis was precipitated some twenty years later by the upheaval provoked by the global free-trade cycle and by the great disorder in the global geopolitical framework.

The corruption that was "unmasked" by the "*mani pulite*" inquiry starting in 1992 was merely the tangible manifestation of transformist negotiations of the 1970s and 1980s. But this corruption concerned not only the many entrepreneurs and politicians who were greasing the skids for their enterprises with bribes; it had become a mass phenomenon as well. The clientelist strategy had become indispensable for getting a job or a pension, even to gain admission to a hospital. But there were other forms of mass corruption. Taxes were relatively low[26] and tax evasion was largely tolerated; interest on public debt was conspicuously high; welfare was practically free. This system was affordable in the boom years, but when it became clear that considerable cuts had to be made, the debate degenerated into a fight of everyone versus everyone, each social group trying to leave to another the honor of saving the national economy.

We arrive at the heart of the problem: as Sergio Romano explained, a regime collapses when the majority of its adherents and its clients abandon it because it is no longer capable of satisfying their demands.[27] This was the case of the subjects of Francis II of the Two Sicilies, of Leopold II of Tuscany, and of the pope, subjects who voted the annexation of Italy with a plebiscite; the case of the millions of Italians who voted for the Fascists in April 1924 having almost all voted anti-Fascist three years earlier; of the millions of members of the Christian Democrats (DC) and the Italian Communist Party (PCI) in 1946 who, three years earlier, had held Fascist party membership; and finally, it explained the mass abandonment of the Christian Democrats and the Socialist Party between 1992 and 1994. The Piedmontese in 1859, the Fascists in 1922, the anti-Fascists in 1943, Berlusconi in 1994,[28] all profited from the collapse of the old regime, but they did not provoke it.

If we follow the timeframe suggested by Sergio Romano, we see political cycles of around twenty years each: the rupture of 1859 to 1861, the transformism of 1876 to 1881, the crisis of the end of the century and Giolittism; the post–World War I period and fascism; World War II and the republic; the "crisis of imbalance" at the end of the 1960s; and the crisis of 1992 to 1994.

Internal Italian quarrels, influenced for a quarter century by a dispute over institutional reform, can lead to the conclusion that the crises were provoked by the lack of or inadequacy of shared rules. In fact, with the exception of the Fascist period, these rules have always formally existed and, in the case of the republican phase, they were shared even by the political forces that, whether government or opposition, had together drawn up the constitution. So the determining cause must be sought elsewhere, and precisely in the degree to which Italy was exposed to international, political, and economic influences.

Regarding 1859, a series of factors linked to European politics—principally that of Napoleon III devising a plan to undermine the balance of power decided in Vienna—shook Italian politics to the point where every old state but one had collapsed. From the late 1870s to the early 1880s, the crisis of the global free-trade cycle and its direct implications on international politics obliged the political class that had run the preceding phase to withdraw gradually from affairs. The turn-of-century crisis had been brutally linked to the encounter with global competition and its political manifestations (especially the colonial wars). The two world wars had a devastating impact on the whole of Italian society, with no traces of the preexisting systems remaining. The "crisis of imbalance" was the product of accelerated industrial development by the integration of Italy into the ascendant phase of the world economic cycle (particularly through integration in the European Economic Community). And the crisis of the 1990s was provoked by the collapse of the Soviet Union, German unification, and above all, the rapid acceleration of development in Asia and its influence on globalization.

But the reasons these international influences touched off a transformist rupture were the primary weakness of the unitary state, the fragility of its institutions, and its chronic lack of legitimacy. Again, we can point out the fundamental problems of the Italian bourgeoisie: its late emergence, its fragmentation, and consequently, its difficulty in finding a balance of power within the state. These inherent weaknesses always made it particularly susceptible to major movements in international economics and politics.

Vera Zamagni reminds us that Italy was a country "of numerous towns and numerous agricultures," and indeed numerous ideologies, thus the profound significance of transformism consists, according to her, in its constant search for "operational convergences allowing the country to be governed in the presence of such plurality of ideologies and interest"[29]: *quod erat demonstrandum*.

Chapter 11

Internationalization Crises and Transformism

The Crisis of Internationalization of 1866

The second half of the 1860s was marked by the early signs of the crisis that would end with the arrival in power of the *Sinistra*. In this phase, social groups previously excluded from power began to wield sufficient weight to disrupt the previous balance, but not enough to allow them to forge a new one.

Between 1861 and 1880, Italian industrial production as a share of total gross domestic product (GDP) shrank from 20.3 percent to 17.3 percent, despite an annual mean growth in industrial production of 1.4 percent to 2.2 percent (depending on the source).[1] The sector was thus undergoing a profound restructuring. This included the disappearance of thousands of small and very small enterprises, halfway between artisanship and home-based production, often closely linked to agricultural activities, and the progressive, but extremely slow birth of a more modern industrial sector, with higher levels of production.

The year 1866 marked a turning point. It was a particularly painful year for Italy, politically, economically, and militarily: with an army of 400,000 men—more than all the forces of the British Empire, according to Denis Mack Smith[2]—and a fleet twice as large as Austria's, Italy was defeated in two major battles, on land near Custoza, and in the Adriatic see, near the island of Lissa.

But the humiliation suffered at the hands of the Austrians was only the most glaring of the misfortunes that struck the kingdom barely five years after its birth. These misfortunes were due largely to its dependence on foreign countries, and in particular France;[3] that is, they reflected the coincidence of an economic crisis and an international political crisis, the effects of which were multiplied in Italy by the coefficient of its economic and political weakness. The country was struck, in a manner of speaking, by the first big "internationalization crisis."

That the crisis of the mid-1860s was rooted in the world market is beyond doubt. It also appears to be a classic example of a crisis provoked by overinvestment during a favorable period (1862–1863), which manifested itself first through a depletion of the money supply in circulation, then by an unprecedented rise in the key rates of the Bank of England (which reached 10 percent in May 1866), and finally, by a recession that spread first through the British Isles and then the continent. But it was also the first manifestation of "globalization," in the sense that Europe was struck with the effects of a political crisis that had exploded in another part of the planet, namely, the United States. During the American Civil War, in fact, a considerable flow of American capital left the country in search of safer investments and poured across the old continent, helping saturate the markets. Later, at the end of the war, not only was part of this capital repatriated, but the resumption of American production led to a drop in the price of cotton, a key area of Italian industrial activity.

Italy was doubly affected: first, because of its economic dependence on other countries; and second, and less directly, because of its political subordination. Thus in 1859 (and later during all the great turning points in international relations), to pursue its own foreign policy objectives, it had to try to insinuate itself into disputes between other powers. Since the armistice of Villafranca, the return of Venice had become, along with the annexation of Rome, one of the two overarching objectives of Italian foreign policy; the tensions between Vienna and Berlin after 1864 were thus considered an occasion not to be missed.

But the major "external constraint" was represented by Napoleon III, who oversaw the peninsula as a sort of "semiprotectorate."[4] Candeloro suggests that the excessive prudence with which the Italians took part in the war—a major reason for the debacles of Lissa and Custoza—was also the consequence of a note slipped by Napoleon III to Costantino Nigra, the ambassador in Paris, recommending that the Italians not fight "with too much vigor."[5]

But the chief cause of the defeat lay elsewhere: not only Italy's military manpower, but also its larger ambitions were greater than what the country's economic potential could afford. The effects of the international crisis were multiplied by internal Italian weaknesses. The run on the banks provoked by credit restrictions was inflamed in Italy by the plunging value of public debt securities as French investors dumped them in mass. This, along with some exceptional financial decisions, soon led to a veritable stampede as war approached.

From that moment on, the country had no choice but to rely on its own resources. On May 1, 1866, the forced circulation of the virtually irredeemable lira put an end to convertibility between the Italian currency and gold. Two other measures were taken at the same time: the imposition of a loan from the Banca Nazionale to the state of 250 million lira at an interest rate of 1.5 percent, and the legal circulation of bills from four preunitary banks, guaranteed by the Banca Nazionale itself.

For finance minister Quintino Sella, the reestablishment of the state's financial authority, by balancing the budget to create conditions favorable to private investors and to expanded industrial activity, quickly became a question of survival for the country. At the same time, economic groups of the center-north began to talk of seeing the state play a larger role in defending industrial interests. The erosion of the old ruling class's bases of power had begun.

Splendor and Decline of Free-Trade Policy

In November 1869 an alliance of mixed interests brought about the fall of the Menabrea government, but without giving rise to an alternative majority.

The most important economic sectors demanding a new political balance within the Italian state were industry, credit, and the southern bourgeoisie. This is a rather schematic breakdown; there does not, of course, exist a single interest of the financial bourgeoisie or, even more obviously, a single interest of the southern bourgeoisie. But what brought these three disparate groups together was their desire to emerge—that is, to transform their economic weight and influence into political weight and influence.

The crisis brought on first a decomposition and then a recomposition of the two traditional political families along the lines of regional fractures and interests: the ultraliberal Tuscan *Destra* found common interests with the southern *Sinistra* more easily than with the northern *Destra*, which, for its part, often joined forces with certain sectors of the radical Milanese *Sinistra* and, in particular, with the "statist" dirigiste and "social" factions of the southern *Destra*.

In its earliest years, the Kingdom of Italy had adopted a policy that was "naturally" pro–free trade, which enjoyed wide support if one considers that the 1863 free-trade convention with France was ratified by a vote of 257 to 49. In the same period, Italy also concluded commercial treaties with the Ottoman Empire (1861), Sweden (1862), Great Britain (1863), Belgium, Denmark, The Netherlands, Russia (1864), Austria and the German Zollverein (1865), Switzerland, Uruguay, Japan, China, Tunisia (1868), and Spain.

The capital needed to develop the "natural industries," and thus to form a vast national market, could be found only through close connections to the world market, as Cavour asserted in his last parliamentary address. In the prime minister's view, a free-trade policy would make it possible for agriculture to accumulate the capital necessary for future industrial development.[6] It is noteworthy that Cavour, on this occasion, was responding to a speech by Quintino Sella, who was to become the finance minister of the *Destra* in 1864, and who was delivering his first address before the Chamber of Deputies to support the possibility of accumulation and development based above all on the "combination of factors available internally within the country."[7] And the necessary precondition for productive internal competition, according to Sella, had to be protection from foreign competition.

Two years later, during the parliamentary debate on the convention with France, a deputy from Turin denounced the parliamentary commission for having failed to consider the fact that thirty of the thirty-one chambers of commerce opposed it, as did the 23,000 heads of enterprise who had signed petitions in opposition to the treaty. During the same debate, the Lombard cotton industrialist Ercole Lualdi listed numerous grievances against England and France, which he accused of preaching free-trade policy only after having conquered every market through the protections they had enjoyed for centuries; he proposed the formation of a commission of inquiry on industry. Giovanni Ricci, a Genoese deputy, demanded that France be stripped of the right to practice *petit cabotage*. Two Garibaldian deputies, Antonio Polsinelli and Antonio Mordini, put forth for the first time the thesis that the country's independence depended on the creation of a state-protected military industry. The Milanese democrat Giuseppe Ferrari accused the majority of lacking confidence in the nation's industry.[8]

The debate and its outcome demonstrate that the industrial group's interests and positions were, at the beginning of the 1860s, largely in a minority within a class that enjoyed near-direct representation in the parliament,[9] but it also shows that ideological weapons were starting to be polished up for use from the late 1870s to the early 1880s in a final attack on the free-traders' last remaining redoubts.

These years had been characterized not only by the beginning of a theoretical dispute, but, above all, by the ascension, the flowering, and the decline of the free-trade cause. By the time the final battle between free-traders and protectionists was engaged in Italy, the other world powers—the United States, Germany, France, Austria, Russia, and, to an extent, even England—had already raised their import taxes or were preparing to do so. Once again, the Italian dynamic and its internal struggles left it trailing in the footsteps of the world market.

A Difficult, Slow-Motion Changing of the Guard

Quintino Sella was one of the rare political leaders of the era who attempted to offer all the disparate interests the outline of a common strategic perspective.

Sella's strategy, as we have seen, was to create favorable conditions for investment and for industrial expansion. His origins, his studies, and his accumulated political experience combined to inspire in him, as in Cavour before him, the conviction that industrial development was the necessary path to lead the country into the modern world. Thus, when he took up his battle to balance the budget—a fundamental precondition necessary to free up capital for productive investment—he found himself in conflict with the financial aristocracy who had drained out most of this money at a time when state securities were more profitable than investments. It was impossible to establish this equilibrium, as Marx wrote in regards to the July Monarchy, "without encroaching on interests which were so many props of the ruling system—and without redistributing taxes."[10]

But Sella felt that redistributing taxes was his "mission," the most important measure in his strategy for balancing the budget.[11] The increase in fiscal charges was accompanied by borrowings from the Banca Nazionale, cuts in the budgets of the military ministries, the transfer to the provinces of the expenses of secondary instruction, the reduction of the royal appanage, and the sale of some Church assets and some state properties (including the rail networks).

The financial aristocracy resisted Sella's policies for another reason, and while this stemmed from something as immaterial as social psychology, it was no less real a force: the conviction that, as the banks held the capital needed by the industrialists, the latter were subordinate to the former. It was a subjective impression, but it strengthened the objective resistance.

Sella, however, was far from being naturally hostile to the capitalist banks. A capitalist himself, he was aware of the irreplaceable role of financial intermediation and he had been, as minister of finance, the protagonist of numerous treaties, including that of November 1864, when the sale of certain of the kingdom's assets was confided to a syndicate formed by the Credito Mobiliare of Turin, the Banco di Sconto e Sete, also of Turin, and the Cassa di Sconto of Genoa. Sella persisted with Cavour's old attempt to discipline the way credit was organized by uniting all the issuing banks into a single bank, then a common practice in the more advanced countries. But like Cavour, his predecessor at the Ministry of Finance, he met stern resistance from numerous local groups, until in the end his attempt failed.[12]

After the fall of Menabrea, a new majority struggled to emerge. Lanza having renounced any interest in forming a government, General Cialdini[13] tried in vain to do so with the leaders of various parliamentary groups. In the end, Lanza was again called on and succeeded in forming a government in which Quintino Sella was the finance minister, and this despite the rivalries between the two politicians and with the Piedmontese *Destra* (although both men were from Piedmont and part of the *Destra*). Despite the fundamental hostility of the Tuscan *Destra*, the government obtained the confidence of parliament, thanks to the favorable vote of Marco Minghetti, who was linked by personal and political connections to Florentine circles, and whose support was supposed to condition, to a degree, the actions of the government. But from the moment the government took office (in December 1869), the deep-seated hostility was transformed into a veritable guerrilla war of attrition. The series of financial measures presented by Sella were examined by no fewer than four parliamentary committees, and the debate, begun in the spring of 1870, produced a positive vote of parliament only on August 11, 1870, barely a month before the annexation of Rome.

The length of the discussions reflected deep divisions within the ruling class, and Mazzini thought the moment was right to launch a series of attempted raids, which led, as usual, to the dispersion of fragile republican groups and the arrest or death of some of their leaders. Nonetheless, the press of the *Destra*, especially that part under Tuscan influence, used this as a pretext to attack the government, accusing it of excessive weakness.

The attempts to overturn Lanza took place not only in the heat of the discussion over his financial intervention plan, but also in the midst of the Franco-Prussian War, at a point in time when much was being asked of the young structures of a state born under international protection. We should add that at the beginning of the war, two of Victor Emmanuel's former counselors, Antonio Gualterio and Luigi Federico Menabrea, had attacked the government with the aim of replacing Lanza with someone closer to the king,[14] and that the king himself had sent General Cialdini on August 3 to attack the system of parliamentary government in order to regain the diplomatic initiative and carry Italy into war alongside France against Prussia.[15]

As we can see, the concept of a "national union" was still far—very far—from seeing the light of day within a ruling class where the numbers of those preferring chaos to the risk of sacrificing even a part of their private interests were still legion.

Chapter 12

Emerging Sectors and Transformism

Finance

If one were to sketch an outline of the history of banks in Italy, one could say that Italian financial institutions, over the course of a century and a half, were numerous, fragile, and protected, and once the state stopped protecting them, directly or indirectly, they became prey to sturdier foreign institutions better versed in the rules of competition. Recent years have seen a rather timid reversal of that trend, but it is too early to draw firm conclusions.

In Italy, banks managed to fashion around themselves an original juridical framework, that of the "universal bank," halfway between the Anglo-Saxon model of total integration with enterprises and the German model of complete separation. The state first intervened directly in the activities of the credit sector in the great rescues of 1888 through 1893 and 1931 through 1936, and later by taking control, after World War II, of 70 percent to 80 percent of all bank activities.[1]

Whatever the case, and whether under a regime in which public property was dominant or one almost exclusively favoring private property, the major banking institutions rarely missed a chance, in the decisive battles, to influence state policy in the direction most favorable to their interests. This battle of influence took different forms: at times it was subtle and indirect, through the banks' presence within industrial groups or financial or insurance companies; at other times through political relations, involving pressure that was more or less legal; and at yet other times through what one might call "confidential" diplomacy, something at which Enrico Cuccia, the most celebrated banker of the second half of the twentieth century, was a master.[2]

According to Gianni Toniolo, the decision to move toward the forced currency for the lira in 1866 was the first important rescue operation undertaken in Italy by the "lender of last resort."[3] It is an interesting point of view, not only because it predates by some three decades the year in which the central bank—in substance if not in form—was established, but also because it corroborates the theses of those for whom the existence of Italy corresponds to the existence, in the country, of an economic system dominated by state capitalism.

When the Banca d'Italia was officially established, in 1893, it began to fulfill the institutional task of "monetary power," supervising the general monetary interests of the country, in keeping with the regular tenets of capitalist development. In this context, the central bank does not play the role of one credit institution among many, defending its particular interests while others do the same; it acts rather as a traffic cop for different private interests, and not only for banking interests but also for all economic sectors as it works to safeguard the "general interest."[4]

This specific role is imposed by facts, not by desire. In 1870, four years after the decision on the forced currency, issuing banks held 66.9 percent of all paper currency in circulation. Ten years later, these same banks held only 36.5 percent.[5] In absolute numbers, the total sum of circulating currency in the hands of the issuing banks had declined by an almost imperceptible amount (going from 621 million lira in 1870 to 557 million lira ten years later); this means that the total mass had grown in the meantime (from 929 million to 1.527 billion), but more importantly, that a slew of new financial actors were now competing for it. In fact, from 1870 to 1874 there was a veritable boom of banking institutions. The number of ordinary credit institutions rose from 36 to 121 and the number of "banche popolari" (industrial cooperative banks) rose from 48 to 109.[6]

The general framework of the Italian economy was beginning to mature. Integration between finance and industry became so evident that the activities of ordinary credit banks began to grow and contract in close conjunction with the cycles of industrial production.

According to an Italian political tradition, the responsibility for these changes was found not in the dynamic of the Italian economy within the world market, but in the subjective choices of governments. Thus, in 1873, Lanza was forced to resign by a new coalition of interests that felt threatened; Minghetti was finally able to take his place, with the goal of reducing the power of the Banca Nazionale by creating a cartel of minor banks, notably southern ones. Around them emerged much of the growing opposition of the *Sinistra*.

The Minghetti government thus constituted a sort of intermediate step toward new balance. But these new equilibria had a difficult time establishing themselves, confronted with the greatest upheaval the Italian social structure had faced in centuries: industrialization.

Industry

To the causes of Italian economic backwardness at the moment of unification, one must add what Alexander Gerschenkron calls "the absence of vigorous ideological encouragement for industrialization." The supporting testimony is near unanimous: for Guido Baglioni, author of a reference text on the subject, "there is no ideological horizon to match the role of the productive bourgeoisie." For Vera Zamagni, the problem lies in the absence of a single ideology of industrialization able to impose itself over all others.[7]

The responsibility for this lack of an "industrialist culture" must be sought, as we have seen, within the bourgeoisie itself. According to historian Guido De

Ruggiero, the bourgeoisie "was a class of uncultured bureaucrats and businesspeople, skeptical about the importance of ideas and programs." More recently, Paolo Farneti generalized that opinion by saying that the bourgeoisie "lacked a broad vision of its class interests in the wider framework of those of the nation."[8]

This situation hardly arose by chance: if the "industrialist" position seemed uninspired it was because it reflected industry's own shortcomings. Even an original opinion like Cavour's—that stimulating the growth of the agricultural surplus would provide a base from which industry could take off—was interpreted by "agriculturalists" as an endorsement of their conservatism, while "industrialists" viewed it as a cunning sabotage of their views on the importance of the development of manufacturing activities.

From the moment of unification, the industrial fractions tended to intervene with state powers more to obtain aid and protection than to influence strategic choices or contribute to the establishment of a common policy aimed at promoting and defending the general interest of their entire class. In this sense, one can say that Italy lacked a national strategy from the beginning. The lag in development, Italian cultural tradition, and the modalities of unification helped create this psychological substratum. By interpreting the events that determined the birth of the unitary kingdom as manifestations of an auspicious "destiny," the Italian bourgeoisie persuaded itself that its own direct involvement in the edification of this destiny was tangential, indeed, superfluous.

Benedetto Croce has given us, as regards successive agricultural cultures in the Puglia region, an exemplary description of the way Italian entrepreneurs attempted to adapt gradually to diverse circumstances rather than seeking to formulate their own development strategy.[9] One finds this same passive adjustment, on the national level, during the economic crisis of 1866, during the Vienna-Berlin conflict of the same year, during the French defeat of 1870, during the rapid rise of steam-powered shipping, during the stock market crisis of 1873, and during the turn toward protectionism in the following decade.

One reason for the breakdown between different societal groups after 1866 lay in a miscalculation—or, one might say, in a lost bet—in Cavour's strategic vision. Beginning in 1846, the future prime minister linked Italy's "magnificent economic perspective" to the organization of commercial traffic along a north-south axis, so as to make of the peninsula "the shortest and most convenient path from the Orient to the Occident."[10] When excavation of the isthmus of Suez began in 1854, Cavour's theories seemed confirmed, for southern Italian ports, linked by railway to northern Italy and to Europe, were considered a natural endpoint for a large part of the traffic that the Suez Canal would be funneling into the Mediterranean.

Things turned out quite differently, and almost all the development projects that were built up around this axis found themselves rather suddenly in dire trouble.[11] There were several reasons for this failure, the most important of which were structural, that is, linked to the weak Italian economic structure: the elevated costs of rail construction, which led to higher freight charges that caused shippers to abandon the Brindisi line in favor of maritime transport; the aging of the Italian commercial fleet that, though it ranked third in Europe in tonnage terms, was almost entirely wind powered, and sail ships were poorly suited for navigating the Red Sea.[12] But there were other factors, one internal—the Brindisi port was too shallow for the high-seas vessels traveling to the Red Sea and back—and one external—the high tolls charged by the canal discouraged a considerable amount of traffic. And finally there was a factor tied to the growth of the world market, which reduced the gap in prices of products and raw materials from different parts of the globe, putting an end to the day when a merchant could derive a profit from the large price differentials between distant markets.

Thus, rather than serving to promote Italy's progress and development, as any good free-marketer might have expected, the newly built Suez Canal merely served to aggravate its backwardness. The Rubattino shipping company, which in December 1869 had purchased a concession in the Bay of Assab in Eritrea as a forward post for Italian commercial penetration in the Red Sea, had to resell it to the government thirteen years later. The shipyards that popped up like mushrooms after rain when the canal opened had to rapidly scale back their ambitions or, in many instances, file for bankruptcy.[13] The involvement of the Italian fleet in international trade, rather than growing, was drastically reduced, and even the share of internal commercial navigation handled by Italian vessels fell from 52.6 percent of the total in 1881 to 31.4 percent in 1891, despite the establishment, in the meantime, of significant protectionist tariffs.[14] Finally, the considerable decline in the price of maritime shipping contributed to a sharp drop in the price of some imported foodstuffs, in particular wheat and rice, thus accelerating the crisis in the country's agricultural sector.

The example of the Suez Canal clearly demonstrates the damage that can result from an incapacity to provide a strategic perspective for Italian capitalist development, leaving it reliant on the "ephemeral favors of fortune."

The Southern Bourgeoisie

In 1873 the world experienced the first great depression of contemporary economic history. It was provoked by the creation, in Germany after the victory of 1870, of joint-stock companies and banks specialized in investments that favored the development of a "bubble" in rail and real-estate values, to the point of triggering the classic mechanism of rising costs and prices and falling markets.

Opinions are divided on the direct influence this crisis had on the Italian situation. For some, the economic weakness of the peninsula helped preserve the country, while for others the impact on the lira was strong, causing its value to plunge[15]; for Cafagna, it had at least the merit of putting an end to the "plaster" economy born in a time of market effervescence.[16]

The impact of this crisis—coming just years after the first major shock of 1866—affected the whole of the Italian ruling class, and in particular, sectors that had scarcely participated in the major political choices, or who considered themselves damaged by the political choices they had made up to that point. With an abstention rate of 55.4 percent of voters (and as much as 70 percent in the large northern cities), the elections of 1870 sent 170 new deputies to the chamber,[17] most of them representing not traditional parties, but local interest groups—an extremely significant signal of the malaise that the crisis of 1873 was to catalyze. The new sectors of the economy, still fragile because of their youth, were naturally more exposed to the effects of the latest crisis and reacted by accentuating their political pressure.

When discussing interest groups keen to play a more consequential role in managing the country's affairs, we must not forget a part of the ruling class, much older and more substantial than those mentioned above, which had been almost totally excluded from national power practically since unification: the southern bourgeoisie. The necessity of integrating it into the management of public life was felt ever more acutely, starting in the late 1860s and especially in the early 1870s, as demonstrated by the attention Minghetti paid to its expectations.

But Minghetti merely added to the frustrated ambitions and dashed expectations of the dominant southern classes, constrained as he was to pursue the rigorous budget-balancing policies inaugurated by the preceding governments. Thus the dominant southern classes definitively cast their lot with the *Sinistra*.

Loyalty to the *Sinistra* was built around the question—crucial to landowners—of the equalization of property taxes. The provisional calculation of property tax assessments, established shortly after unification, favored southern landowners. Faced with a likely reform of this calculation, that group held that differences in property-based revenues owing to different conditions of viability, trade, and culture should have been taken into account. Two separate regimes should have been institutionalized—one for the south and another for the rest of the country—which was the negation of a national unitary policy and which was to be the fundamental characteristic of Italian "dualism."

The results of the 1874 elections—which saw voter participation jump by 10 percentage points from the previous electoral exercise—anticipated this "dualism," giving a territorial character to the political divide between the *Destra* and the *Sinistra*. The *Sinistra* won 100,350 votes, 63.4 percent of them in the south and the islands, and the *Destra* won 116,129 votes, of which 76.5 percent were in the north and the center.[18]

From 1874 to 1876, the political struggle was feverish. Matters descended to the paradoxical level—even more absurd if one thinks of the results of the institutional referendum of seventy years later—of dangling the specter of separation between a republican south and a monarchist north. What is certain is that from 1874 to 1876, the *Sinistra* ended up representing—partly through profound conviction, partly through opportunist calculation—a deeply mixed coalition representing every faction that wanted to confirm the break with what remained of the previous equilibrium. These disparate interests came together around two classically liberal demands: to reduce the tax burden and to defend the free movement of the "invisible hand" against any state interference.

As for taxes, the country felt that the spartan policies imposed by the *Destra* had seen their day. Indeed, it is no coincidence that after the elections of 1874, the Chamber of Deputies rejected any proposed tax increase, although the *Destra* held a majority. And when Silvio Spaventa, minister of public works, suggested putting an end to the hypocrisy of "private" rail companies supported by extensive public aid and proposed nationalizing the sector outright, the "enraged Smithians" (as they were called) of the Tuscan *Destra* and the *Sinistra* found common cause: The day after the announcement that the budget had been balanced, the Minghetti government was disavowed by the chamber and had to resign. As Denis Mack Smith writes, the *Destra* had "completed their task of tightfisted and unspectacular administration. New times called for new men."[19]

Chapter 13

The Southern Question

Dualism and Unequal Development

Literature devoted to the "southern question" began appearing between the elections of 1874 and 1876. The first to specialize in this new discipline were men of the *Destra* who were struggling to understand the reasons for their crushing electoral defeat of 1874 in southern Italy. Thus the Tuscan Leopoldo Franchetti[1] traveled to Sicily to meet the historian Pasquale Villari, author of *Lettere meridionali* [Southern Letters]. Discussions between the two men led to the conclusion that the new laws and the new institutions that unification had brought to the south had worsened conditions in the *Mezzogiorno*, not improved them. In two later texts, Franchetti pointed the finger at the "economic and class relationships that prevented the civil development"[2] of these regions.

The *Sinistra* angrily rejected Franchetti's conclusions, seeing them as an attack on existing property relationships, launched with electoral objectives in mind. The debate on the "southern question," with the themes and position-taking that would accompany it for more than a century, was thus opened.

The theme that cropped up most often in the debate was what Luciano Cafagna described as the *"impostazione rivendicativa risarcitoria"* [demand for damages and compensation]: The *Mezzogiorno*, by this logic, had a right to demand damages, with interest, from the Italian political class for losses provoked by unification.[3] The basis for this view was easily found in the conclusion that Villari and Fortunato had reached during their meeting in 1875: in observing that conditions in the *Mezzogiorno* had worsened after unification, they were describing an incontestable reality; yet by placing all responsibility for this on the new laws and institutions, they were asserting a causal link that was arbitrary to say the least.

For those who have carefully analyzed this question in recent decades, unification simply placed the two parts of the country into a direct relationship within a uniform institutional framework, submitting them to the same policies; yet this attempt to make two such different regions uniform merely focused the gap separating them. Most historians now conclude that, in the first postunitary decades, neither part of the country developed to the detriment of the other. Between north and south, they asserted, there was substantial "economic indifference," in the wider context of an absence of interchange between the different "economic Italies."[4]

In fact, the widening of the north-south gap was due to unification only insofar as unification accelerated the integration of the *Mezzogiorno* into the world market. Postunitary free-trade policies put Italy in contact with the more advanced parts of Europe, favoring agricultural exports from the south as well as the north and sparking an industrial restructuring in all parts of the country. This process would eventually have produced comparable results in the *Mezzogiorno* even without unification.

If unification widened the gap, it did not create it. Even a superficial study of the history of the peninsula demonstrates that this "dualism"—and more generally, all the disproportions between the "economic Italies"—has roots extending long before unification. Pasquale Villani calculated that in the continental *Mezzogiorno* of the late eighteenth century, two-thirds of the population was dependent on ninety families. This level of concentration made it extremely difficult to effect genuine "democratization" of agricultural property by dividing it into small lots.[5] A closed rural economy dominated in the south; an internal market and export flows that were very limited and thus had no need for evolved financial or commercial institutions, nor of an effective transport system. At the moment of unification, the rail network consisted of a mere ninety-nine kilometers of track in the entire kingdom, and the credit system was essentially based on a few private institutes and on two public banks in Naples and Sicily, each of them with a subsidiary in Bari and another one in Catania.[6] As for manufacturing, beyond state-owned industry and a few foreign investments, it was essentially limited to rural and family-based activities, closer to self-consumption than to a market.

Agriculture in the south, of course, faces serious geographical and climatic handicaps, from the mountainous terrain to the limited availability of hydrological resources, from the torrid temperatures six months a year to the narrow, clay-filled plains subject to catastrophic seasonal flooding. But we should avoid the temptation to explain the region's lag in agricultural production by a sort of "geographic determinism," when the shallowest of historic reviews offers a more nuanced picture. We know that in the time of the grandeur of Rome, Sicily was the "granary of the Empire," while during the same period, Lombardy was a desolate and unproductive land. According to David Abulafia, even at the end of the Middle Ages the agricultural production of the southern regions was greater than that of the north.[7] We must conclude that responsibility for the radical changes in the relationship between the two parts of Italy lies in the actions of man and not of nature.[8]

The cumulative effects of the actions of man and the actions of nature form the substratum of later development. This is why the territory of a modern national state is never homogeneous and, when the different parts come in contact, it merely accentuates their respective inequalities and future "dualisms." The case of Italian north-south "dualism" is no exception.

The Universal Character of Unequal Development

Vera Zamagni writes that in most great countries, "including the United States," important dualisms have long existed.[9] Piero Bevilacqua, for his part, notes that at the end of the 1990s, the ratio between the gross domestic product (GDP) of the richest region and the poorest was the same in Italy and in France (2.4) and nearly the same in Germany (2.3).[10]

But these "dualisms" and "inequalities" affect not only territories separated by great distances—geographically or structurally; they can be found even in the interior of regions considered economically and socially more "homogeneous." To take the case of Piedmont, the imbalances between the mountainous zones and the plains or hilly country, as well as the inequalities between the different provinces, are found in every social indicator, sometimes by a ratio of two to one. From 1824 to 1861, the urbanization process in the cities of Novara and Vercelli grew 64 percent, while in Cuneo and Asti, the rate was lower than that of Aosta. In the province of Turin, according to data from 1883, the average life expectancy of a mountain dweller was only thirty-eight years, while in the plain it was forty-five to fifty years. The rates of illiteracy among those called to military service was 24 percent for young men from Cuneo province, 22 percent for those from Alessandria province, 18 percent for those from Novara, and 12 percent for those from Turin. In the same period, the rate of industrial employees among all workers was 2.6 percent in the province of Alessandria, 2.9 percent in the province of Cuneo, 6.2 percent in the province of Turin, and 7.6 percent in the province of Novara.[11]

As for the phenomenon of rural exodus toward urban centers, it first affected the north, and massively so; only in the late nineteenth century did emigration from the south start to take on considerable dimensions. And yet, contrary to widespread belief, since unification the countryside of the north has been depopulated at rates and in numbers far larger than those of the south.[12]

Once we have brought the supposed Italian specificity—and within it the supposed southern specificity—into a more realistic context within the "universal" framework of the laws of development, we must nonetheless reconsider the particular situation of Italian "dualism," and its exponents. That is, we must reexamine the way in which the south's historic backwardness, its uneven development, and the miserable conditions faced by the enormous majority of the population were used by the southern bourgeoisie for political purposes.

Having been inaugurated by intellectuals of the *Destra*, the "southernist" theses, as they were to be called, grew more elaborate, but also more diverse, until they were left with only two points in common: the insistence on southern specificity, and the fact of being exploited by all those for whom the *Mezzogiorno* represents the main flaw of Italian development. On every other question—questions of substance, since they were supposed to concern proposed solutions—the various approaches were miles apart, even totally opposed. From the "social" wing of the *Destra*, "southernism" evolved into one frankly reactionary faction, under Pasquale Turiello, and another into a syndicalist faction, under Arturo Labriola. At the same time, "southernists" included men like Pasquale Villari, Sydney Sonnino,

Napoleone Colajanni, and Francesco Saverio Nitti, all of them partisans to varying degrees of state intervention in economic matters. Alongside them there were intransigent free-traders like Antonio De Viti de Marco and Gaetano Salvemini, federalists like Salvemini and Colajanni, rigorous centralists like Fortunato, imperialists like Leopoldo Franchetti, and also pacifists. According to Salvatore Lupo, the absence of a unique "southernist" discourse can be explained quite simply by the absence of unique southern interests.[13]

All these confused or even antithetical tendencies gave rise to two contradictory movements: on the one hand, the persistent demand for political action to reduce the gap, and on the other, an inability to formulate concrete proposals on how best to do so. It was a contradiction, however, that could be synthesized by the "demand for damages and compensation," as Cafagna calls it. Starting with the protectionist laws enacted progressively from 1878 to 1887 and, more particularly, with the "special legislation," no measure of public intervention was considered sufficient to definitively resolve the problems, which meant more "special legislation" was required, and so on. Thus the gap between north and south, as Gianfranco Viesti wrote, became the pretext employed by a large part of the ruling class to obtain the greatest quantity possible of public allocations.[14]

This attitude highlighted a conception of the function of the state that is the historic product of several heritages: by constantly demanding favors, the southern elites seemed to propose to the liberal state what Paolo Macry calls a "courtisan paradigm."[15] This relationship with the state revealed another of the south's historic handicaps, and not the least important.

The Ruling Southern Class

At the moment of unification, and for fifteen years afterward, the *Destra* governments had excluded even the possibility that the southern ruling classes should play a direct role in managing the affairs of the new state; they were considered too querulous and too preoccupied with managing public matters as if they were private affairs. The "Piedmontized" southern intellectuals were the most determined about this. They refused, on the one hand, to separate the interests of the *Mezzogiorno* from that of the entire nation, while on the other hand, based on their experience in their home regions, they imagined the transformation of Italy into an "ethical state" that could make up for the traditional lack of a civic sense.

According to Aldo Schiavone, in the social psychology of the inhabitants of the peninsula, the notions of state and ethics are most often in contradiction. This mistrust of established power, he asserts, was born from foreign domination, followed by the failure of "the relationship between bourgeois development and the construction of the state" in the fifteenth and sixteenth centuries. As they grew accustomed to this domination from the outside, the Italians began to associate public power with the invader, and force to pillage, thus establishing a direct relationship between the state and the stifling of their own identity.[16] This sentiment, common to the entire peninsula, was displayed most flagrantly in the south due to the almost uninterrupted subjection of these regions to foreign powers, and to the absence of any possibility of a "relationship between bourgeois development and the construction of the state."

The most "Italian" of the southern kings was a German, Frederick II of Hohenstaufen, the founder in the thirteenth century of the Sicilian school of poetry, the first in a "vulgar" language. At the other extreme of the southern Italians' historical experience—chronologically, as well—was Ferdinand IV, son of the Spanish King Charles III, king of the Two Sicilies at the moment of the 1799 revolution, semiliterate, speaking little but the Neapolitan dialect, "*lazzarone*" among "*lazzaroni*" (the *lazzaroni*, or street people of Naples, were fiercely monarchist). The long thread uniting these two seemingly utterly different monarchs is the fact that they were foreigners in their own kingdoms: the former, a Swabian speaking the vulgar tongue and an unknown number of other languages, was as foreign to his people as was the latter, a Neapolitan-speaking Spaniard who, though at home in the Spanish quarters of Naples,[17] was a foreigner in Palermo, in Puglia, and in other parts of the kingdom.

The other factor linking the two is that Frederick II helped, we could say, to lay the bases of power for Ferdinand IV. In effect, the kingdom of the south—born out of the struggle against the communes—lacked the necessary conditions to establish this "relationship between bourgeois development and the construction of the state" which had been attempted, precisely through the communes experience, by other regions of the center and the north.[18] Protected by past history and present domination, the feudal lords of the south were not threatened, either in power or in privileges, by an emerging bourgeoisie. That would have given rise, according to an interesting thesis by Paolo Sylos Labini, to what he defines as a "*lazzarone* absolutism": the king, struggling against the barons, and unable to rely on the bourgeoisie, sought support from the plebes in the cities, to whom he granted all sorts of favors, and from the peasants as well. Thus, continues Sylos Labini, the phenomenon of the "*lazzaroni* kings," from which emerged the popular royalist sentiment, present above all among the lowest layers of the population, and that persisted until very recent times.[19]

Giving rise to "*lazzarone* absolutism" in the south of Italy was the presence of a weak and disjointed civil society in which the central power of the state was organically incapable of exercising its fundamental function in an era of absolutism: that of replacing the "spirit of the bell tower" with centralized control. Instead, the persistence of that spirit contributed, in the *Mezzogiorno*, to the establishment of jealously preserved fiscal privileges, which faithfully reflected these local particularisms.

The southern bourgeoisie, Sylos Labini continues, lagged behind the social groups of feudal origin, both economically and politically, at least until unification. And when they replaced them, as property owners, they were inspired by these two models: the feudal barons, as concerns the economy and society, and "*lazzarone* absolutism," as concerns politics.[20] Yet, given their extreme weakness, they were unable from these models to construct a superior synthesis.

It is thus not surprising that those men of the south who truly understood the social nature of their country—and who, while waiting for the "ethical state" to emerge, concerned themselves with the problems of the actual state—should have judged the new Italian government's moralizing ambitions as not only extravagant, but dangerously out of place. "Do you know," Pasquale Villari wrote Governor Farini on December 9, 1860, "that in Naples, destroying corruption amounts to destroying the country?"[21]

It is also unsurprising that, in these conditions, the Piedmontese would prove reluctant to involve the southern ruling classes in the management of the state; all the more so because Cavour belonged to a generation (and a class) unaccustomed to resolving social problems by creating jobs, of greater or lesser utility, within an administration, and equally unaccustomed, as Cavour himself said, to a "system that consists of reconciling men's differences at the expense of the State treasury."[22]

For fifteen years, the men of the *Destra* lived under the illusion that the practices of transformism and clientelism were the result of free choices, and consequently they rejected them. They could not yet know—and their political culture inhibited such awareness—that these practices constituted what Cafagna considered a "regular and constant tendency" of a democratic state, which would expand as the bases of electoral consensus expanded.[23]

The men of the *Sinistra*, for their part, displayed a more pragmatic approach, progressively adapting to the new situation. Those deputies elected in 1876, accused by their opponents of representing corruption and intrigue, may have lacked the prestige of their predecessors, but they had sufficient moral stature to embody the transformist process—a process, Carocci wrote, "of which the growth of democracy was the cause and the degeneration of democracy was the effect."[24]

The Sublimation of Transformism

The social enlargement of the bases of power having gone hand in hand with geographic enlargement, one can say that the leaders of the *Sinistra* constituted the first truly national governments. At the same time, however, their transformist practices led them to renounce any notion of a "nationalization of the masses," that is, to renounce any structural effort to stifle particularisms in order to seek a theoretical national interest in which Italians might recognize themselves.

The *Sinistra* had been carried to power by a coalition of interests intent, in part, on weakening, if not abolishing, the rigorous restrictions imposed on public spending by the *Destra*. After several years, enlarging the bases of consensus through public spending became the mechanism of ordinary functioning of the state. This mechanism essentially worked in two directions: it extended the electoral base, as per the law of 1882, while expanding the bureaucratic apparatus.

With the law of 1882, the habit of regularly electing a town's notable, particularly in the south, leapt to a new level. The end of the organic relationship between elected and elector led these notables increasingly to entrust the representation of their interests to new political professionals, markedly this "small crowd of Southern lawyers" that Romano describes.[25] The function of the latter was to haggle with each minister, offering their votes in exchange for certain local interests being taken into account.

As for the enlargement of the bureaucracy, the period of 1883 to 1891 brought 13,000 new civil servants, a growth rate of 20.3 percent in eight years.[26] It was now more closely aligned to geographic criteria, unlike the earlier "Piedmontization" of public structures in the first years of the kingdom. This increasing "southernization" mainly affected the lower layers of bureaucracy, while executive functions remained primarily in Piedmontese hands for some time to come. This phenomenon—which gave structure to the "Turin-Naples axis" on which, according to Galli della Loggia, the Italian state project would be built—is one effect of the capacity for negotiation the *Mezzogiorno* acquired after its rise to power (the others being linked to the "policy of compensation" put in place by the special legislation). As Jean Meynaud writes, the "Southernization of public life" was a trend responding to the pressure of a petit bourgeoisie lacking in local perspective or the means to ensure its existence.[27]

The renunciation of the nationalization of the masses resulted directly from what Lanaro calls "transformism as the extreme sublimation of the clientelist relationship."[28] It was a renunciation in terms of national moral cohesion, for transformism implies the loss of all legitimation not founded on negotiation, and a "legitimation" subject to constant challenge can hardly provide a stable marker of identity. And it was a renunciation in terms of the material cohesion of the nation because, as a result of this "sublimation," the center ceded in the face of local pressures and began progressively to adapt different rules for the *Mezzogiorno*.[29]

The special legislation and the enlargement of the bureaucratic apparatus (and later, the military expeditions into Africa) were financed by those regions of Italy that could do so, which is to say, mainly those in the north.[30] This transfer of funds is justified as an imperative of national solidarity that is apparently absolute but that in the real world takes place only to the extent that it corresponds roughly to the interests and social psychology of those controlling the purse strings. The strength and importance of the hesitations and the resistance are always directly proportional to the opacity of the "national contract." When the most important groups and sectors of the dominant class have difficulty seeing the benefits they might gain from representing a supposed "general interest," they tend to tighten their grip on the national purse and to contest the right of those ostensibly representing them to speak in their name. They exploit every means at their disposal to challenge the defined balance.

Thus, in transformist Italy, the versatility of political relationships was the rule. Each time a proposal, an idea, or a demand surfaced somewhere in the country, there was an effort to isolate it from the others and to give a particular, specific response. The "historic bloc" between the industrialists of the north and the big property owners of the south that, according to Gramsci, prevailed throughout the phase that began with the adoption of customs tariffs in 1887 should only be considered as a specific and episodic tactical alliance that brought together, around protectionist demands, powerful interests with little else in common.

Shortly after the arrival in power of Francesco Crispi, it was Milan that set the tone for the campaigns against the government headed by the man whom the Socialist Filippo Turati referred to as the "cynical Sicilian bumpkin." The "true bourgeoisie," Turati declared, had nothing in common with the "brazen banditry and crookedness of the bumpkins and thugs who made Crispi their hired gun."[31]

The opposition of the "State of Milan" marked the collapse of the last attempt by the ruling class of the *Risorgimento* to endow the Italian bourgeoisie with a "positive" political identity, capable of measuring up to the Catholic and Socialist identities. Born from the failure of efforts to base national legitimation on transformist mediation, this attempt foundered on the same reef: the social bases of any plan for a "sacred union" between the classes were still too weak and the habit of pitting different interests against each other in the search for state support drained all meaning from any striving for national concord.

Crispi resorted to the old Garibaldian expedient of attempting to bypass the obstacles of reality through subjective voluntarism, but this transformed him into a sorcerer's apprentice of social movements—riots, insurrections, and military adventures—with catastrophic consequences for the new Italy. In the ensuing crisis, Giovanni Giolitti recognized that the social and political actors no longer had anything in common with those of forty or even twenty years earlier. His attempt to create a new "unique party of the bourgeoisie" marked the final effort to seek a national Italian identity, and it led to two political and military catastrophes: the Libyan War and the Great War.

Part III
Identity and Sovereignty

Chapter 14

A Counter-Reformist Identity

The Disappearance of Italy

In a 1999 essay, the then archbishop of Bologna, Giacomo Biffi, wrote that the gravest error of the Piedmontese ruling class in the 1860s was to underestimate "how deeply rooted Catholic faith is in the Italian soul, and its near consubstantiality with national identity."[1]

The voice of Cardinal Biffi was but one of many to be raised from within the Catholic hierarchy during the 1990s to explain that the fundamental reasons for the identity crisis then shaking Italy lay in the separation between the development of the state and the national spiritual tradition. The bishops were sounding a polemical theme that the Church had previously taken up during the celebrations of the fiftieth anniversary of Italian unification. On that occasion, the Holy See's daily newspaper had observed that the masses were indifferent, even hostile, to the state because liberalism had failed to represent "the true interests of Italy and the Italians."[2] In 1929, immediately after the signing of the Concordat, the Jesuits' review blamed the "Piedmontese government" for the failure of the "national league" proposed by Pius IX in 1848: the pope and the cardinals, far from opposing unification, simply wanted "to achieve it differently."[3] Sixty years later, a revisionist Catholic school of historiography again took up and emphasized these polemical themes, which had been put aside in the name of a Christian Democratic republic: The real trustees of the national identity, according to this school, were not Garibaldi and Victor Emmanuel, but Cardinal Ruffo and Pius IX.[4]

The Church's investment in Italy bore fruit: today, in the peninsula, the voice of the Vatican is not only heard and respected, but it has become the axis around which many great decisions of the country revolve, whatever the coalition in power. This investment, however, does not date from the 1990s, it dates from the moment when the popes renounced any intention to reestablish their temporal power on the right bank of the Tiber in order to devote themselves to the conquest of both banks, that is, of all Italy. It is a long-term strategy, which began with the transformation of the Church from a feudal to a financial power, continued with the creation of the first national Catholic organizations, refined itself with the substantial support of the Italian clergy for the military effort of the Great War, and culminated with the birth of the People's Party in 1919. The

Concordat of 1929, viewed by many as an endpoint, should really be seen as the formalization of a strategy, as an indispensable intermediary step, and as a sort of treaty (signed, if not always respected) with a regime that had its own pretensions of forging a national identity based on its particular concept of Italianness. Afterward came the long period of Christian Democratic domination, the "clerical republic," in the words of the most important (Catholic) historian of Church-state relations in Italy, Arturo Carlo Jemolo.[5] But it was only with the disappearance of Christian Democracy—that is, from the moment when the Church succeeded, with difficulty, in ending its relationship with *one* of the parties—that the Church was able to claim for the first time since unification that it represented the overall population and could assert a "quasi-consubstantiality" between the Catholic and Italian identities.

For Gramsci, Italian Catholicism was a sort of "substitute for a spirit of nationality"[6] after the sixteenth century, that is, from the moment when the Church of Rome asserted itself as the major obstacle to any political unification of the peninsula. Biffi, for his part, places the roots of "consubstantiality" in the fourth century, at the moment when the transition (itself partly a continuity) began from the institutional structures of the declining Roman Empire to the emerging Catholic Church. At that time, the peninsula was subjected to multiple influences, mixing and interacting with the common Latin—and later Catholic—base, giving rise to sometimes very different variations in identity. Disputed by Byzantines, Lombards, Francs, and Arabs, the peninsula would yield up the principles of a common identity only hundreds of years later.

Not until the time of Dante and Petrarch did the name of Italy gain political resonance. According to the two Tuscan poets, torn between Empire and Church, "enslaved Italy"[7] could only have been reconciled by the conjunction of these two powers. Petrarch began to develop the idea of an Italian "lag" compared to other nearby entities, an idea that Machiavelli would carry to its conclusion by suggesting that "certainly a country can never be united and happy, except when it obeys wholly one government"—as had been the case, in very recent history, of "France and Spain."[8]

During the ten centuries from the fall of the Roman Empire to the time of Dante and Petrarch, two major characteristics emerged that would transform the Catholic Church into the pivot of Italian political and social life while fostering a break with the Roman experience: the formation of a state in central Italy and the decline of urban civilization. The pontiffs' state, indispensable in preserving Church autonomy, prevented all direct contact between the north and the south of the peninsula for more than one thousand years. And the reversal of the city-country dynamic saw the clergy taking root in rural areas, where it eventually represented the only social mediating force between the peasants and the rest of the world.

When the cause of an Italian national state appeared compromised in the late fifteenth and early sixteenth centuries, the clearest and most forward-looking thinkers placed the prime—sometimes sole—responsibility on the Catholic Church. The most important of them was, of course, Machiavelli, who expressed this conviction in the clearest and most irrevocable language. To him, "the court of Rome has destroyed all piety and religion in Italy."[9] To this moral grievance he added another that we would now describe as geopolitical: the Church was sufficiently strong to constitute its own state, but not enough to unify the peninsula, often requiring the aid of foreign powers to protect its temporal power.[10] It is interesting to note that even those who, like Guicciardini, did not necessarily view the division of the peninsula as a problem, they nevertheless shared Machiavelli's thesis on the divisive role played by the Church.[11]

But the debate on the failure to unify the peninsula faded as the real possibility of overcoming its division receded. The more distant its prospects became, the larger did Church influence loom over the entire Italian population. Certain historians have observed that the Counter-Reformation shaped Italian anthropological identity as few phenomena have done. The fear of punishment, the habit of acquiescing without necessarily approving, and thus the necessary recourse to duplicity and dissimulation had a depressing moral effect on the Italian mind, not unconnected to the weak public morality of the peninsula's inhabitants.[12] Another important heritage that the Counter-Reformation bequeathed to Italy's later destiny was the progressive but ineluctable decline of intellectuals as a social group, who, though limited in size, were still potentially able to exert and claim a "national" ruling function.

The Disappearance of the Italian Intellectual

The intellectuals' decline should not be seen as a regrettable bit of "collateral damage" from the Counter-Reformation; rather, it was central to the Church's sixteenth-century rebirth from the ashes of the Italian Renaissance. At the moment when the collapse provoked by the Reformation suggested an irreversible decline of the Catholic institutional structure, religious life was surprisingly "ardent and intense."[13] It was a popular religiosity, impregnated with superstition and the residual influence of ancient polytheistic cults. Facing such vitality, Machiavelli and some others hoped to channel it toward mundane political ends; others wanted to purge it of its superstitious elements and restore its original purity; still others wanted to use it to lessen the difficulties facing the Church. It was the latter approach that prevailed.

According to Giordano Bruno Guerri, it was Cardinal Roberto Bellarmino, protagonist of the trials against Bruno, Campanella, and Galileo, who was the first to acknowledge the loss of northern Europe; he advocated a strategic retreat to make it easier to safeguard those border countries that had remained Catholic, starting obviously with Italy.[14] Toward this end, all available weapons were deployed, and not just repressive action. The most important and lasting result was to appropriate the form and contents of popular religiosity by disciplining them and opposing them to the schisms and wars that result whenever one attempts to eradicate a people's most deeply rooted beliefs.[15]

According to the sociologist Enzo Pace, writing about Italians' religious practices in the 1990s, "primary religious socialization" has resisted secularization, still affecting more than 90 percent of the population. Pace used that phrase to define the "sort of comfort" that religion and its structures provide during certain fundamental life experiences, whether suffering, death, marriage, or birth.[16] There is a singular coincidence between the characteristics Pace attributes to "primary religious socialization" and what certain Renaissance intellectuals denounced as the ultimate essence of superstition. In 1539 the Tuscan jurist Enrico Boccella described as superstitious all those who turn to God only in a moment of fear or when faced by a material problem that they do not know how to solve. True religion, Boccella added, should concede nothing to external rites or to the "egoisms of individual appetites."[17]

The Counter-Reformation condemned such positions, which it said were dictated by "haughty intellectuals," and it rose to the defense of the *sancta simplicitas* of the people. During the seventeenth century, Italy witnessed a proliferation of religious cults, miracles, and revelations, and a multiplying of new saints, prodigious images, and religious relics. In this way the Church renewed its traditional ties to the people while marking the limits of its agreement with Reformation theses. For a time, a series of "scholars" were put on trial, even as a systematic campaign was undertaken first against the press—as a technological invention—and then against publishing and books. Pope Paul IV created in 1557 a congregation to monitor the application of the *Index librorum prohibitorum*. When the Inquisitors put a stop to the attempted resistance of Venice, where, by then, two-thirds of Italian books were being printed, they had ten thousand to twelve thousand volumes burned, though the government first obliged them to purchase the tomes to avoid a revolt by bookstore owners and printers.[18]

And yet, the cultural policy of the Counter-Reformation did not consist solely of repressive measures. The trials and the book burnings cannot, by themselves, explain its successes. For Gramsci, the explanation lay in the fact that in Italy, religion did not represent "an element of cohesion between the people and the intellectuals."[19] But there is another reason, again identified by Gramsci: culture had developed in Italy in the Middle Ages in the cities from which the struggle between the bourgeoisie and the feudal nobility began; the premature interruption of this process weakened the bourgeoisie and thereby deprived the royal powers (whatever their form) of the possibility of pitting this class against the nobility to keep both in check. This brings us back to the fundamental problem breaking the straight, ascending line of Italian bourgeois development: the absence of the material conditions indispensable to the formation of absolute states.

In this framework, the pitting of "the simple folk" against the "scholars" is reminiscent of Sylos Labini's thesis regarding "*lazzarone* absolutism" in the Kingdom of Naples. But there was a sizable difference: in the latter case, it was not simply a question of the problematic power of the monarch in Rome (the Pope) over the subjects of his kingdom (the Papal States), but of the power of all ecclesiastical structures over all subjects on the entire peninsula. The "favors of every nature" that the Church was able to dispense to the plebes and peasants were incomparable to what other states could offer. Even if one disregards properly religious questions—and they are hardly negligible—the decisive difference lies in the clergy's capacity to tend to the most elementary needs of society's lower levels, a capacity that for centuries made the Church the only Italian institution that was genuinely popular.

In material terms, this capacity contrasted markedly with the impotence of states in terms of primary services. In Italy, all the structures of what we now would call the "welfare state," such as hospitals, hospices, and aid to the poor, remained the monopoly of ecclesiastical institutions until the end of the nineteenth century. Especially in the countryside, the priest was long a public scribe, a teacher, an intermediary with bureaucracy, and—not negligibly—the holder of everyone's secrets.

The Church thus played a decisive role in what Gramsci calls the "denationalization of intellectuals"[20]: taking their place in "cohesion" with the people; forcing those who would not submit to emigrate; and preparing its personnel for a Catholic universe reaching far beyond the peninsula. Thus, Guerri expounded, the Italy that had dominated science and culture until the sixteenth century essentially became a country of intellectual export. The bases for the creation of an ideology and of a national ruling class were thus definitively destroyed.

The Appearance of the Catholic Party

As mentioned, Counter-Reformist spirit left a deep impression on Italian culture and social habits. The distrust of the written word, for example, channeled a large part of the still-existing creative energies toward visual arts, architecture, and music, which helped make Italians, even today, as famous for their esthetic sense as for their weak penchant for reading.[21]

The actions of the Congregation of the Index pushed men of letters to abandon sensitive subjects and to take refuge in an exaggerated attention to formal problems. Celebrated Italian universities declined rapidly into decadence, leaving to the Jesuits a monopoly on the education of the upper classes. As for the political world, general theoretical explorations of the organization of the modern state were henceforth displaced far from Italy. Geopolitically the peninsula was under near-complete Spanish domination, with the exception of three states that were but partially Italian: Venice, Savoy, and the Papal States. The fight against "scholars" and the loss of resources from wealthy northern Europe led to an impoverishment—qualitative as well—of the court of Rome, and its loss of international prestige. At the moment of the Treaty of Westphalia, for example, Rome's protests against the document's religious clauses left European chancelleries unmoved.

Thus it is not surprising, in this situation of evident decadence, that certain Italian intellectuals accentuated their cosmopolitan character. Gramsci notes that, among men of science and culture, those who represented the more advanced techniques and capacities generally quit the country.[22] Men of letters, having long dealt in light or inoffensive subjects, slowly rediscovered a taste for themes of more general interest. But in doing so, and lacking social reference points, they constructed their polemical edifices on moralist foundations, comporting themselves as the ultimate judges of their contemporaries' virtue and as the sole "official" representatives of the general interest.

What is noteworthy about the generation of great men of letters reaching from the Counter-Reformation to Romanticism is that almost none of them—from

Ludovico Muratori to Pietro Giannone, to Baretti, Vico, Goldoni, Parini, Alfieri, Cuoco, Foscolo, and Leopardi—dealt with the Church or the Catholic religion, and when they did do so, it was to castigate the Church and the religion for their bad influence on Italian behavior.[23] On the contrary, during the Romantic period, the most prestigious group of leading Italian intellectuals who posed the problem of national redemption was formed of Catholics who resolutely proclaimed their religious convictions: from Silvio Pellico to Massimo d'Azeglio, from Cesare Balbo to Carlo Troya, from Niccolò Tommaseo to Vincenzo Gioberti, and from Alessandro Manzoni, naturally, to Antonio Rosmini.

This religious awakening resulted from several converging factors. For Piero Gobetti, the struggle of the *Risorgimento* against the Church was purely political. It did not touch on "dogmatic" issues, for the quest for liberation from the Popes' territorial domination had absorbed all the Italians' energies, preventing them from following the example of other developed countries and devoting themselves to religious Reformation. In this religious renaissance the traditional subordination to French culture also doubtless played a role, as did, surely, the disenchanted realism of much of the postrevolutionary generation.

One principal effect of the upheaval produced by the French Revolution was the secularization of politics, which had deprived the Church of its organic relationship with the power of the state. Candeloro emphasized that if, during the Restoration, there was constant talk of an "alliance between the throne and the altar," it was precisely because this organic relationship had been ruptured and replaced by a simple, temporary agreement between the ecclesiastical structure and a certain type of government against a common enemy.[24] Unable to do so directly, the Church was forced to find new forms of representation for its interests, thus giving rise to a veritable Catholic movement, or to "a party opposed to other parties," in Gramsci's words.[25]

The ruling Italian classes had suffered only a pale echo of the "Great Fear" in France; the peasant masses, for their part, had been either the passive element of the revolution or the active element of the counterrevolution. But there remained what Croce called an "impression of fear," which led to a certain dread of the misdeeds of the "fraternité" and distaste for the promises of "égalité," leaving only "liberté" as an object of bourgeois interest. And the only power in Italy able to combine the struggle for "liberty" with real control of the peasant masses was the Catholic Church. This explains the tendencies of a good part of the liberal Italian bourgeoisie: The ancient faith, as Croce wrote, remained a means—"mythological to be sure, but still an effective means, to soften and appease suffering and pain."[26]

Pius IX may have been the first to notice that, as Croce would write much later, among "liberal Catholics," the emphasis was "on the adjective"—liberal. For this reason the Pope placed the works of Gioberti, Rosmini, and Ventura on the list of prohibited books in May 1849.[27] In any case, the movement played a decisive role in the creation of the myth, denounced by Cattaneo,[28] that the "Guelph Party" in Italy was essentially identical with the national party.

When Pius IX invoked a divine benediction on Italy on February 10, 1848, the clergy and the faithful began considering seriously for the first time the possibility of national unification.[29] Ippolito Nievo recalls that both peasants and city dwellers, the educated and the illiterate, were at that moment united in "the cry of 'Long live Pius IX!'" Yet, when the pontiff ostensibly abandoned the national cause, "this religious link that had united intellectuals and the plebeians of our Italian countryside in common aspirations was broken."[30]

According to Gramsci, the breaking of this bond meant that, in the Italian *Risorgimento*, the democrats—who, in an ideal (and abstract) scheme, should have represented the "Jacobins"—expressed none of the essential demands of the masses[31]; the real "theoretical Jacobins," the true strategists, were the liberal Catholics. This group, however, was destined to fail, for it could only lead the masses to the extent that it was prepared to wed itself fully with the policies of the Church.[32]

The Italian bourgeoisie thus found itself a prisoner of its traditional historical contradiction: that of being a class that both needs change but also fears it. Once again, this fundamental indecision left it as a hostage to the Church. And the Church, once it learned this lesson, exploited to its own benefit this trace of national spirit that it had never had.

Chapter 15

A Civil "Guelph" Religion

The Red and the Black

Throughout the process that empowered the bourgeoisie—from the Reformation to the Italian Army's entry into Rome in 1870, by way of the French Revolution—the Catholic Church witnessed a progressive decline in its doctrinal prerogatives, in its property holdings, and in its material and spiritual influence. The impact in Italy was not nearly as disruptive as had been the case in sixteenth-century Germany or in eighteenth-century France, but it carried the potential of even more dire consequences for the Church.

As had happened elsewhere, development on the peninsula was supposed to eliminate feudal vestiges. Beginning in Piedmont in the 1850s, a series of legislative acts guaranteeing the free circulation of capital were progressively put in place, provoking a violent reaction from local clergy and from Rome.

Most historians agree today that the threat for the Church was far less serious than it seemed at the time, certainly far less so than it might have been. According to the Catholic historian Roger Aubert, anticlerical legislation was often applied flexibly and with moderation.[1] In September 1870, the Italian laws against congregations were not applied throughout the newly conquered Roman region, leaving time for churchmen to sell anything they could. In May 1871, finally, eight months after the taking of Rome, the law known as *"guarentigie"* (the Guarantees Bill) was passed, assuring the Vatican a small independent territory and an annual income of 3,225,000 lira, around 5 percent of the annual budget of the kingdom. The pope firmly rejected both the law and the money, making it known through the *Ubi nos* encyclical that the Church could not receive from the state those rights that are given it by God. Some six months earlier, the same Pius IX had excommunicated the king, the government, and the "subalpine" army; later he forbade Catholics to take part in the political activities of the kingdom. The rupture was real and profound.

During the final phase of the *Risorgimento*, the Catholic Church's material strength had deteriorated rapidly. The coup de grace came in 1860 with the loss of Emilia and the Marche, the two richest regions of the Papal States. Church hierarchies were paralyzed by doubt and uncertainty; a strategy of *reconquista* did begin to emerge only some years later. It was a strategy built on two trump cards: the

Church's still-strong influence in the countryside, and the desire of many bourgeois liberals for appeasement.

Its real *presence* in society's most remote corners allowed the Church to exert the full weight of the political blackmail represented by its *absence* from political competition. This absence was all the more strongly felt since part of the bourgeoisie was beginning to think that the closest peril was no longer represented by *sanfedism* in the interior or by a hostile alliance of Catholic powers in the exterior, but by socialism. Even as a parliamentary discussion continued in Rome on the Law of Guarantees, in Paris, said the Foreign Minister Visconti Venosta, blew "the impious breath that extinguished all moral sense and all sentiment of honor among the masses.". In the Parliament, the former head of government Luigi Federico Menabrea warned against acting like the Byzantines in 1453: "Rather than continuing to wage a war against a group that no longer represents any danger, let us unite to exorcise the common enemy."[2] In the struggle against the "revolutionary peril," the Church undeniably held a solid lead. While it could draw on the capital accumulated during centuries of implacable struggle against "revolution," the Italian bourgeoisie had only just waged its own revolution, and a timid one at that.

The absence of a real workers movement in Italy meant that the repression of Thiers in France sufficed to remove the fear of "red peril" for several more decades. But, Jemolo writes, the "impious breath" had left Church hierarchies and Italian bourgeoisie believing that a society without private property constituted a graver threat than a society that allowed divorce.[3] The accords of 1929 would merely give such thinking a juridical underpinning.

The Conversion of the Church

The real problem facing the Italian state in the early decades of its existence was not to defend itself from the lower classes, which posed no concrete threat, but rather to find broad legitimacy among the ruling class. What united Church and state from the start of the unification process was the vital and primordial problem, for both, of survival. Yet, since their reciprocal hostility was real and unavoidable, the difficulty consisted in finding a balancing point between rapprochement and repulsion.

Thus, Candeloro writes, having eliminated its temporal power, confiscated part of its assets, secularized its laws and some of its structures, "the bourgeoisie satisfied itself with what it had achieved and even offered the Church the possibility of involving itself in the new state of things."[4] The Church, while officially rejecting this implicit truce offering, was not about to ignore the proposal, taking advantage of it to begin the long work of economic and organizational transition.

Underlying this transition, writes the most important historian of the *Azione cattolica*, Gianfranco Poggi, was the clear awareness that a simple attitude of refusal "would have been disastrous." Secularization tended to loosen the attachment of the faithful, an attachment that risked disappearing for good if the Church did not decide to approach the new context with more constructive attitudes.[5] It thus proceeded toward a more rigorous centralization and a broader opening to lay people to give the latter direct responsibilities within ecclesiastical institutions; these were strictly interdependent measures, for the larger the number of lay people speaking in the Church's name, the more necessary it is for them to come under hierarchical control and strict discipline. These choices prefaced the creation of a national organization of coordination of all Catholic associations. During its Congress of 1874, this organization made known its principal demands, particularly concerning education and family policy.

Although it had rejected the notion of a conservative Catholic party, the Vatican nonetheless maintained various forms of organization at the national level, and remained willing to intervene through appropriate political instruments in local situations where it had specific interests to promote or defend, as in the city of Rome.

In the kingdom's new capital, the main act of the Church's metamorphosis was being played out. Having had to abandon its final links to the remnants of the feudal world, the Church was being pushed to make its grand entry into the capitalist system, with the status of a great financial power.[6] In this turning point lies the main explanation for its survival amid the bourgeois tempest.

The liquid capital that the Church had managed to conserve came partly from the custom of "Peter's pence," a sort of economic billows for the universal Church, but above all from the transfer of its property holdings, largely effected in the short period between the conquest of Rome and the application of the laws against the congregations. This capital led to the creation of a vast financial system, which made it possible to buy back some of the same properties that had once been the "inalienable" assets of the feudal Church. A multiplier mechanism kicked in, boosted by the dizzying rise in property values: The banks provided the indispensable capital for property investors and builders, and in turn, these investments, yielding phenomenal profits, supported an unprecedented expansion of the credit sector.

Since Rome had become the country's capital, numerous enterprises had opened offices there and thus came into contact with the Catholic economic forces dominating the city. Productive bonds, at times conflicting, but more often cooperative, were thus forged between Vatican finance and the rest of the Italian capitalist world. In these linkages one finds the fundamental reason that many moderate liberals sought common ground with the Catholics.

At the time of the Libyan War, in 1911, the Banco di Roma—the largest of the Catholic banks, directed by the uncle of the future Pius XII—distinguished itself as a key supporter of the colonial mission.[7] It was no accident if the "baptism by fire" of Italian imperialism in Libya was followed almost immediately by the suspension of the *non expedit* (the Vatican policy, enjoined on Italian Catholics, of abstaining in parliamentary elections), by the concession of universal suffrage, and by the entry into parliament of the first Catholic deputies. During World War I, the Church gained entry among the fundamental forces of the state by institutionalizing its instruments of support, assistance, and comfort.

Social Transformism

Catholics' involvement in the management, direct or indirect, of the affairs of the kingdom was often curbed by the Church hierarchy, but almost never by Italian political officials. Even Crispi, who, as a deputy of the far left, had fought the Guarantees Bill, sang its praises once he had become prime minister.

Crispi was a sort of human hinge of the first decades of the new Italy, since he personified the connection between the "heroic" period of the *Risorgimento* and the early colonial phase. He knew that, in an open war, the Church could have unleashed the peasantry against the state, whereas the mission of Italian "grandeur" necessitated internal concord; he thus created, as Jemolo reminds us, the conditions for an unprecedented rapprochement between the political and religious authorities; no important Catholic, Jemolo adds, was ever excluded from any branch of the administration because of his convictions.[8] The first important public evidence of this rapprochement, as regards colonial ambitions, came with the clergy's participation in the national memorial services, in 1887, for five hundred soldiers killed during a battle against the Abyssinians in Dogali, in Eritrea.

But the truly decisive turning point was represented, in the eyes of many observers, by the events in Milan of May 1898. On this occasion, the ruling liberal class, for the last time, played the card of self-sufficiency, striking equally at the "reds" and the "blacks" to prove itself the sole arbiter of conflicts in Italy. This pretense began to appear, even in the eyes of part of the bourgeoisie, as disproportionate, the symptom of a paranoid syndrome of utter encirclement quite out of keeping with the new situation. The parliament disavowed the government, which was forced to resign, opening the way for a new transformist phase that would take its name from Giovanni Giolitti.

During the following decade, the development of Catholic organizations and of the Socialist Party were only two of the political forms taken amid the country's profound social transformation. As this first Italian "economic miracle"[9] took shape, numerous new financial and industrial actors appeared. Giolitti's approach was to systematize what Crispi had attempted to do: to associate the old social groups in power with those fostered by industrialization, by directly targeting their political representatives.

As for the lower classes, Crispi had, for the first time since the birth of the new state, adopted a "social policy." Thus, while social spending constituted a mere 0.3 percent of total public expenditures in 1870 and 0.5 percent in 1880, it doubled in the Crispian decade to reach 1 percent in 1900. The social portfolio became a fundamental element of Giolitti's policy, to the point that by 1906, it accounted for 2.3 percent of all public spending.[10] But that was not enough to reach the objectives the prime minister had set. As the Italian proletariat had not yet given birth to a "workers' aristocracy" that could be mobilized to defend the established order, the attempt to separate the reformist Socialists from the extremist swamp failed.

With the Catholics, the difficulties were not as large. The great majority of them, Spadolini writes, realized after 1898 that the "anti-state, anti-unitary prejudice" no longer made any sense. The riots of Milan, Spadolini continues, had laid bare the interweaving of the interests of the secular bourgeoisie and the new Catholic bourgeoisie, leading the latter to understand that a collapse of the liberal state would have taken with it many of the group's positions and zones of influence.

Despite the convergence of interests, Giolitti's attempts at a policy of assimilation did not produce the anticipated fruits. This was partly because of the Socialists' irreducibility, but primarily because of the immaturity of Italian capitalist development and the necessity not to break with old social classes that were already integral to the new system. Thus, having failed to define the contours of a "national interest," that is an agenda capable of unifying the conscience of Italians, the ruling liberal class again resorted to a case-by-case negotiation for political consensus, using the same methods Depretis and Crispi had employed: bargaining at every level, corrupt practices, pressures of every sort, seizure of prefectures and their local administrations, and electoral intimidation. A witness of the time, Ettore d'Orazio, described the majority as "the temporary coalition of different groups, having different leaders and divided by tradition, by interests and by tendencies."[11]

To simplify, one could say that the "Giolittian" strategy was based on three principal objectives: to enlarge the parliamentary majority; to integrate the new actors that had arisen from development into the management of the state; and to create a national collective conscience. Of these three objectives, the first was achieved (though at the cost of the most brazen parliamentary maneuvers), the second was not realized (because of the Libyan War and, especially, World War I), and the last failed owing to the constant resort to transformist practice.

In 1911, even a liberal monarchist like Benedetto Croce acknowledged seeing, fifty years after unification, the decline of social unity. Individuals, the philosopher wrote, "no longer feel linked to a grand whole," and if such division cannot be overcome, he concluded, it was vain to hope that "Italy will ever become great."

The "Great War" of the Church

Catholicism came to occupy a predominant place in the collective Italian mind, with each point of transition marked by an accompanying weakening of secular culture. The phenomenon has been widely noted in relation to the crisis between the eighteenth and nineteenth centuries; Gramsci and Jemolo observed it in connection with the crisis between the nineteenth and twentieth centuries; and some are starting to see it in connection with the crisis between the twentieth and twenty-first centuries.

Just as during the first of these critical phases, the central problem during the second had to do with the relationship to the masses, though under different forms, of course. Gramsci dealt with this notion in an article in December 1918: the collision with Catholicism, he wrote, caused the liberal state to shrivel and could lead only to the "subordination of liberalism to Catholicism."[12] Gramsci wrote these words in the aftermath of World War I, during which this "subordination" had become clear.

As we have seen, the Catholic bourgeoisie had realized for some years that its interests did not differ substantially from those of the rest of the Italian bourgeoisie. Thus even those bourgeois Catholics who expected no direct benefit from Italy's participation in the war rallied to the ambient patriotism for fear that they otherwise would be accused of being unpatriotic and might lose, as Candeloro puts it, "the political, economic and administrative positions they had attained in the preceding years."[13]

The Church thus found itself having to manage the contradiction between its universalism (which required it to continue being the Church of Catholics in Austria, France, Belgium, Germany, Ireland, Italy, Poland, etc.) and the "national" interests of the bourgeois Catholics in those countries. It dealt with this awkward position by allowing the faithful to deal with the distinction between the Church's universal position and that of the Catholics in the nations involved in the conflict. Thus, on May 20, 1915, four days before Italy's attack on Austria, Catholic deputies joined their votes to those of the majority (407 to 74) in granting full powers to the prime minister "in case of war." In June 1916, the first Catholic deputy, Filippo Meda, entered the government as minister of Finance.

This transition from neutrality to engagement took place not just at the top of the social ladder, but, more importantly, at its very bottom. The 2,400 army chaplains that the commander in chief of the Italian Army presided over among the 25,000 clergymen mobilized were part of a veritable infiltration of the army. The Pope not only authorized the chaplains to serve but also created a special diocese within the army, with its own bishop—who immediately obtained from the state the rank of general. It was a clear case of *do ut des* ("I scratch your back, you scratch mine") in which each of the contracting parties served its own interests, and it anticipated the Concordat.

During the war, the clergy officially regained its traditional role of social mediator between power and the people, a role that it had never lost despite the secularization that accompanied modernization. The state now recognized the importance of this role, both to boost the morale of the troops and to bolster failing backup. The parishes managed 11,932 charities, 8,088 money and clothing collection centers, 4,177 information offices, 1,963 day-care facilities, and 3,084 committees for civil mobilization and assistance.[14]

Militarily, and in terms of international politics, the Italian war was won by the English and the French, with decisive help from the Americans. Morally, and in domestic political terms, the Italian war was won by the Church.

The Church did not hesitate to present its bill. Not only did the state take it upon itself to increase the emoluments provided to priests, but also, starting in 1920, it undertook serious negotiations to resolve all outstanding disputes. The most significant change, however, came in the birth of the People's Party, which Gramsci described at the time as "the most important event in Italian history since the *Risorgimento*."[15] The Church had renounced the demand for the restoration of the temporal state, because now it harbored a far more vast ambition, involving the identification between the Italian nation and the Catholic nation. The Vatican now aimed, Candeloro writes, for the creation of an integrally Christian state,[16] an ambition that would lead, inevitably, to the confrontation with fascism.

The conviction that a reintegration of God in both legislation and public affairs was under way was reinforced by a series of measures taken by the new fascist government: the return of the crucifix to schools and courtrooms, mandatory religion classes in school, the education reform of 1923 that placed public and private schools on an even footing, and the establishment of Sacred Heart of Milan, the first Catholic university.

When the Concordat was signed in February 1929, the "Roman question" died away for good. It was at that moment that the latent conflict between two religions, both aspiring to provide spiritual direction to the Italian masses, burst into plain sight.

Chapter 16

The Quest for a Civil Italian Religion

The Voluntarist Shortcut

Italy, writes Gian Enrico Rusconi, has known no form of "civil religion"—neither the American form, which emphasizes the noun in that phrase, nor the French form, which accents the adjective. This void, according to Rusconi, was filled by the Church, which exercises the role of a "substitute civil religion."[1] The Italian case is unique in this regard. Unlike other Catholic countries like France, Austria, and even Spain, where the ecclesiastical apparatus has had to confront an entrenched royal power since at least the fifteenth century, in Italy the authority of the Church has long faced no real state obstacles.

At its birth, the Kingdom of Italy lacked all the common qualities that putatively create a sense of belonging to a single nation: unity of language, unity of territory, and unity of tradition. Above all, the new country lacked "a common way of thinking, a common principle, a common goal," that is, the very essence of nationality in Mazzini's eyes. The *Destra* lost little sleep over this. It had other priorities, starting with the need to build structures that could extend state power across the entire peninsula; the national principle was not part of its cultural mentality. The ruling Piedmontese class was accustomed to dealing with subjects, not citizens, and the conditions under which the country had unified gave it little motive to abandon its traditional vision.

It was only when the *Sinistra* arrived in power that the ambition of an Italian "civil religion" began to find practical application. This was not only because of the different cultural education of the men who had come to power in 1876, nor was it simply because the Paris Commune had shown, early in the decade, that the people were not merely a sum of individuals, but a mass whose moods had to be recognized and disciplined. It was also because the *Sinistra* had been the first manifestation of a real enlargement of the bases of power, and it had to attempt to bring a certain form and coherence to the new and composite interests that it had pulled together.

For Francesco de Sanctis, minister of public instruction, but also a literary critic, this task was the responsibility of the schools and of literature, guardians not only of a national identity but also of a national *pedagogy*. That said, the education system was weakened by profound structural inadequacies, as we have seen, and the patriotic literature of De Amicis, Carducci, Pascoli, D'Annunzio, and even the futurists continued for a very long time to address itself to a very limited public with diversified tastes; moreover, this literature was deeply influenced by French literary production.

The attempt to apply the pedagogical virtues of the French Third Republic to Italy had failed not only because Italy was not France but also because the terms of the relationship between the grandeur of the country and a national consciousness in Italy had constantly been reversed. The "nation" was only a abstract concept in France before the distribution of land to the peasants, before the civil code, and before the Napoleonic conquests. British pride, for its part, was not a condition of the creation of the empire, but its consequence. The Americans did not conceive of themselves as a "nation" with the objective of throwing the English into the ocean and creating the first constitutional republic in human history, but rather in the aftermath of these two titanic enterprises. National consciousness is a consequence of real strength. It can grow as a function of the growth of real strength; it never replaces it and, *a fortiori*, never creates it.

In Italy, like in many weaker countries, it is the voluntarist factor that has dominated the concept of nation. De Sanctis's idea that literature could permit Italy to rise above "second-rank" status and aspire even to "convert the modern world into a world that we own"[2] does not date from the *Sinistra's* accession to power. It comes from the conviction, which grew during the *Risorgimento*, that Italy had to be the "educator" of humankind, even the "verb of God among the races," in the words of Mazzini. This idea was popularized, if one can say it, by Vincenzo Gioberti and also by Mazzini himself, who offered historic, cultural, religious, and even geopolitical justifications for it.

This idea of a "civilizing mission" clearly influenced the first leaders of unified Italy—"even the most realistic and those most aware of the country's real conditions," writes Emilio Gentile—to reject the possibility that the new country might limit itself to a modest neutrality in the concert of nations.[3] Given the circumstances of its creation, its objective weight in demographic and economic terms, and its geographic position, Italy had no real possibility of remaining neutral for long. The lack of realism among the leaders of the country thus lay not so much in their thoughts of an impossible neutrality, but in the conviction that the new country could prevail over other powers.

As we have seen, lacking policies of their own, the democrats of the 1850s were in fact guided by Cavour and the moderates. A similar thing occurred on the international policy scene, especially among men of democratic background. In an April 1868 letter, Otto von Bismarck offered a lesson in geopolitics to Mazzini, exploiting the latter's notorious francophobia: Italy and Germany, the Prussian chancellor wrote, "exert their action in such different directions that Italy can never aspire to dominate the Baltic, nor Germany the Mediterranean"; at the same time, "the configuration of the terrestrial globe being unchangeable, Italy and France will always be rivals and often enemies."[4]

The most Mazzinian politician of the new Italy, Francesco Crispi, recognized that the grandeur of Italy and its national conscience would be born of its successes in international politics, notably, if they were achieved through military means. Italy, he asserted in 1866, the year of the humiliations of Custoza and Lissa, "needs a baptism by fire: she owes it to herself, so that the great nations of Europe know that she, too, is a great nation, and that she is sufficiently strong to demand respect in the world."[5] Yet, the "baptisms by fire" that Italy was to experience under Crispi's leadership—Amba Alagi and Macallé in 1895, Adwa in 1896, not to mention the Fasci Siciliani—destroyed Crispi, diminished respect for Italy in the world, and lessened the possibility that Italy might one day be able to construct its own "civil religion."

Italian Fatherlands

On the eve of World War I, the competition between those presenting themselves as the sole true trustees of the "fatherland" was fierce. The conservative liberals pointed to the undeniable progress achieved since 1861 and, in the fiftieth-anniversary celebrations, made official the syncretistic vision of the *Risorgimento* advocated by de Sanctis as early as 1862. The republicans, for their part, condemned the "lie" of an official Italy, which they said was physically but not spiritually united because it "lacked a popular soul." As natural heirs to the Mazzini's "voluntarist shortcut," they conceived the "true fatherland" as the real country purged of its flaws; they made of this a moral postulate.

The living conditions of the people outside the public arena were also a polemical target of the Catholics and the Socialists, hostile to a state seen as "foreign" to Italians' real interests. But, unlike the republicans, the Catholics and Socialists had deep roots among these same people. Because of the continuity of their institutions, the propagation of their religion, and their centuries-long symbiosis with the peasant world, the Catholics also claimed to represent the true fatherland of the Italians, which was naturally different from the liberals'. They knew that so long as they were not called on to manage the state, it could not truly be a state for all, and this, indirectly, would give them political strength. On top of that, they would bring to the negotiating table with the liberals the trump card of their social doctrine. Embodied in state structures, it could provide a dowry to the common fatherland—a solution to the "workers question," that is, social peace.

Among the different fatherlands proposed to the Italians, one was actually Socialist. For Filippo Turati, "Italian, worker and citizen" are but one; separated, they unmasked the "lie" upon which the official Italian state was founded.[6] But here again was an underlying offer of collaboration: the proposal to transform the proletariat into a social pillar of the Italian state. It is not incidental that this suggestion came from the leader of the reformist wing of the party who, during the Giolittian decade, had come close to throwing his support to a majority that today we would call center-left. But the Socialist Party was very divided and, in 1912, it was the maximalist (extremist) faction that emerged to take the reins, declaring war on "bourgeois patriotism" and expelling four of its deputies for their "nationalist and warmonger" positions.

All the political groups mentioned were in fact divided at their cores: the liberals were motivated by their ideals, of course, but also by their transformist management of public affairs; the republicans oscillated between a liberalism barely more radical than that of the government and revolutionary subversivism; and the "modernist" tendencies troubled the consciences of many Catholics, before being energetically condemned by Pius X in his 1907 encyclical *Pascendi Dominici Gregis*.

To be sure, among the republicans and the Catholics there were factions and individuals who were unalterably hostile to the liberal state, but most of Mazzini's heirs seemed more interested in "pursuing their business interests within the shadow of the monarchy" than in overturning it, as one can read in a report by the prefect of Forlì, a republican stronghold.[7] In any case, outside Romagna and the Carrara region, their political influence was negligible. Catholics, for their part, had already begun their slow ascension toward the conquest of the state; their hostility toward it was tactical, though a few took it literally. Support for the Libyan expedition and the elections of 1913—when Catholics were responsible, according to Count Ottorino Gentiloni, for the election of 195 of the 305 deputies in the liberal majority—testified eloquently to this fact.

Outside of these minorities—reactionary Catholics, revolutionary republicans, extremist Socialists, and anarchists—one other political grouping declared open hostility to the liberal state: the nationalists. If the Socialists were the direct product of the Giolittian era's "economic miracle"—representing, as they did, a proletariat that had grown in quantity and in quality[8]—the nationalists were the indirect product, the still uncertain expression of new forces that had begun to raise questions about the old balance but that were not yet able to create new one.

During the Giolittian period, industrial production rose from 50 percent to twice that, depending on the source.[9] Imports tripled and exports rose by a factor of 2.5 in less than twenty years.[10] The agricultural consumption of chemical products rose by 9.25 times between 1893 and 1913, and this had a multiplying effect on the rural exodus.[11] The number of Italians leaving the countryside each year rose from 310,434 in 1896 through 1900 to 679,152 in 1909 through 1913 (having hit a high of 739,661 emigrants per year in 1905 through 1907).[12] At the same time, the cities grew more and more crowded as they went from 24 percent of the population in 1881 to 31.3 percent in 1911 (four-fifths of this increase stemmed from migratory flows).[13]

During the early years of the decade, the combined effects of protectionism, expanded credit and production, plus increasing purchasing power seemed to create a virtuous circle that could satisfy all demands. Transformism as an occasional exchange of favors soared to new heights. But the crisis of 1907, born out of the first great financial panic in the United States, brought to light all the contradictions that growth had hidden. Banks refused to continue long-term financing, creating a liquidity crisis for large industry; industry then demanded more substantial aid from the state and abandoned the policy of direct negotiations with workers. Consumption diminished, and the most export-dependent sectors, which had suffered in a time of protectionist-aided development, tightened further.[14]

At once, the balance that had been assured in a time of impetuous growth broke down, with serial political effects. Among the Socialists, the reformist camp rapidly lost ground; among the Catholics, the factions that had favored lending a helping hand to the liberal state gained strength; among the nationalists, the movement broke free of the limited intellectual circles in which it had been confined. At its heart, the rupture between "free-traders" and "protectionists" became complete, and the nationalists became the political organ of big Italian capital financiers as well as of the frightened new petit-bourgeois groups who were terrified of losing their recently gained prosperity.

The "Dogmatic Vice" of Nationalism

It was only during the Giolittian decade and, in particular, in connection with the 1907 crisis that some in Italy first theorized about the necessity of a "party of the bourgeoisie." This notion arose precisely at the moment when the "sole party of the bourgeoisie," based on transformism, faced a crisis.

The first to seek to give a political conscience to the productive bourgeoisie were the nationalists, united around the journal *Il Regno*. For them, "the life of Italy" was embodied by those "courageous industrialists who increase our production, fight for the markets of England [and] conquer Asia Minor and South America"; their factories, these nationalists continued, would have an advantage over the "word factories" of parliamentary politics.[15]

Francesco Saverio Nitti, however, was the first, or one of the firsts, to speak in terms of an actual party. Writing in 1907, Nitti offered the outlines of a platform meant to reflect the general interest of the bourgeoisie, and in particular of the industrial bourgeoisie; the party was not seen so much as an organization as it was a "conscience."[16] On the creation of a "coherent conscience of the bourgeoisie after the economic malaise of the years after 1907," according to Carocci, the work and action of the economist Vilfredo Pareto, a theoretician, with Gaetano Mosca, also dealt with the power of the economic elites.[17] Pareto would become, over the years, the advocate of a "national" or "imperialist" socialism; and it was with a socialism transposed from class struggle to the struggle between nations that Enrico Corradini, considered the "theoretician" of Italian nationalism, also aligned himself.

The nation, to Corradini—like the proletariat for the Socialists—without theoretical conscience is a class *in itself*, but not a class *for itself*: the task of the Socialists, he said, had been to "teach the proletariat the value of class struggle," while the task for the nationalists was to "teach Italy the value of international struggle."[18] If, for Socialists, class consciousness developed through struggle and strikes, for nationalists, Corradini concluded, national consciousness developed through imperialist war: "Nationalism should give rise in Italy to the desire for victorious war."[19] Corradini drew up a list of seven reasons why, even in 1911, "Italy does not have a developed national conscience": (1) it had never been a nation; (2) it had not had (and still does not have) a national language; (3) it was not the product of a revolution; (4) it was, instead, the product of "diplomatic maneuvers and foreign arms"; (5) it was the theater of too much antagonism; (6) it was the theater of too many social conflicts; and (7) its political class was "the residue of servile times."[20] Beyond the polemical exaggeration, the description is correct, but, as with a borrowing from Marxism, it stops at the surface. Rather than finding "the organic process that necessarily determined these conditions," Gobetti wrote, the nationalists merely "came back to Gioberti's poor dream of despair."[21]

The nationalists celebrated the Libyan War as the beginning of Italian grandeur and the displays of patriotism that accompanied it as the beginning of national consciousness. They had seen only the surface and the potential of economic transformation in the just-ended decade and ignored its contradictions: growth and power for them were merely a question of virtue and desire, and only immorality and a failure of will could stop the triumphal march of the bourgeoisie in Italy.

Over the course of the decade, industrial monopolies, created with the complicity of protectionist policy and with the direct participation of the major banks, had taken on greater and greater importance, to the point that even Luigi Einaudi, a sworn enemy of any state intervention in economic affairs, had begun to worry. Protected from foreign competition, the steel industry long continued to use techniques that necessitated no great capital investments or particularly qualified manual labor, but the steel thus produced cost twice as much as English steel. So it was normal that with each economic slowdown, with each crisis putting Italian production in even slightly greater contact with foreign production, the monopolists felt lost and called on the state to help. In 1911 the Banca d'Italia responded to such appeals by creating, along with the Banca Commerciale and the Credito Italiano—the two largest banks in Italy at the time—a syndicate designed to provide ninety-six million lira to troubled enterprises.[22] Also in 1911, Italy declared war on Turkey and invaded Libya.

The foreign policy of transformism was the exact mirror of domestic policy: Italy was allied with everyone at once and promised its support to all the parties in the various conflicts. In June 1902, Foreign Minister Prinetti signed an accord with France, which was in a state of open hostility with Germany, two days after having signed the renewal of the Triple Alliance with Germany and Austria. In October 1909, Minister Tittoni signed an agreement with Russia against, among others, any Austrian expansion in the Balkans, just four days after having ratified a pact with Vienna providing for compensation for Italy in the event of Austrian expansion in this same region, and committing the two countries to make no agreements with third states on the subject of the Balkans.

The whole "organic process that necessarily determined" the gestures of Italian imperialism was foreign to the nationalists, who made this simply a question of "courage," of "moral integrity," of "national pride."

When Italy launched its Libyan adventure, the patriotic effervescence and the triumphalism of the nationalists joined to conceal international perplexity over the gap between Italian ambitions and the reality of the country's development.[23] The war itself necessitated sending a contingent three times larger than anticipated. It lasted a year and ended in October 1912 with a unilateral retreat of Turkish army from Libya, under pressure from the birth of a hostile coalition in the Balkans. During World War I, the Libyan Arab tribes succeeded in chasing out the Italians, and the "pacification" of the region would be announced twenty-one years after the start of operations there, in January 1932, by Governor Pietro Badoglio.[24]

In fact, despite the performance of the Giolittian decade, Italy's lag behind other great powers was remarkable and, owing to protectionism, had even grown wider. Its share of total world manufacturing production declined from 2.5 percent in 1900 to 2.4 percent in 1913. This also explains the undulating character of foreign policy, buffeted by the military difficulties, but also by the incapacity to find other domestic political balance beyond the transformist approach.

In 1913 Italian industrial production was 2.5 times less than that of France, 3.6 times less than that of Russia, 6 times less than that of Germany or England, and 13.3 times less than that of the United States. Despite the steel-making monopolies, its steel production was only one-third that of France, barely 5.3 percent that of Germany, and a mere 3 percent that of the United States. Its energy consumption, to conclude this brief comparative tableau, was 17.6 percent that of France, 5.8 percent that of Germany, and 2 percent that of the United States Nothing in these data seems to justify the optimism of the editors of *Regno* regarding the capacity of Italy's "courageous industrialists" to fight for English markets or to conquer "Asia Minor and South America."

In 1913 Gaetano Salvemini wrote that the nationalists had a "megalomaniacal vision of the capacities of Italy," and added that he personally felt more like a citizen of "the Italy of today, only beginning to rise up from the intellectual, moral and economic misery of several centuries."[25] For Gobetti, the nationalists were the "grand party of a dreary and infantile Italy." For them, concluded this young liberal—who would be killed by the Fascists in 1926, at age twenty-five—"colonial expansion and militarism are not specific desires, but dogmatic vices."[26] It was these dogmatic vices that would lead Italy to catastrophe during the two world conflicts just ahead.

Chapter 17

A Petit-Bourgeois Fatherland

The Rise and Fall of the Petite Bourgeoisie

Fascism represented the most coherent attempt to create an Italian civil religion—a homogeneous body of values, feelings, and behaviors to be shared among all the peoples of the peninsula.[1] But everyone knows how catastrophically this turned out: in 1945, after two years of civil war, with Italians on both sides swapping accusations of betrayal, all mentions of the nation, the fatherland, or any other symbol even remotely suggestive of the Fascist experience were abandoned.[2]

After the question of national identity resurfaced in Italy following the political crisis of the 1990s, many people said that it was fascism and the war that had kept it on a back burner for more than forty years. Fewer dared to link this "disqualification" of a sense of identity to the successes achieved earlier by the Mussolinian regime in attempting to forge such a sense: a social compromise with the petite bourgeoisie founded on promises that could not be kept.

It may seem paradoxical that the petite bourgeoisie should have become so politically important at the precise moment when it was starting on a downward curve in economic and social affairs—that is, when large numbers of peasants were abandoning the countryside to become hourly laborers, and when small-scale production and distribution were hit by the first big processes of concentration. Historically the petite bourgeoisie has been the first to benefit from the gradual enlargement of political institutions in newly maturing capitalist societies, making it a mass base for liberal democracy, and an unavoidably pivotal social element. Its political importance has helped slow its downward curve, socially and economically, as have legislative initiatives; this braking action has grown more decisive as social and economic decline have become more pronounced.

In Italy, the growth of the *political* strength of the petite bourgeoisie largely took place in just a few years, between the repression of the Milanese riots of 1898 and the entry into World War I in 1915. The group's arrival on the political scene was marked by a pronounced hostility toward the old ruling classes, which the petit bourgeois wanted to replace, and by an equally sharp hostility toward the proletariat, whose demands were seen as a direct threat to the economic well-being and social prestige so recently acquired. Let us not forget that from 1901 to 1913, while average income increased by 17 percent, workers' salaries rose by 26 percent, strengthening the petit-bourgeois conviction that industrial employees were privileged in their own way.[3]

In a 1923 essay, Luigi Salvatorelli explains that this class was democratic and Socialist leaning so long as it thought it had found, in democracy and in socialism, the idealized forms of its interests, and it abandoned them the moment they began to transform into reality and embody its worst nightmares: industrialization and a workers' coalition. In the years of Giolittism, the petite bourgeoisie aligned with nationalism because, Salvatorelli continues, it was "too weak and inconsistent as an organic class—that is, one holding power and economic function"—to measure up to the haute bourgeoisie and the proletariat. Its "class struggle," according to Salvatorelli, consisted in the negation of the very concept of class, replacing it with that of "nation." In the case of the fascist movement, he concludes, "the petit-bourgeois element" is numerically dominant, but above all is "distinctive and directive."[4] Along with Salvatorelli, numerous witnesses of the period—including Gobetti, Gramsci, Ansaldo, and Tilgher[5]—and nearly every historian of the post-Fascist period has insisted on the dominance of the petit-bourgeois element in fascism, as much in social terms as in moral or intellectual terms.

The haute bourgeoisie, for its part, was uninvolved in fascism's birth or its direction, but used it precisely because of its character as a mass movement, able to promote its interests as an "organic class." A similar attitude had been adopted toward nationalism in the period before World War I. From August 1914 to May 1915, the industrial and agricultural sectors, battling for international market share, had remained faithful to Giolitti in the conviction that there was more to gain through neutrality than through war, and in the fear that war would strengthen the protectionist alliance between high finance and heavy industry. They finally gave in when it appeared that Italy would participate in the conflict regardless, for fear of being excluded from what was thought to be the imminent work of defining a new postwar order.

The mass of peasants had always opposed the war. The urban petite bourgeoisie—shopkeepers, artisans, intellectuals—believed that the conflict would mean an end to the Giolittian system, to the tyranny of the trade unions, and to usurious banking practices, and would allow it to satisfy its thirst for a "gentle" patriotism, learned from De Amicis's books, and also its thirst for an aggressive and vengeful patriotism, learned from D'Annunzio's speeches on the war, "the most fertile matrix of beauty ever to appear on Earth."[6] The Italian war, in its three and a half years, would show that the petit-bourgeois were right only in judging that the Giolittian system was a thing of the past.

The Death of Liberal Transformism

The European war immediately transmitted to Italy the effects of the stock market collapse, the interruption of credit and foreign trade, and the consecutive failure of banks and of enterprises, and it caused numerous emigrants to return home.[7] In December 1914 the state created an entity—*the Consorzio per le sovvenzioni sui valori industriali*—to inject capital into troubled banks and industries. The money came from the Banca d'Italia, which, to fund this program, had to enlarge the monetary mass in circulation. When the country entered the war, the new Ministry for Arms and Munitions gave rise to another organization aimed at centralizing industrial production. The 1,976 enterprises connected to it benefited from military orders, easy access to credit, energy, raw materials, transportation, and exemptions from military service for some employees. This was a windfall for many industries—even those that had been hostile to participation in the war—and they absorbed a number of their competitors and saw their turnover, profits, and activities soar. The manufacturing industry's share in gross domestic product (GDP) creation rose from 25 percent to 30 percent.[8] Meantime, workers, though they had been militarized during the war, saw their salaries rise afterward, and the intense social struggles of the period—more than twenty-two thousand days lost to strikes in 1919 and more than thirty thousand in 1920[9]—reinforced this trend, leading to passage of the forty-eight-hour maximum work week, social insurance, and minimum wages.

This tableau would have been depressing enough for the petite bourgeoisie—which had dreamed of resolving all society's complexity in a single "national middle class"—if it had not been for the fact that, while the peasants paid the highest tribute in blood during the war, it was the petit-bourgeois who paid the highest economic cost. The state—to pay its suppliers, prop up the banks and enterprises involved in the military effort, reimburse interest, at least, on the debts contracted with the allies and through the purchase of public securities—resorted to taxes (although they covered only 32 percent of the public deficit in 1918), issuing new state securities, borrowing, and above all, to the printing of paper money. Thus, in 1920, the volume of the monetary mass was six times what it had been in 1915. The lira had depreciated in comparison to the dollar by a factor of five from 1914 to 1919, and the wholesale price index by a factor of 5.9 between 1913 and 1920. Italian inflation, writes Michèle Merger, was the most pronounced in Europe, following that of Germany.[10]

After inflation, forever its most terrible nightmare, the petite bourgeoisie was frightened by the successive waves of labor unrest in industry and agriculture, more so than the haute bourgeoisie, which, for its part, had the economic and organizational strength (the Confederation of Industry was officially founded in April 1919) to resist the shock. Some major employers, bolstered by their substantial war profits, even considered exploiting the trade union struggles of 1919 to 1920 to induce hourly workers and technicians to join a sort of reformist alliance of the productive classes by way of salary and contract concessions.

The fear of expropriation, indeed, of revolution, played in favor of the gradual abandonment of any reformist hypothesis, but the decisive factor, in the end, was the global overproduction crisis of 1920, which culminated a year later in Italy with the collapse of the reference bank of one of the most important Italian industrial groups, Ansaldo. It was only then that the Fascist option began to make headway among industrialists. But whether the preferred solution was reformist or authoritarian, it was clear that Giolittian transformism, already in decline just before the war, had breathed its last.

Attitudes in the run-up to the war were decided outside the usual mediating channels of Giolittism, which were the king's palace, the corridors of the Foreign Ministry, the embassies, the newspapers, and the universities. To the contrary, from the summer of 1914, parliament was consulted only once, to approve a decision already taken, on May 20, 1915. According to Denis Mack Smith, in the first year of the European war, the *Corriere della Sera* became a political institution far more influential than the Chamber of Deputies.[11] Historians of the right, the left, and from abroad have spoken of a "coup d'état" against the monarchy and the government, in favor of a few press organs of the boisterous interventionist minorities that had invaded the streets.[12] Whatever the case, the parliament barely convened through the duration of the conflict, and legislative activity was handled by government decree. The machine for mediation and transformist recomposition had broken down.

At the end of the war, the first elections, in 1919, were dominated by the Socialists and the Catholics, two parties that based their actions more on motivations of a general order than in defense of small interest groups.[13] At the same time, the new electoral law—calling for proportionality, larger districts, and preference to electoral lists and not to candidates—further loosened the bond between deputies and their electors. But more than that, the coup de grâce to Giolittism came from the fact that transformism does not work without constantly integrating new interest groups as soon as they take on social importance. And at this point, the new interests knocking on the door of the state were those of the peasant, worker, and petit-bourgeois masses. In the face of the full social variety of mature capitalism, and shaken by war's calamitous consequences, the political machine of liberal Italy, born in 1861, came grinding to a halt.[14]

Apprenticeship in Consensus

Mussolini and his collaborators were the first representatives of the ruling Italian class called to manage what would later be referred to as a "mass society." As a general rule, the management of a "mass society" requires the "learning of consensus," which is nothing more than what we might define as "the final stage of transformism." This pursuit of consensus can (and to a degree, must) become a veritable creative forge of values; but consensus can never be founded exclusively on a sharing of abstract values. According to Gian Enrico Rusconi, the virtues of "citizenship"—namely, "loyalty" and "civic solidarity"—can be learned only in a "concrete manner." They become shared values only when "citizenship allows access to specific assets," whether these be "rights" or "benefits induced by social policies."[15] By shining a direct light on the close linkage between "citizenship" and "benefits," Rusconi, and Cafagna with him,[16] reveal for us some of the fundamental workings of the mechanism of consensus in developed capitalist societies. It matters little if this is manifested in democratic forms or otherwise. What matters is that the more "benefits" there are to distribute, the broader will be the consensus and the more those enjoying them can aspire to create a collective mythology, a framework of common belonging to the nation.

Mussolini and his regime believed it possible to found a collective Italian identity on the idea of Italy as a great power. But this idea, to enjoy any credibility at all, had to be backed by a tangible demonstration that the well-being of Italy and the well-being of the Italian people could, to some extent, coincide. Thus the second half of the 1920s was characterized by the "battle for *quota 90*" (a rate of 90), a brutally deflationist policy in defense of small savers that aimed to bring the Italian currency back to an exchange rate of 90 lira per pound sterling, after it had sunk to 148.87 in August 1926: and indeed, on April 25, 1927, the lira reached its high point of 85.75 per pound.

Moreover, after having founded, in 1925, the *Opera Nazionale Dopolavoro*—with the mission of organizing "after-work" leisure activities, vacation outings (especially for workers' children), trips, and cultural events—the regime in 1934 instituted the forty-hour work week. The welfare state was reorganized and expanded, notably with the institution of family allowances, temporary layoffs, and public health measures. During the 1930s, public spending steadily increased, rising from 16.5 percent of GDP in 1926 to 33.4 percent in 1936.[17] All of this was built around a promise to end the humiliations suffered by the Italian people in the past, especially those that had led to emigration.

On these bases, fascism attempted to create a national mythology—a "civil religion"—that would reinvigorate the Mazzinian plan for a "fusion of interests and of individual and class rights in the melting pot of fatherland," as Bollati summed it up.[18] Yet, the vicious circle in which Mussolini and his men found themselves was typical of the contradiction that has long hampered the blooming of a national Italian consciousness: to have any chance of creating a true civil religion, one needs tools of social cohesion that go beyond the means the country has at its disposal.

The Mussolinian autarchy was not merely the Italian version of the widespread protectionism of the 1930s, or an ideological backdrop to the lack of raw materials, it was also a sort of sanitary cordon pulled tight around the petite bourgeoisie so that it could contemplate its social betterment without being tempted to compare it to the conditions of the "decadent demo-plutocracies." In fact, based on statistics on living conditions, Zamagni notes that there was not, during the Fascist period, any real improvement of the living conditions of the "middle classes," but rather a "revenge" of the lower classes, a revenge that would reinstate the prewar differences, both materially and in terms of social prestige.[19]

As heir to the profound social transformations of the first twenty years of the century, fascism found itself confronted with the same corrosion of centuries-old social relationships that the Church defines as "secularization." But faced by these processes, the attitudes of the Church and of fascism sometimes converged—as in their common opposition to liberalism and socialism—while at times competing, in a similar ambition to assume "the spiritual leadership" of the Italian masses. For fascism, religion was nothing but an *instrumentum regni*, while for the Church, the fascist regime could be an *instrumentum religionis*. The goal of both parties was to master processes that by their very nature are ungovernable. The conflict between traditional religion and "civil religion" contributed to disorienting Italians and feeding their "ethical and political weakness," which would be, according to De Felice, at the base of the defeatist sentiment during the war.[20]

The Apprentice Sorcerer

The fundamental error of fascism, on a political level, was to take seriously the idea of totalitarianism and to truly believe in the "fusion of interests and of individual and class rights in the melting pot of fatherland." In fact, the party and the regime were nothing but a confederation of "baronies and of big corporative autonomies"[21]—the different groups and factions of the bourgeoisie, the armed forces, the court—that "il Duce" believed he had disciplined into a sort of national and Fascist *reductio ad unum*.

Mussolini built his concept of "totalitarianism" around a confidence in the "primacy of politics" that he had shared with many of his former Socialist friends. He could not have been unaware that certain factions and counterfactions in society are constantly erupting, nor that they express contradictory interests, but he felt certain that politics—the control of the political levers of society—could keep them in check.

The obstacles raised to emigration[22] and the attempt to divert it toward the "fourth shore" (Libya) are perhaps the most striking examples. Another case came with the foolish ambition to lessen the influence of Church and family on young people. Once again, not having resolved the root causes of Italian backwardness—determinate of what would be called "amoral familyism"[23]—fascism attempted a purely superficial operation aimed at "socializing" the family institution through a sort of militarization of youth, even though the economic bases of nuclear family life were still in place.[24]

The desire to "nationalize the masses" by acting such that each social group "could find in the corporatist and totalitarian state a minimum of material and moral advantages"[25] required an ever more intense Italian participation in the competition for a share of the world market, until the ultimate consequences would result. On this subject, the most important historian of fascism, Renzo De Felice, made a significant and inexplicably underestimated observation: one could expect anything from Mussolini, he wrote, "except neutrality; at the extreme, an intervention against Germany was more plausible than neutrality."[26] The entry into World War II was the price the Italian bourgeoisie had to pay in exchange for the generous state aid and social peace that had allowed its businesses to prosper for twenty years.

Given the conditions facing Italy in 1940, as Paul Kennedy has written, only "a miracle, or the Germans, could prevent a debacle of epic proportions."[27] The situation in the year of the "stab in the back" was not so different from that preceding Italy's entry into World War I. The country's industrial production had nearly doubled from 1913 to 1938, but it represented only 2.9 percent of world production, a smaller share than the 3.3 percent of 1929. On the eve of the conflict, its industrial might amounted to barely more than half that of France, one-third that of Great Britain, less than one fourth that of their German ally, one-sixth that of the USSR, and one-tenth that of the United States.[28] In terms of military potential, the gaps were a bit smaller in comparison to France and the Soviet Union, somewhat larger compared to Germany and Great Britain, whereas a gulf separated the military power of the United States—which was 16.7 times greater[29]—though that did not stop Italy from declaring war against America in December 1941.

Certain contemporary observers and a number of historians today hold that some Italians were motivated by a sort of *cupio dissolvi*, an essential defeatism, from the very beginning of the conflict.[30] To some, this pessimism had begun to manifest itself even before Italy's entry into the war. The bellicose enthusiasm that had accompanied the "conquest" of Ethiopia had cooled significantly with the realization that Italy would be facing armies hugely more powerful than that of the Ethiopian Negus. Even Giuseppe Bottai, a Fascist deputy since 1921 and former governor of Addis Ababa, who defined himself as an "insincere interventionist," noted in his journal the coolness with which the crowd assembled on the Piazza Venezia on June 10, 1940, greeted the speech declaring war: "One perceives the difficulty of the small groups of the faithful, full of goodwill to lead the cheers and cries. There was the sensation of a sort of stunned discipline which the Party was unable to brighten with its slogans."[31]

During the first phase of Italian participation in the war, the Germans' victories were accompanied by feelings that oscillated between relief and enthusiasm. But those victories did not entirely compensate for the alarm Italians felt in the face of the Greek counteroffensive in the autumn of 1940, for the declaration of war first against the Soviet Union and then against the United States, followed by the loss of eastern Africa in 1941, well before the decisive defeats of El Alamein and Stalingrad.

For Sergio Romano, a "mass transformism" occurs when most of the followers and clients of a regime abandon it and take up hostile positions. But clients abandon their usual providers only when the latter no longer have much to offer and the degree of loyalty is insufficiently strong to convince them to maintain their confidence even in times of distress. The flame of popular support for fascism had been fed by the myth of a "proletarian nation," a myth based materially on the promise—often implicit—of greater well-being for all. So, from the moment when the regime proved that it was incapable of keeping this promise, the investment of confidence it had benefited from shifted inevitably toward those who seemed better placed to fill this expectant void, thus the "massive phenomenon of servility and transformism" that Galli della Loggia perceived in "the comportment of many of the bourgeois and the petits-bourgeois."[32] Another chapter in Italian transformism had come to a close.

Chapter 18

A Country of Limited Sovereignty

A Geopolitical Capital Up for Bid

According to Sergio Romano, "the founding ideology of the Italian republic" was built on "a lie": that Italy had not lost the war. It was a lie, he said, meant to help the country repair its damaged collective conscience, by offering a comfortable alibi to divert it from its *"Schuldfrage,"* the question of its responsibilities. The alibi, Romano continued, was built on a colossal political bargain: The masses, who not so long before were still acclaiming Mussolini, would agree to be governed by the anti-Fascists so long as the latter would drop any demand for an accounting of their behavior during the preceding quarter century.[1] Romano's thesis is more than plausible, but also consider this: one aspect of this bargain was the extraordinary indulgence with which the anti-Fascists in power treated the Fascists whose places they had taken.

On June 22, 1946, Justice Minister Palmiro Togliatti, leader of the Italian Communist Party (PCI), signed an amnesty decree that freed some ten thousand Fascists, including some who were guilty of torture or massacres, of denouncing others to the police, and of collaborating in the hunt for Jews.[2] After the early and sometimes blind acts of vengeance in the first days after the Germans' hasty retreat, the ostensible "purge" almost did not happen. When trials were held, the largest number of suspects possible were freed. Paul Ginsborg calculated that as late as 1960, 62 of 64 prefects had had public responsibilities under the Fascists, as had all 135 police prefects and 139 subprefects.[3]

In its first decades of existence, the anti-Fascist republic retained the legal codes, the norms, the institutions, the public administration, the civil servants, and the teachers that had been created, educated, and recruited under fascism. This phenomenon, known as "state continuity,"[4] also involved the continuity of a number of state organs or state-related organs created under Mussolini's dictatorship. Even among the political parties there was a certain continuity: Giorgio Galli calculated that the total percentage of Italians belonging to all the anti-Fascist parties after the war (12 percent) corresponded roughly to the number of Fascist Party members immediately before the war.

Official ideology, established in the constitution, was that there had been a rupture with the past, yet the daily practical experience of the general population was one of continuity. This can only be considered a paradox by those who genuinely believed in the "anti-Fascist revolution," or in those, like Benedetto Croce, who believed that fascism was a kind of brief interlude, foreign to Italian history and tradition. For others, who believed that there was never a real social or economic break between the Fascist and post-Fascist periods, "state continuity" was never a surprise.

This gap between reality and the way it is represented made it harder to build any sort of identity or idea of a nation, as Galli della Loggia emphasizes.[5] But was there ever really a desire for such an identity?

The ruling Italian class never saw a lack of concern toward the fatherland as an entirely negative thing. Along with the "fiction" of a "Republic born from the Resistance" and therefore victorious, the absence of a well-defined and declared national interest made it possible to present Italy on the international scene as open to all possibilities. As Sergio Romano writes, the war had cost Italy everything, except its "geopolitical capital."[6] When De Gasperi insisted, on August 10, 1946, at the Paris Peace Conference, on the "meta-national" inspiration of the new Italian leaders—"the humanitarian aspirations of Mazzini, the universalist concepts of Christianity, and the internationalist hopes of the workers"[7]—he was demonstrating this broad readiness to make the country's geopolitical capital available to the highest bidder.

The "clericalization" of Italian political life also pointed it toward "denationalization." The Church and its theoreticians knew that Catholicism in Italy—unlike in Poland or Ireland—had not been a force for national cohesion. The Poles and the Irish, surrounded and oppressed by non-Catholic nations, had made religious identity the distinctive sign of their very right to exist. Nothing comparable has ever happened in Italy, all of whose neighbors are Catholic and which has never been oppressed, in modern history, by any but Catholic powers. Thus, on the Italian side, the equation between Catholicism and Italianity suggested an availability and an openness to universalism, to use the Catholic vocabulary, or to the pursuit of new ties for the Italian national interest, to use the "realist" terminology.

With the end of the war, Europe became the other pole of availability. A European sensibility—which one can view as a desire to dilute Italy in a vast continental whole—was seen even in the late 1910s, when Fiat president Giovanni Agnelli and the free-trader economist Attilio Cabiati drew up a plan for a federal Europe.[8] But when it became clear that Italy needed Europe more than Europe needed Italy, Prime Minister De Gasperi and Foreign Minister Carlo Sforza became the most fervent advocates of continental unification. According to Sergio Romano, this choice presented the dual advantage of salving national injuries by offering the prospect of a larger European nation of which Italy would be the precursor, even while putting all European countries on the same starting line, erasing the distinction between victors and vanquished.[9]

But while the vision of a united Europe was being raised, other identity stand-ins were making an impression on Italians' collective consciences. Above all was that embodied by the American dream.

The Fictions of a Republic

In a small book devoted to Alcide De Gasperi, Giulio Andreotti repeats no fewer than six times that the fundamental reason for the governmental alliance with the PCI lay in the desire, first, to obtain better conditions for the peace and, once that hope was shattered, in the need to share the burdens of the treaty.[10]

The internal debate on the conditions imposed on Italy at war's end is the last explicit defense of a national interest before the "rediscovery" of the 1990s. One explanation for the lurch in this direction is that for once—perhaps for the only time in decades—the entirety of the Italian ruling class was expressing a common will on the international scene *different* from that of its allies of the moment.

Although the capitulation signed on September 3, 1943, was "unconditional," De Gasperi—and with him the whole of the ruling class—maintained the illusion of being able to gain negotiating leverage by raising the role of the Resistance and of the monarchist government's participation alongside the Allies as the war wound down. Foreign Minister Sforza clearly illustrated this ruling-class state of mind when he declared that he felt "a right, given the role played in the war of liberation, and given the real demands of the country, to expect a revision of the diktat."[11] When De Gasperi and Sforza were forced to drop this attempt, they embraced a new strategy: exploiting the divergences between the victorious powers. For this strategy, national identity was superfluous, even deleterious, and a low profile was a must.

A leader of the war of liberation, Vittorio Foa, wrote that the "most profound sense of the Resistance" lay precisely in the need to regain a national identity.[12] Still, the Resistance was unable to give birth to real national sentiment among the Italian people. The very notion of national feeling, as we have seen, had been monopolized by the Fascists, so it carried an almost direct identification with a regime from which the Italians wanted quickly to distance themselves. Furthermore, the Resistance was far from being a mass movement.[13] And finally, among many Resistance fighters, the "need to find a national identity" was hardly the decisive motive for involvement.

The only real mass movement to arise during the war was that of the strikes of March 1943 and March 1944, which mobilized several hundreds of thousands of workers (more than three hundred thousand in the province of Milan alone). This movement certainly had a real impact in giving birth to the Resistance, for the German repression of 1944—two thousand workers were deported—had urgently raised the question of the military defense of the strikes and of the clandestine nature of their organization; but in this movement, trade-union and class considerations outweighed those of a "national" or "patriotic" character. The PCI, thanks to its organizational strength and political homogeneity, subsequently managed to establish hegemony over the workers movement, channeling it toward national objectives in the explicit goal of "assuring Italy a position of strength at the peace table."[14] It was thus that the myth of the Resistance as a "founder" of republican values began to emerge.

The real motivations of the strikers of 1943 and 1944 were cast aside once the season of "national unity" had arrived. For a very long time, silence prevailed about the fact that most of the young people who had embraced the armed anti-Fascist struggle had been pushed to do so only when the battle front drew nearer, and by the decree of the Fascist republic of the north condemning to death those draft dodgers born in 1922 through 1925.

The country, divided in two, also gave rise to at least two opposed nationalisms, each following the traditional reflex that there is no Italian nation without a foreign "godfather": a "German" nationalism on the one side, and a "Russian" and an "American" nationalisms on the other. Naturally the first condition for these three nationalisms to exist was the rejection of any national legitimacy of the other, even the accusation—well-founded in both cases—that the "enemy" was at the service of one or several foreign powers. The abolition for decades of the phrase "civil war" to describe the period from 1943 to 1945 stemmed from the necessity, for the victors, to consider the vanquished (in this case, the Fascists) as foreigners to the civil community in order to promote themselves to the rank of the one and true Italian nation.

The staging of this "new" anti-Fascist Italy, which expected "a revision of the diktat," coincided with the drafting of the republican constitution. This document thus reflected the major themes of the alliance among the "great popular forces." Once the peace treaty had been signed, and in the climate that developed after 1948, the tie was no longer antifascism, but anticommunism. While the Fascists were largely set free, in the years after 1948 the Communist Party witnessed among its numbers 48 deaths, 73,000 arrests, and 15,000 sentencings for a total of 7,598 years in prison, according to Walter Barberis.[15] This new reality, added Galli della Loggia, sparked a sort of constitutional short circuit for, while the constitution derived its legitimacy from antifascism, the actual political system found its own in anticommunism.[16] This short circuit did not lead to political schizophrenia, only because the norms provided for by the constitution were largely side-stepped; nor did this lead to the sort of "constitutional patriotism"[17] that Jürgen Habermas describes, and even less to an American-style "constitutional faith." Indeed, it was precisely thanks to the absence of "patriotism" that Italy was able to regain, at times surreptitiously, an important place among the "concert of nations."

The End of Italian Parties

With fascism and the war in the past, Italy, in the striking phrase of Sergio Romano, was "saved by its enemies,"[18] first of all its international enemies. The treaty of 1947 was tough, it was said, but extraordinarily indulgent when compared to the fate reserved for Germany and Japan. Then came its internal enemies. The Catholics, the Socialists, and the Communists, foreigners all to *Risorgimental* tradition, were better qualified to take on the management of Italy's third incarnation because they had played no major role in leading the first two, saving them any major responsibility for both debacles.

The Catholics and Stalinists had been trained in the national spirit in foreign schools, the former in the school of the Church's universalism, and the latter in that of Russian nationalism. It is not quite accurate, however, to describe the

Christian Democratic Party or the Communist Party of Italy, respectively, as the "Vatican party" or the "Russian party." In his book on "the death of the fatherland," Galli della Loggia describes the PCI's politics of this period as being at times "anti-Italian"[19] and at others "nationalist."[20] In truth—Galli della Loggia himself points this out—the two terms were not in contradiction, since all of Italian political life from 1943 to 1947 was modeled "under the influence of a decisive factor: Italy's total subordination to foreigners, to *lots* of foreigners."[21]

Since unification, Italian politics has always been essentially "hetero-directed," even when the noise of nationalist rhetoric was deafening.[22] After the debacle of 1943 to 1945, anyone who might have attempted to govern the country could not possibly have followed a purely nationalism-inspired policy. The "national unity" of the anti-Fascist parties was the concrete form taken by the alliance between those parties "inspired," directly or indirectly, by the international anti-German coalition: the Christian Democrats and the Partito d'Azione (Action Party) by the Americans, the liberals and monarchists by the British, the Communists and Socialists by the Russians.[23] A shrewd observer, Giuseppe de Luca, wrote in 1946 that it was henceforth impossible to "speak in Italy of an 'Italian' political life, that is, one of Italian inspiration, Italian content, and with Italian finalities, and thus one cannot speak, in the same sense, of 'Italian' political parties—one has to speak of political parties 'in Italy.'"[24]

Nonetheless, for the foreign influence—whether Anglo-American, German, or Russian—to translate into concrete policy in Italy, it was indispensable that the intermediaries have real Italian roots and truly represent Italian interests. Thus the ability to embody the complex dialectic between national and antinational (or, more precisely, between Italy's national interest and that of another country) became a necessary condition for any political approach hoping to play a role in reconstruction.

The British had decided to rely on an institution—the monarchy—that was certainly popular, but irremediably compromised with the fallen regime. Yet they failed, not because they had bet on a lame horse, but because they could no longer punch their weight, in Italy as elsewhere, against the American ally. The United States, with all its economic and military dominance, was able to show greater flexibility and pragmatism in its choice of political agents, all the more so since, unlike London, Washington had begun only very late in the game to take a positive interest in the geopolitical capital of the peninsula.

The Americans did not cast their attention immediately on the Christian Democrats[25]—who were virtually nonexistent in 1943—but on the "liberal" wing of the Action Party. They would turn to the party of De Gasperi only after he was able to prove, through electoral results, that he enjoyed ample popular backing. Meantime, the Christian Democrats' transformation into an "American party" (or better, a "national-American party") would be completed only between the elections of April 1948 and Italy's adherence to the Atlantic Pact, a year later, after the final settling of scores with the party's neutralist and nationalist left wing.

As for the Communist Party, its evolution followed an inverse path. From an exclusively "Russian" party, it transformed itself progressively into a national party (better still, "Russo-national") beginning with the 7th Congress of the Komintern, in 1935, where Togliatti was one of the protagonists. Until then, the national sections of Moscow Central served merely as annexes or substitutes for the Soviet Embassy; politically, they were isolated in each country, just as the Soviet Union was isolated internationally. The USSR's orientation, as we know, changed 180 degrees after Hitler's first foreign policy moves. Thus, in its introductory report to the 1935 congress, the secretary of the Komintern Georgi Dimitrov extolled the alliance between the working class "and the strata of the urban and rural petite bourgeoisie," the "respect for democratic conquests" and the "respect for national sentiments."[26]

Upon his return to Italy in 1944, Togliatti announced his intention to "take up the flag of national interests that fascism has dragged through the mud and betrayed."[27] Thus the policy of "national unity" was, from the Italian Communist Party's viewpoint, the synthesis by which Togliatti attempted to combine Soviet interests with those of the ruling Italian class, which faced the need to reestablish credibility after the country's downfall under fascism. The PCI became "national" because the interests of the USSR demanded it. It should come as no surprise that, each time Italian national interests came into conflict with the national interests of Russia, the party chose Moscow without hesitation. But nor should it be surprising if, once it had become the permanent representative of certain national interests, it dared, with time, to take a certain distance, mainly verbally, from Moscow.

The party of Togliatti lost any hope of representing the "general interests of the country" when it conformed to the Kremlin's directives against accepting Marshall Plan assistance, confirming yet again that the real difficulty in Italy was not that of being a servant to two masters, but rather of being a servant to the right masters.

The National Vatican Party

On September 16, 1929, barely eight months after the signing of the Concordat, Pius XI declared to ecclesiastical members of Catholic Action: "The day will come when we will have need of reliable men, unquestionably honest, and we will think of you again."[28] Despite the ecclesiastical hierarchy's "cordial relations, infused by a spirit of collaboration"[29] with the Fascist regime—as the Catholic historian Arturo Carlo Jemolo describes it—the hierarchy was already thinking and operating with an eye to the future.

Under fascism, the Church always fiercely defended the prerogatives of Catholic Action and other movements linked to it. Its imperative was to preserve the relative autonomy of structures that would allow it to form an independent ruling class, capable, if need be, of replacing the ruling class of the regime. Yet its capacity to remain independent and meticulously prepare the political personnel for a postfascism era, while a necessary condition, was not sufficient to make it the dominant force after the war, let alone to give Italy what Jemolo calls "the cachet of a clerical state."[30]

The Christian Democrats, whose first cadres were largely men who had started out with Catholic Action,[31] were not the only "mass party" of the time. This element alone does not explain why it was the Church that left such a mark on the state. Other factors played a role, above all the popularity of the Church itself.

The point of departure has to be the vast process of societal dislocation brought by war and then defeat. No possibility of a radical social transformation was there to offer the Italians hope, as had been the case during the Great War. This time, too, the Italians were deprived of any "institutional" prospects—of being able, at least potentially, to resort to some trustworthy authority. The state having dissolved itself at the moment of capitulation, on September 8, 1943, ordinary people had to attend to the most urgent matters first, to rebuild connections by turning first to what was nearest at hand for immediate support. The collective tragedy had laid bare a survival instinct that, in normal conditions, is the most private of matters. Other than the few tens of thousands of people taking orders from one of the five authorities disputing control of the peninsula,[32] the great mass of Italians lived a sad and isolated reality of "every man for himself." In this shipwreck, the Catholic Church, the only surviving institution, found itself playing the role of "*defensor civitatis*," rather like during the time of the fall of the Roman Empire, as the secular historian Federico Chabod puts it.[33]

The Church's capacity to exert both civil and institutional authority reinforced its moral authority. But while that alone might have explained its enormous influence, other factors were at play. For example, the identification of ordinary people with the Church could only be strengthened by the common desire to forget the many compromises, large and small, that had been made with the fallen regime; the ordinary people could measure their chances to do so with the successes of the Church. Its close relationship with the peasant world was another major factor, especially in a country where the population was still largely rural. Then, too, a part of the dominant class that was preparing, by force or persuasion, for a regime change wanted to avoid having the new power be dominated by "revolutionary" forces; the Church wanted the same. Finally, the Allies—the true masters of the situation in Italy—were searching for an anti-Fascist power that met these very same criteria.

Starting in the second half of the 1940s, the Church permeated Italian society, influencing the lives of the entire population, independently of individuals' religious or political convictions. Religious authorities intervened directly in numerous decisions affecting public life. They were invited to every ceremony—from the annual report of the Banca d'Italia to the distribution of vaccines in the schools—and, in exchange, organized virtually obligatory religious services in the ministries and in every public establishment. They often had the last word on appointments to public office, and nearly always on any new law or proposal. They controlled school texts, censorship of movies, theater, radio, and later television, with the repressive organs of the state such as the police, the carabinieri, and magistrates keeping close watch to ensure respect for morals and the "common sense of modesty."[34]

Although it was largely the effect of a well-prepared *reconquista* strategy, this strength of the Church also reflected the weakness of the ruling Italian class and its traditional inability to define the contours of the "national interest," an inability aggravated in the early postwar years by the severe constraints of an utterly unfavorable international situation. The Christian Democrats were able to become the pivotal party of Italian politics for more than forty-five years not because they bent, purely and simply, to the will of the Church, but because they knew how to combine its interests with the need of the major part of the productive bourgeoisie for a spokesman within the state after the military defeat.

For De Gasperi, Christian democracy was supposed to be only one branch of the Church's more global strategy of intervention in all of Italian society and, as he himself wrote, "the proper organizational tool to act on a single sector of society, the state."[35] The party's left wing, headed by Giuseppe Dossetti, more responsive to the *desiderata* of Pius XII, believed, on the other hand, that the Christian Democrats were called to mold civil society such that it would conform to the "substantial values of Christianity."[36] While the Christian Democratic left dreamed of a corporatist recomposition of social conflicts, De Gasperi and his colleagues threw a lifeline to the petite bourgeoisie, still shaken by the recent catastrophe, by guaranteeing it the same protection against inflation that Mussolini had guaranteed with the "battle for quota 90."[37] At the same time, they explicitly invited the haute bourgeoisie—the "fourth party"[38]—to take a place within the government.

Even as it worked to represent in its own councils the most diverse interests and to serve as their mediator, the Christian Democratic Party was above all a "northern" party and, more particularly, the party of the industrial triangle (Milan, Turin, Genoa), as illustrated by its deep electoral and organizational roots. In the elections of 1946, while obtaining a nationwide average of 35.2 percent of the vote, the party won 37.3 percent in the north, 30 percent in the center, and 35 percent in the south. As for its members, 54.3 percent were in the north (of which 34.7 percent in the northwest), 16 percent in the center, 22.6 percent in the south, and 7 percent in the islands. In the National Center (the Christian Democrats' "central committee") that arose from the First Congress, one-third of the members came from the industrial triangle alone. The closer one came to the ruling bodies, the more evident was the influence of the northern industrialized regions.[39]

For the party to succeed, it had, above all, to avoid giving in to the "totalitarian temptation" suggested by the Vatican and the party's left wing. De Gasperi knew, Andreotti asserts, "that a party that attains 50% of the vote carries within it very profound contradictions."[40] He knew, as noted earlier, that if all major interests are forced to seek representation within a single political envelope, they will inevitably end up locked in paralysis or, at a minimum, face extremely laborious dialectical confrontations, a major problem for fascism.[41] As Andreotti put it, De Gasperi understood that "if a general synthesis was not possible," it was necessary to try "to obtain at least partial syntheses."[42]

"The sole party of the bourgeoisie," functioning by "partial syntheses," was thus reconstituted, and Christian Democratic transformism reproduced even the external forms of the transformist regimes that had preceded it. This situation, born of the necessity always to have recourse to "partial syntheses," led to the conviction that, whatever happened, the search for a "general synthesis" had become impossible, if not superfluous.

Chapter 19

Identity and Development

The Mythical Transfiguration of Italian Backwardness

In the late 1920s, Italian intellectuals found themselves caught up in a debate that seemed to mirror Italian backwardness. On one side was the *Strapaese* faction, representing a supposed "plebeian tradition" of Italian culture rooted in the values of small towns and the countryside; on the other side was the *Stracittà* faction, which published the French-language journal *900* and urged receptivity to recent international cultural productions.

Stracittà—which embodied the transition between the declining influence of French culture and the rise of American cultural influence—reflected a cosmopolitan aspiration to maintain contact with modernity's leading edge, if only in the artistic domain. *Strapaese* was suspicious of progress, industry, and urban life in general, indeed of all that sociologists mean by "modernity." Curzio Malaparte—one of the group's most eminent members, along with Leo Longanesi and Mino Maccari—summed up its message this way: "Italians are unfit to become modern."[1]

Strapaese might be the most explicit example of what Bollati calls the "Italian Sturm und Drang against modern civilization,"[2] of the opposition mounted since unification by intellectuals, the Church, the political class, and, sometimes, industrialists themselves. Some observers attribute the "molecularity of the collective behavior" of Italians precisely to this will to oppose the national conscience and "modernization."[3]

Fascism's intrinsic limit had been that it represented an overly bottom-heavy synthesis of the Italian bourgeoisie's interests. In seeking to make Italy a great power even while "ruralizing" it, Mussolini's regime was plunging unstoppably toward catastrophe. This "bottom-heavy imbalance" was ideological as well: *Strapaese* was a sort of cultural guarantee of the regime's "Catonist" ideology (which saw the peasant as a savior of the nation), a mythical transfiguration of Italian backwardness, brandishing it as a sign of rigor and virtuous frugality, and aiming to give value to the very modest social ascension of the petite bourgeoisie. To tame its mass base, fascism had to improve the people's material well-being, but the country's real conditions being what they were, frugality had to be made a virtue. Thus the slogans warning against the "comfortable life" coincided with the sugary mirages of the *Telefoni bianchi* and the *Mille lire al mese*.[4]

The dominant political cultures of the postwar period, the Catholic and the Stalinist, were more coherent. Any trend toward consumerism was liable to eat into their power bases. The Church saw the attack as direct, for development and affluence tend to undermine two pillars of its influence: rural life and the family. For the Italian Communist Party (PCI), rooted in a zone where social migration occurred mainly within the petite bourgeoisie (between country dwellers, cooperatives, craftsmen, and small businesses), the direct effects were probably less immediate, but noticeable nonetheless in a growing disaffection for militant political life. So both sides based their prescriptions on the precepts of temperance and abstinence, tinted with a hatred of change built around the presumed "authenticity" of Italian life and tastes.

In a 1946 speech, Pius XII underlined the link between the defense of "authentic rural civilization" and the possibility of perpetuating values like "work, simplicity, purity of life, and respect for authority," without which life would lose its meaning and be transformed into an "unbridled pursuit of personal gain."[5] That same year, the Christian Democrats' secretary (and minister of education), Guido Gonella, depicted modern civilization, and radio in particular, as "an invisible and silent atomic bomb that has torn the family apart."[6] The PCI, not wanting to be left behind, contrasted the hypocrisy of the "bourgeois family" to the "greater modesty and simplicity" of the Soviet-style "Socialist family,"[7] and the Union of Italian Women (UDI), one of the party's "mass" organizations, made the "happy family" the theme of its national congress in 1947.[8] In December 1950, an article in the PCI's youth monthly vehemently condemned the publication in Italy of a review titled "Sexual Digest," with its "disgusting" and "obscene" articles of "evident American origin" and full of "psychoanalytical vocabulary."[9] The Catholics, for their part, did not limit themselves to verbal condemnation: the Central Bureau for Cinematography, headed by Giulio Andreotti and then by Oscar Luigi Scalfaro, provided detailed judgments on what was licit and what was illicit, "advising against," for example, the projection of "scenes likely to excite the senses, such as of kisses or of prolonged and sensual embraces."[10]

These attitudes were the ideological and political mirror of the concerns felt by social classes that had just learned from the Fascist regime that when one toys with the existing equilibrium, immense catastrophes can result.

Republican Transformism

According to Guido Carli, the postunification economic world of Italy harbored both a minority of people open to the world and a majority of "animal spirits" intent on protecting their own immediate interests and fearful of the risks that even their own development might involve.[11] Immediately after World War II, Carli continues, these "animal spirits" rematerialized in those who opposed liberalization and sought a return to the "tranquillizing cocoon of corporative society."[12] In 1945, before the Economic Commission of the Constituent Assembly, Angelo

Costa, the head of the Italian industrialists' union, asserted that big industry in Italy was "against nature." And Gaetano Marzotto, who led the largest garment-making group, even declared that it was necessary to "take a step backwards," because big industry undermined the true character of Italian production, which could never really go beyond the stage of "grand craftmanship."[13]

It is difficult to know whether the major postwar parties represented the interests of small producers and small distributors because of their "antimodern" sensibility or whether, to the contrary, they ended up embracing the *Strapaesane* reservations because of the ideological influence of their social reference classes. Regardless, even while promoting the trend toward a vast economic state network, these parties worked first of all to defend the petit-bourgeois interests they had protected since their birth.

The ideological and political inertia of the PCI and the Christian Democrats were doubtless provoked as well by the international division of labor as well as by their dependence on, respectively, the Soviet Union and the Catholic Church. Moreover, the PCI, by its defense of rural- and village-based national traditions that it said were threatened by "monopolies," the "market," and "America," cut itself off culturally from any chance of becoming the sort of social-democratic labor party that could usefully have contributed, as Gianni Agnelli put it, to a "clarification of Italian political life."[14] The Christian Democrats, for their part, drew on governmental connections to do everything possible to deter the increasing concentration of production and distribution and to open the public administration's doors to some victims of these processes.

To slow a massive rural exodus,[15] a series of laws and decrees were approved beginning in 1948 to facilitate land purchases, so much so that by 1956, some 1.4 million hectares had passed into the hands of small farmers. The number of craftsmen remained stable from 1951 to 1971 and, because of the legislative obstacles to opening supermarkets[16]—the first of them arrived in Milan in 1957—the number of small businessmen actually rose, from 1.35 million to 1.7 million. In 1971, 8.7 percent of the working Italian population consisted of shop owners, compared to 6.6 percent in France (in 1968) and 2.2 percent in Great Britain (in 1966).

The presence of civil servants in the overall workforce grew in direct proportion to the rural exodus, rising in the 1951 to 1971 period from 4.6 percent to 8.1 percent.[17] And then there were the *enti pubblici*—bodies attached to the executive and created to fulfill temporary missions, but often serving to do little more than distribute revenues. They numbered 44,500 in the 1960s, and 70 percent of the public funds allocated to them ended up paying salaries.[18]

The production of such "artificial middle classes," as Lanaro called them,[19] is one form that transformism assumed in its republican version. The PCI, while in the opposition, not only did not seek to block legislation in this direction, but often contributed to it, and decisively so. Most of the laws, and particularly those concerning the sorts of interests we have just discussed, were approved in parliamentary commissions sitting during legislative sessions where each group's vote is distinguishable only over the long term. Thus, according to Musella's review of all votes, the PCI took positions against the majority one time in three in the first legislature, one time in seven in the second, one time in sixteen in the third, and one time in six in the fourth and the fifth.[20]

The constitutional expert Giuseppe Maranini, in 1967, described the republican parliament as "a sort of echo chamber of contracts that had been ratified elsewhere," contracts "between small and mediocre feudal systems, and sometimes between minuscule groups, even individuals; minor contracts which, through the quasi-secret legislative actions of the commissions led to disorder, immorality and incoherence."[21] The description might rather easily have applied to the epochs of Depretis, Crispi, and Giolitti, and it anticipated by exactly twenty-five years the chorus of indignation that arose upon the "discovery," early in the 1990s, of the existence of these mechanisms upon which Italian transformism has resided since the beginning.

The American Dream

Italian culture, up to the early twentieth century, had been a phenomenon of "French provincialism," as Gramsci put it. One might also suggest that during that same century it gradually became a phenomenon of "American provincialism." This again was a question of the absence of a "center" or of a native identity with well-defined contours shared by the entire national community. This vacuum has always been filled by themes, symbols, and even objects from abroad, seasoned to the different tastes found on the peninsula.

During the 1950s, according to Stephen Gundle, Italy was the most receptive country in Europe to American cultural offerings.[22] This trend had begun in the 1930s when intellectuals and part of the petite bourgeoisie began seeing everything American as the fulfillment of their unrequited desires. Fascist voluntarism had bet on what we might call welfare nationalization, but the country's structural weaknesses yielded the opposite of what was intended: the Fascists fanned the growing appetites of the new middle class without being able to satisfy them. Thus Italians welcomed the American "liberators" with wide-open arms because, if they could not drink from the well of affluence, they could watch as its representatives debarked on their shores.

To better respond to the curiosities born during the 1930s, the publisher Valentino Bompiani, in 1938, asked Elio Vittorini to undertake an anthology of the translated works of American authors. Italian writers as important as Eugenio Montale, Alberto Moravia, Guido Piovene, Cesare Pavese, Giansiro Ferrata, and Fernanda Pivano worked on the project, and it led to the publication in 1941 of the book *Americana*, which included texts by Nathaniel Hawthorne, Edgar Allan Poe, Mark Twain, William Faulkner, Ernest Hemingway, Erskine Caldwell, William Saroyan, Herman Melville, and others. Unfortunately, the year was not a propitious one for the celebration of Italian-American friendship, and the publication was sequestered. Nevertheless, *Americana* embodied the hopes and expectations of a generation whose mores, as Corrado Alvaro wrote later, were no longer Italian, "but a mixture of behaviors derived—à l'italienne—from the books, movies, theater, and magazines of the richest and freest of countries, America and England."[23]

In reality, for the American way of life—which intellectuals knew through direct experience, or more often, through their readings—to become a widely shared myth in the peninsula, Italians would have to wait for direct contact with its themes, symbols, and objects, first through the American Army, then through the liberalization of markets. Confidence in the illusory opulence of fascism had to dissipate, as it did through the disaster of war and through the moral and material misery that followed.

America again became the promised land, as it had been for the five million Italians who disembarked at Ellis Island between 1880 and 1950. This time, however, there was a secret hope that "America" could be achieved in Italy. The first step was the imitation of the model, beginning with writers who took inspiration from the dry, fleshless prose of the generation represented in *Americana*, and including the more naively and superficially "Americanizing" behavior gently mocked in a film like Steno's 1954 *Un americano a Roma* with Alberto Sordi, or in Renato Carosone's famous 1956 song *Tu vuò fa' l'americano* ("You want to act as an American", words in Neapolitan, but with a rock 'n' roll rhythm).

The symbols and objects that Italians found so tempting were not just chewing gum or Carosone's "whisky and soda." Nor was it simply the representations of American life contained in the 5,368 films to cross the ocean from 1945 to 1953. It was above all the dollars and the massive assistance to arrive first through the United Nations Relief and Rehabilitation Administration (UNRRA) and then through the European Recovery Program, better known as the Marshall Plan. In 1946 the UNRRA, created in November 1943, had already contributed $450 million to Italy, providing 70 percent of its food aid, 40 percent of its coal, 82 percent of its agricultural equipment, 22 percent of its industrial equipment, and 100 percent of its medical supplies. Between April 3, 1948, and June 30, 1952, the Marshall Plan poured into the peninsula $1.5 billion—80 percent of it in goods and 20 percent as credits—or 11.3 percent of all aid sent to Europe. It was less than the $3.18 billion allocated to Great Britain or the $2.71 billion provided to France, but more than the $1.39 billion for Germany. In any case, the sums were colossal, given the situation on the peninsula.

This manna was not destined for clearly defined uses, and the Americans debated whether the conditions placed on it were appropriately restrictive. Nonetheless, the Marshall Plan—which boosted gross domestic product (GDP) by 2 percent over four years—made it possible to import the wheat and coal the country badly needed, to plug the holes in public finances and stabilize the lira, to modernize industrial infrastructure, to intervene in the *Mezzogiorno*, and to decisively boost the reconstruction of civilian structures. In particular, the equivalent amount of 390 million euros were destined for the construction of 75,000 new housing units; 480 million for the reconstruction of 450,000 dwellings damaged in the war; and 130 million to finance thirty-year, fixed-rate loans (at 4 percent interest) for the purchase of 350,000 new apartments.[24]

If one considers that the bombardment of Milan left 230,000 people (one-third of the population) homeless in the month of August 1943 alone, one realizes the size of the gap between the people's needs and the aid offered. Psychologically, however, it had a resounding effect. The Americans not only helped end the war, but now they were "offering" help with reconstruction. Needless to say, in the people's eyes the responsibility for the damage and destruction lay entirely with the Fascists and the Germans. Much of the population also appreciated the Americans as the major reason the country had not fallen into Communist hands.

Thanks to the example from the other side of the ocean, Italians began to believe that frugality was not, after all, their unavoidable destiny. People even began to see a connection between the "five meals a day" that the Fascists had asserted that the British indulged in[25]—and that the Fascists ritually denounced—and the hegemony that first Great Britain and later the United States had managed to impose on the world.

But for the Church and for the PCI, the "American dream" presented a threat. For Togliatti's party, hostility toward consumerism was reinforced by the political and cultural anti-Americanism flowing from Moscow's new line in the autumn of 1947. Thus, for ten years, through obeisance to the mother party, the PCI marginalized itself. Even while it accentuated its patriotic rhetoric, it fiercely opposed the Marshall Plan and the Atlantic Pact—the two initiatives that gave Italy both the oxygen for reconstruction and the international political context in which to resume business dealings interrupted by war.

This "anti-imperialist" orientation, with its nationalist, populist character, was not unknown in Catholic circles either, particularly by those most attuned to Vatican sensibilities. Those who had done ideological battle with fascism could not stand idly by while what they considered the Trojan horse of secularization and the "unbridled pursuit of profit" penetrated the fortress of Catholicism. But the Christian Democrats, by fair means or foul, had to consider international political imperatives, and De Gasperi, more by fair means than foul, tried to preserve for Italy its room for negotiation and autonomous initiatives. This would play an important role in the years to come.

Despite the massive influence of the Church and the PCI, however, public opinion felt the persistent lure of the American way of life until the new European myth finally began to take hold in the last decade of the twentieth century. That does not mean that other traditional benchmarks had been abandoned: one could devote oneself to the magic rituals of fecundity[26] even while coveting the real or imagined affluence seen in American films. It was a case of "the slum dwellers who had managed to buy a television," as Pasolini complained in 1963. Long after the era of "modernization" opened, it cohabited with lifestyles and ideologies rooted in a long-ago past.

In these "slums," it was the native Italian elements—the hyperlocal nature of the "thousand bell towers"—that divided the inhabitants of the peninsula, while what united them in common hope for a better life were the elements imported from abroad. While the absence of a "center" fed into all the particularities of the outlying areas, popular acculturation was based on models borrowed from the United States.[27]

Later, when the "modernity" that some had tried to neutralize took its revenge, assuming "the resounding form of an immoderate and unstoppable bulimia,"[28] what seemed to be the realization of the American dream emerged as a new model of social integration—the social integration that the national ruling classes had never managed to achieve.

Chapter 20

The Failure of "Democratic Nationalization"

The Shameful Abandonment of Frugality

When mass consumption shifted for the Italians from aspiration to satiation, they gradually began to shrug off the pedagogical grip of the two dominant cultures that found cause for present temperance in the promise of future ethereal happiness. This involved not a peaceful, linear transition, but rather a series of profound upheavals provoked by what we commonly call the "economic miracle."

This phase of intense Italian economic development—generally said to have lasted from 1953 to 1973, or some say from 1958 to 1963, when average annual growth reached 6.3 percent—brought a typical succession of events. The acceleration of the rural exodus sparked by the development of industry (particularly mechanical and chemical) lured millions of people into industrial cities, where their production contributed further to the conditions that had provoked them to abandon the countryside in the first place. In the 1961 census, industrial workers (38 percent) and those in tertiary sectors (32 percent) surpassed farm laborers (30 percent) for the first time. Internal migration in 1955 through 1971 involved nearly one-third of the population, with 9,140,000 people leaving their regions of origin for good. Between 1951 and 1967 the population of Rome rose from 1.65 million to 2.6 million, that of Milan from 1.27 million to 1.68 million; and that of Turin from 719,000 to 1.12 million. Coinciding with these internal movements were the migrations out of Italy of 956,458 people from 1959 to 1968. For the first time, Italy found itself confronting a series of problems linked to immigration and urbanization.

One characteristic of the unequal development that occurs amid accelerating growth was the coexistence of profound social difficulties—many people experienced a clear degradation in their quality of life—with increasing consumption. Thus in the same years when immigrant families were piling four or five to a room in subdivided apartments in central Turin's basements or attics; when infant mortality began rising again and public schools had to operate two or three shifts a day; when manifestations of racism became more frequent and apartments were often not rented to southerners,[1] in these same years per-capita income rose in

Italy more rapidly than in any other European country but Germany: 3.7 times more than in France and 4.2 times more than in Great Britain.

The first "revolution" in Italians' lives was the daily presence of meat on their tables. Once this stage had been reached, everything became simpler and priorities started to change. The physical benefits of durable consumption constituted a new divinity to be worshiped. In the years from 1958 to 1967, the number of families owning a television rose from 12 percent to 49 percent of the population, and of those possessing a refrigerator rose from 13 percent to 55 percent. Between 1950 and 1964, the number of private automobiles increased more than 13.5 times (from 342,000 to 4.67 million), and the number of motorcycles more than 6 times (from 700,000 to 4.30 million).

These new manifestations of wealth represented not only a material conquest but also the fulfillment of a long psychological journey. It had begun with the Mussolinian dream of Italian greatness that ultimately produced the "mass transformism" that led first to the fall of fascism and later, in the 1950s, to an impatient wait for better days. When this aspiration first evolved into a sense of concrete possibility, it was difficult to express openly, often accompanied by a sort of implied guilt, as if those who dared nourish such hopes were foreigners to a national tradition of frugality and sacrifice. Lanaro asserted that material enrichment, and the sharing of new means of expression and communication, meant an "impoverishment of the collective symbolic universe." The move to modernization and its social transformations, the "nationalization of words and of signs" of a people brought together by migration, speaking for the first time one language—that of television—all this came about without any attempt to provide any underlying meaning or value.[2]

As the country continued to develop, the ruling class and certain intellectuals retained a sense of nervous distrust regarding "modernity." The search for collective myths to make sense of material well-being gradually shifted elsewhere, beyond the political and institutional representations Italians had known. The gap between economic development, the functioning of the state apparatus, and the "collective symbolic universe" became brutally clear in the late 1960s. Lanaro speaks of 1968 as a metaphor for "the aspiration to a 'civil life' in keeping with the outsized potential of the 'economic life.'"[3] The student movements represented the demand for social mobility of the recently acculturated middle classes. This demand pointed to the material bases of a new step for transformism: a step that, having not been fulfilled with the co-optation of the ruling Socialists, would impose itself in the form of crisis thirty years later, involving the emergence of original phenomena and political personages.

Low Productivity, Low Wages

There is a close relationship between productivity, increasing revenues, and mass consumption. So long as productive activity remains essentially at a craftsman's level, productivity remains low, costs high, wages low, and the market limited. It is the rise in productivity (through technical innovation and concentration) that reduces costs and unit prices, making possible the creation of less-expensive products, as well as the payment of higher wages, which in turn stimulates the market.

And yet, weak productivity and low salaries did not prevent Italy—before World War I—from joining the fight for economic market share. But the portion of social capital destined for foreign investment was only a small part of a well of overall capital that was also small.[4] Italian imperialism drew great profits from its zones of influence when the relationship was purely economic. Afterward, at the moment of military conquest, the costs of maintaining them always surpassed the benefits and, at times, the political chaos that ensued ultimately depressed economic activity. If the Libyan War cost 1.30 billion lira, emptied the state's treasury and arsenals, and provoked the crisis of the Banco di Roma, for the Mussolinian "empire" it was worse. In Ethiopia, the destruction and the massacres of people and livestock by poison gas provoked a crisis of production and exportation, to the point that the minister of colonies, Alessandro Lessona, was forced to admit that "external trade flourished more during the time of the Negus."[5]

Fascism was certainly voluntarist, and even succeeded in putting into place the beginnings of a welfare state. But as for guaranteeing higher working-class wages, it went in the direction opposite to what Corradini described. The priority was to "nationalize" the petite bourgeoisie, with the costs paid by other sectors of society. Part of this fell on certain groups of the upper bourgeoisie, as in the case of the "battle for quota 90," but the largest part was paid by the working class. According to Sylos Labini, the policy of systematic wage reductions was a distinctive trait of fascism at that time. Up to 1940, he notes, real salaries had fallen in Italy by about 20 percent, much more than the 5 percent in Great Britain or France.[6] This reduction allowed the regime to gain the sympathy of sectors of the bourgeoisie unhappy with the "bottom-leaning synthesis," and because industrial profits were thus increased, to enlarge the shares for pensions, commerce, and taxes.

In the nascent phase of imperialism, Italy had become a favored destination for foreign investors, drawn by its generally low costs and its labor force. It drew the same sort of attention now reserved for certain former Soviet-bloc countries or Southeast Asian nations: foreign entrepreneurs established businesses or subsidiaries there or made investments there.[7] The ample availability of unskilled labor, following the massive rural exodus, helped keep wages low. The policy of salary restrictions boosted competition and helped offset other deficiencies (lack of raw materials, inadequate infrastructure, weak financial system, modest level of technological training, near-total absence of research), but it discouraged fixed investments, postponing indefinitely the solution to the structural problems linked to low productivity.

There was nothing uniquely Italian about this. The specificity lies in fascism's choice to "steer" wage policy as it had "steered" monetary policy. Thus an objective blot on development was transformed into a (subjective) virtuous choice, part of the consoling myth of the "proletarian nation."

The costs of reconstruction after World War II were also essentially paid by wage earners, who were hit by inflation (salaries fell by half in real terms during the war), the role played by trade unions in boosting the "national reconstruction," and by massive layoffs.[8] The path to liberal reconstruction taken by the parties of national unity, including the PCI,[9] resulted from the confluence of three factors: (1) international constraints, which left no alternative; (2) the traditional deficiencies of the productive system, aggravated by the war, which could be only partially offset through wage compression; and (3) the interclass character of the mass parties, which forced them to take measures that did not harm the petite bourgeoisie.

In any case, reconstruction and, later, the "economic miracle" owed much of their success to wage reductions, although such reductions were relative. Amid growth, from 1951 to 1958, of national revenue by 43.93 percent, of imports by 90.18 percent, of exports by 138.93 percent, of net investments by 118.61 percent, and in the face of an 89 percent increase in industrial production from 1953 to 1960 and of productivity by 62 percent, real salaries declined over the same period by 0.6 percent.[10] The situation changed little in the years immediately afterward: Between 1964 and 1968 the annual rate of increase of compensation per worker in industry, including employer-paid national insurance contributions, was the lowest of any country in the European Community, except for Luxembourg. In 1968 the average annual salary of Italian industrial workers was $2,000, just two-thirds of that paid to their German colleagues, a bit more than half that of the French, and less than one-quarter the average salary of American workers.[11]

Even if the largest part of new production was destined for international markets, Italy experienced a strangling effect typical of development. Growth required an enlargement of the domestic market, which necessarily required wage increases, which cut into or even canceled the competitive advantage of Italian industry. Some major entrepreneurs began to think that, in order to consolidate growth, there was an urgent need to break out of the cycle of low salaries and help new social groups enter a sphere of more mature consumption. But, as noted earlier, this option implied the need to drastically boost industrial productivity in particular, and the productivity of the system in general, by overcoming its structural deficiencies.

The transformist political operation that should have made it possible to "shake up" the Italian productive system and enlarge the social bases of democracy was the center-left. But the processes that this operation attempted to launch ended up, yet again, in failure.

The Failure of the "Great Reform"

In 1957 Amintore Fanfani, the Christian Democrats' secretary, declared that the goal of the rapprochement between his party and the Socialist Party was to "recover vast popular social strata, evidently not the conservative ones, for the democratic base of the state."[12] In these words from an architect of the "opening to the left" of the early 1960s, one sees the explicit basis for a new season of transformism. However, to fully understand this political operation—and its failure—one must look beyond a strictly Italian framework and consider the reformist dynamic of the center-left in the context of the international dynamic of the time.

From a macroeconomic viewpoint, the Italian "miracle" meant an increasing presence of "made in Italy" sales, from 2.2 percent of the world market in 1951 to

3.4 percent in 1960 and 4.6 percent in 1970. Its relative weight more than doubled in less than twenty years, causing a proportional increase in influence globally, and particularly in Europe. Italian success would not have been possible without the boost provided by the development period 1945 to 1975 (the so-called *Trente Glorieuses*, the glorious thirty) and without integration into the European market. Against a broader framework of increasing trade worldwide, the volume of merchandise destined for the five European Economic Community (EEC) partners rose twice as fast as the overall increase of exports: between 1953 and 1964, Italian production destined for Germany, France, and the Benelux countries rose from 23 percent to 40.2 percent.[13] Yet constraints increased along with benefits: Italy found itself ever more exposed to the imperatives of the market—from the prices of imported raw materials to those of exported industrial products—while its capacity to influence the latter remained limited. Thus the problems relative to levels of productivity and concentration, always the principal cause of Italy's backwardness, now presented themselves with such urgency that they could no longer be ignored without risk to the gains so recently achieved.

Because of their greater public visibility, the major groups often seem to be the only economic actors in a country, which is never the case. In the Italy of the 1960s, 95 percent of the members of the Confindustria employers association were small or very small entrepreneurs. It was from this group that the greatest resistance emerged. Since the electric monopolies took up the fight against any nationalization of the sector, a "natural" alliance formed between the employers group and the petite bourgeoisie, which had achieved its own miracle thanks to low wages and the absence of trade unions.

Late in the decade, faced with the delaying tactics and timidity of the center-left governments, some large private groups like Fiat, Pirelli, Olivetti, and a major public monopoly like ENI attempted to break this "conservative" alliance in the name of efficiency, which they now proposed as the standard of industrial management, rather than the simple pursuit of profit. These groups represented the most dynamic contingent of the Italian economy. They had had to adapt to a far greater level of competition than they had been used to and thus needed what Lucio Caracciolo referred to, in his mentioned 1994 editorial, as a "country-system" capable of supporting their penetration into external markets. Their proposals, backed by certain press organs and some important research centers, were presented in the form of a vast reformist project, both more organic and ambitious that what big capital had attempted in the aftermath of World War I. Collaboration with the trade unions was foreseen, even a convergence with them on some fundamental objectives that reached far beyond simple industrial relations: the reform of the legal code, public administration, taxation, and education systems; unification of the sanitary system; new housing legislation; and above all, a policy of investment in the *Mezzogiorno*.[14]

All these reformist recipes—particularly when combined with a policy of collaboration between the big industrial groups and the trade unions, which made wage concessions possible—provoked the inevitable hostility of the small production and small commerce sectors, which, in the short term, could only be weakened, if not destroyed, by rising productivity and the rationalization of the apparatuses of production and of the state.

The interclass nature of the political parties thus became an echo chamber for the tensions and conflicts shaking society. These tensions and conflicts interested the Christian Democratic Party in particular, because it was the political shell within which all the interests expressed themselves, confronted one another, and often ensured the failure of both sides. One protagonist of the period, the Socialist economist and minister Francesco Forte, acknowledged that it was difficult to reform certain sectors of society without attacking the Christian Democrats' electoral foundation: the small farmers organized in the all-powerful Coldiretti, the shopkeepers opposed to fiscal rigorousness and the opening of supermarkets, the bureaucracy of the state and of its parallel administrations, and so on.[15] These sectors of society were also organized and protected by other parties, though to a lesser degree: the small farmers of the left by Confagricoltura, and the left-leaning craftsmen within Confartigianato, not to mention the powerful League of the Cooperatives, a holding company directed by the PCI, whose interests often converged with those of the petite bourgeoisie.[16]

Thus many of the reforms envisaged from the beginning of the center-left experience were impeded, delayed, and finally mutilated by the resistance—manifest or covert—that parliamentary action inflicted on the stances of the various parties. When the proposed law for the election of regional councils—which the Constitution had set for 1950 at the latest—was finally presented during the legislative session of 1963, it had to pass through 231 votes in the Chamber and 825 in the Senate, involving 4,300 amendments and 600 speeches, before the legislature adjourned without an actual vote on the law. The proposal, taken up again in 1969, was finally approved in May 1970, without including a clear definition of the powers accorded the elected councils.[17] Similar difficulties hobbled the creation of the *Scuola media unica*—the unified middle school. As for the nationalization of electrical energy, seen by many as the most important, if not only, accomplishment of the center-left, it was the culmination of a process that, begun a decade earlier, led to direct or indirect state control of the greater part of Italy's most technologically advanced sectors. Those who believed that the nationalizations were "the antechamber of socialism," in the end, simply went along. The five private electricity producers operating on Italian territory, for their part, received 2.2 trillion lira in indemnities (around 18 billion euros in 2001)—of which 1.8 trillion went to Edison alone—and thus transformed themselves into new industrial and financial powers, with a debt of recognition and much closer ties to the state that had expropriated them.

The wage storm stirred up by the "hot autumn" of 1969, and the growing sense that the parties and parliament had lost control of social dynamics, fed into a last paroxysm of reformist fever in 1970 when, beyond the law on the regions, lawmakers approved a new labor law and even a law permitting divorce, the latest of thirteen proposals on the subject presented to parliament since 1852, but the first to be approved.

The law on popular referenda, also approved in 1970—so that Catholics could subject the divorce law to the people's judgment—created another instrument for bypassing the institution of parliament. The premature dissolution of the legislature in 1972, effected precisely as a means of delaying this referendum, can be considered as parliament's last feeble attempt at resistance before finally recognizing its capitulation before "civil society." The two chambers—which, during the republican period, had been stripped almost entirely of the constitutional prerogative of expressing defiance to governments—now found themselves denied their traditional role as transformist mediators of different fragmented interests. The various party factions, organizations, trade unions, economic groups, and the Church had by now learned to negotiate directly among themselves, disdaining parliamentary mediation. Governments, whose formal legitimation flows from parliament, were diminished to the point of seeming almost to disappear, as indicated by the titles of several texts published during the decade.[18] Thus opened a new phase of social fragmentation, one in which "clienteles," "counterpowers," and "surrogates," even "shadow states," waged an all-out battle that definitively wrecked the balancing system among the powers of the state.

The "Shadow States"

According to Lanaro, the real failure of the 1964 to 1970 period lay less in the incapacity of the ruling class to reform society than in the lost opportunity to achieve a "democratic nationalization," that is, a sharing of common values, "starting with the predominance of general interests over individual demands."[19]

The center-left not only was born of a loose assembly of differing desires and designs but also had encountered some tenaciously opposed interests, firmly bound to their prerogatives. In fact, what ensured the convergence of such disparate interests was, again, the low-wage policy. So long as wages remained moderate, the "programmation"—this magic word of the center-left—could be seen as an attempt to channel, to tone down, or to dilute the disturbing effects of accelerating global development on Italian society. Urbanization and full employment had sparked a rise in consumption that, though moderate, had enlarged demand in the marketplace. Because the generally low productivity of the Italian system—in particular in agriculture and commerce—were unable to fulfill the new demands, the only way to satisfy consumers was to increase imports. When, as early as 1953, the governor of the Bank of Italy Donato Menichella used his annual report to denounce the new imbalances in Italian society, he was thinking above all about the commercial imbalance. His recipe for reducing imports focused on a "damming up" or "regulation" of consumption.

In 1962, for the first time since the 1940s, the country faced inflationist pressures. Some historians attribute this to a tendency of wages to exceed the ceilings set by national contracts.[20] The relationship between wage growth and inflation is the same as that between the number of ill people and hospitals; and yet no one would suggest that it is hospitals that generate sick people. In the Italy of the "economic miracle," consumption was merely the last act of a process during which the product had to pass through the long gauntlet of a nit-picking bureaucracy full of redundancy and overwhelmed by new tasks, then be transported over a seriously inadequate road network, and, last but not least, face an extremely fragmented distribution system. All of this could only add to the final sales price.

In the immediate postwar period, Italian workers paid a high price in the struggle, first, against inflation provoked by the war, and then by the peculiar monetary policy of the occupation authorities. They paid again in the 1960s to guarantee to the parties their electoral petit-bourgeois clienteles, the true cause of the currency devaluation. As Menichella had done in 1953, Ugo La Malfa devoted part of his efforts in 1962 to establishing a policy of "wage moderation" through an explicit offer of collaboration with the trade-union world, and its insertion into a reformist circuit in which the PCI could not tread directly, owing to international constraints. A few years later it was the Socialist Party that claimed credit for helping to overcome "the most dramatic moment of the economic crisis by imposing two years of austerity on the working masses."[21]

But the events of 1962—the year of the rioting at the Piazza Statuto in Turin against an agreement reached between Fiat and the social-democratic trade union UIL—had taught two important lessons: first, that any serious notion of reform could not avoid the question of increasing productivity and, therefore, wages; and second, that once one meddled with productivity and wages, the result was certain panic among the petite bourgeoisie. The struggles late in the decade for the renewal of collective labor contracts—the celebrated *"autunno caldo"* of 1969— led to a wage increase equal for all, a workweek of forty hours, the extension of union rights for apprentices, the national unification of wage scales that had varied by region, the right to organize paid assemblies during working hours, and so on. The *Corriere della Sera* summed this up by writing that the country had found itself "at the edge of a precipice."[22]

Despite their efforts at self-preservation, the parties saw their role as collectors of clienteles undercut as their former clients attempted to confront their vital problems on their own, or collectively. The traditional political system no longer seemed to respond to the varied expectations of the diverse interests it represented. The Christian Democrats were weakened by a rural exodus that drained its traditional reservoirs of support, and even by the open contestation of a significant part of the Catholic world, including institutions like Catholic Action (AC), Catholic Association of Italian Workers (ACLI), and the Catholic labor union (CISL). The Socialist Party meanwhile suffered a new schism in July 1969, just five years after the first split, in January 1964, with the departure of adversaries of the center-left. As for the PCI, its membership fell from 2.11 million in 1950 to 1.50 million in 1970, with an even more marked loss of influence among the working class. The number of PCI groups in companies dropped from 11,272 in 1950 to 2,977 in 1971. Forced for the first time after the war to confront a movement born outside of, and in opposition to, its directives, the PCI suffered a rupture of its own in 1969, with the exclusion of the group united around the journal *Il Manifesto*.[23]

The traditional "absence of a center" compounded by the "nongovernment" led to a multiplication of independent power centers, which Lanaro defined as an attempt at "unbridled self-government by all the corporations, old and new," the "shadow states."[24] The failure of "democratic nationalization" resulted in a contrary phenomenon. All those wielding even a fragment of power—legal, semilegal, or frankly illegal—considered themselves authorized, by dint of the absence of central authority, to fill the gaps left free, often trampling on prerogatives coveted by other powers in the process.

This applied to the trade unions, economic groups, the media, the Church, and the "street" in general—which the *Corriere della Sera* described in 1969 as *the* new power center in Italy[25]—and, beginning in 1970, to the regions as well, which began the long march toward what would later be called *devolution*. This applied as well to two other phenomena that, in the 1970s and even afterward, would often be considered abroad as the only aspects of Italian life worthy of attention: the Mafia and terrorism.

A growing number of people explain today terrorism as the weapon of a frustrated and frightened petite bourgeoisie. The phenomenon is thus starting to emerge from the fog of the various conspiracy theories in which it was long stuck. But if it has become more common to suggest that the bombing of the Piazza Fontana in December 1969 was a reactionary response to the "hot autumn," there is greater reticence regarding the petit-bourgeois character of the leftist terrorism of the 1970s. The leader of the PCI, Enrico Berlinguer, denounced this character when Aldo Moro was abducted, although more for immediate tactical reasons—the PCI had just entered the governmental majority—than through any in-depth analysis of the social and ideological tensions in the country. In fact, it was the growing joblessness of intellectuals and the timid attempts to slow public spending that, combined with the anti-American campaigns of the 1960s, created a fuse for this new season of violence; a season—whose actual importance was probably less than a few dramatic actions and their media depiction implied—that ended with the arrival of the new "economic boom" of the 1980s.[26]

During the 1960s and part of the 1970s, the most important "shadow state" was not the Mafia or the terrorists, but, as we have seen, the trade-union federations. This was not because of their intrinsic strength, which was actually rather limited, but because of the support they received from those who wanted to free up Italy's "blocked system" through needed structural reforms. The unions added to their explicit job the role of a labor party. This change profited them in the short term in membership growth (the Italian General Confederation of Labor [CGIL] and the CISL grew from 4 million members in 1968 to 6.75 million in 1975), but in terms of pure union strength it did not help them.

Certain sectors of big capital attempted, as we have seen, to forge alliances with the trade unions in the absence of a true labor party. But this coalition was far from being homogeneous or speaking in unison, for it worked within a fragmented framework in which "all the corporations, both old and new" wanted to change the country to suit their own interests. Rather than being reformed by some preestablished design, society ultimately reformed itself, following a disordered (but modern) process of molecular adaptation.

Chapter 21

Italian Metamorphoses

Involuntary Unification

The social earthquakes of the 1960s finally activated the self-preserving instincts of the political system, pushing it into a sort of mad race against changes that were imposing themselves spontaneously and anarchically on society. As we have seen, the laws on the regions and the referendum did little more than simply fill a constitutional void of more than twenty years. Yet the reorganization of certain sectors of state industry and public service—while helping rationalize functional mechanisms of the "country-system"—seemed to better serve the parties to which these sectors and services were linked than the "general interest" of the country. This division inspired the journalist Alberto Ronchey, in 1968, to coin a metaphor that would become greatly popular: that of the *lottizzazione* (parceling out, as in the sale of housing lots) of public property. If the public holding company IRI (Industrial Reconstruction Institute) remained the private hunting ground of the Christian Democrats, the chemical and hydrocarbon giant ENI (National Hydrocarbon Agency) was left to be managed by the Socialist Party, and the EFIM (Agency for Participation and Financing of Manufacturing Industry) was overseen by the other governmental parties, the Republicans and the Social Democrats. Following the RAI (Radiotelevisione Italiana) reform of 1975, the Christian Democrat monopoly was broken; this merely reshuffled the cards. Thus the leading television station—dubbed "national" up to that time—was confirmed as a Christian Democratic fiefdom, the second channel was entrusted to the Italian Socialist Party (PSI), and the newly established third channel went to the Italian Communist Party (PCI). In 1978 the National Healthcare Service was finally unified, and executive positions were strictly *lottizzate*: in 1985, 57 percent of the presidencies were in Christian Democratic hands, 20 percent were held by Socialists, and 23 percent were held by representatives of other parties.[1]

Other measures taken in the early 1970s seemed to respond to trade-union demands. There were the housing reforms of 1971 and 1978, but above all, the *Statuto dei lavoratori* (Labor Bill), approved in May 1970, which guaranteed legal protections for wage earners, while excluding from its terms all enterprises with fewer than fifteen employees, which was to say the great majority of Italian industry.[2]

As for "fiscal reform," wage withholding was confirmed, yet measures to control independent workers remained problematic. In 1977, when the PCI was part of the governing majority, Mario Salvatorelli wrote in *La Stampa* that wage earners deserved "the Oscar for best tax-payer," because they provided 80 percent of declared revenues, even as tax evasion remained massive.[3] At the beginning of the following decade, the first Craxi government risked provoking a crisis when its finance minister, Bruno Visentini, proposed stricter controls on tradesmen, who, on average, declared receipts that were actually less than the wages they paid their employees. When, in 1989, the International Monetary Fund (IMF) reported that housing taxes in Italy produced fiscal receipts that were just half those of similar countries, the president of the Confedilizia (the Association of Building Owners), Attilio Viziano, explained that in fact 50 percent of buildings were simply "unknown to the tax authorities" because the housing law of 1978 imposed a sort of "political rent" that led their owners to expect to be paid the market price, but under the table.[4] By 2005, declarations to the tax administration showed that the situation had not changed; car dealers, for example, claimed revenues less than those of automobile metalworkers. Still in October 2006, Finance Under-Secretary Vincenzo Visco declared to parliament that in certain Italian provinces, there were fiscal irregularities in more than 50 percent of declarations.[5]

As we have seen, the possibility of staging referenda had transferred to the "sovereign people" some parliamentary prerogatives. This was true not only institutionally but also from the viewpoint of the social reality that parliament was supposedly representing through the parties. The most striking demonstration of this came the first time the procedure was used, on May 12, 1974, when Italians were asked to vote on whether to maintain or reject the divorce law of December 1970. A modification of the law, even a wording change, could have averted the referendum. But the intransigent Catholics did everything possible to bring the matter before the people, persuaded that Italians would reestablish the primacy of Christian values that had been undercut by the eruption of "modernity." The Christian Democrats, despite their initial reservations linked to their governmental relationship with the "prodivorce" parties, ultimately followed in the Catholics' footsteps, seeing the referendum as a way to relaunch a party facing a crisis of legitimacy.

The result revealed that the various political powers were far from understanding what the country had become in the course of its "economic miracle": 59.3 percent of the voters supported continuation of the law, with much narrower margins between deeply Catholic parts of the country and others. Moreover, the margins between the north and the south of the country were much smaller than those recorded in 1946 in the referendum between the monarchy and the republic. This trend was confirmed even more clearly seven years later, when the 1978 law on abortion was submitted to a referendum: 67.9 percent of the voters supported it; so did every Italian region except Trentino-Alto Adige, which missed doing so by only 0.3 percent. For the first time in history, Italians had expressed themselves nearly unanimously on a question concerning their whole society.

The referenda on "civil rights," beyond their specific goals, constituted a sort of reactive indicator of a new relationship among Italians, flowing from three major correlated and concomitant changes affecting them all: the growth in consumption, the "melting pot," and the great trade-union struggles.

In this regard, we should recall above all the linguistic unification of the country. Italy, in the second half of the twentieth century, was the European country in which social and regional linguistic distances were most rapidly reduced. According to De Mauro's calculations, in 1955, only 10 percent of Italians correctly spoke the national language, and nearly all of them still used a dialect for their daily communications. After the cinema, which for most Italians was the first "teacher" of Italian, radio and television generalized the use of the national language, while resolving in a practical way the theoretical dilemmas that had divided nineteenth-century linguists. The media, in effect, did not create the language, as De Mauro notes, but adapted themselves to existing tendencies, and those tendencies, since the unification of the country, have developed in the major economic, demographic, political, and intellectual centers of the country: in Turin, in Milan, and in Rome. It was there, and not in Tuscany, that radio and television spontaneously drew their lexical and pronunciation models, which they then spread to the rest of the peninsula: one result was to make the Tuscan pronunciation of Italian seem provincial.[6]

The Transnational Consumer

But the increasing uniformity of some aspects of Italians' behavior did not mean they were being "nationalized." Those who had been brought together by their trade-union demands were only a portion of society, and the very circumstances of their rapprochement ruled out any feeling of "national" solidarity with representatives of the classes who had opposed them in the season of struggles. The solidity of their gains, moreover, was shaken once the big company owners began a counteroffensive. But the chief reason why "modernization" did not generate a common national identity is that even with the standardization of behavior that followed the increasing turn to mass consumption, no "Italian" specificity emerged. Instead, mass consumption brought an inhabitant of Milan closer to a citizen of Paris or New York than to someone from Matera or Cuneo.

The small party that had made itself the herald of "civil rights"—the Radical Party[7]—was referred to quite appropriately as "transnational." Its battles represented the tendency of the upwardly mobile strata of society to align their behavior with that of the social groups in more-developed countries that had already achieved such success.

As marketing experts know, consumption, however massive, remains a fundamentally individual act. Thus the possibility to consume more is always seen as an individual victory and the social behavior that accompanies it is seen as the securing of a long-denied right. There is an almost perfect correlation between crossing a certain threshold of consumption and the appearance of specific social behaviors. The improvement of the quality of life regularly leads to a decrease in the birth rate. Thus even though each couple feels certain it is deciding freely how many children it desires, at the moment when improved living conditions become widespread, most couples respond more to collective behaviors, rather like the sudden and simultaneous movements of a school of fish, than to carefully thought-out individual choices.

In Italy, the fertility rate dropped in 1968 below the 2.4 or 2.5 children-per-woman rates maintained since the 1950s, falling to less than 1.5 in 1984, and stabilizing around 1.2 in the late 1990s. Indeed, for some time, in the mid-1990s, the Italian fertility rate was the lowest in the world.[8] This phenomenon coincided with another characteristic of development: the massive entry of women into the workplace. From 1970 to the end of the century, the employment rate for women rose 70 percent even as male employment stagnated. In parallel, the average age of women at the birth of their first child rose from 24.9 years to 29 years between 1972 and 1990, accentuating the decrease in births.[9]

The combined impact of these factors was that, in the Italian social structure, a still largely absent "labor aristocracy" was replaced by a growing "wage aristocracy." Average wages remained low, even very low, but the average number of revenue earners per family rose as family sizes declined, leading to an overall increase in resources per household.

When one considers that these changes were accompanied by a profound modification of the labor market—an increase in the training levels of hourly workers and of their expectations—one has a better picture of the conditions that favored, in the 1980s, the rise of a significant part of the population to the income level above them. Because of this process, carried out against a backdrop of persistent protectionism, waves of migrants from developing countries began to fill the least-rewarding jobs on the social ladder, responding to a demand that local laborers were less and less available to fill.

Italy thus underwent one of the most radical (and rapid) social metamorphoses of its history: from being a net exporter of labor until the early 1970s to being a net importer of labor at the start of the following decade. This new social reality provided the ideal terrain for the Church to regain a central position in society. It again affirmed itself as the lone institution capable, thanks to its cultural weight and material structures, of handling social phenomena that had overwhelmed a clearly insufficient state.

The Church and the "Unjust Masters"

The new behaviors provoked by the social impact of the economic boom pointed to an ever-clearer emancipation from the cultural guardianship of the two dominant ideologies in the republic's early decades. But while this led to a steady erosion of the influence of the PCI, that of the Church, paradoxically, would be strengthened, to the point that it became an inescapable force in all political equations as matters settled after the earthquake of the 1990s.

Those seeking an explanation for this "miracle" often look to the undeniable weaknesses of "secular thinking," ever more on the defensive for its inability to make sense of the contradictions of "modernity." Some university professors, having successively been Maoists or followers of Sartre, Adorno, or Nietzsche, revealed themselves in the 1980s as Kantian: unable to understand the transformations of Italian society, they lent philosophical dignity to what they called "weak thought": the simple presumption of understanding the world, they said, must be rejected, for it is the antechamber of totalitarian ideologies. The left, rapidly losing its ideal reference points, seized on the "weak thought" theory to justify both the collapse of its myths and its inability to find new ones.

To understand how the Church was able to transform apparent defeat into certain triumph, we must consider not just the wanderings of "secular thought," but the strength and skillfulness of the Church itself. It was able to (and still can) prevail through four points of added leverage: (1) a plurisecular heritage of struggle against "secular" philosophies that allows it to dispose of, with seemingly coherent responses, the concerns and uncertainties raised by "modernity"; (2) a long experience with humankind that has led it to measure historical time not in terms of political or electoral cycles, but through secular perspectives; (3) a long experience with humankind that has led it to analyze events not through their present manifestations, but in terms of their dynamic aspects; and (4) a consolidated and increasingly centralized organizational structure that allows it to "give legs" to the three points of strength mentioned above by grounding its roots in the social terrain.

The Catholic defeat in the divorce referendum certainly marked the end of the supposed identification of the Italian nation with Catholicism. It left the Church in the minority. But it is precisely in its awareness of the need to adapt in "secularized" societies to minority status that the Church launched its spectacular rebound. It is difficult to know whether the line that developed around the concept of "minority Church," explicitly defended by Cardinal Joseph Ratzinger in a 1996 text,[10] was adopted after this referendum or whether the rearguard battle on divorce was not already part of this strategy of adaptation. It appears fairly evident, however, that contrary to widespread belief, the battle over abortion constituted an essential moment.

The defeat at the ballot box had little importance for the Church because, as Ratzinger put it, "statistics is not one of God's measurements." The church is not, he continued, "a business operation that can look at the enterprise to measure whether [its] policy has been successful". The results of its actions are not visible in the short-term; what is important, Ratzinger continued, is to plant "mustard seeds."[11] The battle against abortion was such a seed. On the one hand, it helped the Church assure the cohesion of the faithful—at least some of them—by involving them in battles of principle over "difficult" subjects. On the other hand, it became the central axis of a campaign on a key problem overhanging the country's future and, more generally, that of the Christianized West: the demographic deficit.

In Italy, the legacy of the Fascist period did not help in coping with the birth crisis and its attendant problems. The dark memory of the Mussolini regime's natalist policy long provoked a more or less conscious repression of the demographic question. Moreover, the persistence of Fascist legislation meant that the release of information on birth control or family planning was for years deemed a misdemeanor, and Article 533 of the Penal Code, which punished the use of contraceptives, was not abrogated by the Constitutional Court until 1971. All this fed into an atmosphere of massive illegality, which only grew as "modernity" imposed its laws. Thus when the drop in the birth rate began to create labor shortages, lawmakers found themselves bankrupt for ideas; not so, needless to say, the Church.

These shortages could be overcome, at least partially, only through immigration, but this was likely to produce a negative, identity-centered reaction, at least psychologically. Over these social and psychological repercussions, the Church was able to recover some of its credit in the eyes of the country.

In a series of articles published in February 1989 on the occasion of a closed-door session of the Italian episcopal conference on the question of immigration, the bishops' semiofficial journal, *Avvenire*, offered an analysis of the phenomenon. Immigration, the Catholic journal wrote, is inevitable for three key reasons: (1) the demographic imbalance between the north and south coasts of the Mediterranean, (2) the fact that many immigrants came from oil-exporting countries, and (3) the demands of the Italian labor market. "An industrial country," said a commentary in *Avvenire*, "needs reserves of low-cost manual labor: farm workers, domestics and seasonal laborers."[12] This was thus an inevitable destiny in the eyes of the bishops, but also a threat to the social equilibrium of the country, and one that in *Avvenire's* estimation only the Church could prevent. For it had known how to defeat slavery in the Roman Empire "not by opposing it, but by telling the slaves: Subjugate yourselves to unjust masters, too."[13]

The Italian secular culture, which in the meantime had ceded to Catholic culture the monopoly of ideals, of solidarity, and of the means to practice it, could only follow the Church's path on questions that had long split it between its do-good instincts and apprehensions that were more or less culturally justified. Faced with a proposal by Biffi in a pastoral note of September 13, 2000, that immigration from Catholic—or at least Christian—countries should be favored, the most famous Italian political scientist, Giovanni Sartori, wrote "in his capacity as a layman" that the remarks of the cardinal of Bologna were "holy words, to say the least. And very responsible."[14]

Thus some twenty years after the referendum on divorce, the authority of the Church had again begun to radiate a light so bright that few shadows dared intrude, and the supposed superposition of the Catholic and the Italian identities was restored to prominence with scarcely any resistance from intellectuals or the public authorities of the peninsula.

Chapter 22

Between Europe and the Mediterranean

The "Pedagogy of Austerity"

The Italian crisis of the 1990s began in the early 1970s in Washington, D.C., Basel, and Kuwait City. The end of the gold-dollar standard, announced from the White House on August 15, 1971, by President Richard Nixon, the creation of the European monetary "serpent," decided in the Swiss city on April 10, 1972, and, finally, the oil crisis that followed the decision by the Organization of Petroleum Exporting Countries (OPEC), on October 17, 1973, in Kuwait, to raise the price of oil from $3 to $5.15 a barrel touched off a seismic movement whose aftershocks would shake the entire Italian system twenty years later.

With the failure of a timid deflationist policy decided after the wage increases of 1969, each Italian social and economic actor reacted, once again, by pursuing its own immediate interests. Many small and medium entrepreneurs closed their businesses or profited from the largess of the state, either by selling troubled businesses or by profiting from the generous financing meant to support investment in the *Mezzogiorno*.[1] Others decided simply to export their capital abroad, while some shifted higher production costs to consumers; nearly all of them practiced a sort of fiscal self-indemnification, seeking to pay the lowest taxes possible.

Public enterprises, for their part, continued to produce at a loss. At the end of 1978, Castronovo points out, while private enterprises were reporting 613 lira of debt per 1,000 lira of turnover, state-owned companies were declaring more than 1,100 lira; in other words, debt exceeded their turnover.[2] In 1971 the state-owned EFIM (Agency for Participation and Financing of Manufacturing Industry), IRI (Industrial Reconstruction Institute), ENI (National Hydrocarbon Agency), and IMI (Istituto Mobiliare Italiano), each of them loss-makers, gave birth to GEPI (Società per le Gestioni e Partecipazioni Industriali), whose aim was, as its founding statute declared, to "contribute to the maintenance and the growth of jobs compromised by the transitory difficulties of industrial enterprises," that is, to purchase private companies poised at the brink of bankruptcy.[3] Thus, from 1969 to 1973, state involvement in economic affairs grew steadily, increasing from 19.9 percent of all employees to 25.2 percent, and from 31 percent of capital to 39.2

percent, a trend that would continue until the 1980s.[4] From 1970 to 1975, the flow of public money destined to enterprises rose from 6 trillion to 17 trillion lira, and in 1992 the European commissioner Lord Leon Brittan complained that 28 percent of the country's deficit went to subsidizing companies.

Bit by bit, a new "social compromise" took shape, thanks to the Keynesian and protectionist policies of the state, supported by public debt, which rose from 38 percent of gross domestic product (GDP) in 1970 to 55 percent in 1982, reaching 120.2 percent in 1997. This policy took three directions: direct (subsidies) and indirect support (orders, trade and fiscal protection, etc.) to industry; expansion of the bureaucratic apparatus; and, above all, an inflationist policy intended to support exports.

After the February 1973 decision to allow the lira to float on currency exchanges, the mechanism of "competitive devaluation" thus became the principal weapon of the "doped-up" competition of the 1970s and 1980s. While the great powers were beginning successively to follow the painful path of deregulation, Italian industry kept afloat thanks to this expedient. Not until the arrival of the single currency was Italy definitively deprived of the option of resorting to this form of competition.[5]

The other weapon was also a return to tradition: the attempt to reestablish pre-1969 wage conditions. If the aims remained the same—and helped re-create "class solidarity" between the petite and the grand bourgeoisie, between the private and public sectors—the methods could not help but change. Gianni Agnelli, president of Confindustria since 1974, had two years earlier described the perspective of this new phase of social relations thus: "We have only two possibilities," he said. "Either a frontal shock to impose a lowering of wages or a series of courageous initiatives to eliminate the more intolerable phenomena of waste and inefficiency. Needless to say, we have chosen the latter."[6]

In short, this was a new attempt to adopt the path of "great reform," but this time employing every decisive force influencing the agents of society. The simultaneous launching—just days before the oil crisis of the fall of 1973—of a political plan for "historic compromise" by the secretary of the Italian Communist Party (PCI), Enrico Berlinguer, was more than simple coincidence. The strategic objectives of the head of Fiat and the boss of the PCI were in agreement, even to the choice of words: Berlinguer, too, effectively committed himself to fight "waste and dissipation, the exaltation of the most immoderate particularities and individualism, the most brazen consumerism."[7]

The PCI was welcomed into the governmental majority less than three years later, in the summer of 1976. Its willingness to play the role that, ten years earlier, had belonged to the Italian Socialist Party (PSI) enjoyed trade-union support—support the center-left never had—for a veritable "pedagogy of austerity." The secretary-general of the Italian General Confederation of Labor (CGIL; the union close to the PCI), Luciano Lama, announced that this austerity would consist of "not marginal, but substantial sacrifices": wage moderation, restriction of the wages guarantee fund mechanisms, "real" mobility for hourly workers, and "an end to the system of permanently subsidized labor."[8] Arguing that unemployment tends to rise when wage levels are too high in comparison to productivity, Lama presented his as the only way to defend employment. In fact, he was defending the traditional practice of attacking wages in order to avoid dealing with low productivity. Real wages diminished without reducing unemployment, which in fact rose from 5.9 percent in 1975 to 7.7 percent in 1979. Still, thanks to a series of successive devaluations beginning in the first half of 1976, exports revived, creating the conditions that would allow the adventures of the *nuovi condottieri* in the 1980s.[9]

In legislative terms, the period of "national solidarity"—the name given to the phase of Christian Democrat–PCI collaboration that would last until 1979—produced modest results, probably less important than the achievements a decade earlier during the first years of center-left rule. Disappointment was even more crushing since the PCI had presented its participation in the governing majority as the act through which the working class would "become" the state (*"si fa Stato"*), as per the famous slogan of 1977. In the elections of 1979, the PCI paid dearly for its policy of austerity, especially in big-city working-class neighborhoods and among the young. Even as its overall share of the vote dropped by 11.75 percent compared to 1976, the loss among voters age eighteen to twenty-one saw the PCI's share fall by more than a third (−35.41 percent). The progressive decline, which would lead to the party's ultimate dissolution a decade later, had begun.[10]

But the failure of "national solidarity" went beyond the fortunes of the parties that had promoted it. One could say about this new "missed opportunity" just what Galli della Loggia had said about the impossibility of building national sentiment on the fiction of a "republic born from the Resistance": it "clashed too obviously with the concrete experience of the majority of the population."[11] The "pedagogy of austerity" and the ethic of sacrifice were not in tune with the transformations of Italian society and with the relative enrichment of multi-income families, who measured their social progress in terms of consumption. To be convincing, wrote Enzo Pace, an ideology must seduce both emotionally and rationally, but also must "produce useful social effects, both in collective terms and in individual incentives."[12] "National solidarity" did neither.

Among the electorate there also arose, in the following decade, "a new political animal." This voter, as the journalist Mariella Gramaglia portrayed him in 1987, loved money and power, was "irritated by egalitarianism," and was seduced by "guts and effrontery as virtues that he would like to possess and that he imitates as best he can."[13] This "political animal," who voted in the 1980s for the PSI of Bettino Craxi, would become the protagonist, in the 1990s, of the Berlusconian "revolution."

"External Constraints"

In August 1974, the Bank of Italy was constrained to pledge part of its gold reserves in exchange for a $2 billion loan from the Bundesbank. Afterward, the lira's international standing was downgraded to a level below that of the Mexican peso. The subordination to Germany that was formalized by this loan provided added proof that international factors would play an ever greater role in determining the situation of Italy. This became even more evident after the oil crisis and the recession of 1974 to 1975.

The crisis of the early 1970s revealed a new global configuration after thirty years of unequal development. In 1974, while the industrialized countries saw their manufacturing production drop by 0.5 percent, that of the newly industrialized countries continued to grow at an annual rate of 7.2 percent. For the old powers, the need to deregulate and to restructure the productive apparatus of the state began to appear urgent and inevitable if they were to stay ahead of these dynamic countries, so rich in labor and free of parasitic burdens and social preoccupations. The need to deal with these new actors would lead to a new global free-trade cycle and a new liberal cycle in the domestic politics of different countries. Margaret Thatcher, Ronald Reagan, Helmut Kohl, and François Mitterrand (after 1983) would be the political agents of this crisis of restructuring.

In Italy, on the other hand, the free-market tendencies long remained weak. Adding to the difficulties arising from a political world born and nourished by a planned economy was the resistance of a productive apparatus that hoped indefinitely to postpone its technological reconversion by relying on its traditional resources: the depreciation of the lira and low wages. Wages, according to *Le Monde*, had risen in 1974 by 4.9 percent in Germany, 1.6 percent in Great Britain, 5 percent in France, and 1.3 percent in Japan. In Italy, in contrast, they had fallen by a full 5 percent.[14] Though often overshadowed by "competitive devaluation," low-wage policies would long be characteristic of Italian competitiveness. Twenty years after the data cited by *Le Monde*, an Organization for Economic Development and Cooperation (OECD) estimate found that Italians were working more for less pay than were workers in other industrialized countries.[15]

The Italian monetary authorities quickly sounded the alarm about the inherent risks of resorting systematically to these expedients to avoid dealing with the structural problem of low productivity. It was no accident if Guido Carli, Carlo Azeglio Ciampi, and Lamberto Dini (two former governors and a former director general of Banca d'Italia) occupied leading positions in Italian political life starting in 1991. They were the first to argue that if Italy was unable to reform itself, changes ultimately would be imposed by constraining European mechanisms, or by what Carli called an "external constraint."[16]

The first of these "constraints"—meant to impose on Italy an ability to compete not by "the degradation of the lira," but by "limiting costs and increasing productivity"—was, according to Ciampi, adherence to the European Monetary System (EMS), in March 1979. When the effects of entry into the EMS began to be felt "in June 1980," Ciampi said, companies came to understand that "their reorganization could no longer be postponed."[17]

Ciampi himself did his best to help them understand. Giangiacomo Nardozzi recounts what happened in the summer of 1980 when the president of Fiat, Gianni Agnelli, visited the governor of Banca d'Italia to ask for a new lira devaluation: Ciampi turned him down "politely but firmly."[18] That September, Fiat sent out fifteen thousand dismissal notices. After a twenty-day strike that brought down the government, the dismissals were transformed into "temporary" layoffs, but for twenty-three thousand workers. In the end, only a few dozen were rehired. In the years to follow, Fiat closed its facilities in Lingotto and Chivasso. The victory of the Turinese group in its strong-arm confrontation with the trade unions marked a turning point, the official beginning of industrial restructuring in Italy. Nardozzi estimates that this restructuring yielded an increase in per-employee productivity of 50 percent during the 1980s.[19]

Adherence to the EMS, as we have seen, was hardly the fruit of a coherent strategic vision by Italy's governing classes. In some ways it was not even the fruit of a deliberate choice; it was, to employ an oxymoron, an obligatory choice. Indeed, while it provided special terms for Italy—a 6 percent range of fluctuation for the lira, compared to 2.25 percent for other currencies—the EMS involved a monetary discipline that the national solidarity government attempted to evade until Germany finally posed an ultimatum. At that point, the head of the government, Giulio Andreotti, obtained approval for the decision by a narrow parliamentary margin in a late-night session on December 12, 1978.

The "general law" of external constraint, as Sergio Romano describes it, was confirmed. The country, Romano wrote, "can permit itself a few diplomatic liberties and marginal autonomy so long as the international events or decisions of its most important allies do not suddenly restrain its field of action; in such circumstances, it has no choice but to conform in order not to lose contact with those upon whom, ultimately, its prosperity and political stability depend."[20]

"Party of Europe" and "Party of Inflation"

The same "general law" had characterized the Italian Atlanticism of the preceding three decades. As Francesco Cossiga summed up the situation, Italy depended entirely on the international policies of the United States and NATO, but this loyalty allowed it to exploit "the marginal utility, the geopolitical 'income' that came from being a frontier country with an internal frontier which, moreover, accommodated on its territory the Holy See."[21] Romano explains in concrete terms how this "marginal utility" was expressed: Italy accepted its subordination to the United States, in exchange reserving itself the right to flirt "with the enemies of its principal friend: the Soviet Union, the PLO of Arafat, Gaddafi's Libya, and the Ethiopia of Mengistu."[22]

Tacitly authorized by the Americans, this "Mediterranean Atlanticism" had, of course, to be very discreet. Often this policy sidestepped the Foreign Ministry and was conducted instead by economic groups, by Catholic organizations, and, naturally, by the PCI, which was the privileged intermediary for matters on the other side of the Iron Curtain. The case of Enrico Mattei, who, as president of ENI, bypassed governments and the big international petroleum companies to establish direct relationships with the oil-producing countries of the Mediterranean, was surely the most famous example of this "parallel diplomacy," but hardly the only one.[23]

"Mediterranean Atlanticism" was the essence of republican Italy's international political projection until the caesura of 1989 to 1991, when it was succeeded by the phase of "passive Europeanism" or "impotence," of which the "forced" membership in the EMS had provided a foretaste in the 1970s. Beyond its impact on the productive system, this membership also affected the strategic debate of the governing class. It clearly exposed a double fault line that followed rather clear geopolitical lines, internal and international. On the one side were the economically free-market-leaning groups and tendencies of the north; they relied on Germany to help them seek advantage over the other side—the "Mediterranean" groups and tendencies—which were largely protectionist.

The theses supported by some entrepreneurs in the north can be summed up thus: even if the lands south of the Mediterranean form an attractive market, Germany is the locomotive of the European economy and is the country capable of absorbing the bulk of Italian exports; it is thus to Europe that Italian interests must be tied. The opponents of this line, continued the northern businessmen, are defending backward sectors of production by use of monetary protection. The true line of demarcation, they concluded, is the one that separates the "party of Europe" from the "party of inflation."[24]

This debate had inevitable political echoes. Interest groups closer to the markets of the "deutsche mark zone" began in the late 1970s to support a rising political phenomenon—"localism"—which was explicitly anticentralist. Transborder associations that included Italian, Swiss, Austrian, and German regions of the eastern Alps intensified their encounters. A "Working Community of Eastern Alpine Regions," referred to as the "little EEC of the Alps," included as its members not only Veneto, Friuli, Carinthia, Styria, and Upper Austria but also Slovenia and Croatia, a dozen years before the breakup of Yugoslavia. All these regional groupings posed rather explicitly the problem of using the north's resources to develop trade with the rest of Europe rather than "wasting" it on the unproductive consumption of Rome and the *Mezzogiorno*.

The backers of the "party of Europe" could not help but find sympathy for their beliefs within the traditional parties. At the end of November 1978, a certain Christian Democratic university professor from Bologna joined the government. He was the head of the Il Mulino publishing house, Romano Prodi. Early the following month, Prodi was, along with others including Beniamino Andreatta, Giuseppe De Rita, and Umberto Agnelli, the promoter of a symposium launching a Christian Democratic "free-trade" faction. But the party that felt most invested in this "mission" was the small Republican Party of Italy, headed by Ugo La Malfa, long the party of reference of the great capital of the north. In late 1978 the Republican Party attacked the PCI for its opposition to the EMS.

Adherence to the EMS in December 1978 marked the end of "national solidarity." Within the PCI, not only had the traditional pro-Russian and anti-German reflexes prevailed, but so had the factions linked to Mediterranean trade. In December 1978, Claudio Petruccioli, a party leader, dismissed the economic and political demands of the north as a "wave of provincial neoliberalism." But that was not all. The conviction also prevailed within the PCI that the monetary rigor required by membership in the EMS had negative effects on employment and wages: a rather unfortunate outcome for a working class that was supposed to "become the state."

When Andreotti resigned, Italian President Sandro Pertini turned, on February 22, 1979, to Ugo La Malfa to form the new government. Despite the failure of this effort, it was the first time in republican Italy that this role had been assigned to a political leader who was not a Christian Democrat.

In the meantime, other forces and other men prepared to face the future. In early December 1978, under orders from the new pontiff, the Italian Church organized in Varese a meeting on "Christian Europe" to which was invited the head of the Bavarian Christian Social Union, Franz Josef Strauss. For its part, *L'Osservatore Romano*, the Holy See daily, expressed the desire that one day the European Community would be able to include Eastern Europe. On the "secular" front, among the "provincial neoliberals" mocked by Petruccioli, a Milanese industrialist, important in the business world but unknown to the general public, was mulling the possibility of creating, in Milan, local electoral lists because, as he said, "if we do not succeed in finding a successor to this political class, dark days await us." His name: Silvio Berlusconi.

Chapter 23

The Internationalization Crisis of the 1990s

The "Recycling of Public Spending"

Despite Italy's adherence to the European Monetary System (EMS), the liberal northern groups had merely won a battle. They were not yet sufficiently powerful to remake state policies according to their demands.

The Italian situation in the 1980s was rather like Penelope's tapestry: Italy, goaded by European legislation, was beginning cautiously to dismantle certain forms of protectionism, but new ones were constantly being created, particularly through the uncontrolled growth of public spending and what Carli described, in the rather baroque language of a Banca d'Italia official, as "the allocation of undue sums in order to distend the natural mechanisms of competition and to subtract a large part of the country's economy from selective confrontation with the market."[1] His style aside, Carli's description illustrates the protectionist character of corruption, and it points to the reasons that the signing of the Maastricht Treaty coincided almost exactly with the opening of the operation known as "Clean Hands."[2]

The political interpreter of this pendulum swing between the heritage of a planned economy gone wild and the first timid steps toward free trade was the Socialist Party secretary, Bettino Craxi, the first Milanese to lead the government in Italian history. Under his government—which set a record for longevity in the republican period surpassed only by Silvio Berlusconi—the contradiction evoked by Carli would underlie a new form of "social compromise," a well from which all society's actors, including many wage earners, would drink. The mechanism of this compromise was the "recycling of public spending." The state hired, and to hire it had to indebt itself. To pay its debt, it issued high-interest securities. These were then purchased by the people the state had hired (and debt-service payments required the continual issuance of new high-interest securities, and so on).[3] Each social faction urgently advocated reductions in public spending, so long as it was other factions who were renouncing their benefits. This explains the ample support Craxi received from those who had dared say "Enrich yourselves!"

The Socialist chief, of course, engendered mistrust from part of the Catholic world (but at the same time, the enthusiasm of certain pragmatic Catholic movements, like *Comunione e Liberazione*, for which money had long ceased to be *stercus diaboli*), and the implacable hostility of the PCI. There were various motivations for this opposition, but the principal one, summing up all others, lay in Craxi's proposal to repeat in Italy the French experience of strengthening the Socialist Party at the Communists' expense. This operation was meant to be built on the modern, dynamic, and casual character of the Socialist Party, in contrast to the archaic nature of the PCI, which was presented as moralistic and pauperistic, for it had spent years preaching sacrifice and austerity. The attack on the PCI came on the worker front. Craxi not only demonstrated that public-debt securities brought more money to families, and more quickly, than protests and struggle, but he worked to dismantle the mechanisms that still guaranteed negotiating power to unions.

For a time, the electoral results seemed to confirm the Socialist leader's hypothesis. While the PCI was steadily losing favor in voters' eyes, the Socialist Party passed from 9.6 percent of votes cast in 1976, when Bettino Craxi was elected secretary, to 14.3 percent in 1987, when he left the prime ministership, meaning it had grown by nearly half, even if it did not pick up the entire eight percentage points lost by the PCI. The Socialist Party had also managed to draw into its orbit some of the intellectuals who had distanced themselves progressively from Berlinguer's party as it lost power and prestige, as well as some of those who had, until then, adhered to the wanderings of a reduced extreme left (the list that included survivors of the group once known as "extraparliamentary" ranged from 1.4 percent to 1.7 percent of the vote in those years).

This *in partibus infidelium* breakthrough made Craxi public enemy number 1 of the PCI, to the point that Berlinguer, in 1984, actually declared him "a danger to democracy."[4] Despite this hostility, conveyed in daily attacks by *La Repubblica*, the secretary of the PSI managed to gain the backing of PCI sympathizers and leaders in September 1985, when he demanded that American forces turn over to him the leader of a Palestinian terrorist group intercepted in Sicily who had just hijacked an Italian cruise ship and killed a Jewish American tourist. The PCI, all the anti-American factions, and the small number of self-described "nationalists" applauded the firmness of the head of government, which was seen as an act of defiance toward the "American imperialists."[5]

In short, during the "Craxi years" people began to believe that the distance separating the official country and the real country had narrowed, that Italy had evolved on the international scene onto an equal footing with other powers, and that feelings of national pride could legitimately be displayed, even outside sporting events. Contributing to these impressions were the events just described: unprecedented governmental stability, Craxi's main role in the Socialist International, and the signing of the new Concordat, which had been in the works for decades but which the Christian Democrats had been unable to bring to fruition given the risk of political insider trading. But above all was the conviction that the Italian political class had finally become progrowth. Italians were seeing their income soar; inflation was falling (from 10.4 percent to 4.9 percent in the five years of the Craxi government); gross domestic product (GDP) was rising (in 1987, the prime minister announced that Italy had become the fifth leading world power, having passed Great Britain); the "Third Italy" of small businesses was showing its dynamism; the *nuovi condottieri*—Carlo De Benedetti, Raul Gardini, Silvio Berlusconi, Luciano Benetton—launched their assault on the world, starting with France; and Italians were no longer emigrating. For the first time, affluence, money, and profit were becoming positive notions in the collective imagination, and the inhabitants of the peninsula, growing richer, suddenly realized they could do so without a sense of guilt.

Still, this social compromise revealed its continuing fragility when it encountered its intrinsic limits—the risk of a state bankruptcy or new inflation—and, above all, the limits imposed by its European competitors. Once Germany gave up its politically subordinate role, the cards were on the table. The overarching requirement for any country wanting to remain in Europe was to fight against its public deficits and accumulated debt. For Italy, accepting this rule meant killing the goose that laid the golden egg.

From that moment, the king was declared naked. If Great Britain had indeed been surpassed, it was only because of a change in the way GDP was calculated. If inflation had been defeated, it remained the highest in Europe. If industrial productivity had increased, services, distribution, and administration had not followed suit. Above all, even if Italians were undeniably growing richer, public spending had risen by 8 percent of GDP during the decade.

The first sign that this new era of milk and honey was nearing an end was the retreat of the *nuovi condottieri*, who, one after the other, had to shelve their dreams of international glory. Even the lord of all the *condottieri*, Gianni Agnelli, after some flashes of brilliance during the "Craxi years," faced a lengthy crisis, from which Fiat has only quite recently emerged. At the end of the 1980s, the "disappearance of industrial Italy" would brutally accelerate. For the "disappearance of political Italy," such as it had been known, the wait would not to be so long.

European Constraints

At the beginning of the 1990s, the international upheaval provoked by German reunification and the collapse of the Soviet Union coincided with a crisis of the Italian political system. The disappearance of the international architecture built after World War II had drastically depreciated the country's "geopolitical capital." Italy, no longer a frontier country, lost much of its importance in American eyes, without, however, gaining any in the eyes of the new reference power, Germany, or of its privileged partner in the creation of the European Union, France.

The peninsula's urgent need to revalue its geopolitical capital among the French and Germans flowed from the *horror vacui* that afflicts Italy. As history has amply demonstrated, the country cannot exist without an intimate linkage to one or more great reference powers. Thus the weakening of America's interest had to be compensated for by a strengthening of the interest of another power to which Italy would swear utmost fidelity, as it had for more than forty-five years to the

United States—at least officially. But there was another reason for urgency. The country's fear, given the accelerating European pace, that it might definitively lose contact with the rest of the continent and slide progressively into the Mediterranean. This fear was sharpest in the north, particularly in Milan. For Lombardy, one of the three richest regions of Europe, along with Bavaria and the Paris region, the thought of a distancing from the heart of the continent was intolerable. Any other solution was preferable.

Milan had "made" Craxi; now Milan "unmade" him. From the Lombard capital emanated first the political challenge and then the judiciary challenge to the system of power that had reigned throughout postwar Italy and was now seen as the chief culprit behind the risk of exclusion from Europe. The many anticentralist local electoral lists found their federating force, at the regional level and then beyond, in a leader with both the vices and virtues of the increasingly well-off petite bourgeoisie of the north—which he embodied down to his very verbal tics and gestures, and with uncommon flair and political flexibility: Umberto Bossi. Joining him were, among others, Gianfranco Miglio, former faculty president of the School of Political Science at the Catholic University of Milan, a Craxi-era theoretician, who brought as a dowry his long experience as an analyst of political thought.

But the Northern League was only the best known and, until 1994, the most successful of the many attempts at a metamorphosis of the political system. Early in the 1980s the Republican Party was the object of a major political investment by the large groups and their leading daily newspapers—*Corriere della Sera* and *La Stampa*—and it dreamed briefly of becoming the third major power in the Italian political panorama, representing rigor and efficiency. Then came the turn of "Craxi-ism," which, as already seen, came closer to the goal of breaking up the Christian Democrat–Communist Party duopoly. In the early 1990s, it was the son of the former president of the republic, the Sardinian Christian Democrat Mario Segni, who left his party to give birth to a grand federation of all those who saw the proportional electoral system as underlying the country's problems. The federation had its moment of glory when, in a 1993 referendum, 82.7 percent of voters (63.68 percent of those registered) cast ballots for the abolition of the proportional voting law for the Senate. Between the two decades, even the PCI attempted a break with the past. The disappearance of the Soviet Union relieved it of its international obligations, and it tried to recycle itself as a "liberal" European party, as its last secretary, Achille Occhetto, put it in declaring war on "ineffective, corrupt, bureaucratic statism" in the name of "civil society."[6]

From 1991 to 1993 Italians were called to vote in nine referenda, eight of them on laws regulating the relationship between citizens and the state. Along with the electoral system of the Senate, they abolished the single preference on electoral lists for the Chamber (by 95.6 percent of voters); the law on public financing of parties (90.3 percent); the laws concerning the designation of the heads of public banks (89.8 percent), of certain sanitary services (82.6 percent), and of three ministries: agriculture (70.2 percent), tourism (82.3 percent), and state participations (90.1 percent), the "owner" of public industry in Italy.

Given that in 1978 another referendum for the abolition of the same law on public financing of parties had been rejected by 56.4 percent of voters, one can measure, even quantify, how much the rejection of traditional political groupings had grown over fifteen years, reflecting the evolution of liberal sentiment within "civil society." In 1970 Jacques Nobécourt described the small Liberal Party as the party of all those for whom "the demand for liberty meant the preservation of all that they themselves had acquired or constructed."[7] Twenty years later the Liberal Party had disappeared, but the number of those who had acquired or constructed something worth preserving now measured in the millions.

If they were able to ride it and at times exploit it, an ex-Christian Democrat and an ex-Communist could certainly not channel and stably organize this "liberal" and "antiparty" wave with its determination to break with the past. The Northern League's campaign against "*Roma ladrona*" (Rome the thief) had a greater chance of succeeding. The party of Bossi and Miglio passed from the 186,000-vote mark in 1987 to 3.4 million in 1992, an eighteen-fold increase in its electoral base in just five years. Thus the Italian political earthquake clearly began well before the *annus terribilis* of 1992. But the fact that in 1992 the traditional parties were caught unprepared indicates that earlier predictions of this earthquake had been too cautious. The predictors were considering not only the League's folkloristic character but also its intrinsic, structural limits, represented by its geographic confines. It could not be the party to unite and represent the discontent and appetite for change of all Italians because it quite simply was not an Italian party, it was a northern regional party.

Channelling this will for change would require a force present nationwide, of a clearly liberal nature, and which seemed to keep a certain distance from the party system, and indeed from politics in general. In this sense, Forza Italia represented both the "final stage" and the fruition of all the trends that were transforming Italian society. The most elemental aspect of Silvio Berlusconi's success lay in the fact that his eruption into a political world in profound upheaval could have succeeded only by presenting itself as completely foreign to that world.

But Berlusconi, as innovative and "impolitic" as he was, suffered—for different reasons, and perhaps acutely—from the same malady that afflicts the political world in general and its Italian version in particular: subjectivism. This disease helped persuade the political actors of the 1990s that Europe was something of their own making, not the other way around. For without the gravitational pull exerted by Europe, Italian political life would have taken an entirely different direction. Berlusconi's first government fell only months after it was established, after a fatal miscalculation that it could resuscitate the Atlantic linkage *quo ante* in order to avoid European constraints. Similarly, the Northern League was "European" in the way Molière's Monsieur Jourdain spoke in prose (though he was surprised to learn it). If the rise of Forza Italia at first did not erode the League's electoral basis—even while competing on the same northern Italian playing field—the Bossi's party lost more than half of its votes in the 2001 elections, after the risk of a break with the rest of Europe had been warded off.[8]

The strength of the various center-left coalitions—starting with the one that took the place of Berlusconi in 1994 (led by his former economy minister Lamberto Dini and supported by the Northern League)—consisted of the capacity to submit passively to European directives. In September 1996, four months after becoming head of the government, Romano Prodi had attempted, it is true, to obtain the support of Prime Minister Jose Maria Aznar of Spain in order to modify the Maastricht parameters. When the latter refused, the former doubled overnight the level of cuts foreseen in the proposed budget, from 32,500 billion lira to 62,500 billion lira. Economics Minister Ciampi, freshly back from a meeting of his European counterparts in January 1997, added a further 40,000 billion lira. From that moment on, Europe was to become both the zenith and the nadir of center-left actions.

The co-option into the Euro club on May 3, 1998, was welcomed by a sense of general jubilation. Italy had averted the fate that had been suffered by the Soviet Union and Yugoslavia and that would strike Argentina in 2001 to 2002. But in the chorus of satisfaction one could also hear pride for having so quickly attained an objective that, after the departure from the Monetary System in September 1992, had seemed permanently unreachable.

When he became prime minister again in 2006, Romano Prodi could brag of far closer relations with Brussels than he had enjoyed ten years earlier, relations made even more solid by the presence in his government of Giuliano Amato, the former vice president of the Constitutional Convention, and of the former director of the European Central Bank Tommaso Padoa Schioppa. These were "pro-European credentials," which, as Quentin Peel wrote in the *Financial Times*, compensated for the parliamentary weakness of the new executive and its political minority in Lombardy.[9] In charge of the Foreign Ministry, Massimo D'Alema, who had been prime minister when Italy was involved in the Kosovo war, inaugurated a new phase in Italian diplomacy, one that might be called "Atlantic Europeanism," relaunching Italy's Mediterranean interests under both European and American cover.

Thus it was that Italy was to furnish, in August 2006, the bulk of the European contingent for the United Nations mission in Lebanon. According to a view largely shared by important press outlets, the country, having regained credibility in European eyes, was now restoring its credibility—and usefulness—in the eyes of the Americans.

The Lebanon mission seemed to mark a first, the birth of a genuine, autonomous foreign and defense policy, as the editor of *La Repubblica* suggested.[10] Or did it? Was it instead the latest version of the "Crimean syndrome," leading Italian political leaders to attach themselves to military expeditions—even highly risky ones—with the sole objective of increasing the country's international credibility, as Sergio Romano asserted?[11] Regardless, the Italian Army embarked for Lebanon accompanied by the cheers of the left and the pacifists and by the cautions of the right and the nationalists. Could anyone have imagined a more paradoxical epilogue to a 145-year history replete with paradoxes?

The "Advantage of Backwardness"

The slowing of the European process after the 2005 French referendum on the European constitution eclipsed another debate concerning the near-term future of Italy, a more theoretical but still interesting debate, which followed the acceptance of European constraints: that of the "advantage of backwardness."[12]

The European constraints, as we have seen, involve a progressive cession of sovereignty. This process confers on Italy, at least theoretically, two advantages. All European countries, to the extent that they integrate into the process of continental unification, entrust part of their sovereignty to European authorities. In Italy, unlike countries like France or Great Britain, a cession of sovereignty actually involves the loss of very little. To the contrary, its historic tradition and its difficulty in synthesizing differing local interests made Italy a sort of trailblazer for the "Europe of regions." Its lag in creating a national state could become a trump card when national states were being dissolved into a supranational European whole.

This view, embraced by some, abhorred by others, seems to have faded a bit as the European process has slowed since 2005. But that leaves two possibilities: either the march toward Europe resumes and Italy can again play the card of the "advantage of backwardness," or the stagnation continues and Italy, having found a balancing point in Europe, will again suffer. In the final months of 2006, the latter view led the British think tank Centre for European Reform to formulate a new hypothesis, which is the paradoxical reversal of a paradox. Given its low productivity, if Italy had retained the lira, it would have suffered from a crisis of confidence and a "currency crash," doubtless forcing it to embrace needed reforms, as in the early 1990s. The European safety net, according to the Centre, would thus have made the governing class even lazier and more conservative, exposing it to the risk of having to "abandon the Euro zone."[13]

Beyond this hypothesis, meant perhaps to create a new bogeyman, the Centre for European Reform's analysis should be completed with a consideration of the history from which we started: foreign policy makes Italy more than Italy makes foreign policy.

Since 1861 the Italian state has been unable to exist without submitting to a determinative relationship with a reference power. That was the case when it was still too weak to engage in the battles of European competition, and it was true when it began to measure itself against larger competitors still of the same general order of magnitude. It is true now, when international competition has sized up the continental powers and left Europe itself suddenly looking quite small. And it is even more true today, given new qualitative and quantitative challenges, above all demography and migration. If Europe should slow its pace, Italy will slow its own. If Europe loses sight of its structural problems, Italy will do so as well.

This subordination to international policy applies to Italy, but it does not apply to one of the political forces acting in Italy or, more precisely, from Italy: the Catholic Church. As an Italian, European, and global power, the Church has succeeded, as Cervetto wrote in 1978, in "adapting itself to the structural movement of the past 30 years and can, better than any other, project itself into the social demands and future demographics of Italian capitalism."[14]

The "advantage of backwardness" has also, and perhaps even more so, this characteristic.

Conclusion

Paraphrasing the seventeenth-century English philosopher James Harrington, the Italian economics minister Giulio Tremonti wrote in 1993 that "empire follows property, that is, political power depends on a society's economic structure." But, Tremonti continued, "if the latter internationalizes, then the former loses, especially if it continues to operate as if nothing had changed."[1] Europe's impact on Italy produced some absolute new realities on the political level—above all, the regular change in government of two coalitions and newfound governmental stability—and some relative changes on the economic level—above all, the drastic weakening of the entrepreneurial state for the first time since the 1930s.

Most importantly, power followed property when the latter, in monetary form, deserted the Banca d'Italia to flow to the towering headquarters of the European Central Bank (ECB) in Frankfurt. It was then that Italian industry lost the last of its protections and was abandoned to the *mare magnum* of international competition. Before fixed exchange rates took effect, the combination of the small scale of the production, credit, and distribution sectors, the weakness of the lira, and the opening of the market transformed the country into a great bazaar where foreign groups—primarily French and German—came bargain-hunting, particularly in sectors where deregulation had been the slowest. Thus began the debate on Italian "decline."

Toward the middle of the first decade of this century, certain indices—important ones, though of uncertain long-term effect—seemed to augur fundamental change. In 2006, after a few years of de facto stagnation, Italian gross domestic product (GDP) experienced growth of about 2 percent, owing essentially to, as the Banca d'Italia governor Mario Draghi put it, "investments and the expansion of external demand, especially from Germany."[2] In May 2006, industrial production had already begun to grow, at a 2.9 percent pace, largely because of the growth of the automobile sector, which was 94.1 percent greater than the year before.[3]

In the credit sector, in June 2005, the second-largest Italian bank group, Unicredit of Milan, took over the second-largest German group, Hypovereinsbank of Bavaria, thereby joining the elite list of Europe's ten largest banks. Unicredit became the number one bank in Austria, Poland, Croatia, Bosnia, and Bulgaria, and also became a major player in the Turkish and Russian financial markets.[4] Thus strengthened, the Milanese institution proceeded to merge, in May 2007, with Capitalia of Rome, giving birth to the world's sixth-largest bank (in capitalization terms). This put at least a momentary halt to the latest takeover attempts from abroad, following the conquest of Banca Nazionale del Lavoro by BNP-Paribas and of Antonveneta by ABN Amro. At the same time, it opened other battlefronts, in particular over Mediobanca and Generali. The merger between Banca Intesa of Milan and SanPaolo IMI of Turin, announced in August 2006 and concluded in December that same year, was important not only because it gave birth to the second-largest Italian group (before being passed by Unicredit-Capitalia) but also for its repercussions both on international finance and on Italian economic geography.[5]

The Unicredit-Hypovereinsbank merger involved two of the richest European regions—Lombardy and Bavaria—which joined together to gain financial domination of the markets of Eastern Europe, previously under Russian political domination. The marriage of Intesa and Sanpaolo opened new perspectives for the Italian economy in Europe. Luigi La Spina, an editorial writer for *La Stampa*, saluted this accord as the opening of a new chapter in the country's history: "The Italy of the 19th century, when the sub-Alpine capital was the suspicious cousin of the city that was heiress to Austrian Lombardy-Venice, has finally been buried."[6] If we further note that the Unicredit-Capitalia accord broke two other taboos—the hostility between "secular" finance and "Catholic" finance, as well as the supposed incompatibility of Milan and Rome—we can see just how greatly the Italian geo-economic panorama was being transformed.

The process of Europeanization also finally brought typical Italian polycentrism—the simultaneous existence of several power centers—into an institutional framework. Despite the rigid formal centralism that has characterized the country from unification up through the creation of the regions in 1970, and including the Fascist period, the major cities and regions have always defended their interests without worrying overly much about whether those interests corresponded to the larger interests of the country. The European framework now allows these centers to establish direct relationships with the European Union, as well as with other European metropolises, while bypassing the mediation of Rome.

* * *

In this book we have barely mentioned two other major areas of change that affect not just Italy, but also other countries: the demographic crisis and immigration. We have done so not because these matters are of lesser importance, but rather because each deserves a specific and much more detailed treatment.

According to the Italian National Statistics Institute (ISTAT), in 2003, while the population of native-born Italians declined by 45,405 (544,063 births to 586,468 deaths), the number of inhabitants on the peninsula rose considerably because of a migratory influx of 407,521 people. In 2005 the native-born population was still in decline, but by only 13,282. In fact, while the number of newborn Italians had declined by 1.5 percent from the year before, immigrants themselves were having 9.4 percent more children. According to the United Nations Population Fund, in 2050 the population of Italy could reach 58 million, up from today's 50.9 million. The trends appear to point, however, to an Italy peopled with ever fewer Italians, a worrying perspective for some.

The only institution in Italy that is prepared to confront the dual challenge represented by demographic decline and immigration growth is the Catholic Church. In this book we have described some of the principal steps along the path that has made the Church one of the most important social and political actors on the peninsula; indeed, the only inescapable one.[7] As we have noted, the struggles—considered rear-guard battles—against divorce, and especially against abortion, contraception, and homosexuality, are part of a long-term probirth strategy that has begun to bear fruit.

The failure of the 2005 referendum against the law that strictly regulates stem cell research was determined by a massive abstention of voters, an abstention called for by the president of the Italian bishops of the period, Camillo Ruini. The result, some said, was revenge for the referenda lost by the Catholics on divorce in 1974 and on abortion in 1981. This was generally viewed as proof that, in Italy, it had again become impossible to govern or legislate against the will of the Church.

This, too, may be thorny terrain that Italy is in the process of clearing for the rest of Europe. The Church tests, in the laboratory of the peninsula, its strategies for fighting against individualism—consciously or unconsciously Malthusian—and for an immigration policy founded on a clever mixing of welcoming attitude and doctrinal intransigence. If immigration is not just inevitable, but necessary to the country's economic survival, the new immigrants must be welcomed in all Christian virtues, without ceasing for a moment to point out that these virtues are Christian. Benedict XVI has stated that the peoples of Asia and Africa do not fear the West because it is modern, but because it attempts to exclude God from public life.

In an Italy and a Europe facing the difficult geopolitical and geoeconomic challenges of the twenty-first century, the Church is preparing to play a role rather larger than that simply of a "stand-in" for identity.

Biographies

Giovanni Agnelli (Gianni, nickname: "l'Avvocato," "the Lawyer"), 1921–2003

Grandson of Senator Giovanni Agnelli, the founder of Fiat. Mobilized during World War II, he fought in Russia and Africa, and was a liaison officer with the Allies toward the end of the conflict, helping spare Fiat's Turinese facilities any serious devastation. He became president of Fiat in 1966, succeeding Vittorio Valletta, shortly after the signing of an agreement to produce vehicles in the Soviet Union.

At the end of the 1960s he embodied, with a few other big industrialists of the north and the ENI, the sectors of Italian capitalism that saw a need to deal with workers struggles by collaborating with trade-union organizations. In keeping with that line, he was elected president of the Confindustria employers organization in 1974, remaining in that position until 1976.

In 1980, faced with the refusal of the governor of the Bank of Italy, Carlo Azeglio Ciampi, to again devalue the lira, Agnelli undertook the most sweeping housecleaning of the postwar period, laying off twenty-four thousand Fiat workers and profoundly restructuring its factories.

Having absorbed Lancia in 1970, Fiat took over Alfa Romeo in 1987 and Ferrari in 1988. Agnelli gave up the group presidency in 1996 to Cesare Romiti, but remained one of its central protagonists until his death.

He was also president, among other things, of the publishing house La Stampa and of Juventus, the Turin-based soccer team. In 1991 he was named senator-for-life.

Giulio Andreotti, 1919–

President of the Catholic university students from 1942 to 1945, deputy in the Constituent Assembly (1946), he was repeatedly reelected before being named senator-for-life in 1991. A close collaborator of Alcide De Gasperi, and undersecretary in his governments from 1947 to 1953, he became a minister in 1955 and, for a rather long period (1959–1966), was minister of defense. Named head of the government in 1972, he served in that position a total of seven times up to 1992. In 1973 Andreotti led a center-right executive branch that excluded the Socialists, yet in 1976, he became the head of the first government to be supported by the PCI. In the Ministry of Foreign Affairs almost without interruption in the 1980s, he again became president of the Council of Ministers in 1991, during the Gulf War.

Accused of several offenses, notably for links between some of his Sicilian friends and the Mafia, he was always acquitted. He authored more than thirty books and memoirs, and heads two Catholic magazines, including *30 Giorni*. Despite his denials, he was considered *the* Vatican's man in Italian politics. In 1999, two days after having been accused of playing an intermediary role in a political murder, Andreotti was publicly blessed by the pope.

Silvio Berlusconi (nickname: "il Cavaliere"), 1936–

He has headed the government three times: in 1994, between 2001 and 2006, and since 2008.

An entrepreneur in the construction sector since 1960, in 1978 he created one of the first private television networks, "Telemilano," which became "Canale 5" in 1980, after the birth of the financial/media company Fininvest. He followed this with the purchase in 1982 of "Italia 1" from the Rusconi publishing house, and in 1984 with the purchase of "Retequattro" from Mondadori. At the invitation of François Mitterrand, he founded "La Cinq" in France (1986), attempting to enlarge his activities throughout Europe, along with "Telefünf" in Germany (1987) and "Telecinco" in Spain (1989). In 1990, a law was passed in Italy declaring an end to the state's monopoly on television.

His publishing activities, which began with his investment in Indro Montanelli's *Giornale* in 1977, continued with the purchase of the biggest Italian publishing house, Mondadori, in 1989. Berlusconi also moved into the distribution, insurance, and financial products sectors, with *Mediolanum* and *Programma Italia*. Since 1986 he has owned the Milan AC soccer team.

Until then, very close to the Craxi's Socialist Party, a few weeks before the parliament elections of 1994, he founded his own party, Forza Italia, which carried the elections. He formed his first government with the former fascist National Alliance and the Northern League, which would quit the coalition that December. He was defeated in the legislative elections of 1996 because he was unable to make an arrangement with the Northern League. He changed that in 2001, with the serious electoral decline of the party of Umberto Bossi. Berlusconi set a record for the survival of a postwar Italian government. In the 2006 elections his coalition was defeated, by a margin of slightly more than twenty thousand votes. In the 2008 elections his new coalition with National Alliance and Northern League succeeded by and large.

On *Forbes* magazine's list of the richest men in the world, published in March 2009, Silvio Berlusconi ranked seventieth.

Guido Carli, 1914–93

Employed by the IRI, he was a Liberal Party deputy in the Constituent Assembly. In 1947 Carli was named the Italian representative to the executive board of the International Monetary Fund (IMF). In 1957 he became minister of external commerce and, in 1959, director general of Banca d'Italia. In 1960 he became its governor, a position he kept for fifteen years. In 1976 he was elected president of Confindustria, where, until 1980, he represented continuity with the Agnelli line. A Christian Democratic senator, he was Treasury minister until 1991. In that position, Carli was an architect of the single currency and helped bring about the compromise that led to the signing of the Maastricht Treaty.

Carlo Cattaneo, 1801–69

Milanese, a Latin professor in 1820, beginning in 1835 he worked as a publicist, editing economic and technical texts. His reformist proposals rendered him suspect in the eyes of the Austrian authorities. He criticized Mazzini's strictly unitary hypotheses and the neo-Guelphism of Gioberti, urging a federal solution for Italy, without being hostile to the Austrian Empire. The insurrection of Milan in March 1848, however, chose him as its leader. Victorious, he left the city when it was occupied by the Piedmontese army. Elected a deputy after unification, he never set foot in parliament, to avoid having to swear allegiance to the king.

Between 1839 and 1844, then again from 1860 to 1863, he headed *Il Politecnico*, a journal that had the subtitle "Monthly Review of Applied Studies on Prosperity and Social Culture." With Cavour and Quintino Sella, Cattaneo was one of the rare men of the *Risorgimento* who insisted on the necessity of industrializing the country.

Camillo Benso, count of Cavour, 1810–61

Lieutenant in the Engineer Corps in 1827, he took part in the fortification of the Alps. A partisan of the liberalism, à *la* Louis Philippe, in punishment he was sent to Fort Bard fortress in Val d'Aosta. After leaving the army he became mayor of the commune where his family owned property. In 1835 he traveled through northwest Europe, drawn by the economic and technical progress of Great Britain. On May 1, 1846, the *Revue nouvelle* published his essay "*Des chemins de fers en Italie par le comte Petitti, conseiller d'État du royaume de Sardaigne*" (On the Railways of Italy, by Count Petitti, state counselor of the Kingdom of Sardinia), which earned him an "invitation" to leave the kingdom. The same year he became the leading shareholder in the railway linking Turin to Genoa. In 1847 he founded, with Cesare Balbo, *Il Risorgimento*, a liberal journal.

As a deputy in 1848, Cavour was minister of commerce and of agriculture, and of the navy in 1851, and became president of the council (prime minister) the following year. In 1857 he launched a tunnel project under Mont Cenis that would make possible a rail link from Paris to Turin and open, according to his idea in 1846, a link from London to India via Brindisi and Suez. Having resigned after the armistice of Villafranca in 1859, he was persuaded by the English ambassador to Turin to return to his post in early 1860 to take the reins of the unification process then under way. He remained prime minister until his death.

Charles Albert of Savoy Carignan, 1798–1849

King of Sardinia beginning in 1831. Close to Piedmont's moderate liberal circles, he accepted the regency after the abdication of Victor Emmanuel I following the 1821 riots and conceded to the constitution. Disavowed by Charles Felix, a pretender to the throne, he left for exile in Florence. From there, he claimed Austrian support for his ambitions to the throne, which he obtained in exchange for a promise to retain an absolutist regime in Turin. As king, he respected that promise, even refusing to grant clemency to his comrades of 1821, in prison for ten years. Having expelled Cavour in 1846 because of his pamphlet on the railways, he authorized him to establish a liberal newspaper in 1847. In March 1848, facing the threat of revolution in Turin, he granted the statute that bears his name (*Statuto albertino*) and that would later become the Fundamental Law of a unified Italy until 1947. That same month he invaded Lombardy, which had declared itself independent, chasing the democrats from power in Milan. Defeated by the Austrians, he went to war against them again in March 1849 to prevent a revolution or a coup d'état in Turin. Defeated in Novara, he abdicated in favor of his son Victor Emmanuel.

Benedetto Craxi (Bettino), 1934–2000

A Socialist leader in a "red" suburb of Milan, Sesto San Giovanni, in the 1950s, he moved into the party leadership in 1965, following the line of Pietro Nenni, who favored greater autonomy vis-à-vis the PCI. A deputy in 1968, he became secretary of the PSI in 1976, following its worst electoral showing since the war. He was a severe critic of the Christian Democrats and the PCI, attempting to create a "third pole" at the moment of the governmental alliance between the country's two most important parties. He was the only influential politician to favor negotiations with the Red Brigades to save the life of Aldo Moro.

The PSI then experienced what Craxi called a "groundswell" of electoral growth, without however reaching the goal of becoming the leading party of the Italian left. Craxi brought his party back into the government in 1980, after a five-year absence. Named president of the council in 1983, he headed the executive twice up to 1987, thus giving the impression that the country had achieved domestic political stability and new international prestige.

The chief accused in the corruption scandals that were revealed starting in 1992, he explained, in a memorable speech to the Chamber of Deputies, the mechanisms by which all the parties had financed themselves. He then left the country and took refuge in Tunisia, where the local government protected him from several international arrest warrants issued following his repeated convictions in Italy.

He was vice president of Socialist International.

Francesco Crispi, 1818–1901

A Sicilian lawyer, he was a leader of the Palermo insurrection of January 1848. Exiled to Piedmont during the counterrevolution, he became a journalist. Active in all the Mazzinian conspiracies, Crispi had to take refuge in Malta, then in France. In 1860 he organized the arrival of the Garibaldians in Sicily and was an official in the new provisional government. Distanced from the leadership because of his republican and anti-Piedmontese sentiments, Crispi was, as of 1861, a deputy of the far left, even after his conversion to the monarchy (1864). A supporter of the war of 1866 and of an alliance with France in 1870, he became a minister in the first governments of the *Sinistra*, despite his polemics against transformism. As prime minister in 1887, he attempted to consolidate the national fabric of the country through his effort to solve the "Roman question," with the enlargement of the up-to-then nearly nonexistent welfare state, with the repression of social movements, and with an expansionist policy on the international scene. A supporter of the Triple Alliance, he was the instigator of the colonial missions to Ethiopia, which came to an end in 1895 with the defeat at Adwa, which forced him to resign. He was elected to parliament a final time in 1898.

Benedetto Croce, 1866–1952

Philosopher, historian, literary critic, and politician, he first met Antonio Labriola in the 1890s and, having fallen under the influence of Marxism, broke with it resoundingly at the end of the decade. This experience was, however, at the origin of his sense of history, which he wrote about in his journal *La Critica*, founded in 1903 and later one of the jewels of the Laterza publishing house of Bari.

Named senator in 1910, he was minister of public instruction under Giolitti in 1920. Having followed with intense interest the rise of fascism, he broke with it after the murder of Matteotti in 1924. He was at the origins, in 1925, of the Manifesto of Anti-Fascist Intellectuals. He took to the Senate floor in 1929 to express his opposition to the Concordat with the Church. He again became minister during the Badoglio and Bonomi governments (1944). President of the Liberal Party, he was elected to the Constituent Assembly.

Alcide De Gasperi, 1881–1954

Born in Trento, an Austrian subject, he studied at the University of Vienna. Beginning in 1905, he edited the newspaper of the local diocese. Elected municipal counselor of the Austrian People's Party in 1909, he became a deputy in the Austrian Parliament in 1911. A neutralist in 1914, he came into contact in Rome with politicians and the Church hierarchy with the aim of averting the conflict. Later, he spoke in the Vienna Parliament in favor of more humanitarian treatment of Italian war prisoners. Having become Italian himself in 1918 after the annexation of his native region, he took part in the founding of the People's Party in 1919, and became a deputy in 1921. He voted in favor of the first Mussolini government and, in 1923, replaced Luigi Sturzo as leader of the PPI, who had been pushed aside by the Church because of his opposition to fascism. After a final semiclandestine party congress in 1925, he sought refuge in Austria, but was arrested and condemned for possession of fake documents. Freed after sixteen months in prison, he worked, beginning in 1929, for the Vatican library, while also contributing to some Catholic journals.

In 1944 he became national secretary of the Christian Democratic Party and minister, beginning with the first Bonomi government (1944). He became head of the government in 1945 and continued in that role until 1953. He was a strong advocate of European integration, and the first president of the European Coal and Steel Community.

Agostino Depretis, 1813–87

Born near Stradella, in the province of Pavia (at that time part of the Kingdom of Savoy), he was an early disciple of Giuseppe Mazzini. Elected deputy at the Turin Parliament in 1848, since 1862 he was several times a minister in governments led by the *Destra*, in particular as minister of the navy during the catastrophic war against Austria in 1866. After some *Destra* representatives joined the *Sinistra*, he was called upon to form the first *Sinistra* cabinet in March 1876, which he led until 1878. Again prime minister in May 1881, he retained that office until his death.

Amintore Fanfani, 1908–99

A student at the Catholic university of Sacred Heart of Milan, he studied economics under Agostino Gemelli. He became a proponent of fascism, sharing its corporatist conception of society, which was close to the social doctrine of the Church. In 1938, as a professor of economic history at the same university, Fanfani signed the Manifesto of the Race, supporting the anti-Semitic laws voted on that same year. After the war he was part of the fundamentalist social-left faction within the Christian Democratic Party and rose to official rank in the party's propaganda office.

Involved in the drafting of the Constitution, he is known for having penned the phrase with which it begins: "Italy is a democratic republic founded on work." As minister of labor in 1947, he linked his name to a vast project for the construction of subsidized housing units, made possible by Marshall Plan financing. He became the Christian Democrats' secretary in 1954, just as De Gasperi was leaving the scene. Late in the decade he was among the advocates of the "opening to the left." He headed the first executive branch supported by the Socialists in 1962. Thrown into the minority in his party, he was for two years president of the General Assembly at the United Nations. As Christian Democrat secretary again in 1973, Fanfani suffered a crushing defeat in the referendum on divorce. As head of government for the sixth and last time in 1987, he took part in refounding the People's Party after the end of the Christian Democrats and gave a vote of confidence to the Prodi government in 1996. He was president of the Senate five times.

Giuseppe Garibaldi, 1807–82

Joined the merchant marine at the age of fifteen as a ship's boy and traveled to Odessa. Close to the Mazzinian republicans, he was sentenced to death in 1834 following an aborted conspiracy. Taking refuge in Latin America, he took part, between 1835 and 1843, in the continent's political and military struggles, in particular for the defense of the Rio Grande do Sul, which was in revolt against the Brazilian empire. At the moment of the 1848 revolution, Garibaldi swore loyalty to the King of Sardinia and became head of the provisional army of the government of liberated Milan. In 1849 he took on the same position in the new Roman republic and in that role inflicted minor defeats on the French Army, which had come to reestablish papal power. During the Sicilian insurrection of 1860, he raised a volunteer army (the "Mille", or "Red Shirts"), supported by the king and the British and tolerated by the Piedmont government, with which he was able to rout the Neapolitan Army. Having conquered Naples, Garibaldi restored the kingdom to the hands of Victor Emmanuel II. He twice attempted (1862 and 1867) to attack the Latium, which remained in the Pope's hands, but he was stopped once by the Italians and once by the French. In 1866 he fought the sole victorious battle against the Austrians, at Bezzecca, but the king ordered him to pull back. Elected to parliament in 1861, he organized in 1870 a volunteer corps to defend the French Republic against the Prussians, and then the Paris Commune against Thiers. In the 1871 election, he was elected to the French National Assembly.

Giovanni Giolitti, 1842–1928

A government functionary, he was elected to parliament in 1882 and became minister for the first time in 1889, at the Treasury, under Crispi. Head of the government in 1892, he was accused of receiving bribes from the Banca Romana, which was in crisis after the collapse of its real-estate investments, and had to resign. A minister again in 1901, he finally became head of the government, almost without interruption, until 1914. In this decade Italy experienced its first major wave of industrialization. Hostile to Italian participation in the European conflict of 1914, he remained in the shadows throughout the war. In 1920 Giolitti was called for the fifth and last time to serve as prime minister. Having assembled an electoral alliance that brought Fascist deputies into the parliament for the first time, he later opposed the Mussolini government.

Antonio Gramsci, 1891–1937

A student at the University of Turin, he made contact with the city's workers groups and joined the Socialist Youth in 1913. An interventionist from the beginning of the war, he later had a change of heart, and in 1916 began working with the Turinese edition of the party's journal *Avanti!*. He took part in the insurrection of August 1917 and, in 1919, he was an organizer and, above all, a theoretician of the experiment with factory councils, considered the Italian laborers' form of the

Soviets. The same year he founded the Communist journal *L'Ordine Nuovo* and was, the year afterward, involved in the efforts that led to the birth of the Communist Party of Italy, in January 1921. As a deputy in 1924, he founded *L'Unità* and headed the group that, on Moscow's orders, ousted Amadeo Bordiga from party leadership. He was arrested in November 1926 and sentenced to twenty years and four months in prison. It was during his detention that he wrote his notes on the ruling class and Italian intellectuals, of which a large part, following the "purging" desired by Togliatti, would be published after the war under the title *The Prison Notebooks*. He was freed just days before his death.

Niccolò Machiavelli, 1469–1527

Secretary of the Florentine chancellery in 1498, he undertook diplomatic missions for the republic to other Italian and foreign states. Upon his return from the Medicis in Florence, in 1512, he was accused of conspiracy and imprisoned. Freed and banished from Florence, he withdrew to his country home, where he devoted his existence to the study and production of historical and political texts: among others, he wrote *The Discourses on Livy* and *The Prince*. He returned to Florence in 1515 and wrote the comedy *La Mandragora (The Mandrake)* and, from 1520 to 1526, *The History of Florence*.

Alessandro Manzoni, 1785–1873

Born in Milan, he was Jacobinian during the French domination of Italy. He moved to Paris in 1805, where he frequented the literary salons and met his future wife, Henriette Blondel. In 1810 he converted to Catholicism and returned to Italy, where he composed the first of his *Hymns*, devoted to the chief religious festivities. In 1821 he began writing a novel that, after four different versions—the last of them completed in 1840—would become *I promessi sposi (The Betrothed)*. He also wrote two tragedies and several poems, including *March 1821*, in which he expressed his hopes for war with Austria, and *The Fifth of May*, on Napoleon and the limits of human action. After the 1827 version of *Promessi sposi* he decided to go to Florence to "purify" his language (to "rinse his laundry in the Arno," according to a famous phrase). A moderate liberal, he maintained his distance from active political life, but dealt actively with linguistic problems. Named a senator in 1860, he headed the Committee for Linguistic Reform and, after 1870, he agreed to become an honorary citizen of Rome, despite the interdiction decreed by Pius IX.

Giovanni Maria Mastai Ferretti (Pius IX), 1792–1878

Ordained a priest in 1819, he was sent to work in the apostolic nunciature of Santiago de Chile in 1823. Archbishop of Spoleto in 1827, then of Imola, he was named cardinal in 1840. Elected pope in 1846, he granted a broad amnesty to political prisoners and undertook some timid liberal reforms, including a customs league with the other Italian states. Faced with the spread of the revolutionary movement in 1848, Mastai Ferretti condemned the war against Austria and, in November, was himself overthrown by the proclamation of the republic in Rome. Restored to power by the French Army, he adopted a firm policy toward liberal and national ideas. In 1864 he published the *Syllabus*, a list of eighty ideas condemned by the Church, including rationalism, liberalism, and modern society in general. In 1854 and 1870 came two of the Church's defining dogmas: the immaculate conception and papal infallibility. In 1870, during the Italian conquest of Rome, he closed himself up in the Vatican, excommunicated the king, the government, and its military, and rejected the law of guarantees offered by the new peninsular state. His pontificate was the longest in Church history. He was beatified on September 3, 2000, by John Paul II.

Giuseppe Mazzini, 1805–72

As a law student at the University of Genoa, he published in 1827 a literary essay on Dante. After spending time in the secret societies of the *Carboneria*, in 1831 he founded the republican and unitary movement *Giovane Italia* (Young Italy). After an attempted insurrection in Savoy, he was sentenced to death and fled to Switzerland, where he founded the movement Young Europe, for the liberation of oppressed nationalities. Taking refuge in London, he published his fundamental text *Doveri dell'uomo (Duties of Man)* and organized a series of plots, conspiracies, and attacks. Back in Italy during the revolutionary tempest of 1848, he ultimately found himself at the head of the Roman Republic in 1849, with two other patriots, Carlo Armellini and Aurelio Saffi. Returning to London after the defeat of the revolution, he again began organizing plots and insurrections, concentrating his political hatred on the France of Napoleon III. Among his plans were a plot to dynamite Notre-Dame during the marriage of a relative of the emperor. He was among the founders of the Workers' International, but distanced himself from it to defend a religious conception of policy. In 1865 he was elected a deputy, but his election was invalidated because of his past convictions. In 1870 he returned to Italy with the goal of proclaiming a republic. Arrested, he was amnestied and exiled to Switzerland. He returned soon afterward, under an assumed name.

Aldo Moro, 1916–78

National president of Catholic university students, he became a professor of penal law in Bari in 1941. A deputy to the Constituent Assembly, he was junior minister under De Gasperi and minister from 1955. He began to play an important role in the Christian Democratic Party during the preparation of the center-left, which he saw as a means to eliminate social and political conflicts in Italy. Secretary of the party in 1959, he also continued as a university professor. In December 1963 he headed the first government to include Socialists. The crisis of the center-left in the late 1960s and early 1970s led to his ignoring for some time his most important political responsibilities. He was, nevertheless, minister of foreign affairs in the early

1970s, a position in which he accentuated the pro-Arab character of Italian policy. As head of the government again in 1975, he was the architect of the entry of the PCI into the majority one year later. In 1976 he became president of the Christian Democratic Party. Kidnapped by the Red Brigades in March 1978, he was abandoned by his party and killed by the terrorists fifty-five days later.

Benito Mussolini, 1883–1945

A militant socialist, in 1900 he fled to Switzerland to avoid military service and there encountered the works of Georges Sorel. Back in Italy, he did his service and then lived by his wits before becoming a teacher and contributor to numerous socialist journals. His growing influence within the party led him to take the offensive against the moderates, in particular during the Libyan War, which he fiercely opposed. Having distinguished himself at the PSI congress at Reggio Emilia, which was dominated by the far left wing, he was named chief-editor of *Avanti!*, the party journal. He was involved in the "red week" of Romagna, a series of strikes and clashes with security forces in June 1914. A pacifist when the war broke out, in October 1915 he became an interventionist and was immediately expelled from the Socialist Party. With his new journal, *Il Popolo d'Italia*, he led a violent campaign in favor of intervention, and was mobilized in 1915.

After the war he organized a political front formed of veterans, nationalist intellectuals, and revolutionary anarcho-syndicalists, along republican, anticlerical, and corporatist positions: the *Fasci italiani di combattimento* (Italian League of Combat). After two years with little influence, his movement took the leadership of the antiunion movement in late 1920, and was responsible for a growing number of acts of violence against trade-union and cooperative organizations and its political adversaries. With the violence reaching its peak, in the autumn of 1922 the king asked him to form a government, which also included the People's Party and the liberals.

After a crisis following the assassination of the Socialist deputy Matteotti, Mussolini claimed full moral responsibility for the actions of the Fascists and dismantled all political and labor organizations, except those linked to the Fascist Party and the Church, as well as the Confederation of Industrialists. From then until his death, three days after the general anti-German insurrection of April 1945, his personal history and that of the country were inseparable.

Eugenio Pacelli (Pius XII), 1876–1958

Grandson of Prince Marcantonio Pacelli, one of the founders of the daily *Osservatore Romano*, cousin of Ernesto Pacelli, founder and president of the Banco di Roma, he studied theology at the Gregorian University and was ordained a priest in 1899. Chamberlain of Pope Pius X, he was a consultant to the Holy Office in 1911 and subsecretary for foreign affairs on the eve of World War I. Papal nuncio in Bavaria in 1917, he was transferred to Berlin in 1925. In February 1930 he was named secretary of state (prime minister) of the Vatican, under Pius XI, and signed the concordats with Austria, Yugoslavia, and Nazi Germany.

In March 1939 he was elected pope after a single day of conclave. Having worked to prevent the conflict, Pacelli maintained an attitude of silent neutrality—an attitude that, notably, as concerns the Shoah, fueled endless discussions and debate. His visit to the neighborhoods of Rome bombed during the war was the first official trip by a pope outside Vatican walls since 1870. Upon the liberation of the capital in June 1944, Pacelli supported the Christian Democrats and mobilized Church structures in favor of the party. In 1949 the Holy Office announced the excommunication of "the communists and their allies." Pacelli was an active partisan of the re-Christianization of Italian society.

Romano Prodi, 1939–

A graduate of the Catholic university of the Sacred Heart in Milan, he was a professor of economics and industrial policy at the University of Bologna. President of the Il Mulino publishing house in Bologna from 1974 to 1978, he took part, with his political mentor, Beniamino Andreatta (who had been his boss at the university), in the birth of a free-trade faction within the Christian Democratic Party. Minister of industry in 1978, Prodi founded the Nomisma research center in 1981, from which many of his future collaborators would emerge. In 1982 he was named to head the largest industrial and financial holding company in Italy, the publicly funded Institute for Industrial Reconstruction (known by its Italian initials, IRI), overseeing the majority of big Italian industries, heavy industry, naval shipyards, nearly all banks, Alitalia, and the television system. Under his leadership, IRI erased a large part of its deficit. After his term expired in 1989 he was called back to service by the head of the government, Carlo Azeglio Ciampi, with the aim of overseeing a substantial privatization of state properties.

With Andreatta's support, Prodi was chosen as a candidate for prime minister by the center-left coalition of the *Ulivo* (Olive Tree) in the 1996 elections. Victorious, thanks to the divisions of the center-right, Prodi remained as head of the government for two years, succeeding first in returning the lira to the European Monetary System and later ushering it into the euro zone. He was ousted from the government by Massimo D'Alema, leader of the Democrats of the Left (DS), and was "indemnified" with the presidency of the European Commission. Under his leadership, the euro would become the effective currency of eleven countries in the European Union (EU), and ten new member countries would be co-opted in the EU as of May 1, 2004.

Back in Italy after his term ended, he was again named leader of the center-left coalition, narrowly carrying the elections of April 2006, and on May 16 he was named president of the Council of Ministers. His government, which had more than one hundred ministers and undersecretaries, resigned two years later.

Achille Ratti (Pius XI), 1857–1939

Enrolled in a Lombard seminary in 1867, he was ordained to the priesthood in 1879. With degrees in philosophy, canon law, and theology from the Gregorian University, he was, from 1888 to 1912, curator of the Ambrosian Library, before being named prefect of the Vatican Library in 1914 by the new pope, Benedict XV. As apostolic nuncio in Warsaw once the Polish state was reconstituted, he was profoundly marked by the siege of the city by the Red Army in August 1920. At a time when the fate of Silesia was not yet decided, he threw in his lot with Germany, as Pius XII would do twenty-five years later, disavowing the primate of Poland Stefan Wyszynski.

Archbishop of Milan in 1921, he was elected pope the following year. His platform, aiming to "*instaurare omnia in Christo*," clashed with the Fascist attempt to create a civil religion in Italy. Despite the support offered to fascism at the moment when he took power, notably with the abandonment of Sturzo and of the People's Party, and despite the signature of the Concordat and of the Lateran accords in 1929, Ratti was involved in two major crises with the Mussolini regime, in 1931 and 1938, which allowed the Church to maintain the independence of its organizations, especially among youth and university students. In 1937 Ratti published, in German, the encyclical *Mit brennender Sorge* (With Great Concern), in which he denounced the persecutions of Catholics in Hitler's Germany, without, however, mentioning the situation of the Jews. Five days later he published another encyclical, the *Divini Redemptoris*, in which he violently attacked communism. In 1938, during Hitler's visit to Rome, he polemically left the capital.

Luigi Sturzo, 1871–1959

Ordained to the priesthood in 1894, he earned a degree in theology in 1896. In 1900 Sturzo was among the founders of the Christian Democratic movement, disavowed by Pope Pius X. Deputy mayor of his native city Caltagirone, in Sicily, from 1905 to 1920, he served in 1912 as deputy president of the Association of Italian Communes. Secretary of Catholic Action in 1915, four years later he was among the founders of the People's Party and became its national secretary. Opposed to any agreement with the liberals, Sturzo voted, with his colleagues, in favor of the first Mussolini government. A year later, at the head of the faction hostile to any collaboration with the Fascists, Sturzo was disavowed by his own party and forced to resign. Abandoned as well by the Church, he was "invited" to leave Italy. He spent a lengthy exile in New York, where he published numerous historical and political texts. He returned to Italy at the end of the war, despite attempts by the ecclesiastical authorities to dissuade him. In 1952 he was named senator-for-life. That same year Pius XII invited him, against the advice of Chrstian Democrat secretary De Gasperi, to seek an agreement between the Christian Democrats of Rome and the Fascist far right to prevent the parties of the left from prevailing in municipal elections in the capital. After this attempt failed, Sturzo—isolated and ill—withdrew from active political life. The process of his beatification was opened in 2002.

Palmiro Togliatti, 1893–1964

Member of the Socialist Youth in Turin, where he was a university student, he was an interventionist at the start of the war and, for that reason, was not invited to the 1921 congress where the Communist Party was born. Collaborated with Gramsci on *L'Ordine nuovo*, and for some time was a faithful collaborator of secretary Amadeo Bordiga. After the latter's arrest, Togliatti formed a new majority around Gramsci, more responsive to directives from Moscow. Following Gramsci's own arrest in 1926, Togliatti became secretary of the party. Taking refuge in the USSR, he became number two in the Komintern and a faithful executor of Stalinist policy. He was commissioned to repress the internationalists and the anarchists in Spain, took part in the elimination of numerous Communists who had sought refuge in the Soviet Union, and signed with his own hand the dissolution of the Polish Communist Party in 1939, on the eve of the accord with Hitler. Back in Italy in 1944, he supported the Badoglio government and promoted the theses on "the Italian path to socialism." As minister of justice in 1946, he signed a decree of amnesty for thousands of Fascists, including some admitted collaborators. Victim of an terrorist attack in July 1948, shortly after the electoral defeat of his party, he urged his comrades to react calmly. After breaking in 1948 with Tito—dubbed a "Fascist"—Togliatti severely condemned the "Fascist" insurrection in Hungary and, that same year, attempted to prevent the publication in Italy of Khrushchev's secret report to the twentirth Communist Party Congress (PCUS). Upon his death the Russian industrial city of Stavropol was renamed Togliattigrad.

Victor Emmanuel II of Savoy, 1820–78

A soldier during the wars against Austria in 1848 and 1849, he became king of Sardinia upon the abdication of his father, Charles Albert, following the defeat at Novara, in 1849. Having concluded peace with Austria, he dissolved parliament. He named Cavour prime minister, and a long diatribe began between the two, each trying to diminish the authority, even the prerogatives, of the other. He maintained close contacts with the conspirators, both democrats and republicans, and, according to some sources, even with Felice Orsini, just days before the latter threw a bomb at Napoleon III in Paris. He threatened to dismiss Cavour when the latter agreed to cede Nice and Savoy to France in exchange for its war against Austria. In 1859, after the armistice of Villafranca, he signed the peace with Vienna, and Cavour resigned. At that point Victor Emmanuel accused the prime minister of "playing at making a revolution" and, a few months later, made contact with Garibaldi and encouraged his plan for the invasion of the Kingdom of the Two Sicilies.

Parliament named him king of Italy in March 1861. He decided to keep the dynastic numeral "II" to underline continuity with the Kingdom of Sardinia and the Kingdom of Italy.

Victor Emmanuel III of Savoy, 1869–1947

Son of King Humbert I, he ascended to the throne upon his father's assassination in 1900. Considered a liberal, he left substantial latitude to his prime ministers, in particular Giovanni Giolitti. During the early years of his reign, Italy evolved toward a system of constitutional monarchy. During the war he participated actively in overturning alliances that led Italy to be at war against the central empires. In October 1922, when the Fascists invaded the capital, he refused to sign the state of siege, and gave to Mussolini responsibility to form the new government. After the murder of Giacomo Matteotti, he was a key supporter of the Fascist head of the government. Removed from real responsibility, after the conquest of Ethiopia he was proclaimed emperor, and after the conquest of Albania, its king. In 1938 he signed the laws against the Jews, making them enforceable. When the end of the conflict was in sight, he organized a coup d'état and had Mussolini arrested, replacing him with Marshal Pietro Badoglio. When the armistice was announced on September 8, 1943, he fled with the latter and a large part of the new government, without leaving any directive to the military, and sought Anglo-American protection. While Mussolini, freed by the Germans, gave birth to the social republic, Victor Emmanuel declared war on Germany. Having confided the regency to his son Humbert, he abdicated only a month before the institutional referendum of June 1946, which transformed Italy into a republic.

Notes

Introduction

1. According to the International Monetary Fund (IMF), the GDP of the People's Republic of China and Hong Kong was $1.817 billion in 2004, while that of Italy was $1.680 billion. According to the World Bank, China and Hong Kong had a GDP of $1.812 billion, while that of Italy was $1.672 billion. IMF, World Economic Outlook database, September 2005; World Bank, World Development Indicators database, July 1, 2006. According to these Washington-based organizations, China had also surpassed France and Great Britain in terms of GDP.
2. For the range of statistical information, see Vera Negri Zamagni, *Dalla periferia al centro. La seconda rinascita economica dell'Italia (1861–1990)* (Bologna: Il Mulino, 1990), 465. For the 2005 estimate see https://www.cia.gov/cia/publications/factbook/rankorder/2078rank.html. According to the same source, calculating purchase power parity, the GDP of Italy was eighth in the world rankings in 2006 after the United States, China, Japan, India, Germany, the UK, and France.
3. Sergio Romano, interviewed in *Specchio*, supplement of *La Stampa*, February 1, 1997.
4. The European Innovation Scoreboard, a body of the European Union (EU), ranked the Italian education system twenty-first out of twenty-five in 2006 (http://trendchart.cordis.lu). According to data gathered by Marc Lazar, in 2002 spending on research and development represented 1.16 percent of GDP, "well below that of the European average." In terms of high-tech patents, Italy had only 7.1 per million inhabitants, compared with a European average of 26.45 in Germany and 32 in France and the UK. Lazar, *L'Italie à la derive: Le moment Berlusconi* (Paris: Perrin, 2006), 132. According to the World Economic Forum, Italy was in forty-second place (out of 115 countries studied) in 2006 for its level of investment in research and development, its cooperation between universities and business, and the quality of scientific education; in ninety-first position regarding the rubric "absorption of technology into business practice." Statistics offered by Giuseppe Cassini, *Gli anni del declino: La politica estera del governo Berlusconi, 2001–2006* (Milan: Bruno Mondadori, 2007), 18.
5. Luciano Gallino, *La scomparsa dell'Italia industriale* (Turin: Einaudi, 2003), 3.
6. Zeffiro Ciuffoletti, *Stato senza nazione. Disegno di storia del Risorgimento e dell'Unità d'Italia* (Naples: Morano, 1993), 311, 312.
7. G. Mammarella and P. Cacace, *La politica estera dell'Italia. Dallo Stato unitario ai giorni nostri* (Bari: Laterza, 2006), vi. These authors return to this question at several points, from section 4, chapter VIII, sections 1 and 2 of chapter IX, in particular pages 277, 278, 280, and 281.

8. Giulio Bollati, *L'Italiano. Il carattere nazionale come storia e come invenzione* (Turin: Einaudi, 1983), 40.
9. Sergio Romano, *Histoire de l'Italie du Risorgimento à nos jours* (Paris: Seuil, 1977), 201.
10. "Europe should be again to us the External Commissary, the Bogeyman who force this anarchical and bungling country to pull itself together" Federico Rampini, *Germanizzazione: Come cambierà l'Italia* (Bari: Laterza, 1996), 20.
11. Mario Monti, *Intervista sull'Italia in Europa,* under the direction of Federico Rampini (Bari: Laterza, 1998), 164.
12. Statistics taken from the annual report of the governor of the Banca d'Italia Mario Draghi (see *Corriere della Sera,* June 1, 2006); Hugues Portelli, *L'Italie de Berlusconi* (Paris: Buchet Chastel, 2006), 14; Marc Lazar, *L'Italie à la derive,* 111, 112; Cassini, *Gli anni del declino,* 18, 19.
13. Register (or Fund) for the South, created in 1950 in order to stimulate economic growth and development in the south of the country. It was given a new status in 1984.
14. The Institute for Industrial Reconstruction (IRI) was an organization set up by the Italian government in 1933, initially to rescue floundering companies that could no longer afford to repay their creditors. In the postwar period, the IRI owned many diverse businesses such as the highway system, public television, Alitalia Airlines, 80 percent of the most important banks, telecommunications companies, and several industries (food, iron and steel, shipyards, vehicles, Alfa Romeo, etc.).
15. In Italy, deputies have immunity from legal prosecution as long as Parliament is in session, unless Parliament itself authorizes the prosecution of one of its members.
16. Raffaele Romanelli, *L'Italia liberale* (Bologna: Il Mulino, 1990), 212. The use of *Sinistra* and *Destra* in Italian allows us to distinguish from the left and right defined by the parliamentary "geography" of the twentieth century.
17. This phrase was made famous by Massimo D'Alema's book *Un paese normale. La Sinistra e il futuro dell'Italia* (Milan: Mondadori, 1995).
18. *Shoeshine* (Italian: *Sciuscià,* 1946) and *Ladri di biciclette* (released in English as *The Bicycle Thief* or *Bicycle Thieves,* 1948) are two of Vittorio De Sica's major neorealist works.
19. Edward C. Banfield, *Moral Basis of a Backward Society* (New York: Free Press, 1958), 118, 139, 155, 156, 161.
20. Roberto Cartocci, *Mappa del Tesoro: Atlante del capitale sociale in Italia* (Bologna: Il Mulino, 2007), 13.

Foreword

1. Piero Gobetti, "*Motivi di storia italiana,*" *La Rivoluzione liberale,* May 1, 1923.
2. Valerio Castronovo, *Storia economica d'Italia* (Turin: Einaudi, 1995), 6–10; Giacomo Perticone, *La politica estera italiana dal 1861 al 1914* (Turin: ERI, 1961), 13; Tullio De Mauro, *Storia linguistica dell'Italia unita* (Bari: Laterza, 1965), 37, 38; V. Zamagni, *Dalla periferia al centro. La seconda rinascita economica dell'Italia (1861–1990)* (Bologna: Il Mulino, 1990), 42, 43; www.stradeanas.it.
3. Antonio Gramsci, *Il Risorgimento* (Turin: Einaudi, 1949), 42, 43.
4. Maximilien Misson credits this phrasing to Victor Amadeus II (1666–1732), the first king of the House, in his *Voyage d'Italie, avec un Mémoire contenant des avis utiles à ceux qui voudront faire le mesme voyage* (The Hague: Chez Henry van Belderen, 1702).
5. Quoted by Denis Mack Smith, "L'Italia," in *Storia del mondo moderno,* vol. X (Cambridge: Cambridge University Press, 1972), 705.
6. Quoted by Giuseppe La Farina, *Storia d'Italia dal 1815 al 1850,* vol. II (Milan: Casa Editrice Italiana, 1861), 474.
7. Gramsci, *Il Risorgimento,* 49.

8. Quoted by Giorgio Candeloro, *Storia dell'Italia moderna*, vol. II, *Dalla Restaurazione alla rivoluzione nazionale, 1815–1846* (Milan: Feltrinelli, 1958), 27. The Kingdom of Italy included, in 1810, the regions of Lombardy (augmented by the province of Novara and the zone of Tortona), Veneto, and part of Emilia, Romagna, and the Marche.
9. This approximate valuation comes from different calculations suggested by J. M. Roberts, *Italia, in Storia del mondo moderno*, vol. x (Milan: Garzanti, 1969), 499; Marco Meriggi, "Borghesie," in *Dizionario storico dell'Italia unita*, ed. Bruno Bongiovanni and Nicola Tranfaglia (Bari: Laterza, 1996), 73, 74; Didier Musiedlak, "*Construction politique et identité nationale*," in *L'Italie, une nation en suspens*, ed. I. Diamanti, A. Dieckhoff, M. Lazar, D. Musiedlak (Brussels: Editions Complexe, 1995), 30.
10. Carlo Cattaneo, *L'insurrezione di Milano nel 1848 e la successiva guerra* (Turin: Loescher, 1968), 6 (first edition, Paris, September 1848). By some calculations, the Austrian treasury absorbed some two-thirds of the annual active budget of the Lombard–Venetian Kingdom. Candeloro, *Storia dell'Italia moderna*, 23–24.
11. Smith, "L'Italia", 722.
12. Quoted by Gramsci, *Il Risorgimento*, 109. Massimo d'Azeglio served as prime minister of the Sardinian kingdom on several occasions.
13. Paul Kennedy, *The Rise and Fall of the Great Powers* (London: Fontana Press, 1989), 234.
14. The phrase was created by Francesco Crispi: "*Cavour? What did he finally do, Cavour? Nothing but to diplomatize the revolution* » - as cited in Gramsci, *Il Risorgimento*, 149.
15. Gramsci, *Il Risorgimento*, 149.
16. Sergio Romano, *Histoire de l'Italie du Risorgimento à nos jours* (Paris: Seuil, 1977), 14.
17. Quoted by Smith, *L'Italia*, 732.
18. "Napoleon III will conclude a peace with Austria and stifle all efforts of the Italians to carry on the war . . . but, should Austria be worsted in the fight, that peace will be concluded on the Adige, which will leave the whole of Venice and part of Lombardy in the hands of the hated Austrians." Karl Marx, in the *New York Daily Tribune*, January 24, 1859.
19. Romano, *Histoire de l'Italie du Risorgimento à nos jours*, 9.
20. Senate minutes relative to the session of June 4, 1912.
21. "Se vogliamo che tutto rimanga come e, bisogna che tutto cambi"; this is the affirmation made famous by the novel *Il Gattopardo* by Giuseppe Tomasi de Lampedusa.
22. The revolutionary republic of Rome (February to July 1849) provided Garibaldi with his first opportunity to make his military virtues known: he defeated the French disembarked in Civitavecchia and repulsed the Neapolitans in Palestrina and Velletri; he was, however, defeated in the battle of Gianicolo on June 3. For the battles of Aspromonte, Bezzecca, and Mentana, see the biographical profile.
23. Italo Balbo, in *Critica fascista*, May 24, 1932, quoted by Gramsci, *Il Risorgimento*, 165.
24. Romano, *Histoire de l'Italie du Risorgimento a nos jours*, 21.

Chapter 1

1. Quoted by Mario Vinciguerra, "Depretis e la nuova classe politica italiana," in *Il centenario del Parlamento, 8 maggio 1848–8 maggio 1948* (Rome: Chamber of Deputies, 1948).
2. The word "mafia" is used for the first time in a theater comedy *Li mafiusi di la Vicaria di Palermu* in 1862 and 1863. The prefect of Palermo, Filippo Gualtiero, was the first to speak of Mafia "officially" in April 1865. S. Lupo, *Storia della mafia dalle origini ai giorni nostri* (Rome: Donzelli, 1996), 13.

3. Giampiero Carocci, *Il trasformismo dall'unità ad oggi* (Milan: Unicopli, 1992), 7.
4. P. Bevilacqua, *Breve storia dell'Italia meridionale* (Rome: Donzelli, 2005), 146–59; G. Viesti, *Abolire il Mezzogiorno* (Rome: Laterza, 2003), 4; Vera Zamagni, "*Les difficultés économiques de la Seconde République,*" in *L'Italie aujourd'hui: Situation et perspectives après le séisme des années 90*, ed. Manlio Graziano (Paris: L'Harmattan, 2004), 121.
5. Quoted by Valerio Castronovo, *L'industria italiana dall'Ottocento a oggi* (Milan: Mondadori, 1980), 9.
6. Quoted by V. Castronovo, *Storia economica d'Italia. Dall'Ottocento ai giorni nostri!* (Turin: Einaudi, 1995), 42.
7. Quoted by Denis Mack Smith in *Storia d'Italia dal 1861 al 1997* (Rome-Bari: Laterza, 1998), 85.
8. See Gino Luzzatto, *Breve storia economica dell'Italia medievale* (Turin: Einaudi, 1958), 182.
9. Vera Zamagni, *Dalla periferia al centro. La seconda rinascita economica dell'Italia (1861–1990)* (Bologna: Il Mulino, 1990), 23.
10. Zamagni, *Dalla periferia al centro*, 19.
11. Maurice Aymard, "La transizione dal feudalesimo al capitalismo," in *Storia d'Italia Annali I. Dal feudalesimo al capitalismo*, ed. Ruggiero Romano and Corrado Vivanti (Turin: Einaudi, 1978), 1133–92.
12. See Luzzatto, *Breve storia economica*, 111–14; and Zamagni, *Dalla periferia al centro*, 18, 19.
13. Paul Kennedy, *The Rise and Fall of the Great Powers* (London: Fontana Press, 1989), 4.
14. See Fernand Braudel, *Le modèle italien* (Paris: Flammarion, 1994).

Chapter 2

1. José Gil, "*Nazione,*" in *Enciclopedia Einaudi*, vol. IX, ed. Ruggiero Romano (Turin: Einaudi, 1980), 851.
2. Emmanuel Joseph Sieyès, *Écrits politiques* (Paris: Edition des archives contemporaines, 1994), 121.
3. *Limes* 1993, no. 1–2:10. The first article in this edition was a discussion on the theme "In Search of the National Interest."
4. This monograph-style edition had the thematic title "*A che serve l'Italia*" (What good is Italy) and the subtitle "*Perché siamo una nazione*" (This is why we are a nation).
5. Lucio Caracciolo, "Editorial," *Limes* 1994, no. 4:9.
6. Federico Fubini, "*A Bruxelles è tramontato il tricolore,*" *Limes* 1996, no. 3:208. Fubini is a researcher and a journalist for the *Corriere della Sera*.
7. Carlo Jean, "*La nostra sicurezza nel mondo balcanizzato. Linee-guida per una politica estera e di difesa coerente,*" *Limes* 1994, no. 4:202. General Jean was at the time the president of the *Centro Alti Studi per la Difesa* (Center for Advanced Defense Studies).
8. Patrizio Bianchi, "*Dove stanno i nostri interessi economici,*" *Limes* 1994, no. 4:214. At the time he wrote the article, Bianchi was a professor of economics for the European Community in Bologna.
9. Jacopo Turri, "*Scene da una secessione,*" in *Limes* 1996, no. 3:.
10. *Corriere della Sera*, June 8, 1995.
11. *La Stampa*, November 1, 1995.
12. *Corriere della Sera*, June 1, 1996.
13. Sergio Romano, "*Così muore una nazione,*" *La Stampa*, January 11, 1996.
14. Interview with Romano Prodi, *Limes* 1996, no.3:24.

15. Antonio Maccanico was secretary to the president of the republic under Sandro Pertini and Francesco Cossiga, president of Mediobanca (1987–1988), senator and minister on several occasions, notably minister of institutional reforms in the Prodi and D'Alema governments.

Chapter 3

1. Antonio Gramsci, *Letteratura e vita nazionale* (Rome: Editori Riuniti, 1975), 88.
2. Gramsci, *Letteratura e vita nazionale*, 138.
3. Giorgio Rumi, "*Povera Padania, triste storia la sua*," *Liberal*, October 1996.
4. See Silvio Lanaro, "*Le élites settentrionali e la storia italiana*," *Meridiana*, no. 16, 1993.
5. The text was C. Cattaneo, *Notizie naturali e civili su la Lombardia* (1844), now *Storia della Lombardia* (Milan: Rusconi, 1992).
6. *La città considerata come principio ideale delle istorie d'Italia* (1855), now *Storia della Lombardia*.
7. G. Rumi, "*Povera Padania, triste storia la sua*," *Liberal*, no. 19, October 1996.
8. Cattaneo, *Notizie naturali e civili*, 138.
9. Cattaneo, *Notizie naturali e civili*, 163. According to the calculations of Vera Zamagni, in 1857 Lombardy produced a value corresponding to 238 lira per hectare, which was slightly less than 1.5 times the production of Piedmont (169 lira), approximately twice that of Tuscany (117 lira), 3 times that of the Kingdom of the Two Sicilies (81 lira), and 3.5 times that of the State of the Church (68 lira). *Dalla periferia al centro. La seconda rinascita economica dell'Italia (1861-1990)* (Bologna: Il Mulino, 1990), 42.
10. Cattaneo, *Notizie naturali e civili*, 167.
11. Marco Meriggi, *Breve storia dell'Italia settentrionale, dall'Ottocento ad oggi* (Rome: Donzelli, 1996), 152.
12. Fausto Fonzi, *Crispi e lo Stato di Milano* (Milan: Giuffrè, 1965). The "State of Milan" was, according to Francesco Crispi's polemical description, a coalition between Milanese industry, the democrats, the Socialists, and a part of the Catholic world organized against the Africa policy of the Sicilian prime minister. During hostile street demonstrations organized in Milan during the Abyssinian War, people shouted slogans of support for the Ethiopian Negus Menelik. Felice Cavallotti (*1842–98*) was a radical politician, poet, and dramatic author.
13. Filippo Turati, "Proemio al programma comunale dei socialisti milanesi" *Critica Sociale*, 20(9): 134–37, May 1, 1910.

Chapter 4

1. See Ernesto Galli della Loggia, *L'identità italiana* (Bologna: Il Mulino, 1998), 81.
2. This was in "*Il carattere nazionale come storia e come invenzione*," published in 1976 in the first volume of *La Storia d'Italia* (Turin: Einaudi), and republished as a book under the very similar title *L'Italiano. Il carattere nazionale come storia e come invenzione* (Turin: Einaudi, 1983).
3. "*Il carattere nazionale come storia e come invenzione*," 40.
4. Galli della Loggia, *L'identità italiana*, 130, 131.
5. The revolt known as "the Sicilian Vespers" was organized in Palermo by the Sicilian nobility to "avenge" the Swabians, who had recently been vanquished by the Plantagenets after the death of Frederick I Barbarossa. It was at the beginning of Spanish

domination of the Aragonese and, some say, the birth of the Mafia. The revolt of the Ciompi (wool workers) of Florence in 1378 was probably the revolt in which the class characteristics of the protagonists were the clearest. Nonetheless, it also led to the uprising of the "very slim people" under the impulse of a leader, Michele di Lando, who did not hesitate to betray the Ciompi and pass over to the "Arti maggiori" (Major Guilds) This revolt ended with the workers' defeat and the definitive political crisis of the Commune of Florence. Masaniello (1620–1647; his real name was Tommaso Aniello), led the revolt of the Neapolitan commoners of 1647 against tax-collection bureaus. Named "captain general of the most loyal people" by the viceroy of Naples, he was later killed by his own partisans. Finally, Cola di Rienzo took advantage of the vacancy in the pontifical seat in Rome in 1347 and was named "tribune of the people" with the support of Clement VI, one of the Avignon popes. A victim of his own ambition, he defied Emperor Charles IV, who imprisoned him. Returned to Rome, he ended the anarchy of the city before being captured and killed by the populace.

6. Indro Montanelli and Roberto Gervaso, *L'Italia dei secoli d'oro* (Milan: Rizzoli, 1967), 135; Luigi Barzini, *The Italians: A Full-Length Portrait Featuring Their Manners and Morals* (New York: Touchstone, 1996); Giuseppe Prezzolini, *The Legacy of Italy* (New York: Vanni, 1948).
7. This image, which appeared in the *Römische Geschichte*, was repeated by G. Prezzolini.
8. Johann Gottlieb Ficthe, *Discours à la nation allemande* (*Addresses to the German Nation*), Paris: Imprimerie nationale, 1992), 54.
9. Galli della Loggia, *L'identità italiana*, 155.
10. Galli della Loggia, *L'identità italiana*, 131.
11. The phrase comes from Anne-Marie Thiesse, *La création des identités nationales. Europe XVIIIème-XXème siècle*, Paris: Seuil, 1999, 161.
12. "Catonism," according to the American sociologist Barrington Moore, is the "rhetorical glorification of the peasant as the backbone of society." Barrington Moore, Jr., *Social Origins of Dictatorship and Democracy. Lord and Peasant in the Making of the Modern World* (Boston: Beacon Press, 1993), 491–96.
13. Tommaso Garzoni, *Piazza universale di tutte le professioni del mondo, e nobili et ignobili* (Venice: Gio Battista Somascho, 1586); Giuseppe Baretti, *An Account of the Manners and Customs in Italy: With Observations on the Mistakes of Some Travelers, With Regard to That Country* (London: T. Davies, 1768).
14. Prezzolini, *The Legacy of Italy*, 220.
15. Quoted by Claudio Varese, "Teatro, prosa, poesia," in *Storia della Letteratura Italiana*, vol. V, ed. Emilio Cecchi and Natalino Sapegno (Milan: Garzanti, 1967), 736.
16. Vareses, "Teatro, prosa, poesia," 58.
17. Paolo Greppi, *La Rivoluzione francese nel carteggio di un osservatore italiano*, vol. 1 (Milan: Hoepli, 1900–1904), 360. Greppi was the "finance minister" of the Cisalpine Republic, of which Melzi d'Eril was vice president.
18. "Our revolution being a passive one, the only way it could prevail was by conquering the opinion of the people," wrote Cuoco in his famous *Saggio storico sulla rivoluzione napoletana del 1799*. In order to return King Ferdinand IV to the throne, Cardinal Fabrizio Ruffo di Bagnara organized the Army of the Holy Faith (whose adherents were thus referred to as Sanfedisti), led by famous and pitiless outlaws, but enjoying vast support among the peasant masses of the kingdom.

Chapter 5

1. Paolo Greppi, *La Rivoluzione francese nel carteggio di un osservatore italiano* (Milan: Hoepli, 1900–1904), 364. Greppi (1748–1800), a nobleman and a tradesman, was also a diplomat who was close to Napoleon, both in Paris and in Milan.
2. Greppi, *La Rivoluzione francese*, 380.
3. G. Bollati, *L'Italiano. Il carattere nazionale come storia e come invenzione* (Turin: Einaudi, 1983), 58.
4. Quoted by Ettore Passerin d'Entreves, "Ideologie del Risorgimento," in *Storia della Letteratura Italiana*, vol. VII, ed. Emilio Cecchi and Natalino Sapegno (Milan: Garzanti, 1969), 240.
5. These quotations, taken from articles published in the *Giornale italiano*, are mentioned by Bollati, *L'Italiano*, 66–68.
6. Bollati, *L'Italiano*, 77. It is Bollati who emphasizes this.
7. A. Gramsci, *Letteratura e vita nazionale* (Rome: Editori Riuniti, 1975), 98, 99.
8. Bollati, *L'Italiano*, 81.
9. Augustine of Hippo, *De civitate Dei contra paganos (413–426)*, XIX, 13.
10. Having completed his first version of the *Promessi Sposi* (which in fact was his third, after *Fermo e Lucia* and *Gli sposi promessi*) in 1827, Manzoni's linguistic preoccupation led him to travel to Florence "to rinse his laundry in the Arno." From this linguistic revision, founded on the spoken language cultivated in the Tuscan capital, the definitive version of *Promessi Sposi* (The Betrothed) was born in 1840.
11. A. Manzoni, "*Sulla morale cattolica*, part II," in *Tutte le opere*, vol. ii (Milan: Mondadori, 1963), 534.
12. E. Galli della Loggia, *L'identità italiana* (Bologna: Il Mulino, 1998), 131.
13. A. Gramsci, *Il Risorgimento* (Turin: Einaudi, 1949), 116.
14. "Their instinctive tendency was to oppose any patriotic army which requisitioned their scanty food supplies and hence were usually a counterrevolutionary force in politics. In 1848 the Lombard peasants opened the irrigation dikes against the invading Piedmontese. In 1849, as in 1799, they had fought for the old dynasties in both North and South, because their dislike of royal tyranny was less than their hatred of the local lawyer, the usurer and the factor who managed the landowner's estate." Denis Mack Smith, *Storia d'Italia dal 1861 al 1997* (Roma: Laterza, 1997), 49, 50).
15. Giuseppe Pecchio, *Il Conciliatore*, July 8, 1819. The same year, Giuseppe Pecchio became a deputy of the provincial assembly of Milan. In 1829, he wrote *Storia dell'economia pubblica in Italia*, A. Levasseur, Paris, 1830.
16. Published in the review *Annali universali di statistica*, vol. XIX (1829).
17. Carlo Ilarione Petitti di Roreto, *Del lavoro de' fanciulli nelle manifatture*, (May 20, 1841) Turin, Memorie della Regia Accademia delle scienze di Torino, 1841.
18. *Cenni statistici sulla condizione economica e morale della città di Parigi* (1839), quoted by G. Bollati, *L'Italiano*, 105.
19. Quoted by G. Bollati, *L'Italiano*, p. 105.
20. V. Gioberti, *Del primato morale e civile degli Italiani*, part I (Naples: Stamperia del Vaglio, 1861), 166.
21. Gioberti, *Del Primato morale*, 52. In the second part (*Théologie des nations européennes*), Gioberti states: "The salvation of England comes from Catholicism."
22. Paul Kennedy, *The Rise and Fall of the Great Powers* (New York: Random House, 1987), 385.
23. Kennedy, *The Rise and Fall of the Great Powers*, 337.

24. Quoted by Elena Aga Rossi, *Dal partito popolare alla democrazia cristiana* (Bologna: Cappelli, 1969), 22.
25. Giuseppe Mazzini, *Dei doveri dell'uomo* (Genoa: Giovanni Ricci Editore, 1922), 18.
26. Tullio De Mauro, *Storia linguistica dell'Italia unita* (Bari: Laterza, 1963), 43, 44.

Chapter 6

1. According to figures suggested by Raffaele Romanelli, the movement led to 257 deaths, 1,099 injuries, and 3,788 arrests. Rosario Romeo, *L'Italia liberale* (Bologna: Il Mulino, 1990), 156.
2. Giacomo Devoto, *Il linguaggio d'Italia* (Milan: Rizzoli, 1974), 306, 308.
3. T. de Mauro, *Storia linguistica dell'Italia unita* (Rome: Laterza, 1984), 16.
4. T. de Mauro, *Storia linguistica dell'Italia unita*, 92, 93. Examples of the structural inadequacy cover more than five pages of de Mauro's text.
5. E. Galli della Loggia, *L'identità italiana* (Bologna: Il Mulino, 1998), 107.
6. T. de Mauro, *Storia linguistica dell'Italia unita*, 46.
7. A thesis on dialectology written in 1968 was entirely devoted to the "differences, especially of a lexical character, between one zone of the city and another" of the town of Asti. Maria Grazia Socco, "*Per una topografia linguistica di Asti*" (thesis, University of Turin, 1967–68), 1, 2. Keep in mind that, when the research published in this thesis was carried out, Asti had only some 75,000 inhabitants (76,151 in the 1971 census).
8. Antonio Gramsci, *Gli intellettuali e la formazione della cultura* (Turin: Einaudi, 1953), 23.
9. Among others, Luigi Settembrini, Edoardo Scarfoglio, Carlo Dossi, as well as the Tuscans Giosuè Carducci and Pietro Fanfani.
10. The data come from the ministerial survey of 1864–65; quoted by de Mauro, *Storia linguistica dell'Italia unita*, 40.
11. This sociolinguistic distinction between the countryside and the cities was introduced by Marcel Cohen in *Pour une sociologie du language* (Paris: Albin Michel, 1956), 139–40.
12. Matteo Giulio Bartoli, "*I dialetti dell'Italia settentrionale*," in *Piemonte*, 5th ed. (Milan: Touring Club Italiano, 1930), 83.
13. Gramsci, *Gli intellettuali*, 39.
14. Amadeo Bordiga, *I fattori di razza e nazione nella teoria marxista* (Milan: Iskra Edizioni, 1976), 80.
15. Gramsci, *Gli intellettuali*, 40.
16. Galli della Loggia, *L'identità italiana*, 123.
17. Galli della Loggia explains that "in France, in Spain and in Austria—which is to say in all the other large Catholic countries—a religiously inspired political and ideological perspective ... was consciously assumed by the national monarchy" (*L'identità*, 127).
18. Gramsci, *Gli intellettuali*, 63.
19. G. Prezzolini, *The Legacy of Italy* (New York: Vanni, 1948), 237.
20. Gramsci, *Gli intellettuali*, 59, 60.
21. Eugene of Savoy-Carignan-Soisson (1663–1736) led the Austrian army in its victorious campaigns against the Turks of Zenta in 1697 and again in Petrovaradin, in Temesvar, and, especially, in Belgrade (1716–1717), and against the French during the War of Spanish Succession. He was also governor of Milan and a diplomat (the peace of Rastadt in 1709 and of Passarowitz in 1718).
22. Gramsci, *Gli intellettuali*, 60.

23. Pasquale Villari, *Di chi è la colpa? O sia La Pace e la guerra* (Milan: Tipografia di Zanetti Francesco, 1866), 31. Villari (1826–1917) was a famed historian. The "quadrilateral" was a territory controlled by four Austrian fortresses that had allowed Vienna's army—during the wars of 1848, 1859, and 1866—to defend the western accesses to Venice while also guarding communications avenues with the center of the empire via Trentino and the Tirol.
24. A. Gramsci, *Letteratura e vita nazionale* (Rome: Editori Riuniti, 1975), 86.
25. Manlio Graziano, "Le philosophe militant," in *L'Internationaliste* no. 17–18, July–August 2001.
26. Melchiorre Cesarotti (1730–1808) was a teacher of rhetoric and ancient literature. The text from which the quotation is taken is the *Saggio sulla filosofia delle lingue applicata alla lingua italiana* (Padoua: Penada, 1785).
27. French became an official language of the Italian departments of the empire in 1809 (including, roughly speaking, the modern regions of Piedmont, Liguria, Tuscany, and Latium), along with Italian.
28. Vittorio Alfieri, *La vita* Turin: Unione Tipografico Editrice Torinese, 1948, 168, 169.
29. Francesco de Sanctis, *Storia della letteratura italiana* (Milan: Bietti, 1963), 810, 811. De Sanctis (1817–1883), the most important Italian literary critic of the nineteenth century, took part in the revolution of 1848 in Naples. Later (1878–1882), he was minister of education.
30. Quoted by T. de Mauro, *Storia linguistica*, 281.
31. Carlo Muscetta, "*Niccolò Tommaseo*," in *Storia della letteratura italiana*, vol. VII, ed. Emilio Cecchi and Natalino Sapegno (Milan: Garzanti, 1969), 750.
32. Edoardo Scarfoglio, *Il libro di don Chisciotte* (Naples: L'Editrice Italiana, 1919), 103, 104.
33. S. Romano, *Histoire de l'Italie du Risorgimento à nos jours* (Paris: Seuil, 1977), 33.
34. Gramsci, *Letteratura e vita nazionale*, 252.

Chapter 7

1. Quoted by Gianfranco Lotti, *L'avventurosa storia della lingua italiana* (Milan: Bompiani, 2000), 121. Balbo's text is *Del naturale dei Piemontesi* (Florence, 1855).
2. Quoted by Aurelio Lepre in *Italia, addio? Unità e disunità dal 1860 a oggi* (Milan: Mondadori, 1994), 41.
3. E. Galli della Loggia, *L'identità italiana* (Bologna: Il Mulino, 1998), 61.
4. See Gaston Tuaillon, "*Le frontiere linguistiche (Il caso Piemonte),*" in *La frontiera da Stato a nazione. Il caso Piemonte*, ed. Carlo Ossola, Claude Raffestin, and Mario Ricciardi (Rome: Bulzoni, 1987), 221.
5. The royal family's entrance into the new capital of Turin took place on February 7, 1563. In October 1581, Montaigne wrote of Turin: "French is widely spoken here, and all the people of the country seem quite affectionate toward France. The common language has only Italian pronunciation but it is essentially composed of our own expressions." M. de Montaigne, *Journal du voyage de Michel de Montaigne en Italie par la Suisse & l'Allemagne en 1580 & 1581* (Paris: Chez Le Jay Librairie, 1774), 154.
6. Dante Alighieri, *De vulgari eloquentia*, vol. I, XV, 7
7. Quoted by T. de Mauro, *Storia linguistica dell'Italia unita* (Rome-Bari: Laterza, 1984), 287. After 1848 Costanza Arconati (1800–1871), born in Vienna, followed her husband, the Milanese marquis Giuseppe, to Belgium and to Turin, where she held a political and literary salon open to exiles of the other Italian states.

8. See M. Meriggi, *Breve storia dell'Italia settentrionale dall'Ottocento ad oggi* (Rome: Donzelli, 1996), 9.
9. G. Bollati, "Osservazioni sul carattere dei piemontesi," in an appendix to *L'Italiano. Il carattere nazionale come storia e come invenzione* (Turin: Einaudi, 1983), 185.
10. The phrase comes from Cesare Balbo, *Del naturale dei Piemontesi* (Florence, 1855).
11. Cesare Balbo, "*Del naturale dei Piemontesi*," quoted by Meriggi, *Breve storia dell'Italia settentrionale*, 8, 9. The quality that makes Piedmontese stand out from other Italians is, according to Balbo, that they are less subject to "the excitation of passions," less subject to inconstancy and to "infidelity." The *"sodezza"* [solidity] of which he speaks has to be understood more in a psychological sense (i.e., a taste for the concrete) than in a physical sense. "It is solidity [*sodezza*]," he concludes, "that makes men happy."
12. Meriggi, *Breve storia dell'Italia settentrionale*, 9, 10.
13. Romeo cites, in particular, the lower Novarese region, the region of Vigevano (Lomellina), and a large part of the provinces south of the Po, where social relationships were certainly much closer to those of Lombardy than to those that existed in Piedmont itself. Meriggi, *Breve storia dell'Italia settentrionale*, 8.
14. Guido Quazza, *Le riforme in Piemonte nella prima metà del Settecento*, vol. I (Modena: STEM, 1957), 53.
15. "Born around 1690, dead in 1737, he was the leading philosopher of the Enlightenment on the Peninsula, before Giannone, Verri and Beccaria," wrote Pietro Gobetti, who devoted to him the first chapter of his *Risorgimento senza eroi* (Turin: Edizioni del Baretti, 1926, p. 37).
16. G. Procacci, *Histoire des Italiens* (Paris: Fayard, 1970), 231.
17. Procacci, *Histoire des Italiens*, 234.

Chapter 8

1. G. Leopardi, "*Discorso sopra lo stato presente del costume degli Italiani*" (1824), in *Tutte le opere*, vol. 1 (Firenze: Sansoni, 1969), 971.
2. S. Cassese, *Lo Stato introvabile. Modernità e arretratezza delle istituzioni italiane* (Rome: Donzelli, 1998), 53.
3. So said the deputy Niccola Marselli, quoted by Alberto Caracciolo, *Stato e società civile. Problemi dell'unificazione italiana* (Turin: Einaudi, 1960), 69.
4. Open letter from Sicily to the former Prime Minister Massimo d'Azeglio, in August 1861. D'Azeglio had resolutely opposed the Roman solution starting in March 1861.
5. The phrase comes from the Milanese federalist Giuseppe Ferrari, quoted by Denis Mack Smith, *Storia d'Italia dal 1861 al 1997* (Rome: Laterza, 1997), 73.
6. A. Caracciolo, *Stato e società civile*, 28.
7. A. Caracciolo dated from the 1910s the beginning of this "anti-Roman polemic." *Roma capitale. Dal Risorgimento alla crisi dello Stato liberale* (Rome: Editori Riuniti, 1999), 63. Emilio Gianni notes that, in the first fifteen years of the twentieth century, the Latium influence in governments doubled when compared to forty years earlier, reaching 6.1 percent of all ministers. E. Gianni, "*Le influenze regionali nei poteri governativi*," in *Lotta comunista* 1985, nn. 182, 183, 185.
8. Quoted by A. Caracciolo, *Stato e società civile*, 67.
9. G. Salvemini, *L'Italia politica nel secolo XIX* (1925), today in *Scritti sul Risorgimento* (Milan: Feltrinelli, 1961), 433.
10. P. Gobetti, "*Motivi di storia italiana. Socialismo di Stato*," *La rivoluzione liberale* no. 15, May 22, 1923.
11. See A. Gramsci, *Il Risorgimento* (Turin: Einuadi, 1949), 69, 70.

12. E. Gianni, "*Le influenze regionali nei poteri governativi*," art. cit. One should keep in mind that some of the men elected in regions other than Piedmont, such as the Tuscan Ricasoli and the Emilians Minghetti and Farini, were considered "Piedmontized," having spent the majority of their political careers in Piedmont as exiles. A particular case is that of Agostino Depretis, who had been elected to the Piedmontese parliament starting in 1848 as a deputy of Stradella, a city in Piedmont until 1859, when it was incorporated into the province of Pavia and, consequently, "Lombardized." It is thus not entirely accurate to consider Depretis, who headed most of the thirteen ministerial teams during the Sinistra period (1876–91), as representing Lombardy.
13. The data come from a study by Francesco Saverio Nitti, *Il bilancio dello Stato dal 1862 al 1896–97* (Naples, 1900), cited by A. Caracciolo, *Stato e società civile*, 124.
14. E. Ragionieri, *Politica e amministrazione nella storia dell'Italia unita* (Rome: Editori Riuniti, 1979), 136, 137. One must consider that the prefects who had been career bureaucrats were but a minority in a corps dominated by men who had come directly from political careers, leaving one to suppose—for want of specific data—that the incidence of Piedmontese among prefects was much greater than what is cited above.
15. During World War I, the Lombards, for the first time, had a greater presence in Italian government (15.2 percent of ministerial posts) than the Piedmontese (13.1 percent); under fascism, the subalpine presence dropped further, to 6.1 percent.

Chapter 9

1. Note sent to Italian embassies abroad on August 24, 1861, quoted by S. Romano, *Histoire de l'Italie du Risorgimento à nos jours* (Paris: Seuil, 1977), 28.
2. G. Prezzolini, *L'Italia finisce, ecco quel che resta* (Milan: Rusconi, 1994), 210–22.
3. See G. Candeloro, *Storia dell'Italia moderna*, vol. V, *La costruzione dello Stato unitario, 1860–1871* (Milan: Feltrinelli, 1968), 47; Christopher Seton-Watson, *L'Italia dal liberalismo al fascismo* (Bari: Laterza, 1973), 31; V. Zamagni, *Dalla periferia al centro* (Bologna: Il Mulino, 1990), 37–39, 92; Denis Mack Smith, *Storia d'Italia dal 1861 al 1997* (Rome-Bari: Laterza, 1997), 50.
4. Smith, *Storia d'Italia*, 52.
5. According to Romeo, the southern emigrants, who composed nearly the entirety of the provisional government of the south (in the autumn of 1860) were "fierce adversaries" of autonomy (R. Romeo, *Dal Piemonte sabaudo all'Italia liberale* [Rome: Laterza, 1974], 274), and they had "become almost strangers to the country" (G. Candeloro, *La costruzione dello Stato unitario* [Milan: Feltrinelli, 1968], 127).
6. Out of hatred for France, Mazzini had described the Sanfedisti revolt of 1799 as "an atrocious war, but a national one." Franco Della Peruta, *Politica e società nell'Italia dell'Ottocento. Problemi, vicende e personaggi* (Milan: Franco Angeli, 1999), 13.
7. Salvatore Lupo, "*Mezzogiorno*," in *Dizionario storico dell'Italia unita*, ed. B. Bongiovanni and N. Tranfaglia (Rome: Laterza, 1997), 584.
8. Romano, *Histoire de l'Italie*, 27.
9. The quotations come from Galli della Loggia, *L'identità italiana* (Bologna: Il Mulino, 1998), 66, A. Lepre, *Italia, addio? Unità e disunità dal 1860 a oggi* (Milan: Mondadori, 1994), 4, and A. Caracciolo, *Stato e società civile. Problemi dell'unificazione italiana* (Turin: Einaudi, 1960), 68); on the Garibaldians, A. Lepre, *Storia del Mezzogiorno nel Risorgimento* (Rome: Editori Riuniti, 1974), 283, and E. Ragionieri, *Politica e amministrazione nella storia dell'Italia unita* (Rome: Editori Riuniti, 1979), 91.

10. Quoted by Ragionieri, *Politica e amministrazione*, 98.
11. After 1848, Cavour said that the "spectre of communism ... is keeping many worried minds in suspense" (quoted by Romeo, *Dal Piemonte sabaudo*, 120).
12. Federigo Paolo Sclopis, private letter dated February 9, 1848 (quoted by Romeo, *Dal Piemonte sabaudo*, 115). The statute granted by Charles Albert was not, as we have seen, the Piedmont government's only reaction to the threat of political and social upheaval: the war against Austria, and particularly its 1849 phase, was equally conducted with the objective of preventing a revolution in Turin and ending it in Milan.
13. Candeloro provides some quantitative indications of the size of this phenomenon, calculating that in 1849 the number of political émigrés in Turin was "perhaps" 50,000, and between 1850 and 1858 their number ranged from 20,000 to 30,000. *Storia dell'Italia moderna*, vol. IV, *Dalla rivoluzione nazionale all'Unità 1849–1860* (Milan: Feltrinelli, 1964), 21.
14. As of the end of 1857, only 2,300 refugees were in public jobs or functions, and only one, the Venetian Pietro Paleocapa, was among Cavour's ministers. Candeloro, *Storia dell'Italia moderna*, 211–13.
15. When we speak of the "spectre of 1799," we are referring not only to the Sanfedisti revolt but also more generally to the open or tacit hostility of the peasant masses toward the French army and the "patriots." The insurrection of Binasco, near Pavia, was in fact the most important of a much wider insurrectional movement that affected the cities of Milan, Lodi, Varese, Como, and Pavia beginning on May 23, 1796 (Bonaparte entered Milan on May 15).
16. Quoted by Romeo, *Dal Piemonte sabaudo*, 275.
17. Quoted by Smith, *Storia d'Italia*, 53.
18. R. Romeo, *Risorgimento e capitalismo* (Rome-Bari: Laterza, 1998), 29–33. "It is significant," the author continues, "that the celebrated domain of Cavour in Leri was originally owned by the Abbey of Lucedio, confiscated and conceded by Napoleon to Prince Borghese, and then sold to the Marquis Michele di Cavour."
19. Zamagni, *Dalla periferia al centro*, 75, 76.
20. Karl Marx, *Capital*, part 8, chapter XXVII, "*Expropriation of the Agricultural Population from the Land.*"
21. Franco Bonelli, "Il capitalismo italiano. Linee generali di interpretazione," in, *Storia d'Italia. Annali I. Dal feudalesimo al capitalismo* (Turin: Einaudi, 1978), 1196.
22. The aristocracy, Candeloro writes, "had largely become bourgeois-ified, and did not disdain banking and commercial activities." *Storia dell'Italia moderna*, vol. IV, *Dalla rivoluzione nazionale all'Unità 1849–1860* (Milan: Feltrinelli, 1964), 14.
23. Indro Montanelli, *L'Italia del Risorgimento* (Milan: Rizzoli, 1972), 656, 657.
24. Quoted by Romeo, *Dal Piemonte sabaudo*, 122.
25. The electoral corps grew more in 1882 than even in 1912, when the principle of "universal suffrage" was adopted. It grew by a factor of 1 to 2.9 in 1912, but from 1 to 3.3 in 1882. See Giovanni Sabbatucci, *Il trasformismo come sistema* (Bari: Laterza, 2003), 53.
26. The data reflect the total of the Italian regions (Venice and Rome included), not that of Italy in 1861.
27. The data were synthesized based on numerous sources suggested by Zamagni, *Dalla periferia al centro*, 42, 43.
28. The following data come from a graph in Paul Kennedy's *The Rise and Fall of the Great Powers* (New York: Random House, 1987), 220, describing the gross national product (GNP) of Russia, France, England, Germany, the Austrian Empire, and Italy, calculated in billions of U.S. dollars in 1960.

Chapter 10

1. Among the most important texts are the 1989 essay by Carlo Tullio-Altan, "Populismo e trasformismo" and the article by Giovanni Sabbatucci, "La soluzione trasformista. Appunti sulla vicenda del sistema politico italiano" in *Il Mulino* (March–April 1990), which was the point of departure for the book *Il trasformismo come sistema* (Rome: Laterza, 2003); Giampiero Carocci, *Il trasformismo dall'unità ad oggi* (Milan: Unicopli, 1992); Riccardo Nencini, *Il trionfo del trasformismo* (Firenze: Loggia de' Lanzi, 1996); Sandro Rogari, *Le origini del trasformismo* (Rome-: Laterza, 1998); and perhaps the most complete, Luigi Musella, *Il trasformismo* (Bologna: Il Mulino, 2003). In addition are essays such as that by Piero Melograni, "*Trasformismo vizio italiano*," published in *Corriere della Sera* (March 17, 1993), and that of Alfio Mastropaolo, "Innovation ou transformisme? D'une classe politique à l'autre . . ." in *Politique à l'italienne* (Paris: Presses Universitaires de France, 1997).
2. Raymond Grew, "Il trasformismo: ultimo stadio del Risorgimento," in *Il Risorgimento e l'Europa*, ed. Vittorio Frosini (Catania: Bonanno, 1969).
3. A. Gramsci, *Il Risorgimento* (Turin: Einaudi, 1949), 70. Musella's book begins with the first of these two quotations.
4. See E. Galli della Loggia, *L'identità italiana* (Bologna: Il Mulino, 1998), 99; L. Musella, *Il trasformismo* (Bologna: Il Mulino, 2003), 9, 173; G. Carocci, *Storia d'Italia dall'Unità ad oggi* (Milan: Feltrinielli, 1975), 43.
5. Raffaele Romanelli, *Il transformismo* (Bologna: Il Mulino, 1990), 212.
6. R. Grew, quoted in Romanelli, *Il transformismo*, 59.
7. For Gramsci, the transformist operation certainly weakened the influence of the aristocracy and landowners in the life of the state, but "it is impossible to speak of the substitution of one class for another." Romanelli, *Il Risorgimento*, 57.
8. Speech by Chateaubriand in the French House of Lords, on the death of the Count of Sèze (*Moniteur*, June 20, 1828), quoted by Rosario Romeo, *Cavour e il suo tempo* (Bari: Laterza, 1969), 283.
9. Quoted by Giampiero Carocci, *Agostino Depretis e la politica interna italiana: 1876–1887* (Turin: Einaudi, 1956), 612. By "disorganization," Spaventa means what today we probably would call "disarticulation."
10. S. Romano, *Histoire de l'Italie du Risorgimento à nos jours* (Paris: Seuil, 1977), 72–74.
11. Gramsci, *Il Risorgimento*, 58.
12. Gramsci, *Il Risorgimento*, 58.
13. See Arturo Carlo Jemolo, *Chiesa e Stato in Italia. Dall'unificazione ai giorni nostri* (Turin: Einaudi, 1974), 3, 44.
14. Stefano Jacini explores these themes in an 1879 text, *I conservatori e l'evoluzione naturale dei partiti politici in Italia*. See Giorgio Candeloro, *Il movimento cattolico in Italia* (Rome: Editori Riuniti, 1982), 178, and Gabriele de Rosa, *I conservatori nazionali. Biografia di Carlo Cantucci* (Brescia: Morcelliana, 1962), 32–43.
15. Edoardo Soderini, *Il pontificato di Leone XIII*, vol. II (Milan: Mondadori, 1932), 20.
16. See G. Candeloro, *Il movimento cattolico in Italia* (Rome: Editori Riuniti, 1982), 178.
17. Benedetto Croce, *History of contemporary Italy (1871–1915)* (Paris: Payot, 1929), 26.
18. *La Repubblica*, July 2, 1988.
19. Gianfranco Pasquino, "Interprétations du système politique italien," in *L'Italie aujourd'hui. Situation et perspectives après le séisme des années 90*, ed. Manlio Graziano (Paris: L'Harmattan, 2004), 52.
20. C. Seton-Watson, *L'Italia dal liberalismo al fascismo 1870–1925* (Bari: Laterza, 1973), 109 (original edition: Methuen, 1967)

21. The stability of power offered by Depretis, Romanelli states, lies in the "capacity to turn the classic institution of the vote of confidence through an attentive management of extra-parliamentary crises, of sudden resignations, followed by an immediate renewal." R. Romanelli, *L'Italia liberale* ((Bologna: Il Mulino, 1990), 210. Let us remember that all 51 governments from 1945 to 1992 revolved around the Christian Democratic Party, and 31 of them were led by only six prime ministers (De Gasperi, Fanfani, Moro, Andreotti, Rumor, and Craxi). Sabino Cassese remarked that the length of service of many Italian ministers was no less than that of their counterparts in France or in Great Britain in the same period. "Histoires et caractéristiques de l'État italien," in *Portrait de l'Italie actuelle*, ed. Sabino Cassese (Paris: La Documentation Française, 201), 27.
22. V. Zamagni, *Dalla periferia al centro. La seconda rinascita economica dell'Italia (1861–1990)* (Bologna: Il Mulino, 1990), 210, 211. Concerning the incidence of the public debt on GDP, it was 45 percent in 1861, 95 percent in 1876, 116 percent in 1889, and 119 percent in 1896, its high point.
23. S. Cassese, "Introduction," in *Portrait de l'Italie actuelle* (Paris: La documentation française, 2001), 13.
24. The statistics come from annual general records of the State Accounts Department. Regarding the decrease, we have to consider that entire sections of the public administration (post and telecommunications from 1993, the agency of national roads - ANAS - from 1995, the railways, etc.) are removed from the statistical sheets once the process of their privatization began.
25. Arrigo Cervetto, "La tendenza generale del capitalismo italiano," in *L'ineguale sviluppo politico: 1968–1979* (Milan: Editore Lotta Comunista, 1991), 86.
26. The tax rate in Italy was 25.8 percent of GDP in 1960 and 31.0 percent in 1980 (an increase of 20.1 percent in 20 years); it rose to 39.5 percent of GDP in 1990 (an increase of 24.05 percent in 10 years).
27. S. Romano, *L'Italia scappata di mano* (Milan: TEA Storica, 1995), 11.
28. In 1992 the Christian Democrats and Italian Socialist Party won 43.3 percent of the vote, in 1994 they received 13.3 percent, and in 1996 they received 6.8 percent.
29. Zamagni, *Dalla periferia al centro*, 139, 149.

Chapter 11

1. For Valerio Castronovo (*Storia economica d'Italia* [Turin: Einaudi, 1995], 49, 51) growth was 1.44 percent from 1862 to 1878; for ISTAT, it was 2.0 percent (1861–1881); and for Stefano Fenoaltea, it was 2.2 percent for the same period (quoted by V. Zamagni, *Dalla periferia al centro* [Bologna: Il Mulino, 1990], 108).
2. Denis Mack Smith, *Storia d'Italia* (Rome: Laterza, 1995), 98.
3. After the signing of the convention on navigation and the treaty on commerce between Italy and France in 1863, imports from France rose from 233 million lire in 1862 to 346 million in 1865 (an increase of 48.5 percent) and exports to France went from 189 million lire to 188 million. G. Candeloro, *Storia dell'Italia moderna*, vol. V, *La costruzione dello Stato unitario 1860–1871* (Milan: Feltrinelli, 1968), 242. A large part of the public debt issuances (which rose from 21 percent of total public spending in 1861 to 31 percent in 1866 through 1870) were subscribed abroad, and notably in France. Christopher Seton-Watson, *L'Italia dal liberalismo al fascismo, 1870–1925* (Bari: Laterza, 1980), 24. Moreover, for the period 1861 through 1870, 325 million of the 789 million lire of gross investment (or 41.2 percent) came from abroad. See. R. Romeo, *Risorgimento e capitalismo* (Bari: Laterza, 1959), 106.

4. The phrase comes from Candeloro, *Storia dell'Italia moderna*, 289.
5. Quoted by Candeloro, *Storia dell'Italia moderna*, 292.
6. For Cavour's speech of late May 1861, see Candeloro, *Storia dell'Italia moderna*, 238–40, and Romeo, *Risorgimento e capitalismo*, 36.
7. Quoted by Candeloro, *Storia dell'Italia moderna*, 239, 240.
8. For this debate, see Roberto Casella, "1863: *I primi passi dello scontro tra protezionisti e liberoscambisti in Italia*," in *Lotta comunista* (September 1984); Giuseppe Are, *Alle origini dell'Italia industriale* (Naples: Guida, 1974), 152–61; Zamagni, *Dalla periferia al centro*, 148, 149; Candeloro, *Storia dell'Italia moderna*, 239–41.
9. In the elections of 1861, only 239,583 of 418,696 registered voters cast ballots, yielding only about one deputy for 550 voters.
10. Karl Marx, "*Les luttes de classes en France*," (1850) in, *Oeuvres*, vol. IV, *Politique I* Paris: Gallimard, 1994), 239.
11. Benedetto Croce discusses Quintino Sella's sense of "mission" in *Histoire de l'Italie* (Paris: Payot, 1929), 56.
12. See Zamagni, *Dalla periferia al centro*, 179, 180.
13. The victor of the siege of the fortress of Gaeta, the last bastion of the Kingdom of Two Sicilies, had been a lieutenant of the king in Naples since July 1861 and led the military fight to suppress the *brigantaggio*.
14. See Denis Mack Smith, *Vittorio Emanuele II* (Milan: Mondadori, 1994), 242.
15. See Denis Mack Smith, *Storia d'Italia*, 118.

Chapter 12

1. The estimate comes from Vera Zamagni, *Dalla periferia al centro* (Bologna: Il Mulino, 1990), 464.
2. Enrico Cuccia (1907–2000) went to work for the Banca d'Italia in 1932, for the IRI in 1934, and for the Banca Commerciale in 1938; he was cofounder (in 1946) and director (from 1982 until his death, honorary chairman) of Mediobanca SpA, the largest Italian merchant bank following the suppression of mixed banks in 1936.
3. Gianni Toniolo, *Storia economica dell'Italia liberale, 1850–1918* (Bologna: Il Mulino, 1988), 104. Remember that in the modern sense, the "lender of last resort" is the central bank.
4. When Bonaldo Stringher became its director-general in 1900 (a position he held until 1928, when he was named governor, a role he kept until his death in 1930), the Banca d'Italia had a privileged clientele, in competition with other banks. This proves that its transformation into an organ of "monetary power" was the result of a process and not of a preestablished plan.
5. The banks in question were the Banca Nazionale, Banco di Napoli, Banca Nazionale Toscana, Banco di Sicilia, and Banca Toscana di Credito. The Banca Nazionale played a central role among all these issuing banks, with (as of December 31, 1873) 67.7 percent of total capital.
6. Zamagni, *Dalla periferia al centro*, 182.
7. Alexander Gerschenkron, *Il problema storico dell'arretratezza economica* (Turin: Einaudi, 1965), 84; Guido Baglioni, *L'ideologia della borghesia industriale nell'Italia liberale* (Turin: Einaudi, 1974), 120; Zamagni, *Dalla periferia al centro*, 140–45.
8. Paolo Farneti, *Sistema politico e società civile* (Turin: Giappichelli, 1971), 171. For the quote from De Ruggiero (1888–1948), see Renzo De Felice, *Gli intellettuali di fronte al fascismo* (Rome: Bonacci, 1985), 50. We should point out the different conclusion

reached by Silvio Lanaro, who, in *L'Italia nuova. Identità e sviluppo, 1861–1988* (Turin: Einaudi, 1988), states that, from the beginning of unitary history, "with the exception of a few modest Catholic groups, Italian nationalism was markedly industrialist" (p. 161).
9. B. Croce, *Histoire de l'Italie contemporaine* (Paris: Payot, 1929), 62, 63.
10. C. Cavour, "*Des chemins de fer en Italie par le comte Petitti, Conseiller d'État du Royaume de Sardaigne*," quoted by G. Candeloro, *Storia dell'Italia moderna*, vol. V, *La costruzione dello Stato unitario, 1860–1871* (Milan: Feltrinelli, 1968), 37, 38.
11. Among the major works projects linked to this hypothesis we should mention the extension of rail service to Brindisi (completed in January 1865) and the construction of the Fréjus tunnel, inaugurated in 1871.
12. In 1862 only 1.59 percent of global tonnage was steam powered, compared to 11.1 percent of English tonnage and 9.71 percent of French; moreover, the average vessel was a mere 69 tons, compared to 170 tons for both British and French ships (see Candeloro, *Storia dell'Italia moderna*, 40, 41). Zamagni notes that "even in 1913, one-third of the Italian merchant marine was wind-powered" (*Dalla periferia al centro*, 131).
13. In Genoa alone, the number of shipyards rose from eight in 1868 to nineteen in 1873, and having built, from 1870 to 1875, a yearly average of 70,000 tons of capacity, all Italian shipyards combined produced only 14,000 tons in 1880 and 11,000 the year after.
14. R. Romanelli, *L'Italia liberale* (Bologna: Il Mulino, 1979), 236.
15. The former thesis is supported by Romanelli (*L'Italia liberale*, 164), the latter by C. Seton-Watson (*L'Italia dal liberalismo al fascismo* (Bari: Laterza, 1980), 74).
16. Luciano Cafagna, *Dualismo e sviluppo nella storia d'Italia* (Venice: Marsilio, 1989), 269. The same observation is made by G. Candeloro in *Storia dell'Italia moderna*, vol. VI, *Lo sviluppo del capitalismo e del movimento operaio, 1871–1896* (Milan: Feltrinelli, 1970), 21.
17. The number of new deputies comes from Romanelli (*L'Italia liberale*, 144), although Candeloro puts the number at 184 (*Storia dell'Italia moderna*, 387).
18. In describing the regional vote breakdown, we consider the south to be the provinces of the former Kingdom of the Two Sicilies plus Sardinia, the center to be the regions of the former Papal States plus the former Grand Duchy of Tuscany, and the north to be the other provinces (Piedmont, Liguria, Lombardy, and Venice).
19. D. Mack Smith, *Storia d'Italia* (Rome: Laterza, 1995), 132.

Chapter 13

1. Leopoldo Franchetti (1847–1917) would become a deputy in 1888. According to Luciano Cafagna, *Nord e Sud, non fare a pezzi l'unità d'Italia* (Venice: Marsilio, 1994), 23, Franchetti was the first to use the term "clientelism."
2. Quoted by R. Romanelli (*L'Italia liberale* (Bologna: Il Mulino, 1979), 189). The texts in question are "*Condizioni economiche e amministrative delle Province Napolitane*" and "*Inchiesta sulla Sicilia*," written with Sidney Sonnino.
3. Cafagna, *Nord e Sud*, 58.
4. Romanelli, *L'Italia liberale*, 22. G. Carocci, *Storia d'Italia dall'Unità a oggi* (Milan: Feltrinelli, 1975), 37; Salvatore Lupo, "Mezzogiorno," in *Dizionario storico dell'Italia unita*, ed. B. Bongiovanni and N. Tranfaglia (Rome: Laterza, 1997), 584; Alberto Caracciolo, *La storia economica* (Turin: Einaudi, 1973), 511, 512. Vera Zamagni quantifies this "economic indifference," saying that at the moment of unification, less than 20 percent of the Italian states' trade was among those states. Zamagni, *Dalla periferia al centro. La seconda rinascita economica dell'Italia (1861–1990)* (Bologna: Il Mulino,

1990), 101. Among the indicators of this "indifference," we should also include the near-total absence of any migratory flow between the two parts of the country (see Cafagna, *Nord e Sud*, 46).
5. See Pasquale Villani, *Mezzogiorno tra riforme e rivoluzione* (Bari: Laterza, 1973), 195–197.
6. Zamagni, *Dalla periferia al centro*, 37–39.
7. David Abulafia, *Le due Italie. Relazioni economiche tra il Regno normanno di Sicilia e I comuni settentrionali* (Naples: Guida, 1977).
8. Zamagni, *Dalla periferia al centro*, 38.
9. Zamagni, *Dalla periferia al centro*, 60.
10. P. Bevilacqua, *Breve storia dell'Italia meridionale* (Rome: Donzelli, 2005).
11. See Valerio Castronovo, "*Il Piemonte*," in *Storia d'Italia. Le regioni dall'Unità a oggi* (Turin: Einaudi, 1977), 4, 5, 146, 149.
12. From 1871 to 1881, the migration balance (emigration minus immigration) was negative, by 34,000 people a year for the north and 2,000 for the south; from 1881 to 1901, 62,000 people left the north and 47,000 left the south every year; and from 1951 to 1967, in total, some 2.6 million people left the northern countryside and 1.5 million left the south. Paolo Sylos Labini, *Problemi dello sviluppo economico* (Bari: Laterza, 1974), 116.
13. S. Lupo, "*Mezzogiorno*," in *Dizionario storico dell'Italia unita*, 591.
14. Gianfranco Viesti, *Abolire il Mezzogiorno* (Rome-Bari: Laterza, 2003), 7.
15. Paolo Macry, *La società contemporanea. Una introduzione storica* (Bologna: Il Mulino, 1992).
16. A. Schiavone, *Italiani senza Italia. Storia e identità* (Turin: Einaudi, 1998), 103.
17. This was the neighborhood built in the southwestern area of the city, at the feet of the Sant'Elmo hill during the reign of Charles V, under Vice-King Pierre of Toledo. It was the working-class neighborhood.
18. One of the paradoxes of national Italian mythology is that it promotes the anti-imperial leagues of the communes to the rank of founders of a supposed national conscience against the invader from the north, whereas these leagues played a fundamental role in the struggle to prevent Ghibelline unification against the papacy. The defeat of the emperors allowed the pope to remain as arbiter of a fierce struggle between the "thousand bell towers" until the eve of unification of the peninsula, without, however, succeeding in spreading the communal system through the kingdom of the south.
19. Sylos Labini, *Problemi dello sviluppo economico* (Bari: Laterza, 1974), 111. Labini places the beginning of this process in the Bourbon era.
20. Labini, *Problemi dello sviluppo economico*, 112.
21. Letter quoted by A. Lepre, *Italia, addio? Unità e disunità dal 1860 a oggi* (Milan: Mondadori, 1994), 33.
22. Letter from Cavour to Nigra, ambassador to Paris, on March 4, 1861.
23. Luciano Cafagna, *La grande slavina. L'Italia verso la crisi della democrazia* (Venice: Marsilio, 1993), 19, 20.
24. G. Carocci, *Il trasformismo dall'Unità a oggi* (Milan: Unicopli, 1992), 14.
25. S. Romano, *Histoire de l'Italie du Risorgimento à nos jours* (Paris: Seuil, 1977), 77. Between 1861 and 1882, 29.7 percent of the lawyers present in the chamber were of the *Destra* and 37.5 percent were of the *Sinistra* (without counting the extreme left); from 1882 to 1900, only 15 percent of lawyers in the chamber were of the *Destra*, compared to 40 percent of the *Sinistra*. See Fulvio Cammarano, "*Sinistra storica*," in ed. Bongiovanni and Tranfaglia, *Dizionario storico dell'Italia unita*, 830, 831.
26. Data cited by A. Caracciolo, *Stato e società civile. Problemi dell'unificazione italiana* (Turin: Einaudi, 1960), 119.

27. Jean Meynaud, *Rapporto sulla classe dirigente italiana* (Milan: Giuffrè, 1966), 44. Meynaud refers to the post–World War II situation, when this phenomenon, qualitatively comparable, was to undergo a powerful quantitative acceleration.
28. S. Lanaro, *L'Italia nuova. Identità e sviluppo. 1861–1988* (Turin: Einaudi, 1988), 110.
29. The 1904 law on the southern region of Basilicata would mark a veritable resort to "special legislation" until the war in 1915. See Zamagni, *Dalla periferia al centro*, 218, 219.
30. At the time of the first African expeditions, the Milan newspaper *Italia del popolo* calculated that the Milanese were paying 89.85 lira in taxes per inhabitant, while the national average was only 47.95 lira. Quoted by Lepre, *Italia, addio?* 81.
31. Filippo Turati, in *Critica Sociale*, October 16, 1891. Quoted by Lepre, *Italia, addio?* 83.

Chapter 14

1. Giacomo Biffi, *Risorgimento, Stato laico e identità nazionale* (Casale Monferrato: Edizioni Piemme, 1999), 44. About the role of the Church in Italy, see Manlio Graziano, *Identité catholique et identité italienne. L'Italie laboratoire de l'Église* (Parigi: L'Harmattan, 2007), whose following chapters are a modest and necessarily partial synthesis.
2. "Sciopero e patriottismo," *L'Osservatore Romano*, March 27, 1911.
3. *Civiltà cattolica*, March 16, 1929, quoted by A. Gramsci *(Il Risorgimento* (Turin: Einaudi, 1949), 146).
4. Among the works of the revisionist camp, we would cite that of Angela Pellicciari, *L'altro Risorgimento. Una guerra di religione dimenticata* (Casale Monferrato: Edizioni Piemme, 2000).
5. Arturo Carlo Jemolo, *Chiesa e Stato in Italia. Dalla unificazione ai giorni nostri* (Turin: Einaudi, 1977), 314–315.
6. Gramsci, *Il Risorgimento*, 12.
7. "Ah, Italy enslaved, abode of misery, pilotless ship in a fierce tempest tossed, no mistress over provinces but a harlot!" (Dante, *La Divina Commedia*, "Purgatorio," canto vi, 76–78).
8. Niccolò Machiavelli, *Discorsi sopra la prima deca di Tito Livio*, book I, chapter XII, ed. C. Vivanti (Turin: Einaudi, 1983)
9. Machiavelli, *Discorsi sopra la prima deca di Tito Livio*, book I, chapter XII.
10. Machiavelli, *Discorsi sopra la prima deca di Tito Livio*, book I, chapter XII.
11. Francesco Guicciardini, *Considerazioni intorno ai discorsi di Machiavelli*.
12. This thesis was first formulated by Francesco de Sanctis in 1869. Others who took it up were E. Galli della Loggia, *L'identità italiana* (Bologna: Il Mulino, 54; G. B. Guerri, *Gli italiani sotto la Chiesa* (Milan: Mondadori, 1992), 128; and Adriano Prosperi, "*Intellettuali e Chiesa all'inizio dell'era moderna*," in *Storia d'Italia, Annali*, vol. IV, *Intellettuali e potere* (Turin: Einaudi, 1981), 187.
13. Delio Cantimori, "*Le idee religiose del Cinquecento. La storiografia*," in *Storia della letteratura italiana*, vol. V, *Il Seicento*, ed. E. Cecchi and N. Sapegno (Milan: Garzanti, 1967), 7.
14. Guerri, *Gli italiani sotto la Chiesa*, 126.
15. According to Ortensio Lando (1512–1553), writer and first translator of Thomas More in Italy, "Scholars give birth only to discord, schism and pestilential heresies. The heresies come from men of letters, and from the illiterate, veritable saintliness . . . Once a scholar reads a composition on any possible subject, he immediately gives birth to some bizarre controversy [*alcuna strana contradittione*]." Quoted by Adriano Prosperi,

NOTES   235

       Intellettuali e Chiesa all'inizio dell'era moderna, in *Storia d'Italia*, vol. IV, *Intellettuali e potere* (Turin: Einaudi, 1978), 195.
16. Enzo Pace, *La nation italienne en crise* (Paris: Bayard, 1998), 122, 123.
17. Quoted by Prosperi, *Intellettuali e Chiesa all'inizio dell'era moderna*, 181.
18. Guerri, *Gli italiani sotto la Chiesa*, 132.
19. Gramsci, *Il Risorgimento*, 34.
20. Gramsci, *Gli intellettuali e la formazione della cultura* (Turin: Einaudi, 1953), 39.
21. On this subject, read chapter 5 (*The Means of Seduction*) of the T. Jones book, *The Dark Heart of Italy* (London: Faber & Faber, 2003), 109–30.
22. Gramsci, *Gli intellettuali*, 57.
23. We must exclude from this list a series of minor authors, like Daniello Bartoli (1608–1685), a historian and apologist for the Society of Jesus; Emanuele Tesauro (1592–1672), an ex-Jesuit and theoretician of baroque poetry; and Giovanni Botero (1540–1617), an ex-Jesuit and a theoretician of "raison d'État."
24. G. Candeloro, *Il movimento cattolico in Italia* (Rome: Editori Riuniti, 1982), 13. Benedetto Croce, *Storia d'Europa nel secolo decimonono* (Milan: Adelphi, 2007), 36, also discusses the temporary agreement between the Church and a part of the "vanquished states and classes."
25. Antonio Gramsci, *Note sul Machiavelli, sulla politica e sullo Stato moderno* (Rome: Editori Riuniti, 1971), 307.
26. Croce, *Storia d'Europa nel secolo decimonono*, 36.
27. Croce, *Storia d'Europa nel secolo decimonono*, 35.
28. C. Cattaneo, *"Vita di Dante" di Cesare Balbo*, quoted by E. Passerin d'Entreves, "Ideologie del Risorgimento," in *Storia della letteratura italiana*, vol. VII, ed. E. Cecchi and N. Sapegno (Milan: Garzanti, 1969), 326.
29. See Roger Aubert, "*L'Eglise catholique de la crise de 1848 à la Première Guerre mondiale*," in *Nouvelle Histoire de l'Eglise*, vol. V, *L'Église dans le monde moderne*, ed. J. Danielou, L.-J. Rogier, R. Aubert, and D. Knowles (Paris: Seuil, 1975), 32.
30. Ippolito Nievo, *Opere* (Naples: Riccardo Ricciardi Editore, 1952), 1079, 1080.
31. Gramsci, *Il Risorgimento*, 72.
32. Gramsci, *Il Risorgimento*, 146.

Chapter 15

1. R. Aubert, "*L'Église catholique de la crise de 1848 à la Premiere Guerre mondiale*," in *Nouvelle Histoire de l'Église*, vol. V, *L'Église dans le monde moderne*, ed. J. Daniélou, L.-J. Rogier, R. Aubert, and D. Knowles (Paris: Seuil, 1975), 93.
2. Quoted by Federico Chabod, *Storia della politica esiera italiana dal 1860 al 1896* (Bari: Laterza, 1951), 430, 435.
3. A. C. Jemolo, *Chiesa e Stato in Italia. Dalla unificazione ai giorni nostri* (Turin: Einaudi, 1977), 81.
4. G. Candeloro, *Il movimento cattolico in Italia* (Rome: Editori Riuniti, 1982), 136.
5. Gianfranco Poggi, *Il clero di riserva. Studio sociologica sull'Azione Cattolica Italiana durante la presidenza Gedda* (Milan: Feltrinelli, 1963), 22.
6. See A. Caracciolo, *Roma capitale. Dal Risorgimento alla crisi dello Stato liberale* (Rome: Editori Riuniti, 1999), 173, 174; G. B. Guerri, *Gli italiani sotto la Chiesa* (Milan: Mondadori, 1992), 219, 220; Jemolo, *Chiesa e Stato in Italia*, 53. Aubert, for his part, asserts that despite the expropriations, the Church "seems to have managed to maintain substantial liquid capital." Aubert, "*L'Église catholique de la crise de 1848*," 93.

7. See Candeloro, *Il movimento cattolico*, 344; Guerri, *Gli italiani sotto la Chiesa*, 250; D. Mack Smith, *Storia d'Italia dal 1861 al 1997* (Rome: Laterza, 1997), 325; Luigi Goglia and Fabio Grassi, *Il colonialismo italiano da Adua all'Impero* (Bari: Laterza, 1981), 139, 140; E. Ragionieri, *Italia giudicata 1861–1945*, vol. II (Turin: Einaudi, 1976), 385; Pietro Grifone, *Il capitale finanziario in Italia. La politica economica del fascismo* (Turin: Einaudi, 1971), 21; V. Castronovo, *Storia economica d'Italia* (Turin: Einaudi, 1995), 182.
8. Jemolo, *Stato e Chiesa in Italia*, 57, 63.
9. The phrase "first economic miracle" comes from Michèle Merger, *Un siècle d'histoire industrielle en Italie (1880–1970). Industrialisation et sociétés* (Paris: Sedes, 1998), 37.
10. V. Zamagni, *Dalla periferia al centro. La seconda rinascita economica dell'Italia (1861–1990)* (Bologna: Il Mulino, 1990), 210.
11. Quoted by L. Musella, *Il trasformismo* (Bologna: Il Mulino, 1998), 84.
12. Antonio Gramsci, "I cattolici italiani," in *Avanti!*, ed. Piemontaise, December 22, 1918; available in A. Gramsci, *Scritti politici*, vol. I (Rome: Editori Riuniti, 1973), 225, 226.
13. Candeloro, *Il movimento cattolico*, 375.
14. The data are from Guerri, *Gli italiani sotto la Chiesa*, 256.
15. Gramsci, "I cattolici italiani," 228.
16. Candeloro, *Il movimento cattolico*, 25.

Chapter 16

1. Gian Enrico Rusconi, "*Religione civile e identità italiana*," in *Il Mulino*, no. 5 (2003):833.
2. F. de Sanctis, *Storia della letteratura italiana* (1870) (Milan: Bietti, 1963), 859.
3. E. Gentile, *La Grande Italia. Il mito della nazione nel XX secolo* (Rome: Laterza, 2006), 46.
4. Quoted by Giacomo Perticone, *La politica estera italiana dal 1861 al 1914* (Turin: ERI, 1961), 154, 155.
5. Quoted by A. Lepre, *Italia, addio? Unità e disunità dal 1860 a oggi* (Milan: Mondadori, 1994), 74, 75.
6. Filippo Turati, "*1° maggio 1911*," in *Critica Sociale*, April 16, 1911.
7. Quoted by G. Belardelli, "*Una nazione 'senza anima': la critica democratica del Risorgimento*," in *Due nazioni. Legittimazione e delegittimazione nella storia dell'Italia contemporanea*, ed. L. Di Nucci and E. Galli della Loggia (Bologna: Il Mulino, 2003), 49.
8. The Socialist Party went from representing 2.95 percent of votes cast in the election of 1897 (15 deputies) to 6.5 percent in 1900 (33 deputies), 8.7 percent (41 deputies) in 1909, and 17.7 percent (52 deputies) in 1913 (not to mention the 5.2 percent of votes and the 27 deputies of the two other Socialist parties that took part for the first time in this election). We should note that the elections of 1913 were the first involving universal suffrage for men.
9. According to the Italian Statistical Institute (ISTAT), it rose by 51 percent between 1900 and 1911; A. Gerschenkron estimated that it rose by 74 percent during that same period, while S. Fenoaltea reports a rise of 118 percent. M. Merger, *Un siècle d'histoire industrielle en Italie (1880–1970). Industrialisation et sociétés* (Paris: Sedes, 1998), 145. One also gains a better understanding of the industrial dynamism of the period from energy production, which doubled between 1898 and 1913 (while production of electrical energy soared by a factor of 20). See V. Zamagni, *Dalla periferia al centro. La seconda rinascita economica dell'Italia (1861–1990)* (Bologna: Il Mulino, 1990), 125.
10. Merger, *Un siècle d'histoire industrielle*, 50. The period in question was 1895 through 1913.
11. See Zamagni, *Dalla periferia al centro*, 89.
12. Merger, *Un siècle d'histoire industrielle*, 148.

13. Merger, *Un siècle d'histoire industrielle*, 37. The percentages are based on cities of more than 20,000 inhabitants.
14. On the crisis of 1907, see Merger, *Un siècle d'histoire industrielle*, 51; P. Grifone, *Il capitale finanziario in Italia. La politica economica del fascismo* (Turin: Einaudi, 1971), 18; Richard A. Webster, *L'imperialismo industriale italiano. Studio sul prefascismo 1908–1915* (Turin: Einaudi, 1974), 45.
15. *Il Regno*, May 22, 1904, quoted by E. Gentile, *La Grande Italia*, 70.
16. Francesco Saverio Nitti, *Il Partito Radicale e la nuova democrazia industriale. Prime linee di un programma di un Partito Radicale* (Turin: Sten, 1907).
17. Giampiero Carocci, *Giolitti e l'era giolittiana* (Turin: Einaudi, 1971), 149.
18. E. Corradini, *Principii di nazionalismo* (1910), in *Scritti e discorsi*, ed. L. Strappini (Turin: Einaudi, 1980), 173, 174.
19. *Principii di nazionalismo*, 174.
20. E. Corradini, *Le nazioni proletarie e il nazionalismo* in *Scritti e discorsi*, ed. L. Strappini, Turin: Einaudi, 1980, 186, 187.
21. P. Gobetti, "*Il nazionalismo italiano*", in *La Rivoluzione Liberale*, September 20, 1922, in *La Rivoluzione liberale. Saggio sulla lotta politica in Italia*, Turin: Einaudi 1995, 116.
22. See Merger, *Un siècle d'histoire industrielle*, 50, 51; Grifone, *Il capitale finanziario in Italia*, 18, 19.
23. See. E. Ragionieri, *L'italia giudicata, 1861–1945, vol. II* (Turin: Einaudi, 1976), 385.
24. On the Libyan War, see Angelo del Boca, *Gli italiani in Libia* (Rome: Laterza, 1986) and *Italiani, brava gente?* (Venice: Neri Pozza, 2005).
25. G. Salvemini, "*Alla ricerca di una formula*," in *L'Unità*, March 14, 1913, quoted by Gentile, *La Grande Italia*, 88.
26. Gobetti, *Il nazionalismo italiano*, 117, 119.

Chapter 17

1. E. Pace talks about "the most coherent attempt" in *La nation italienne en crise* (Paris: Bayard, 1998), 72, 73. As to the Fascist "secular religion," see Emilio Gentile, *Il culto del littorio. La sacralizzazione della politica nell'Italia fascista* (Rome-Bari: Laterza, 1993).
2. The military defeat of Fascist Italy seems "to disqualify forever the slightest reference to the nation," wrote Marc Lazar, who dealt with this subject in the essay "*La gauche, la République et la nation*," in I. Diamanti, A. Dieckhoff, M. Lazar, and D. Musiedlak, *L'Italie, une nation en suspens* (Brussels: Editions Complexe, 1995), 66.
3. For the data, see V. Castronovo, *Storia economica d'Italia* (Turin: Einaudi, 1995), 174.
4. Luigi Salvatorelli, *Nazional fascismo* (Rome: Libero, 2004), 22, 25, 28.
5. Giovanni Ansaldo (1895–1969), a contributor to *La Rivoluzione liberale*, asserted, in a debate with Salvatorelli, that fascism's origins were not among petit-bourgeois intellectuals, but among the productive petite bourgeoisie ("*La piccola borghesia*," in *Il Lavoro*, Genoa, June 3, 1923). Ansaldo later became one of the most important journalists of the Fascist era. Adriano Tilgher (1887–1941), a philosopher and literary critic, in his essay "*Piccoli borghesi al bivio*" (*Il Tempo*, December 7, 1919, then in *La crisi mondiale e saggi di socialismo e marxismo* [Bologna: Zanichelli, 1921]), emphasized the hostility toward the working class.
6. Speech delivered in late May 1915, quoted by D. Mack Smith, *Storia d'Italia dal 1861 al 1997* (Rome-Bari: Laterza, 1997), 354.
7. According to S. Romano, 470,000 emigrants returned to Italy in the first months of the European conflict, including 150,000 from France. *Histoire de l'Italie du Risorgimento à nos jours* (Paris: Seuil, 1977), 163.

8. See M. Merger, *Un siècle d'histoire industrielle en Italie (1880-1970). Industrialisation et sociétés* (Paris: Sedes, 1998), 61–63.
9. V. Zamagni, *Dalla periferia al centro. La seconda rinascita economica dell'Italia (1861–1990)* (Bologna: Il Mulino, 1990), 307. The number represents the total of strike days by industrial and farm laborers. This gauge of social conflict would only be exceeded in 1969, with 37,824 strike days.
10. The inflation data come from Merger, *Un siècle d'histoire industrielle en Italie*, 64.
11. Smith, *Storia d'Italia*, 346.
12. The phrase "coup d'état" is used by, among others, Indro Montanelli and Mario Cervi, *L'Italia del Novecento* (Milan: Rizzoli, 1998), 23; G. Procacci, *Histoire des Italiens* (Rome: Laterza, 2006), 367; and D. Mack Smith, *Storia d'Italia*, 356.
13. In the elections of November 1919, the Socialist Party obtained 1,834,792 votes (32.3 percent of those cast, electing 156 deputies) and the Catholics of the People's Party obtained 1,167,354 votes (20.5 percent and 10 deputies). Of 508 deputies, the liberals of all factions elected 149; the Social Democrats, 60; the Combatants Party, 20; and the Economic Party, 7; while all the other seats (272) went to groupings that were more or less openly hostile to the liberal state (Socialists, Catholics, republicans).
14. Renzo De Felice also sees the crisis of the liberal state as a consequence of its habit of "absorbing the leaders" of opposition parties "without having the capacity to integrate the masses into the heart of the State." R. De Felice, *Intervista sul fascismo* (Bari: Laterza, 1975), 45.
15. Gian Enrico Rusconi, "Question nationale et question démocratique en Italie. Thèses pour un patriotisme républicain," in "Italie. La question nationale," *Herodote*, no. 89 (1998):24.
16. Among the elements constituting "the forms of acquisition of consensus" in a mass society, there is, according to Cafagna, "a very wide gamut of obligations of transference" based on "social considerations, and those of political involvement." L. Cafagna, *La grande slavina. L'Italia verso la crisi della democrazia* (Venice: Marsilio, 1993), 20.
17. V. Zamagni, *Dal centro alla periferia, La seconda rinascita economica dell'Italia (1861–1990)* (Bologna: Il Mulino, 1990), 316.
18. G. Bollati, *L'Italiano. Il carattere nazionale come storia e come invenzione* (Turin: Einaudi, 1983), 109.
19. Zamagni, *Dal centro alla periferia*, 397, 398. According to calculations by Sylos Labini, *Problemi dello sviluppo economico* (Rome: Laterza, 1974), 156; during the Mussolinian period, until 1940 workers' real salaries diminished by about 20 percent, while civil servants saw their pay rise slightly, by 3 percent.
20. Renzo De Felice, *Mussolini. L'alleato (1940–1945)*, vol. II (Turin: Einaudi, 1990), 770. On the conflict between the Fascist state and the Catholic Church, see M. Graziano, *Identité catholique et identité italienne: L'Italie laboratoire de l'Eglise* (Paris: L'Harmattan, 2007), chap. 4.
21. S. Romano, *L'Italia scappata di mano* (Milan: TEA Storica, 1995), 20.
22. From 2.6 million emigrants in the 1920s, for a net emigration of 1.5 million, the total declined to 113,000 in the 1930s. Underlying this trend, the effects of the Great Depression must be cited, as well as the restrictions put in place by the United States in 1921 and 1924. See Zamagni, *Dalla periferia al centro*, 398, 399). According to the calculations of Anna Treves, during the 1930s an average of 1,200,000 people changed residence each year. A. Treves, *Le migrazioni interne nell'Italia fascista* (Turin: Einaudi, 1976), 168.
23. According to Edward Banfield, "amoral familism" is "the inability of villagers to act together for their common good or, indeed, for any end transcending the immediate,

material interest of the nuclear family." E. Banfield, The Moral Basis of a Backward Society, New York: The Free Press, 9-10.
24. See Renzo De Felice, *Un totalitarisme a l'italienne*? (Paris: Presses de la Fondation Nationale des Sciences Politiques, 1988), 138–40.
25. P. Milza and S. Bernstein, *Le fascisme italien. 1919–1945* (Paris: Seuil, 1980), 277.
26. R. De Felice, *Intervista sul fascismo* (Rome: Laterza, 1975), 60. It is interesting to note that the Hungarian-British journalist George Mikes (1912–1987), in his book on the Italians, published in 1956, offered the same observation as the great historian of fascism. He added an almost banal further observation that seems to have escaped those who have criticized the feeble patriotic enthusiasm of the Italians and their army on the eve of the war of 1940: "One cannot expect an army to put all its soul into a battle if it knows that the decision to fight, on one side or the other, was taken by the flip of a coin." G. Mikes, *Italy for Beginners* (London: Allan Wingate, 1956), 76.
27. P. Kennedy, *The Rise and Fall of the Great Powers: Economic Change and Military Conflict from 1500–2000* (New York: Random House, 1987), 383.
28. Kennedy, *The Rise and Fall of the Great Powers*, 386, 426.
29. Kennedy, *The Rise and Fall of the Great Powers*, 430.
30. Thus, for example, contended Corrado Alvaro in 1944: "A large part of Italy hoped for defeat from the first day of the war." C. Alvaro, *L'Italia rinunzia*? (Palermo: Sellerio, 1986), 34.
31. Giuseppe Bottai, *Diario. 1935–1944* (Milan: Rizzoli, 1982), 193.
32. Ernesto Galli della Loggia, *La morte della patria* (Rome: Laterza, 1996), 95.

Chapter 18

1. Sergio Romano, "Perché gli italiani si disprezzano," in *Limes* no. 4 (October–November 1994):161.
2. See Mimmo Franzinelli, *L'amnistia Togliatti. 22 giugno 1946: Colpo di spugna sui crimini fascisti* (Milan: Mondadori, 2006).
3. Paul Ginsborg, *Storia d'Italia dal dopoguerra ad oggi. Società e politica, 1943–1988* (Turin: Einaudi, 1988), 121.
4. On this question, see Claudio Pavone, "La continuità dello Stato. Istituzioni e uomini," in *Italia 1945–1948. Le origini della Repubblica* (Turin: Giappichelli, 1974).
5. E. Galli della Loggia, *La morte della patria* (Rome: Laterza, 1996), 84.
6. S. Romano, *Guida alla politica estera italiana. Dal crollo del fascismo al crollo del comunismo* (Milan: Rizzoli, 1993), 14.
7. Quoted in *Un uomo solo in difesa dell'Italia. Discorso del Presidente del Consiglio on. Alcide De Gasperi alla Conferenza di Pace di Parigi, il 10 agosto 1946*, available at http://www.democraticicristiani.it/documenti/degasperi3.html.
8. G. Agnelli and A. Cabiati, *Federazione europea o Lega delle nazioni* (Pordenone: Studio Tesi, 1986). The same ideas had been advanced in articles in the *Corriere della Sera* by another economist, the future head of the Bank of Italy and the future president of the republic, Luigi Einaudi.
9. Romano, *Guida alla politica estera italiana*, 62.
10. Giulio Andreotti, *Intervista su De Gasperi* (Bari: Laterza, 1977), 36, 37, 65, 66, 69, 78.
11. Declaration of the foreign minister to the Constituent Assembly (July 24, 1947), quoted by Giuseppe Intersimone, *L'Italia e il trattato di pace del 10 febbraio 1947* (Rome: Trevi Editore, 1970), 93.

12. Vittorio Foa, *Il cavallo e la torre* (Turin: Einaudi, 1991), 137. Vittorio Foa was a founder of the Action Party and was one of the most important postwar Socialists, with the CGIL, the union linked to the PCI.
13. Estimates range from around 100,000 active members "if one excludes the 11th-hour converts," a figure advanced by Paul Ginsborg (*Storia dell'Italia contemporanea* (Turin: Einaudi, 1988), 90), to the 223,639 "fighting partisans" suggested by Gianni Oliva (*I vinti e I liberati* [Milan: Mondadori, 1994], 590).
14. Pietro Secchia, *Aldo dice 26 x 1. Cronistoria del 25 aprile* (Milan: Feltrinelli, 1973), 155. Pietro Secchia (1903–1973) was the no. 2 man in the Communist Party during the Resistance.
15. W. Barberis, *Il bisogno di patria* (Turin: Einaudi, 2004), 84.
16. E. Galli della Loggia, *La morte della patria*, op. cit., p. 70. "Naturally," Galli della Loggia continued, "the Republic will always be obliged to deny, at least officially, this double truth. In the official declamations, in solemn written documents, in school books, it will always, and only, be anti-Fascist."
17. Jürgen Habermas, "L'identité des Allemands, une fois encore." in *Ecrits politiques. Culture, droit, histoire* (Paris: Editions du Cerf, 1986), 245–63.
18. S. Romano, *Histoire de l'Italie du Risorgimento à nos jours* (Paris: Seuil, 1977), 232–34.
19. E. Galli della Loggia, *La morte della patria*, 61. Moreover, he describes it as "radically and manifestly foreign to the national community" (p. 72).
20. Galli della Loggia, *La morte della patria*, 128.
21. Galli della Loggia, *La morte della patria*, 67.
22. Remember that the Mussolinian adventure had begun under the auspices (and with the money) of the French government and of the SFIO, the French Socialist party, before finishing its arc with its hands and feet tied to Germany. See P. Milza and S. Bernstein, *Le fascisme italien. 1919–1945* (Paris: Seuil, 1980), 93, among others.
23. The Action Party, founded in 1942 and dissolved in 1947, was a very heterogeneous mixture of diverse tendencies, united in the attempt to federate the non-Stalinist anti-Fascists, but irremediably divided at the moment it proposed a governmental action plan.
24. Quoted by S. Lanaro, *Storia dell'Italia repubblicana* (Venice: Marsilio, 1992), 160. Monsignor de Luca (1898–1962) was a close collaborator of Cardinal Gasparri in the 1930s, then of Cardinal Montini (the future Paul VI) and John XXIII. He was a mediator in the Vatican's contacts with the Communist Party and the Soviet Union.
25. See Gianni De Michelis, *La lunga ombra di Yalta* (Venice: Marsilio, 2003), 21, 22.
26. Quoted by Giuseppe Boffa, *Storia dell'Unione Sovietica. 1917–1941. Lenin e Stalin. Dalla rivoluzione alla seconda guerra mondiale* (Milan: Mondadori, 1976), 504.
27. Palmiro Togliatti, *La via italiana al socialismo* (Rome: Editori Riuniti, 1972), 38.
28. Quoted by Antonio Pellicani, *Il papa di tutti. La Chiesa cattolica, il fascismo e il razzismo. 1929–1945* (Milan: Sugar, 1964), 31.
29. A. C. Jemolo, *Chiesa e Stato in Italia. Dalla unificazione ai giorni nostri* (Turin: Einaudi, 1977), 270.
30. Jemolo, *Chiesa e Stato in Italia*, 313.
31. See Renato Moro, *La formazione della classe dirigente cattolica (1929–1937)* (Bologna: Il Mulino, 1979).
32. The "official" government of Badoglio and of the king; the "Italian Social Republic" of Mussolini; the National Liberation Committee; the German military governor; and the Allies.
33. Federico Chabod, *L'Italia contemporanea (1918–1948)* (Turin: Einaudi, 1994), 125.
34. See A. C. Jemolo, *Chiesa e Stato in Italia*, 314, 315; Guido Verucci, *La Chiesa nella società contemporanea. Dal primo dopoguerra al Concilio Vaticano II* (Bari: Laterza, 1988), 231, 232.

35. Alcide De Gasperi, 1946, quoted by Lanaro, *Storia dell'Italia repubblicana*, 103.
36. See Gianni Baget Bozzo, *Il partito cristiano al potere. La DC di De Gasperi e di Dossetti (1945–1954)*, vol. I (Florence: Vallecchi, 1974), 255. Giuseppe Dossetti (1913–1996), a university professor and resistance militant, was vice secretary of the Christian Democratic Party in 1945. A deputy since the Constituent Assembly, he abandoned political life in 1958 to become a priest. He took part in the work leading up to the Second Vatican Council and was a patron of Romano Prodi's candidacy for prime minister in 1996.
37. For De Gasperi, as Andreotti writes, the defense of the currency was "the best guarantee for savers, for employees, for the little people." Andreotti, *Intervista su De Gasperi*, 106.
38. According to an ex-minister of the Communist Party, De Gasperi said, during a ministerial meeting in April 1947: "Experience has taught me that it is impossible today to govern Italy without drawing into the new government, in one form or another, the representatives of this fourth party, of the party of those who have the money and the economic power." Quoted by P. Ginsborg, *Storia dell'Italia contemporanea*, 100, 101.
39. Emilio Gianni, "La DC nasce come partito nordista," in *Lotta Comunista* no. 149, January 1983.
40. Andreotti, *Intervista su De Gasperi*, 103. In the elections of 1948, the Christian Democrats obtained 48.5 percent of the votes cast and won 305 of the 507 seats in the Chamber of Deputies.
41. Manlio Graziano, "Trois idées sur les mutations de la vie politique italienne," in *L'Italie aujourd'hui. Situation et perspectives après le séisme des années 90*, ed. M. Graziano (Paris: L'Harmattan, 2004), 17.
42. Andreotti, *Intervista su De Gasperi*, 33.

Chapter 19

1. Curzio Malaparte, *Italia barbara* (1925), quoted by G. Bollati, *L'Italiano. Il carattere nazionale come storia e come invenzione* (Turin: Einaudi, 1983), 122.
2. Bollati, *L'Italiano*, 119.
3. The phrase quoted is from Silvio Lanaro, *L'Italia nuova. Identità e sviluppo. 1861–1988* (Turin: Einaudi, 1988), 240. Others have offered similar observations, including L. Cafagna, "Legittimazione e delegittimazione nella storia politica italiana," in *Due nazioni. Legittimazione e delegittimazione nella storia dell'Italia contemporanea*, ed. L. Di Nucci and E. Galli della Loggia (Bologna: Il Mulino, 2003), 20; E. Galli della Loggia, *L'identità italiana* (Bologna: Il Mulino, 1998), 140; and Guido Carli, *Cinquant'anni di vita italiana* (Bari: Laterza, 1993).
4. *Telefoni bianchi* and *Mille lire al mese* are two famous samples of cultural production under fascism, as illustrated by the lyrics to the song (*Mille lire al mese*) by Gilberto Mazzi (1939): "... A modest job, without pretension / I can work / to finally find peace. / A little house / on the edge of town / a little wife, young and pretty / ... If I could have 1,000 lira a month / ... I would buy, among all things / the most beautiful, those that you desire."
5. Speech delivered by Eugenio Pacelli (Pius XII) to the First Congress of the *Confederazione dei coltivatori diretti* (Coldiretti, the leading trade union of property-owning peasants) in 1946. Available at http://www.vatican.va/holy_father/pius_xii/speeches/1946.
6. Report to the First Congress of the Christian Democratic Party, quoted by P. Ginsborg, *Storia d'Italia dal dopoguerra ad oggi. Società e politica, 1943–1988* (Turin: Einaudi, 1988), 99.

7. Thus said the famous literary critic Luigi Russo in 1953, quoted in *Nemici per la pelle. Sogno americano e mito sovietico nell'Italia contemporanea*, ed. Pier Paolo D'Attore (Milan: Franco Angeli, 1991).
8. Pina Nuzzo, *Congressi dal 1944 al 1968*. Available at www.udinazionale.org, Archivio centrale – Memoria.
9. Franco Paparo, "*Pubblicazioni sulle questioni sessuali*," in *Gioventù Nuova* no. 11–12 (November–December 1950). In the review *Sexual Digest*, translated from the French, one finds articles by Jacques Prévert, Francis Carco, and Roland Dorgelès, and in the Italian version, pieces by Giovanni Papni, Luigi Barzini, Jr., and even texts by father Agostino Gemelli and Pius XII.
10. Quoted by S. Lanaro, *Storia dell'Italia repubblicana* (Venice: Marsilio, 1992), 207. In 1950, according to Marta Boneschi, only 72 of 104 films obtained the censor's stamp of approval. Boneshi, *Poveri ma belli. I nostri anni cinquanta* (Milan: Mondadori, 1995), 287.
11. Carli, *Cinquant'anni di vita italiana*, 3, 4. It is noteworthy that Carli uses the phrase "animal spirits" here in a sense opposite to that used by Keynes, to the extent that, for the latter, the phrase referred to irrational behaviors when private investment is left to itself.
12. Carli, *Cinquant'anni di vita italiana*, 3, 4.
13. Quoted by Lucio Villari, *Il capitalismo italiano del Novecento* (Bari: Laterza, 1972), 484, 522.
14. G. Carli, *Intervista sul capitalismo italiano* (Rome: Laterza, 1977), 89
15. V. Zamagni calculates that the number of farmers dropped from 8.6 million to 2 million from the end of the war to the 1990s, and their share in the creation of GDP fell from 23 percent to 5 percent. Zamagni, *Dalla periferia al centro. La seconda rinascita economica dell'Italia (1861–1990)* (Bologna: Il Mulino, 1990), 442.
16. The law "for the defense of the consumer" was signed by the Christian Democrat Giuseppe Togni in 1950, laying out a series of rules intended to block the rise of big retailers.
17. The data were reported by Lanaro, *Storia dell'Italia repubblicana*, 183; Paolo Sylos Labini, *Saggio sulle classi sociali* (Bari: Laterza, 1975), 49, 158; and Ginsborg, *Storia dell'Italia dal dopoguerra a oggi*, 186, 187, 323.
18. Jacques Nobécourt, *L'Italie à vif* (Paris: Seuil, 1970), 45–48. The figure quoted comes from a 1967 study. According to the government, Nobécourt says, they numbered 2,000; those who wanted to cut into this forest, he concludes, were never able even to "carry out a count of the trees."
19. Lanaro, *Storia dell'Italia repubblicana*, 183.
20. L. Musella, *Il trasformismo* (Bologna: Il Mulino, 2003), 155, 156. For the functioning of the commissions, see Nobécourt, *L'Italie à vif*, 56. On the nearly regular contribution of the PCI to the majority, see L. Cafagna, *La grande slavina. L'Italia verso la crisi della democrazia* (Venice: Marsilio, 1993), 40; Carli, *Cinquant'anni di vita italiana*, 17; and R. Cartocci, "*L'Italia di tangentopoli e la crisi del sistema partitico*," in *La coscienza civile degli italiani. Valori e disvalori nella storia nazionale*, ed. C. Tullio-Altan (Udine: Gaspari Editore, 1997), 225.
21. Giuseppe Maranini, *Storia del potere in Italia 1848–1967* (Milan: Corbaccio, 1995), 511.
22. Stephen Gundle, "*L'americanizzaione del quotidiano. Televisione e consumismo nell'Italia degli anni Cinquanta*," *Quaderni Storici* no. 62 (August 1986):561–94.
23. C. Alvaro, *L'Italia rinunzia?* (Milan: Bompiani, 1945), 33.
24. The data come from Ginsborg, *Storia d'Italia dal dopoguerra ad oggi*, 102, 103; *Missione Americana per l'ERP in Italia, Divisione Informazioni*, June 1951; George

C. Marshall Foundation, Marshall Plan Information, http://www.marshallfoundation.org/marshall_plan_information.htm. The numbers expressed in euros are calculated based on the corresponding value of the dollar in 2000.
25. Under fascism, the English were often presented to the Italians as "the people of five meals."
26. The rituals linked to "magico-Christian syncretism" were the object of some varied but equally rich studies by Ernesto De Martino, notably *Sud e magia* (Milan: Feltrinelli, 2001) and Alfonso di Nola, *Gli aspetti magico-religiosi di una cultura subalterna italiana* (Turin: Bollati Boringhieri, 2001).
27. Despite appearances, this was not true of the language. Indeed, by the middle of the twentieth century, 94.8 percent of the lexicon was of Italian origin, while Gallicisms and Anglicisms of recent import constituted a mere 1.6 percent of the total. Beginning in the 1950s, however, the new acquisitions were more often Anglicisms. Of a statistical sampling of seventy-eight foreign phrases, writes De Mauro, "we counted 60 Anglicisms, 9 Gallicisms and 9 foreign expressions of other nature." T. De Mauro, *Storia linguistica dell'Italia unita* (Rome: Laterza, 1963), 202, 210.
28. Lanaro, *Storia dell'Italia repubblicana*, 217.

Chapter 20

1. The most complete text on this subject is that of Goffredo Fofi, *L'immigrazione meridionale a Torino* (Milan: Feltrinelli, 1964).
2. S. Lanaro, *Storia dell'Italia repubblicana* (Venice: Marsilio, 1992), 290. This lack was also underlined by E. Galli della Loggia, *La morte della patria* (Rome: Laterza, 1996), 136.
3. Lanaro, *Storia dell'Italia repubblicana*, 241.
4. See V. Zamagni, *Dalla periferia al centro. La seconda rinascita economica dell'Italia (1861–1990)* (Bologna: Il Mulino, 1990), 17 for the period that preceded World War I; Adriana Castagnoli and Emanuela Scarpellini, *Storia degli imprenditori italiani* (Turin: Einaudi, 2003), 154–160, on the history of Italian businessmen abroad; and Richard A. Webster, *L'imperialismo industriale italiano. Studio sul prefascismo 1908–1915* (Turin: Einaudi, 1974), 357–74, on Italian economic expansion in the Balkans and in Eastern Europe before 1914.
5. Telegram from A. Lessona, November 11, 1937, quoted by Fabienne Le Houerou, *L'épopée des soldats de Mussolini en Abyssinie, 1936–1938* (Paris: L'Harmattan, 1994), 156. Coffee exports fell from 15,822 tons in 1935 to 200 tons in 1939, and pelts from 4,984 tons in 1936 to 48 tons in 1939. While the commercial balance with Ethiopia was active in 1935 (28.497 billion lira in imports and 21.508 billion lira in exports), in 1937 Italy was obliged to send merchandise to its colony worth 86.998 billion lira, and in 1939 it imported goods worth only 480 million lira. Richard Pankhurst, "A charter in Ethiopian commercial history: Developments during the Fascist occupation, 1936–1941," in *Ethiopia Observer* vol. XIV (1971).
6. P. Sylos Labini, *Problemi dello sviluppo economico* (Rome: Laterza, 1974), 156.
7. Among the foreign entrepreneurs who "emigrated" to Italy, we should mention Giorgio Enrico Falck, Heinrich Mylius, Pietro Krumm, Giulio Richard, Roberto Lepetit, Ulrico Hoepli, Otto Joel, and Federico Weil. From 1880 to 1890, foreigners held about 15 percent of industrial capital, a figure that had declined to 8 percent by 1913. The foreign presence was more evident in the credit sector. The Banca Commerciale was formed with 99 percent foreign capital, and the Credito Italiano owed its creation to the capital of two German banks and one Italian bank. See Zamagni, *Dalla periferia*

al centro, 168–171; M. Merger (*Un siècle d'histoire industrielle en Italie (1880–1970). Industrialisation et sociétés* (Paris: Sedes, 1998), 40–44.
8. According to P. Ginsborg, in February and March 1946, 240,000 workers, 13 percent of the southern industrial labor force, were laid off. Ginsborg, *Storia d'Italia dal dopoguerra ad oggi. Società e politica, 1943–1988* (Turin: Einaudi, 1988), 125.
9. On the "resolutely and uncritically liberal" choice of the first economic conference of the PCI (August 21–23, 1945), see Lanaro, *Storia dell'Italia repubblicana*, 86, and C. Daneo, *La politica economica della ricostruzione (1945–1949)* (Turin: Einaudi, 1975), 106. Italo Calvino describes the Communist Party of these years as "an ideal liberal party, which had never before existed." Calvino, *La giornata di uno scrutatore* (Turin: Einaudi, 1963), 37.
10. See Lanaro, *Storia dell'Italia repubblicana*, 194, 195; and Eugenio Scalfari, *Rapporto sul neocapitalismo in Italia* (Bari: Laterza, 1961), 101.
11. Data quoted by J. Nobécourt, *L'Italie à vif* (Paris: Seuil, 1970), 202, 203.
12. Quoted by L. Musella, *Il trasformismo* (Bologna: Il Mulino, 2003), 144.
13. See Zamagni, *Dalla periferia al centro*, 465; and Ginsborg, *Storia d'Italia dal dopoguerra ad oggi*, 289.
14. The basic text of this big-capital reformist policy is *Una politica per l'industria*, of May 1969, compiled by a group of young industrialists—among them Leopoldo Pirelli, Giovanni Agnelli, Roberto Olivetti, Enrico Salza, and Renzo Vallarino Gancia—and by intellectuals of the "Einaudi" Center such as Valerio Zanone, Giuliano Urbani, Mario Deaglio, Piero Ostellino, and Giorgio Rota. See Paolo Soddu, "*Strategie e generazioni industriali,*" available at www.sissco.it/attivita/sem-set-2003/relazioni/soddu.rtf. On this question, see also Nobécourt, *L'Italie à vif*, 146–53. Ginsborg, *Storia d'Italia dal dopoguerra ad oggi*, 357.
15. Quoted by Lorenzo Parodi, *Riformismo da piccolo cabotaggio* (1966), in *Critica del sindacato riformista* (Milan: Edizioni Lotta Comunista, 1987), 651, 652. The *Confederazione nazionale coltivatori diretti*, commonly referred to as "Coldiretti," was the small-farmers' trade group. According to Nobécourt, *L'Italie à vif*, 74, in the elections of 1968, it had delivered as a sort of dowry to the Christian Democrats three million votes, thus guaranteeing the election of eighty-five deputies and twenty-nine senators. At the time, it organized 1.6 million small landowners, controlled 7,000 of the 7,200 farm societies, as well as the Agriculture Commission in the Chamber. Nobécourt also lists the "*Enti pubblici*" or "*para-pubblici*" that existed with the sole purpose of financing the parties and maintaining their electoral bases, and he concludes that no one had any interest in "killing this chicken with the golden eggs" (pp. 45–49).
16. In 2005, the *Lega delle cooperative* boasted 7.5 million associates.
17. See Nobécourt, *L'Italie à vif*, 223, 224.
18. Among them: Percy A. Allum, *Italy. A Republic without a Government* (New York: Norton and Company, 1973), and Giuseppe Palma *Surviving without Governing. The Italian Parties in Parliament* (Berkeley: University of California Press, 1976). In Italy: Ugo La Malfa, *Intervista sul non-governo* (Bari: Laterza, 1977), and Sabino Cassese: *Esiste un governo in Italia?* (Roma: Officina Edizioni, 1980).
19. Lanaro, *Storia dell'Italia repubblicana*, 351.
20. Parodi reports these data on wage growth beyond the ceilings: 0.2 percent in 1960; 2.9 percent in 1961; 3.6 percent in 1962; 3.5 percent in 1963. The reason for these increases, Parodi adds, lay in the raises proposed by the industrialists themselves in order to attract qualified workers. Parodi, *Riformismo da piccolo cabotaggio*, 651.
21. See *La Stampa*, June 2, 1968.
22. Edition of February 22, 1970, quoted by Denis Mack Smith, *Cento anni di storia italiana visti attraverso il Corriere della Sera* (Milan: Rizzoli, 1978), 547.

23. For the data on the PCI, see Marc Lazar, *Maisons rouges. Les partis communistes français et italien de la Libération à nos jours* (Paris: Aubier, 1992), 397, 398.
24. Lanaro, *Storia dell'Italia repubblicana*, 363.
25. Edition of February 2, 1969, quoted by Smith, *Cento anni di storia italiana*, 546.
26. According to the Association of Victims of Terrorism, the political violence of the left caused, between 1970 and 1989, the deaths of 118 people, including 18 between 1969 and 1977, 90 between 1978 and 1982, and 10 between 1983 and 1989 (see *www.vittimeterrorismo.it*). In the same years, the five attacks of the *Questura* on Milan (December 12, 1969, and May 17, 1973), Brescia (May 28, 1974), the Rome–Brenner train (August 4, 1974), and the Boulogne station (August 2, 1980), which can certainly not be blamed on leftist terrorism, claimed a total of 125 victims.

Chapter 21

1. On the reform of the public sanitary service, see P. Ginsborg, *Storia d'Italia dal dopoguerra ad oggi. Società e politica, 1943–1988* (Turin: Einaudi, 1988), 528.
2. At the beginning of the 1980s, in the manufacturing sector, 90.6 percent of companies had fewer than fifty employees (and, according to 1998 data, nearly 75 percent of these had fewer than fifteen employees).
3. *La Stampa*, July 24, 1977.
4. Quoted by A. Cervetto, "*Nuovi aspetti del riciclaggio sociale*" (February 1989), in Cervetto, *Forze e forme del mutamento italiano* (Milan: Edizioni Lotta Comunista, 1997), 209.
5. "*I gioiellieri guadagnano meno dei maestri*," in *Corriere della Sera*, October 14, 2006.
6. See Tullio De Mauro, "*La culture et la langue*," in *Portrait de l'Italie actuelle*, ed. S. Cassese (Paris: La Documentation Française, 2001), 136–43, and *Storia linguistica dell'Italia unita* (Bari: Laterza, 1963), 120–26.
7. Created in 1956 by the union of a small liberal group and a group of intellectuals linked to the weekly *Il Mondo* (notably its celebrated editor, Mario Pannunzio), the Radical Party enjoyed some media success thanks to its battles first for the right to divorce and later for abortion rights.
8. Massimo Livi Bacci, "*La population italienne*," in Cassese, *Portrait de l'Italie actuelle*, 100–105. See also Stefano Molina, *L'equazione demografica italiana: variabili e costanti* (Turin: Fondazione Giovanni Agnelli, 2004).
9. Paul Ginsborg, *L'Italia del tempo presente. Famiglia, società civile, Stato. 1980–1996* (Turin: Einaudi, 1998), 139.
10. "The Church of tomorrow [. . .] will be a Church of a minority" (*Salt of the Earth: The Church at the End of the Millennium*. An Interview With Peter Seewald, San Francisco: Ignatius Press, 1997, 265.
11. Ratzinger, *Salt of the Earth*, 16.
12. Quoted by Guido La Barbera, *Crisi di internazionalizzazione. L'Italia degli anni Novanta* (Milan: Edizioni Lotta Comunista, 2000), 58.
13. La Barbera, *Crisi di internazionalizzazione*, 58.
14. Giovanni Sartori, "*Ma quanto è laico, Eminenza! È un uomo di Chiesa a dare una lezione ai ministri dello Stato sul problema immigrati*," in *L'Espresso*, September 29, 2000.

Chapter 22

1. The *Cassa per il Mezzogiorno* reimbursed 20 percent of initial investments and financed 70 percent of this through a 4 percent loan reimbursable over fifteen years. In his 1970 text, Nobécourt cited the case of industrialists who, having received financing to create businesses in the south, closed them not long afterward and brought back to the north the machines purchased with the state's money. J. Nobécourt, *L'Italie a vif* (Paris: Seuil, 1970), 213.
2. V. Castronovo, *Storia economica d'Italia* (Turin: Einaudi, 1995), 495, 496.
3. The statute of the GEPI (Gestioni e partecipazioni industriali) is quoted by Luciano Barca, *Dizionario di politica economica* (Rome: Editori Riuniti, 1979), 164. It is interesting to note that, in chronological order, the IMI (in 1939), the IRI (1933), and the EFIM (1947) were created at different moments with the same objective, but wound up becoming state holding companies.
4. S. Lanaro, *Storia dell'Italia repubblicana* (Venice: Marsilio, 1992), 439. Between 1977 and 1982, the number of the workers of the state-owned factories grew 31.9 percent.
5. The comment by Jacques Chirac, in September 1996, that "the devaluation of the lira has done a lot of harm to a certain number of European countries, and in particular France" (see www.elysee.fr) was followed by near-general indignation in Italy, led by Deputy Prime Minister Walter Veltroni. Two governors of Banca d'Italia, Paolo Baffi, in 1979 (see G. Carli, *Cinquant'anni di vita italiana* [Rome: Laterza, 1996], 350), and Carlo Azeglio Ciampi, in 1980 (*Il Sole 24 Ore*, October 27, 1985), had already denounced the risks of a recovery "doped" by the continual depreciations of the lira.
6. Gianni Agnelli, interview with Eugenio Scalfari, *L'Espresso*, November 19, 1972.
7. Enrico Berlinguer, *Austerità, occasione per trasformare l'Italia* (Rome: Editori Riuniti, 1977), 13.
8. Interview with Eugenio Scalfari, *Repubblica*, January 24, 1978. Luciano Lama's line was approved by the Congress of the CGIL in February 1978.
9. P. Ginsborg, *Storia d'Italia dal dopoguerra a oggi. Società e politica, 1943–1988* (Turin: Einaudi, 1988), 601.
10. In 1976 the PCI obtained 34.37 percent of all votes cast; in 1979 this fell to 30.38 percent; in 1983 to 29.89 percent; and in 1987 to 26.57 percent. In 1992 the two parties born of its dissolution won a total of 21.73 percent.
11. E. Galli della Loggia, *La morte della patria* (Rome: Laterza, 1996), 84.
12. E. Pace, *La nation italienne en crise* (Paris: Bayard, 1998), 107.
13. Mariella Gramaglia in *La questione socialista. Per una possibile reinvenzione della sinistra*, ed. Gaetano Arfé, Vittorio Foa and Antonio Giolitti (Turin: Einaudi, 1987)
14. Quoted by A. Cervetto, *L'ineguale sviluppo politico. 1968–1979* (Milan: Edizioni Lotta Comunista, 1991), 216.
15. *La Stampa*, January 7, 1996. The OECD estimate comes from October 1995.
16. Carli, *Cinquant'anni di vita italiana*, 5.
17. Ciampi, *Il Sole 24 ore*, October 27, 1985.
18. Giangiacomo Nardozzi, *Miracolo e declino. L'Italia tra concorrenza e protezione* (Rome-Bari: Laterza, 2004), 68.
19. Nardozzi, *Miracolo e declino*, 69.
20. Romano, *Guida alla politica estera italiana*, 192.
21. Francesco Cossiga, "Perché contiamo poco," interview with Lucio Caracciolo, *Limes*, May 1995. Cossiga (1928) was the Christian Democratic interior minister when Aldo Moro was abducted. He was president of the republic from 1985 to 1992.
22. S. Romano, *L'Italia scappata di mano* (Milan: TEA Storica, 1995), 120, 121.

23. On "Mediterranean Atlanticism," see also Arrigo Cervetto, *Forze e forme del mutamento italiano* (Milan: Edizioni Lotta Comunista, 1997), 147, who coined the phrase; Romano, *Guida alla politica estera italiana*, 85, 86, and *L'Italia scappata di mano*, 120, 121; L. Caracciolo, *Terra incognita. Le radici geopolitiche della crisi italiana* (Rome: Laterza, 2001), 14, 15. In English, see Manlio Graziano, "The Rise and Fall of the 'Mediterranean Atlanticism' *in the Italian Foreign Policy: the Case of the Near-East*," *Modern Italy*, vol. 12, no. 3 (November 2007).
24. Thus said the president and director-general of *Toro Assicurazioni* (Fiat Group), Antonio Mosconi, before an assembly of northern entrepreneurs in January 1979. Quoted by Sergio Motosi, *Scritti. Indagine scientifica e passione rivoluzionaria* (Milan: Edizioni Lotta Comunista, 2003), 469.

Chapter 23

1. G. Carli, *Cinquant'anni di vita italiana* (Rome: Laterza, 1996), 5.
2. The Maastricht Treaty was signed on February 7, 1992. The arrest of Mario Chiesa, which marked the beginning of the operation known as "Mani pulite" (Clean Hands), took place on February 17, 1992.
3. See M. Graziano, "*Trois idées sur les mutations de la vie politique italienne*," in *L'Italie aujourd'hui. Situation et perspectives après le séisme des années 90*, ed. M. Graziano (Paris: L'Harmattan, 2004), 19. The phrase "social compromise based on the recycling of public spending" comes from Guido La Barbera, *Crisi di internazionalizzazione. L'Italia degli anni Novanta (Milan*: Edizioni Lotta Comunista, 2000), 104. On this mechanism, also read the first chapter of *La grande slavina. L'Italia verso la crisi della democrazia* (Venice: Marsilio, 1993), by Luciano Cafagna, in particular pages 17 through 30, and Alfredo Reichlin, Acts of Congress organized by the journal *Italianieuropei* (May 2, 2000).
4. Paolo Franchi, "*Un socialista italiano*," in *Corriere della Sera*, January 20, 2000.
5. On this episode, see M. Graziano, 2007, "The rise and fall of 'Mediterranean Atlanticism' in Italian foreign policy: The case of the Near East."
6. *L'Unità*, March 18, 1991. The Congress that saw the dissolution of the PCI and its transformation into the Democratic Party of the Left (PDS) took place in February 1991.
7. J. Nobécourt, *L'Italie à vif* (Paris: Seuil, 1970), 111.
8. The presence of Forza Italia in the 1994 elections led to a loss of only around 150,000 votes for the Northern League, which declined from 8.65 percent of total 1992 votes to 8.36 percent. In the 2001 elections, on the other hand, the Northern League lost nearly 1.8 million votes and fell to 3.94 percent of the total.
9. Quentin Peel, "*Fear Unites Factions in Prodi Cabinet*," *Financial Times*, May 19, 2006.
10. Ezio Mauro, "*Il tramonto dell'illusione unilaterale*," in *La Repubblica*, August 26, 2006.
11. Sergio Romano, "*La sindrome di Crimea. Missioni all'estero e ricerca di reconoscimenti*," *Corriere della Sera*, August 25, 2006.
12. The phrase comes from Lucio Caracciolo, *Terra incognita. Le radici geopolitiche della crisi italiana* (Rome: Laterza, 2001), 102.
13. Editorial, "*Silvio Berlusconi's bequest: The soft underbelly*," *The Economist*, September 16, 2006.
14. A. Cervetto, "*La disfunzione dei partiti parlamentari*," in *L'involucro politico* (Milan: Edizioni Lotta Comunista, 1994), 87.

Conclusion

1. Giulio Tremonti, *Il futuro del fisco*, in F. Galgano, S. Cassese, G. Tremonti, T. Treu, *Ricchezza senza nazioni. Nazioni senza ricchezza*, Bologna: Il Mulino, 1993.
2. Mario Draghi, *Considerazioni finali per l'anno 2006*, general meeting of the Banca d'Italia, exercise CXIII, Rome, May 31, 2007, p. 8.
3. Data from ISTAT, July 11 and 12, 2006.
4. Unicredit was created through the progressive merger, begun in 1998, of Credito Italiano, Credito Romagnoolo, Cassa di Risparmio di Verona, Vicenza Belluno e Ancona, Cassa di Risparmio di Torino, Cassamarca (Cassa di Risparmio della Marca Trivigiana), Cassa di Risparmio di Trento e Rovereto, and Cassa di Risparmio di Trieste.
5. Banca Intesa is the result of the merger, between 1998 and 2001, of Cassa di Risparmio delle Provincie Lombarde (Cariplo), Banco Ambroveneto (in turn created by the merger of Banco Ambrosiano and Banca Cattolica del Veneto), and Banca Commerciale Italiana.
6. Luigi La Spina, "*Prime prove di megalopoli*," *La Stampa*, August 25, 2006.
7. For a more complete analysis of this subject, allow me to refer the reader to my own *Identité catholique et identité italienne: L'Italie laboratoire de l'Église* (Paris: L'Harmattan, 2007).

References

History of Italy

Banfield, E. 1958. *The moral basis of a backward society.* Glencoe, IL: Free Press [Italian ed., *Le basi morali di una società arretrata.* Bologna: Il Mulino, 1976].
Barberis, W. 2004. *Il bisogno di patria.* Turin: Einaudi.
Barzini, L. 1996 [1964]. *The Italians: A full-length portrait featuring their manners and morals.* New York: Touchstone.
Becchi, A. 1995. La questione meridionale. In *La politica italiana. Dizionario critico 1945–95*, ed. G. Pasquino. Rome: Laterza.
Bevilacqua, Piero. 2005. *Breve storia dell'Italia meridionale.* Rome: Donzelli.
Biffi, G. 1999. *Risorgimento, Stato laico e identità nazionale.* Casale Monferrato: Piemme.
Bobbio, N. 1969. Profilo ideologico del Novecento. In *Storia della letteratura italiana*, vol. IX, eds. E. Cecchi and N. Sapegno. Milan: Garzanti.
Bocca, G. 1962. *Miracolo all'italiana.* Milan: Edizioni Avanti!
Bollati, G. 1983. *L'Italiano. Il carattere nazionale come storia e come invenzione.* Turin: Einaudi.
Cafagna, L. 1989. *Dualismo e sviluppo nella storia d'Italia.* Venice: Marsilio.
———. 1994. *Nord e Sud. Non fare a pezzi l'unità d'Italia.* Venice: Marsilio.
———. 2003. Legittimazione e delegittimazione nella storia politica italiana. In *Due nazioni. Legittimazione e delegittimazione nella storia dell'Italia contemporanea*, eds. L. Di Nucci and E. Galli della Loggia. Bologna: Il Mulino.
Candeloro, G. 1982. *Il movimento cattolico in Italia.* Rome: Editori Riuniti.
Caracciolo, A. 1994. *Roma capitale sta in fondo allo Stivale.* Limes 4.
Carocci, G. 1975. *Storia d'Italia dall'Unità ad oggi.* Milan: Feltrinelli.
———. 1992. *Il trasformismo dall'unità ad oggi.* Milan: Unicopli.
Cassese, S. 1998. *Lo Stato introvabile.* Rome: Donzelli.
———. 2001. Histoire et caractéristiques de l'État italien. In *Portrait de l'Italie actuelle*, ed. S. Cassese. Paris: La Documentation Française.
Castronovo, V. 1977. Il Piemonte. In *Storia d'Italia. Le regioni dall'Unità a oggi*, ed. V. Castronova. Turin: Einaudi.
Cattaneo, C. 1957. *Scritti.* Florence: Sansoni.
Ciuffoletti, Z. 1993. *Stato senza nazione. Disegno di storia del Risorgimento e dell'Unità d'Italia* Naples: Morano Editore.
Diamanti, I., A. Dieckhoff, M. Lazar, and D. Musiedlak. 1995. *L'Italie, une nation en suspens.* Brussels: Editions Complexe.
Galli della Loggia, E. 1998. *L'identità italiana* Bologna: Il Mulino.
Gentile, E. 2006. *La Grande Italia. Il mito della nazione nel XX secolo.* Rome: Laterza.
Gianni, E. 1985. Le influenze regionali nei poteri governativi. *Lotta Comunista*, 182–84.
Goglia, L., and F. Grassi. 1981. *Il colonialismo italiano da Adua all'Impero.* Rome: Laterza.

Guerri, G. B. 1992. *Gli italiani sotto la Chiesa*. Milan: Mondadori.
Jemolo, A. C. 1977 [1955]. *Chiesa e Stato in Italia. Dalla unificazione ai giorni nostri*. Turin: Einaudi.
Lanaro, S. 1988. *L'Italia nuova. Identità e sviluppo. 1861–1988*. Turin: Einaudi.
———. 1993. Le élites settentrionali e la storia italiana. *Meridiana. Rivista di storia e scienze sociali*.
Leopardi, G. 1969 [1824]. *Discorso sopra lo stato presente del costume degli Italiani*. In *Tutte le opere*, vol. I, ed. Walter Binni. Florence: Sansoni.
Lepre, A. 1994. *Italia, addio? Unità e disunità dal 1860 a oggi*. Milan: Mondadori.
Livi Bacci, M. 2001. La population italienne. In *Portrait de l'Italie actuelle*, ed. S. Cassese. Paris: La Documentation Française.
Lupo, S. 1993. *Storia della mafia dalle origini ai giorni nostri*. Rome: Donzelli.
———. 1997. Mezzogiorno. In *Dizionario storico dell'Italia unita*, eds. B. Bongiovanni and N. Tranfaglia. Rome: Laterza.
Mack Smith, D. 1978. *Cento anni di vita italiana visti attraverso il Corriere della Sera*. Milan: Rizzoli.
———. 1998. *Storia d'Italia dal 1861 al 1997*. Rome: Laterza. (*Modern Italy: A political history*. Ann Arbor: University of Michigan Press, 1997).
Manzoni, A. 1963 [1835]. *Osservazioni sulla morale cattolica*. In *Tutte le opere*. eds. A. Chiari and F. Ghisalberti Milan: Mondadori.
Maranini, G. 1995 [1967]. *Storia del potere in Italia 1848–1967*. Milan: Corbaccio.
Meriggi, M. 1996. *Breve storia dell'Italia settentrionale, dall'Ottocento ad oggi*. Rome: Donzelli.
———. 1997. Borghesie. In *Dizionario storico dell'Italia unita*, eds. B. Bongiovanni and N. Tranfaglia. Rome: Laterza.
Miège, J.-L. 1968. *L'impérialisme colonial italien de 1870 à nos jours*. Paris: SEDES.
Milza, P. 2005. *Histoire de l'Italie. Des origines à nos jours*. Paris: Fayard.
Molina, S. 2004. *L'equazione demografica italiana: Variabili e costanti*. Turin: Fondazione Giovanni Agnelli.
Montanelli, I., and M. Cervi. 1998. *L'Italia del Novecento*. Milan: Rizzoli.
Musella, L. 2003. *Il trasformismo*. Bologna: Il Mulino.
Pace, E. 1998. *La nation italienne en crise*. Paris: Bayard.
Prezzolini, G. 1948. *The legacy of Italy*. New York: Vanni [Italian ed., *L'Italia finisce*. Milan: Rusconi, 1994].
Procacci, G. 2006 [1970]. *Storia degli italiani*. Rome: Laterza.
Prospero, M. 1999. *Storia delle istituzioni in Italia*. Rome: Editori Riuniti.
Ragionieri, E. 1976. *Italia giudicata, 1861–1945*. Turin: Einaudi.
———. 1979. *Politica e amministrazione nella storia dell'Italia unita*. Rome: Editori Riuniti.
Romano, S. 1977. *Histoire de l'Italie du Risorgimento à nos jours*. Paris: Seuil [Italian ed., *Storia d'Italia dal Risorgimento ai giorni nostri*. Milan: Mondadori, 1978].
———. 2005. *Libera Chiesa. Libero Stato? Il Vaticano e l'Italia da Pio IX a Benedetto XVI*. Milan: Longanesi.
Rumi, G. 1996. Povera Padania, triste storia la sua. *Liberal*, no. 19 (October).
Rusconi, G. E. 1998. Question nationale et question démocratique en Italie. Thèses pour un patriotisme républicain. *Hérodote*, no. 89.
———. 2003. Religione civile e identità italiana. *Il Mulino*, 5.
Sabbatucci, G. 2003. *Il trasformismo come sistema*. Rome: Laterza.
Salvadori, M. L. 2003. Legittimazione politica e storiografia italiana. In *Due nazioni. Legittimazione e delegittimazione nella storia dell'Italia contemporanea*, eds. L. Di Nucci and E. Galli della Loggia. Bologna: Il Mulino.
Schiavone, A. 1998. *Italiani senza Italia. Storia e identità*. Turin: Einaudi.

Sylos Labini, P. 1975. *Saggio sulle classi sociali*. Rome: Laterza.
Verucci, G. 1988. *La Chiesa nella società contemporanea. Dal primo dopoguerra al Concilio Vaticano II*. Rome: Laterza.
Viesti, G. 2003. *Abolire il Mezzogiorno*. Rome: Laterza.
Woolf, S. J. 1973. La storia politica e sociale (1700–1860). In *Storia d'Italia*, vol. III, *Dal primo Settecento all'unità*, eds. Ruggiero Romano and Corrado Vivanti. Turin: Einaudi.

From the Middle Ages to the Nineteenth Century

Abulafia, D. 1977. *The two Italies: Economic relations between the Norman kingdom of Sicily and the northern communes*. Cambridge: Cambridge University Press [Italian ed., *Le due Italie. Relazioni economiche tra il Regno normanno di Sicilia e i comuni settentrionali*. Naples: Guida, 1977].
Aymard, M. 1978. La transizione dal feudalesimo al capitalismo. In *Storia d'Italia*, vol. I, *Dal feudalesimo al capitalismo*, eds. Ruggiero Romano e Corrado Vivanti. Turin: Einaudi.
Braudel, F. 1974. Due secoli e tre Italie. In *Storia d'Italia*, vol. II, *1476–1700: Politica, società, religione*, eds. Ruggiero Romano e Corrado Vivanti. Turin: Einaudi.
Cantimori, D. 1967. Le idee religiose del Cinquecento. La storiografia. In *Storia della letteratura italiana*, vol. V, *Il Seicento*, eds. E. Cecchi and N. Sapegno. Milan: Garzanti,
Guicciardini, F. 1983 [1519]. Considerazioni intorno ai Discorsi del Machiavelli. In *Discorsi sopra la prima deca di Tito Livio*, ed. C. Vivanti. Turin: Einaudi.
Luzzatto, G. 1958. *Breve storia economica dell'Italia medievale*. Turin: Einaudi.
Machiavelli, N. 1983 [1513]. *Discorsi sopra la prima deca di Tito Livio*, ed. C. Vivanti. Turin: Einaudi.
Misson, M. 1702. *Nouveau Voyage d'Italie, avec un Mémoire contenant des avis utiles à ceux qui voudront faire le mesme voyage*. La Haye: Chez Henry Van Bulderen.
Montaigne, M. de. 1774. *Journal du voyage en Italie par la Suisse & l'Allemagne en 1580 & 1581*. Paris: Chez Le Jay Librairie.
Montanelli, I., and R. Gervaso. 1967. *L'Italia dei secoli d'oro*. Milan: Rizzoli.
Prosperi, A. 1981. Intellettuali e Chiesa all'inizio dell'era moderna. In *Storia d'Italia*, vol. IV, *Intellettuali e potere*, eds. R. Romano and C. Vivanti. Turin: Einaudi.
Quazza, G. 1957. *Le riforme in Piemonte nella prima metà del Settecento*. Modena: STEM.
Raffestin, C. 1987. L'evoluzione del sistema delle frontiere del Piemonte dal XVI al XIX secolo. In *La frontiera da Stato a nazione. Il caso Piemonte*, eds. C. Ossola, C. Raffestin, and M. Ricciardi. Rome: Bulzoni.
Recuperati, G. 1987. Cultura di frontiera e identità italiana nelle vicende del Piemonte settecentesco. In *La frontiera da Stato a nazione. Il caso Piemonte*, eds. C. Ossola, C. Raffestin, and M Ricciardi. Rome: Bulzoni.

The Risorgimento

Belardelli, G. 2003. Una nazione "senza anima": La critica democratica del Risorgimento. In *Due nazioni. Legittimazione e delegittimazione nella storia dell'Italia contemporanea*, eds. L. Di Nucci and E. Galli della Loggia. Bologna: Il Mulino.
Candeloro, G. 1958. *Storia dell'Italia moderna*, vol. II, *Dalla Restaurazione alla rivoluzione nazionale, 1815–1846*. Milan: Feltrinelli.
———. 1964. *Storia dell'Italia moderna*, vol. IV, *Dalla rivoluzione nazionale all'Unità 1849–1860*. Milan: Feltrinelli.

Carpi, U. 1981. *Egemonia moderata e intellettuali nel Risorgimento*. In *Storia d'Italia*, vol. IV, *Intellettuali e potere*, eds. R. Romano and C. Vivanti. Turin: Einaudi.

Casella, R. 1984. *1863: I primi passi dello scontro tra protezionisti e liberoscambisti in Italia*. Lotta Comunista September.

Cattaneo, C. 1968 [1849]. *L'insurrezione di Milano nel 1848 e la successiva Guerra*. Turin: Loescher.

Della Peruta, F. 1973. *Democrazia e socialismo nel Risorgimento*. Rome: Editori Riuniti.

———. 1999. *Politica e società nell'Italia dell'Ottocento. Problemi, vicende e personaggi*. Milan: Franco Angeli.

Duriez, É. 1905. *Les principes de l'annexion dans les Traités de 1815*. Paris: Henri Jouve.

Ferrero, G. 1996. *Talleyrand à Vienne (1814–1815)*. Paris: Éditions de Fallois.

Gianni, E. 2006. *Liberali e democratici alle origini del movimento operaio italiano. I congressi delle società operaie italiane (1853–1893)*. Milan: Edizioni Pantarei.

Gioberti, V. 1861. *Del Primato morale e civile degli Italiani*. Naples: Stamperia del Vaglio.

Gobetti, P. 1926. *Risorgimento senza eroi*. Turin: Edizioni del Baretti.

Gramsci, A. 1949. *Il Risorgimento*. Turin: Einaudi.

Greppi, P. 1900–1904. *La Rivoluzione francese nel carteggio di un osservatore italiano (Paolo Greppi)*. Milan: Hoepli.

Lepre, A. 1974. *Storia del Mezzogiorno nel Risorgimento*. Rome: Editori Riuniti.

Mack Smith, D. 1967. *Italy*. In *The New Cambridge Modern History*, vol. 10, *The Zenith of European Power*. Cambridge: Cambridge University Press [Italian ed., *Italia*, Milan: Garzanti, 1972].

———. 1969. *Il Risorgimento italiano. Storia e testi*. Rome: Laterza.

———. 1994. *Vittorio Emanuele II*. Milan: Mondadori.

Marcelli, U. 1970. *Interpretazioni del Risorgimento*. Bologna: Patron.

Marx, K., and F. Engels. 1959. *Sul Risorgimento italiano*. Rome: Editori Riuniti.

Mazzini, G. 1922 [1860]. *Dei doveri dell'uomo*. Genoa: Giovanni Ricci Editore.

Montanelli, I. 1972. *L'Italia del Risorgimento*. Milan: Rizzoli.

Nievo, I. 1952. *Opere*. Naples: Riccardo Ricciardi Editore.

Nobili, M., and S. Camerani, eds. 1945. *Carteggi di Bettino Ricasoli*. Rome: Istituto Storico Italiano per l'età Moderna e Contemporanea.

Pedio, T. 1987. *Brigantaggio meridionale (1806–1863)*. Lecce: Capone Editore.

Romeo, R. 1969. *Cavour e il suo tempo*. Rome: Laterza.

———. 1998 [1959]. *Risorgimento e capitalismo*. Rome: Laterza.

Rosselli, N. 1967. *Mazzini e Bakunin: Dodici anni dimovimento operaio in Italia (1860–1872)*. Turin: Einaudi.

Russo, V. 1999. *Pensieri politici e altri scritti*. Naples: Generoso Procaccini.

Salvemini, G. 1961. *L'Italia politica nel secolo XIX*. In *Scritti sul Risorgimento*, eds. P. Pieri, C. Pischedda. (Milan: Feltrinelli.

1861–1922

Aubert, R. 1975. *L'Église catholique de la crise de 1848 à la Première Guerre mondiale*. In *Nouvelle Histoire de l'Église*, vol. V, *L'Église dans le monde moderne*, eds. J. Daniélou, L.-J. Rogier, R. Aubert, and D. Knowles. Paris: Seuil.

Candeloro, G. 1968. *Storia dell'Italia moderna*, vol. V, *La costruzione dello Stato unitario, 1860–1871*. Milan: Feltrinelli.

———. 1970. *Storia dell'Italia moderna*, vol. VI, *Lo sviluppo del capitalismo e del movimento operaio, 1871–1896*. Milan: Feltrinelli.

Caracciolo, A. 1960. *Stato e società civile. Problemi dell'unificazione italiana.* Turin: Einaudi.
———. 1999 [1956]. *Roma capitale. Dal Risorgimento alla crisi dello Stato liberale.* Rome: Editori Riuniti.
Carocci, G. 1956. *Agostino Depretis e la politica interna italiana 1876–1887.* Turin: Einaudi.
———. 1971 [1961]. *Giolitti e l'età giolittiana.* Turin: Einaudi.
Chabod, F. 1951. *Storia della politica estera italiana dal 1860 al 1896.* Rome: Laterza.
Corradini, E. 1980. *Scritti e discorsi. 1901–1914.* Turin: Einaudi.
Croce, B. 1955. *Cultura e vita morale. Intermezzi polemici.* Bari: Laterza.
———. 2004 [1928]. *Storia d'Italia dal 1871 al 1915.* Milan: Adelphi.
———. 2007 [1932]. *Storia d'Europa nel secolo decimonono.* Milan: Adelphi.
Fonzi, F. 1965. *Crispi e lo Stato di Milan.* Milan: Giuffrè.
Grew, R. 1969. *Il trasformismo: Ultimo stadio del Risorgimento.* In *Il Risorgimento e l'Europa*, ed. V. Frosini. Catania: Bonanno.
Isnenghi, M. 2007. *Garibaldi fu ferito. Storia e mito di un rivoluzionario disciplinato.* Rome: Donzelli.
Martini, F. 1928. *Confessioni e ricordi. 1859–1892.* Milan: Treves.
Nitti, F. S. 1907. *Il Partito Radicale e la nuova democrazia industriale. Prime linee di un programma di un Partito Radicale.* Turin: Sten.
Passerin d'Entrèves, E. 1969. *Ideologie del Risorgimento.* In *Storia della letteratura italiana*, vol. VII, eds. E. Cecchi and N. Sapegno. Milan: Garzanti.
Roberts, J. M. 1965. *Italy.* In *The new Cambridge modern history*, vol. 9, *War and peace in an age of upheaval 1793–1830.* Cambridge: Cambridge University Press.
Romeo, R. 1974. *Dal Piemonte sabaudo all'Italia liberale.* Rome: Laterza.
Seton-Watson, C. 1973. *L'Italia dal liberalismo al fascismo 1870–1925.* Rome: Laterza.
Soderini, E. 1932. *Il pontificato di Leone XIII.* Milan: Mondadori.
Spadolini, G. 1972. *Gli uomini che fecero l'Italia.* Milan: Longanesi.
———. 1974. *Giolitti e i cattolici (1911–1914).* Milan: Mondadori.
Villari, P. 1866. *Di chi è la colpa? O sia La Pace e la guerra* Milan: Tipografia di Zanetti Francesco.

1922–1945

Bottai, G. 1982. *Diario. 1935–1944.* Milan: Rizzoli.
Cammarano, F. 1997. *Sinistra storica.* In *Dizionario storico dell'Italia unita*, eds. B. Bongiovanni and N. Tranfaglia. Rome: Laterza.
Chabod, F. 1994. *L'Italia contemporanea (1918–1948).* Turin: Einaudi.
De Felice, R. 1965. *Mussolini il rivoluzionario. 1883–1920.* Turin: Einaudi.
———. 1975. *Intervista sul fascismo.* Rome: Laterza.
———. 1985. *Gli intellettuali di fronte al fascismo.* Rome: Bonacci.
———. 1988. *Le fascisme. Un totalitarisme à l'italienne?* Paris: Presses de la Fondation Nationale des Sciences Politiques.
———. 1990. *Mussolini. L'alleato (1940–1945).* Turin: Einaudi.
Foa, V. 1991. *Il cavallo e la torre.* Turin: Einaudi.
Gobetti, P. 1995 [1964]. *La Rivoluzione liberale. Saggio sulla lotta politica in Italia.* Turin: Einaudi.
Gramsci, A. 1973. *Scritti politici.* Rome: Editori Riuniti.
Le Houerou, F. 1994. *L'épopée des soldats de Mussolini en Abyssinie, 1936–1938.* Paris: L'Harmattan.
Mikes, G. 1956. *Italy for Beginners.* London: Allan Wingate.

Milza, P., and S. Bernstein. 1980. *Le fascisme italien. 1919–1945.* Paris: Seuil.
Oliva, G. 1994. *I vinti e i liberati.* Milan: Mondadori.
Pankhurst, R. 1971. A charter in Ethiopian commercial history: Developments during the fascist occupation 1936–1941. *Ethiopia Observer* 15 (1).
Pellicani, A. 1964. *Il papa di tutti. La Chiesa cattolica, il fascismo e il razzismo. 1929–1945.* Milan: Sugar.
Rocca, G. 1993. *Avanti Savoia! Miti e disfatte che fecero l'Italia 1848–1866.* Milan: Mondadori.
Salvatorelli, L. 2004 [1923]. *Nazional fascismo.* Rome: Libero.
Secchia, P. 1973. *Aldo dice 26 x 1. Cronistoria del 25 aprile.* Milan: Feltrinelli.
Tilgher, A. 1921. *La crisi mondiale e saggi di socialismo e marxismo.* Bologna: Zanichelli.
Treves, A. 1976. *Le migrazioni interne nell'Italia fascista.* Turin: Einaudi.

1945–1992

Aga Rossi, E. 1969. *Dal Partito popolare alla Democrazia cristiana.* Bologna: Cappelli.
Ajello, N. 1979. *Intellettuali e PCI. 1944–1958.* Rome: Laterza.
Andreotti, G. 1977. *Intervista su De Gasperi.* Rome: Laterza.
Baget Bozzo, G. 1974. *Il partito cristiano al potere. La Dc di De Gasperi e di Dossetti (1945–1954).* Florence: Vallecchi.
Berlinguer, E. 1977. *Austerità, occasione per trasformare l'Italia.* Rome: Editori Riuniti.
Boneschi, M. 1995. *Poveri ma belli. I nostri anni cinquanta.* Milan: Mondadori.
Calise, M., and R. Mannheimer. 1982. *Governanti in Italia. Un trentennio repubblicano. 1946–1976.* Bologna: Il Mulino.
Casella, R. 1989. *La crisi sindacale degli anni ottanta.* Milan: Edizioni Lotta Comunista.
Cassese, S. 1980. *Esiste un governo in Italia?* Rome: Officina Edizioni.
Cervetto, A. 1991. *L'ineguale sviluppo politico. 1968–1979.* Milan: Edizioni Lotta Comunista.
———. 1997. *Forze e forme del mutamento italiano.* Milan: Edizioni Lotta Comunista.
Crainz, G. *Storia del miracolo italiano. Culture, identità, trasformazioni fra anni cinquanta e sessanta.* Rome: Donzelli.
Farneti, P. 1971. *Sistema politico e società civile.* Turin: Giappichelli.
Franzinelli, M. 2006. *L'amnistia Togliatti. 22 giugno 1946: Colpo di spugna sui crimini fascisti.* Milan: Mondadori.
Galli, G. 1966. *Il bipartitismo imperfetto.* Bologna: Il Mulino.
Galli della Loggia, E. 1996. *La morte della patria.* Rome: Laterza.
Gianni, E. 1983. La DC nasce come partito nordista. *Lotta comunista,* 149.
Ginsborg, P. 1988. *Storia d'Italia dal dopoguerra ad oggi. Società e politica, 1943–1988.* Turin: Einaudi.
———. 1998. *L'Italia del tempo presente. Famiglia, società civile, Stato. 1980–1996.* Turin: Einaudi.
Gundle, S. 1986. L'americanizzazione del quotidiano. Televisione e consumismo nell'Italia degli anni Cinquanta. *Quaderni Storici,* 21(2).
La Malfa, U. 1977. *Intervista sul non-governo.* Bari: Laterza.
Lanaro, S. 1992. *Storia dell'Italia repubblicana.* Venice: Marsilio.
Lazar, M. 1992. *Maisons rouges. Les partis communistes français et italien de la Libération à nos jours.* Paris: Aubier.
Lupo, S. 2004. *Partito e antipartito. Una storia politica della prima Repubblica (1946–1978).* Rome: Donzelli.
Motosi, S. 2003. *Scritti. Indagine scientifica e passione rivoluzionaria.* Milan: Edizioni Lotta Comunista.

Nobécourt, J. 1970. *L'Italie à vif.* Paris: Seuil.
Palma, G. 1976. *Surviving Without Governing. The Italian Parties in Parliament.* Berkeley: University of California Press.
Parodi, L. 1987. *Critica del sindacato riformista.* Milan: Edizioni Lotta Comunista.
Pasquino, G. 2004. Interprétations du système politique italien. In *L'Italie aujourd'hui. Situation et perspectives après le séisme des années 90*, ed. M. Graziano. Paris: L'Harmattan.
Pavone, C. *La continuità dello Stato. Istituzioni e uomini.* In *Italia 1945–1948. Le origini della Repubblica.* Turin: Giappichelli.
Sartori, G. 1982 [1967]. Bipartitismo imperfetto o pluralismo polarizzato? In G. Sartori, *Teoria dei partiti e caso italiano.* Milan: Sugarco.
Scalfari, E. 1961. *Rapporto sul neo-capitalismo in Italia.* Rome: Laterza.
Sonnino, E. 1995. La popolazione italiana dall'espansione al contenimento. In *Storia dell'Italia repubblicana*, vol. II., Turin: Einaudi.
Togliatti, P. 1972a. *Il Partito.* Rome: Editori Riuniti.
———. 1972b. *La via italiana al socialismo.* Rome: Editori Riuniti.

1992–2007

Berselli, E. 2003. *Post-Italiani. Cronache di un paese provvisorio.* Milan: Mondadori.
Cafagna, L. 1993. *La grande slavina. L'Italia verso la crisi della democrazia.* Venice: Marsilio.
Cartocci, R. 1997. L'Italia di tangentopoli e la crisi del sistema partitico. In *La coscienza civile degli italiani. Valori e disvalori nella storia nazionale*, ed. C. Tullio-Altan. Udine: Gaspari Editore.
———. 2007. *Mappa del tesoro. Atlante del capitale sociale in Italia.* Bologna: Il Mulino.
D'Alema, M. 1995. *Un paese normale. La sinistra e il futuro dell'Italia.* Milan: Mondadori.
Damilano, M. 2006. *Il partito di Dio. La nuova galassia dei cattolici italiani.* Turin: Einaudi.
Diamanti, I. 1996. *Il male del Nord. Lega, localismo, secessione.* Rome: Donzelli Editore.
Fubini, F. 1996. A Bruxelles è tramontato il tricolore. *Limes* 3.
Graziano, M. 2004. Trois idées sur les mutations de la vie politique italienne. In *L'Italie aujourd'hui. Situation et perspectives après le séisme des années 90*, ed. M. Graziano. Paris: L'Harmattan.
Jones, T. 2003. *The Dark Heart of Italy.* London: Faber & Faber.
La Barbera, G. 2000. *Crisi di internazionalizzazione. L'Italia degli anni Novanta.* Milan: Edizioni Lotta Comunista.
Lazar, M. 2006. *L'Italie à la dérive. Le moment Berlusconi.* Paris: Perrin.
Monti, M. 1998. *Intervista sull'Italia in Europa.* Rome: Laterza.
Nencini, R. 1996. *Il trionfo del trasformismo.* Florence: Loggia dei Lanzi.
Portelli, H. 2006. *L'Italie de Berlusconi.* Paris: Buchet Chastel.
Rampini, F. 1996. *Germanizzazione. Come cambierà l'Italia.* Rome: Laterza.
Riccardi, A. 2005. Papa Ratzinger e l'eredità di Wojtyla. *Limes*, 2.
Rizzo, S., and G. A. Stella. 2007. *La casta. Così i politici italiani sono diventati intoccabili.* Milan: Rizzoli.
Romano, S. 1994. Perché gli italiani si disprezzano. *Limes*, 4.
———. 1995. *L'Italia scappata di mano.* Milan: TEA Storica.
Sacco, G. 2005. *Critica del nuovo secolo.* Rome: Luiss University Press.
Turri, J. 1996. Scene da una secessione. *Limes*, 3.

Italy and International Relations

Caracciolo, L. 2001. *Terra incognita. Le radici geopolitiche della crisi italiana*. Rome: Laterza.
Cossiga, F. 1995. *Perché contiamo poco*, intervista con L. Caracciolo. *Limes*, 3.
De Michelis, G. 2003. *La lunga ombra di Yalta*. Venice: Marsilio.
Graziano, M. 2007. The rise and fall of "Mediterranean Atlanticism" in Italian foreign policy: The case of the Near East. *Modern Italy* 12 (3): 287–308.
Jean, C. 1994. *La nostra sicurezza nel mondo balcanizzato. Linee-guida per una politica estera e di difesa coerente*. *Limes*, 4.
Mammarella, G., and P. Cacace. 2006. *La politica estera dell'Italia. Dallo Stato unitario ai giorni nostri*. Rome: Laterza.
Perticone, G. 1961. *La politica estera italiana dal 1861 al 1914*. Turin: ERI.
Quaroni, P. 1965. *Il mondo di un ambasciatore*. Milan: Ferro Edizioni.
Romano, S. 1993. *Guida alla politica estera italiana. Dal crollo del fascismo al crollo del comunismo*. Milan: Rizzoli.
Vigezzi, B. 1997. *L'Italia unita e le sfide della politica estera*. Milan: Unicopli.

Italian Economic History

Agnelli, G. 1983. *Intervista sul capitalismo moderno*. Rome: Laterza.
Are, G. 1974. *Alle origini dell'Italia industriale*. Naples: Guida.
Baglioni, G. 1974. *L'ideologia della borghesia industriale nell'Italia liberale*. Turin: Einaudi.
Bairoch, P. 1982. International industrialization levels from 1750 to 1980. *Journal of European Economic History* 11 (2): 269–333.
Bianchi, P. 1994. *Dove stanno i nostri interessi economici*. *Limes*, 4.
Bianco, M. 2003. *L'industria italiana. Numeri, peculiarità, politiche della nostra economia industriale*. Bologna: Il Mulino.
Bonelli, F. 1978. *Il capitalismo italiano. Linee generali di interpretazione*. In Storia d'Italia, vol. I, *Dal feudalesimo al capitalismo*, eds. R. Romano and C. Vivanti Turin: Einaudi.
Caracciolo, A. 1973. *La storia economica*. Turin: Einaudi.
Carli, G. 1977. *Intervista sul capitalismo italiano*. Rome: Laterza.
———. 1996. *Cinquant'anni di vita italiana*. Rome: Laterza.
Castagnoli, A., and E. Scarpellini. 2003. *Storia degli imprenditori italiani*. Turin: Einaudi.
Castronovo, V. 1980. *L'industria italiana dall'ottocento a oggi*. Milan: Mondadori.
———. 1995. *Storia economica d'Italia*. Turin: Einaudi.
Daneo, C. 1975. *La politica economica della ricostruzione (1945–1949)*. Turin: Einaudi.
Flamant, M., and J. Singer-Kerel. 1993. *Les crises économiques*. Paris: Presses Universitaires de France.
Gallino, L. 2003. *La scomparsa dell'Italia industriale*. Turin: Einaudi.
Gerschenkron, A. 1965. *Il problema storico dell'arretratezza economica*. Turin: Einaudi.
Grifone, P. 1971 [1945]. *Il capitale finanziario in Italia. La politica economica del fascismo*. Turin: Einaudi.
Luzzatto, G. 1968. *L'economia italiana dal 1861 al 1894*. Turin: Einaudi.
Nardozzi, G. 2004. *Miracolo e declino. L'Italia tra concorrenza e protezione*. Rome: Laterza.
Sapelli, G. 1993. *Sul capitalismo italiano. Trasformazione o declino*. Milan: Feltrinelli.
Sylos Labini, P. 1974. *Problemi dello sviluppo economico*. Rome: Laterza.
Toniolo, G. 1988. *Storia economica dell'Italia liberale. 1850–1918*. Bologna: Il Mulino.
Villari, L. 1972. *Il capitalismo italiano del Novecento*. Bari: Laterza.

Webster, R. A. 1974. *L'imperialismo industriale italiano. Studio sul prefascismo 1908–1915.* Turin: Einaudi.
Zamagni, V. 1990. *Dalla periferia al centro. La seconda rinascita economica dell'Italia (1861–1990).* Bologna: Il Mulino.
———. 2004. *Les difficultés économiques de la Seconde République.* In *L'Italie aujourd'hui. Situation et perspectives après le séisme des années 90,* ed. M. Graziano. Paris: L'Harmattan.

Italian Language and Literature

Bartoli, M. G. 1930. *I dialetti dell'Italia settentrionale.* In *Piemonte,* ed. L. V. Bertarelli. Milan: Touring Club Italiano.
De Mauro, T. 1963. *Storia linguistica dell'Italia unita.* Rome: Laterza.
———. 2001. *La culture et la langue.* In *Portrait de l'Italie actuelle,* ed. S. Cassese. Paris: La Documentation Française.
De Sanctis, F. 1963 [1873]. *Storia della letteratura Italiana.* Milan: Bietti.
Devoto, G. 1974. *Il linguaggio d'Italia.* Milan: Rizzoli.
Gramsci, A. 1953. *Gli intellettuali e la formazione della cultura.* Turin: Einaudi.
———. 1975 [1950]. *Letteratura e vita nazionale.* Rome: Editori Riuniti.
Lotti, G. 2000. *L'avventurosa storia della lingua Italiana.* Milan: Bompiani.
Marazzini, C. 1992. *Il Piemonte e la Valle d'Aosta.* In *L'italiano nelle regioni,* ed. F. Bruni. Turin: Utet.
Socco, M. G. 1967–68. *Per una topografia linguistica di Asti* (thesis, University of Turin).
Tagliavini, C. 1969. *Le origini delle lingue neolatine.* Bologna: Patron.
Tuaillon, G. 1987. *Le frontiere linguistiche (Il caso Piemonte).* In *La frontiera da Stato a nazione. Il caso Piemonte,* eds. C. Ossola, C. Raffestin, and M. Ricciardi. Rome: Bulzoni, 1987.
Varese, C. 1967. *Teatro, prosa, poesia.* In *Storia della letteratura italiana,* vol. V, eds. E. Cecchi and N. Sapegno. Milan: Garzanti.

Other Texts

Agnelli, G., and A. Cabiati. 1986. *Federazione europea o Lega delle nazioni.* Pordenone: Studio Tesi.
Boffa, G. 1976. *Storia dell'Unione Sovietica. 1917–1941. Lenin e Stalin. Dalla rivoluzione alla seconda guerra mondiale.* Milan: Mondadori.
Bordiga, A. 1976. *I fattori di razza e nazione nella teoria marxista.* Milan: Iskra Edizioni.
Cohen, M. 1956. *Pour une sociologie du langage.* Paris: Albin Michel.
De Martino, E. 2001. *Sud e magia.* Milan: Feltrinelli.
Di Nola, A. 2001. *Gli aspetti magico-religiosi di una cultura subalterna italiana.* Turin: Bollati Boringhieri.
Fichte, J. G. 1992 [1808]. *Discours à la nation allemande.* Paris: Imprimerie Nationale.
Gil, J. 1980. *Nazione.* In *Enciclopedia,* vol. IX, ed. R. Romano. Turin: Einaudi.
Graziano, M. 2007. *The Catholic Church and the 'others': A universalist strategy. Geopolitical Affairs,* 2.
Habermas, J. 1986. *Écrits politiques. Culture, droit, histoire.* Paris: Editions du Cerf.
Hobsbawm, E. J., and T. Ranger. 1983. *The invention of tradition. Cambridge:* Cambridge University Press [Italian ed., *L'invenzione della tradizione,* Turin: Einaudi, 1987].
Hogan, M. 1989. *The Marshall Plan: America, Britain, and the reconstruction of Western Europe, 1947–1952.* Cambridge: Cambridge University Press.

Kennedy, P. 1987. *The rise and fall of the Great Powers: Economic change and military conflict from 1500–2000*. New York: Random House.

La Barbera, G. 2006. *L'Europa e lo Stato*. Milan: Edizioni Lotta Comunista.

Marx, K. 1975a. *Il Capitale. Critica dell'economia politica*. Turin: Einaudi.

———. 1975b. *Opere. Lotta politica e conquista del potere*, ed. G. M. Bravo. Rome: Newton & Compton.

Moore, B., Jr. 1993. *Social origins of dictatorship and democracy. Lord and peasant in the making of the modern world*. Boston: Beacon Press.

Ratzinger, J. 1997. *Il sale della terra. Cristianesimo e Chiesa cattolica nella svolta del millennio*. Cinisello Balsamo: Edizioni San Paolo.

Sieyès, E.-J. 1994 [1789]. *Écrits politiques*. Paris: Édition des Archives Contemporaines.

Thiesse, A.-M. 1999. *La création des identités nationales. Europe XVIIIème-XXème siècle*. Paris: Seuil.

Tremonti, G. 1993. *Il futuro del fisco*. In *Ricchezza senza nazioni. Nazioni senza ricchezza*, eds. F. Galgagno, S. Cassese, G. Tremonti, and T. Treu. Bologna: Il Mulino.

Index

Abruzzi, 51
absence of the masses in Italian unification, 15, 16, 19, 24, 43, 49, 56, 58–61, 83, 94, 121, 126, 127
Abulafia, David, 112
Action Party, 157
Agnelli, Gianni, 10, 163, 184, 186, 193
Agnelli, Giovanni, 154
Agnelli, Umberto, 188
Albertine Statute, 76, 83, 86, 92
Alfieri, Vittorio, 51, 66, 126
Alighieri, Dante, 51, 70, 122
Alvaro, Corrado, 164
Amato, Giuliano, 8, 95, 196
Andreatta, Beniamino, 188
Andreotti, Giulio, 155, 160, 162, 187, 188
Ansaldo, Giovanni, 146
Aosta, 69, 113
Arafat, Yasser, 187
Arconati, Costanza, 71
Artom, Isacco, 83
Ascoli, Graziadio Isaia, 63
Aspromonte, 23, 24
Asti, 69, 113
Atlantic Pact (NATO), 157, 166, 187
Aubert, Roger, 129
Augustine of Hippo, 51
Avvenire, 182
Aymard, Maurice, 31
Aznar, Jose Maria, 196

Badoglio, Pietro, 143
Baglioni, Guido, 106
Balbo, Cesare, 69, 71, 126
Banca d'Italia, 37, 106, 142, 147, 159, 173, 185, 186, 191, 199
Bandiera brothers (Attilio and Emilio), 58
Barberis, Walter, 156

Baretti, Giuseppe, 52, 126
Bari, 112
Bartoli, Matteo Giulio, 64
Barzini, Luigi, 50
Basilicata, 51
Bellarmino, Roberto, 123
Bellegarde Heinrich Joseph de, 17
Benedict XVI (Joseph Ratzinger), Pope, 181, 201
Benetton, Luciano, 193
Berchet, Giovanni, 56
Bergamo, 18, 53
Berlinguer, Enrico, 175, 184, 192
Berlusconi, Silvio, 7, 9, 10, 24, 38, 40, 97, 189, 191, 193, 195
Bevilacqua, Piero, 113
Bianchi, Patrizio, 39
Biffi, Giacomo, 121, 122, 182
Bismarck, Otto von, 14, 138
Boccella, Enrico, 124
Bollati, Giulio, 3, 49, 53, 55, 57, 71, 149, 161
Bologna, 31, 121, 182, 188
Bompiani, Valentino, 164
Bonaparte, Louis (Napoleon III), 14, 21, 22, 93, 97, 100, 211, 215
Bonaparte, Napoleon (Napoleon I), 4, 16, 17, 53, 66, 72, 210
Bonelli, Franco, 85
Bordiga, Amadeo, 64
Borsieri, Pietro, 56
Bossi, Umberto, 40, 194, 195
Bottai, Giuseppe, 151
Brindisi, 107, 108
Brittan, Leon, 184
Brofferio, Angelo, 86
Bruno, Giordano, 123
Bülow, Bernhard von, 4

Cabiati, Attilio, 154
Cacace Paolo, 2
Cafagna, Luciano, 108, 111, 114, 116, 148
Calabria, 24, 51
Caldwell, Erskine, 164
Campanella, Tommaso, 123
Candeloro, Giorgio, 100, 126, 130, 134
Caracciolo, Lucio, 171
Carducci, Giosue, 51, 138
Carli, Guido, 6, 162, 182, 186, 191
Carocci, Giampiero, 116, 141
Carosone, Renato, 165
Carrara, 140
Cartocci, Roberto, 94
Cassese, Sabino, 75, 95
Castronovo, Valerio, 183
Catania, 112
Catholic Church (Vatican), 3, 9, 16, 17, 22, 28, 31, 49–51, 59, 60, 64, 73, 81, 82, 93, 94, 102, 121–27, 129–34, 137, 149, 150, 154, 156–63, 166, 173, 175, 180–82, 189, 197, 201
Cattaneo, Carlo, 17, 18, 44, 45, 59, 126
Cavour, Camillo Benso, Count of, 3, 14, 16, 20–24, 59, 62, 63, 76–79, 83–87, 92, 93, 101–3, 107, 116, 138
Cenni, Enrico, 69
Cervetto, Arrigo, 96, 197
Cesarotti, Melchiorre, 65
CGIL. *See* Italian General Confederation of Labor
Chabod, Federico, 159
Charles Albert of Savoy Carignan, King of Sardinia, 15, 19, 20, 83
Charles Emmanuel III of Savoy, King of Sardinia, 70
Charles Felix of Savoy, King of Sardinia, 19
Charles III, King of the Two Sicilies, 115
Charles VIII, King of France, 44
Christian Democratic Party (DC), 9, 10, 37, 94, 97, 122, 157, 158, 160, 162, 163, 166, 172, 174, 177, 178, 185, 188, 192, 194
Cialdini, Enrico, 103
Ciampi, Carlo Azeglio, 37, 186, 196
Cicero, Marcus Tullius, 51
CISL. *See* Italian Confederation of Free Workers
Ciuffoletti, Zeffiro, 2
Clean Hands operation ("Mani Pulite"), 7, 92, 96, 191

Cobden, Richard, 30
Colajanni, Napoleone, 114
Columbus Christopher, 65
competitive devaluation of lira, 1, 6, 184–88
Comunione e Liberazione, 192
Confalonieri, Federico, 17
Confederation of Industry (Confindustria), 147
Constitution of the Italian Republic, 37, 78, 97, 153, 156, 172
Corradini, Enrico, 141, 169
Correnti, Cesare, 59
Corriere della Sera, 148, 174, 175, 194
Cossiga, Francesco, 187
Costa, Angelo, 163
Craxi, Bettino, 1, 7, 9, 10, 45, 95, 178, 185, 191–94, 204, 206
crisis of internationalization, 3, 5, 6, 14, 38, 41, 97, 99–103, 183, 186–88, 191
Crispi, Francesco, 46, 117, 118, 132, 133, 139, 164
Croce, Benedetto, 9, 91, 94, 107, 126, 133, 154
Croce, Giulio Cesare, 52, 53
Cuccia, Enrico, 105
Cuneo, 113, 119
Cuoco, Vincenzo, 53, 56, 126
Custoza, 99, 100, 139

D'Alema, Massimo, 40, 196
D'Annunzio, Gabriele, 66, 138, 146
D'Azeglio Taparelli, Massimo, 20, 30, 126
DC. *See* Christian Democratic Party
De Amicis, Edmondo, 138, 146
De Benedetti, Carlo, 193
de Cesare, Carlo, 30
De Gasperi, Alcide, 9, 24, 154, 155, 157, 160, 166
de Gaulle, Charles, 30
De Laugier, Cesare, 69, 70
de Luca, Giuseppe, 157
de Maistre, Joseph, 59
De Mauro, Tullio, 60, 62, 63, 179
Denina, Carlo, 65
Depretis, Agostino, 9, 92, 95, 133, 164
De Rita, Giuseppe, 188
De Ruggiero, Guido, 107
de Sanctis, Francesco, 16, 27, 66, 137–39
Destra (historical right), 9, 28, 30, 75, 92, 101, 103, 109–11, 113, 114, 116, 137

De Viti de Marco, Antonio, 114
Devoto, Giacomo, 62
Dini, Lamberto, 40, 186, 195di Rienzo, Cola, 50
d'Orazio, Ettore, 133Dossetti, Giuseppe, 160
Draghi, Mario, 199

Einaudi, Luigi, 142
Emilia, 21, 28, 75, 77, 79, 129
Emmanuel Philibert, Duke of Savoy, 70, 71
Eugene of Savoy-Carignan, 65

Fanfani, Amintore, 170
Farini, Luigi Carlo, 79, 82, 116
Farneti, Paolo, 107
fascism, 9, 27, 37, 59, 78, 79, 97, 134, 135, 143, 145–47, 149–51, 153–62, 164–66, 168, 169, 181, 200
Faulkner, William, 164
Ferdinand IV, King of the Two Sicilies, 115
Ferrari, Giuseppe, 102
Ferrata, Giansiro, 164
Fichte, Johann Gottlieb, 51
Fini, Gianfranco, 39
Florence, 18, 22, 33, 62, 66, 72, 76
Foa, Vittorio, 155
Fonzi, Fausto, 46
Forlì, 140
Forte, Francesco, 172
Fortunato, Giustino, 30, 111, 114
Forza Italia, 41, 195
Foscolo, Ugo, 126
Franchetti, Leopoldo, 111, 114
Francis II, King of the Two Sicilies, 96
Frederick II of Hohenstaufen, Holy Roman Emperor, King of Sicily, 115
Friuli, 53, 188

Gaddafi, Muammar al-, 187
Galilei, Galileo, 123
Galli, Giorgio, 153
Galli della Loggia, Ernesto, 49, 52, 57, 64, 69, 117, 151, 154, 156, 157, 185
Gallino, Luciano, 2
Gardini, Raul, 193
Garibaldi, Giuseppe, 4, 16, 20, 22–24, 77, 82, 121
Garzoni, Tommaso, 52
Genoa, 15, 44, 86, 103, 160

Gentile, Emilio, 138
Gentiloni, Ottorino, 140
Gerschenkron, Alexander, 106
Gianni, Emilio, 79
Giannone, Pietro, 73, 126
Ginsborg, Paul, 153
Gioberti, Vincenzo, 43, 56, 57, 59, 126, 138, 142
Giolitti, Giovanni, 24, 118, 132, 133, 139, 146, 164
Gobetti, Piero, 79, 126, 142, 143, 146
Goldoni, Carlo, 126
Gozzi, Carlo, 63
Gramaglia, Mariella, 185
Gramsci, Antonio, 14, 17, 21, 43, 56, 58, 63–65, 67, 79, 91–93, 95, 117, 122, 124–27, 133, 134, 146, 164
Greppi, Paolo, 53, 55, 56
Grew, Raymond, 91, 92
Gualterio, Filippo Antonio, 103
Guerri, Giordano Bruno, 123, 125
Guicciardini, Francesco, 123
Gundle, Stephen, 164

Habermas, Jürgen, 156
Habsburg, House of, 72
Hawthorne, Nathaniel, 164
Hemingway, Ernest, 164

Italian Communist Party (PCI), 6, 9, 10, 40, 97, 153, 155–58, 162, 163, 166, 170, 172, 174, 175, 177, 178, 180, 184, 185, 187, 188, 192, 194
Italian Confederation of Free Workers (CISL), 59, 175
Italian General Confederation of Labor (CGIL), 59, 175, 184
Italian language, 49, 57, 60–63, 66, 67, 70, 71, 137, 141, 168, 179
Italian Republican Party (PRI), 188, 194
Italian Socialist Party (PSI), 7, 28, 60, 94, 97, 132, 133, 139, 141, 148, 157, 170, 174, 177, 184, 185, 191, 192

Jacini, Stefano, 78, 93
Jean, Carlo, 39
Jemolo, Arturo Carlo, 122, 130, 132, 133, 158

Kennedy, Paul, 20, 32, 59, 150
Kohl, Helmut, 186

Labriola, Arturo, 113
lack of general (national) interest, 2, 4, 11, 27, 28, 36, 37, 40, 60, 75, 76, 78, 79, 91, 96, 97, 102, 103, 106, 107, 116–18, 125, 133, 137, 141, 148, 151, 154, 159, 173, 183, 197, 200
Lama, Luciano, 184
La Malfa, Ugo, 174, 188
La Marmora, Alfonso, 79Lanaro, Silvio, 163, 168, 173, 174
Lanza, Giovanni, 79, 103, 106
La Spina, Luigi, 200
Legnago, 65
Leopardi, Giacomo, 11, 75, 126
Leopold II, Grand Duke of Tuscany, 96
Leo XIII (Gioacchino Pecci), 59, 94
Lesseps, Ferdinand de, 22
Lessona, Alessandro, 169
Liberal Party (PLI), 195
Limes (Italian Journal of Geopolitics), 36, 37, 39, 40
Lissa, 65, 99, 100, 139
Livy (Titus Livius), 51
Lombardy, 3, 14, 17, 18–20, 38, 41, 43–47, 49, 55, 57, 61, 71, 72, 75, 77, 86, 112, 194, 196, 200
Longanesi, Leo, 161
low productivity of Italy, 1, 2, 5, 8, 13, 142, 161, 163, 168–74, 184–87, 197
Lualdi, Ercole, 101
Lupo, Salvatore, 82, 114

Maccanico, Antonio, 41
Maccari, Mino, 161
Machiavelli, Niccolò, 51, 56, 122, 123
Mack Smith, Denis, 20, 58, 82, 99, 110, 148
Macry, Paolo, 114
Mafia (Camorra), 24, 29, 175
Maino Gandhi, Sonia, 4
Malaparte, Curzio (Kurt Erich Suckert), 66
Mammarella, Giuseppe, 2
Manfredini, Federico, 53
Manifesto, Il, 174
Mantua, 65
Manzoni, Alessandro, 56–58, 62, 63, 66, 126
Maranini, Giuseppe, 164
Marche, 22, 129
Marinetti, Filippo Tommaso, 66
Marsala, 24

Marshall Plan (European Recovery Program), 158, 165, 166
Marx, Karl, 85, 102
Marzotto, Gaetano, 163
Masaniello (Tommaso Aniello), 50
Matera, 179
Mattei, Enrico, 187
Mazzini, Giuseppe, 16, 20, 51, 58, 60, 92, 103, 137–40, 149, 154
Meda, Filippo, 134
Medici, House of, 72
"Mediterranean Atlanticism," 187
Melville, Herman, 164
Melzi d'Erli, Francesco, 53, 55
Menabrea, Luigi Federico, 79, 101, 103, 130
Mengistu, Haile Mariam, 187
Menichella, Donato, 173, 174
Mentana, 23, 24
Merger, Michèle, 147
Meriggi, Marco, 45
Metternich, Klemens von, 15, 18
Meynaud, Jean, 117
Miglio, Gianfranco, 194, 195
Milan, 14, 17–20, 33, 41, 44–46, 56, 59, 72, 76, 78, 117, 118, 132, 133, 135, 155, 160, 163, 165, 167, 179, 189, 191, 194, 199, 200
Minghetti, Marco, 79, 103, 106, 109, 110
Mitterrand, François, 7, 186
Modena, 22
Mohammed Said Pasha (Sa'id of Egypt), 22
Mommsen, Theodor, 50
Montaigne, Michel Eyquem de, 70
Montale, Eugenio, 164
Montanelli, Indro, 50, 86
Monti, Mario, 7
Moravia, Alberto, 164
Mordini, Antonio, 101
Mosca, Gaetano, 141
Murat, Joachim, 20
Murat, Lucien, 20
Muratori, Ludovico, 126
Musella, Luigi, 163
Mussolini, Benito, 10, 24, 50, 51, 59, 148–50, 153, 160, 161, 168, 181

Naples, 14, 16–19, 21, 23, 24, 33, 53, 55, 61, 72, 75–78, 83, 112, 115–17, 124
Nardozzi, Giangiacomo, 186, 187
National Alliance (Alleanza nazionale), 39

NATO. *See* Atlantic Pact
Negri Zamagni, Vera, 31, 85, 95, 97, 106, 113, 149
neo-Guelphism, 16, 17, 57. *See also* Gioberti, Vincenzo
Nievo, Ippolito, 126
Nigra, Costantino, 100
Nitti, Francesco Saverio, 114, 141
Nixon, Richard, 183
Nobécourt, Jacques, 195
Northern League (Lega Nord), 39–41, 45, 194, 195
Novara, 20, 113

Ochetto, Achille, 194
Orsini, Felice, 21
Osservatore Romano, L', 189

Pace, Enzo, 123, 124, 185
Padoa Schioppa, Tommaso, 10, 196
Palermo, 24, 50, 63, 77, 115
Paolo IV (Giovanni Pietro Carafa), Pope, 124
Pareto, Vilfredo, 141
Parini, Giuseppe, 126
Pascoli, Giovanni, 138
Pasquino, Gianfranco, 95
Pavese, Cesare, 164
PCI. *See* Italian Communist Party
Pecchio, Giuseppe, 58
Peel, Quentin, 196
Pellico, Silvio, 126
People's Party (PPI), 121, 134
Persano, Carlo Pellion di, 24, 65
Pertini, Sandro, 188
Peschiera, 65
Petitti di Roreto, Carlo Ilarione, 58
Petrarch (Francesco Petrarca), 51, 122
Petruccioli, Claudio, 188, 189
Piedmont, 14–16, 18, 20–22, 30, 61, 62, 69–73, 75–79, 82, 83, 85–87, 97, 103, 113, 116, 117, 121, 129, 137
Piovene, Guido, 164
Pisacane, Carlo, 58
Pius IX (Giovanni Maria Mastai Ferretti), Pope, 17, 22, 23, 93, 96, 121, 126, 127, 129
Pius X (Giuseppe Melchiorre Sarto), Pope, 140
Pius XI (Achille Ratti), Pope, 158
Pius XII (Eugenio Pacelli), Pope, 131, 160, 162
Pivano, Fernanda, 164

Poe, Edgar Allan, 164
Poggi, Gianfranco, 130
Polsinelli, Antonio, 101
Prezzolini, Giuseppe, 50, 52, 65, 81
PRI. *See* Italian Republican Party
Prinetti, Giulio, 142
Procacci, Giuliano, 72, 73
Prodi, Romano, 8, 10, 37, 40, 41, 188, 196, 208
PSI. *See* Italian Socialist Party
Puglia, 107, 115

Quazza, Guido, 72

Radical Party, 179
Radicati di Sostegno, Alberto, 73
Rampini, Federico, 7
Rattazzi, Urbano, 79, 85, 92
Ratzinger, Joseph. *See* Benedict XVI
Reagan, Ronald, 186
Repubblica, La, 192, 196
Ricasoli, Bettino, 20, 79, 81, 82
Ricci, Giovanni, 101
Romagna, 22, 140
Romagnosi, Gian Domenico, 58
Romanelli, Ruggero
Romano, Liborio, 82
Romano, Sergio, 1, 6, 21, 23, 24, 41, 67, 82, 92, 93, 95–97, 116, 151, 153, 154, 156, 187, 196
Rome, 14, 18, 23, 29, 33, 38, 50, 51, 55, 59, 63, 64, 66, 75, 76, 78, 94, 100, 103, 112, 122, 124, 125, 129–31, 167, 179, 188, 195, 199, 200
Romeo, Rosario, 85, 91, 92
Ronchey, Alberto, 177
Rosmini, Antonio, 126
Rubattino shipping company, 24, 108
Ruffo di Bagnara, Fabrizio Dionigi (Army of the Holy Faith), 53, 121, 130
Ruini, Camillo, 201
Rumi, Giorgio, 44
Rusconi, Gian Enrico, 137, 148
Russo, Vincenzio, 53, 55, 56, 58

Salvatorelli, Luigi, 146
Salvatorelli, Mario, 178
Salvemini, Gaetano, 78, 114, 143
Santarosa, Santorre de' Rossi di, 19
Saroyan, William, 164

Sarkozy, Nicolas, 11
Sartori, Giovanni, 182
Savoy, House of, 3, 15, 19–22, 65, 69–72
Scalfaro, Oscar Luigi, 162
Scarfoglio, Edoardo, 66
Schiavone, Aldo, 114
Sclopis, Federigo Paolo, 83, 85
Segni, Mario, 194
Sella, Quintino, 100–103
Seton-Watson, Christopher, 95
Settembrini, Luigi, 63
Sforza, Carlo, 154, 155
Sforza, Ludovico (Ludovico il Moro), 44
Sicily, 3, 4, 21–24, 66, 75, 77, 111, 112, 192
Sieyès, Emmanuel-Joseph, 35
Sinistra (historical left), 9, 27, 30, 86, 92, 93, 95, 99, 101, 106, 109–11, 116, 137, 138
Soderini, Edoardo, 94
Sonnino, Sidney, 113
Sordi, Alberto, 165
Spadolini, Giovanni, 132, 133
Spaventa, Silvio, 20, 92, 109
Stampa, La, 178, 194, 200
Steno (Stefano Vanzina), 165
Strauss, Franz Josef, 189
Susa, 69
Sylos Labini, Paolo, 115, 124, 169

terrorism, 21, 175
Thatcher, Margaret, 1, 7, 186
Thiers, Adolphe, 130
"Third Italy," 28, 193
Tilgher, Adriano, 146
Tittoni, Tommaso, 142
Togliatti, Palmiro, 153, 158, 166
Tommaseo, Niccolò, 57, 66, 126
Toniolo, Gianni, 105
transformism, 5, 27, 85, 86, 91–97, 116–18, 133, 143, 151, 160, 163, 164, 170

Tremonti, Giulio, 199
Trentino-Alto Adige, 178
Treviglio, 18
Troya, Carlo, 126
Turati, Filippo, 46, 117, 118, 139
Turiello, Pasquale, 113
Turin, 14–18, 20–24, 44, 69–73, 76–78, 85, 86, 99, 101, 103, 113, 117, 160, 167, 174, 179, 200
Turri, Jacopo, 40
Tuscany, 21, 28, 62, 72, 75, 79, 96, 179
Twain, Mark (Samuel Langhorne Clemens), 164

Umbria, 22
Ungaretti, Giuseppe, 66

Veneto, 17, 28, 188
Venice, 18, 33, 44, 72, 100, 124, 125
Ventura di Raulica, Gioacchino, 126
Vercelli, 113
Verga, Giovanni, 66
Verona, 22, 65
Vico, Giambattista, 126
Victor Amedeus II, Duke of Savoy, 72
Victor Emmanuel I, Duke of Savoy, then King of Sardinia, 19
Victor Emmanuel II of Savoy, King of Sardinia, then King of Italy, 16, 22, 79, 103, 121
Viesti, Gianfranco, 114
Villafranca, 22, 23, 77, 100
Villani, Pasquale, 112
Villari, Pasquale, 65, 111–13, 116
Virgil (Publius Vergilius Maro), 51
Visco, Vincenzo, 178
Visconti Venosta, Emilio, 130
Visentini, Bruno, 178
Viziano, Attilio, 178

Printed in the United States of America